Planning for Retirement

by Jeffrey B. Mershon

ISBN: 978-0-9726772-6-4

TABLE OF CONTENTS

Chapter 5: The Use of Annuities in Retirement Planning

Chapter 6: Employer-Sponsored Tax-Advantaged Plans

Chapter 7: Qualified Plans: Rules for Qualification

Chapter 8: Keogh Plans/Retirement Plans for the Self-Employed

Chapter 9: Profit-Sharing Plans

Chapter 10: Stock Bonus Plans/Employee Stock Ownership Plans (ESOPs)

Chapter 11: 401(k) Plans

Chapter 12: Other Defined Contribution Retirement Plans

Chapter 13: Traditional Defined Benefit Plans

Chapter 14: Cash Balance Pension Plans

PREFACE

The ability to retire at a particular age and at a comfortable standard of living is usually a primary goal of most financial planning clients. Normally, the amount of money necessary to achieve this goal is substantial and, just like the satisfaction of any other financial goal, requires significant planning. In order to provide comprehensive financial planning services, a financial planner needs to develop this specialized skill set.

Planning for retirement is a process, rather than a one-time event. The retirement planning process parallels that of the six-step personal financial planning process, beginning with establishing and defining the client-planner relationship and progressing through gathering client data, including goals; analyzing and evaluating the client's financial status; developing and presenting retirement planning recommendations and/or alternatives; implementing the retirement planning recommendations; and ending with monitoring the retirement planning recommendations. It should be understood that this is an ongoing process that perhaps will be performed several times for a given client (e.g., every 3 to 5 years). The primary reason for this is the long-term unpredictability of the various factors that enter into the retirement planning process, such as inflation, the after-tax investment return, life expectancy, and other unanticipated goals that may detract from retirement planning savings.

Retirement planning involves the determination of a client's retirement need and the identification of retirement income sources to address that need. Financial planners often compare the retirement income sources to a "three-legged stool", with the first leg consisting of government-sponsored retirement plans (such as Social Security) and the other legs consisting of personal savings and employer-sponsored plans. This book addresses all three legs of the retirement income stool.

This book is designed to serve primarily as the textbook for the fifth course of a personal financial planning education program registered with Certified Financial Planner Board of Standards Inc. (CFP Board) and satisfying the education component of CFP Board's requirements for earning the CERTIFIED FINANCIAL PLANNER™ certification*. Specifically, it covers topic numbers 59 through 67 of the 89 topics appearing in CFP Board's 2004 Job Analysis Study.

This book has been written at the upper undergraduate (junior and senior) and graduate levels and may be used in introductory courses in retirement planning offered at colleges and universities. Also, it may be used by individuals interested simply in enhancing their knowledge of retirement planning. Each of the 18 chapters opens with an introduction of the chapter subject and a list of learning objectives. At the end of each chapter, there is a list of important concepts, questions for review, and suggested additional readings.

This book is used as the textbook for Planning for Retirement, the fifth course in Kaplan University's Online Certificate in Financial Planning program and in Kaplan's accelerated classroom education program. In the online course, it is supplemented by brief online readings, exercises, quizzes at the end of each of 10 lessons, and a Final Exam containing 60 multiple-choice questions (some of which are related to a case situation) similar to those appearing on CFP Board's Certification Examination. Students in Kaplan's online financial planning education program also have the use of a message board where they can pose questions online to qualified instructors.

ACKNOWLEDGMENTS

The author is indebted to all the academicians and personal financial planning practitioners who have created the body of knowledge contained in this text not only by practicing their respective professions in an exemplary manner but by participating in the several Certified Financial Planner™ job analysis studies conducted by CFP Board of Standards. Moreover, I thank the countless volunteers who have donated literally lifetimes to the development and advancement of the personal financial planning profession by serving in various capacities with both CFP Board and the financial planning membership organizations.

I particularly thank Keith Fevurly, MBA, JD, LLM (Taxation), CFP® , who performed a technical review of the manuscript of this text and added significant value through his many useful suggestions for improvement in the content and wording.

In addition, I wish to thank Kaplan University's Daniel Moore and John Howard who endured several rounds of revisions and produced the final document in a highly professional manner.

Jeffrey B. Mershon
MBA, CPA/PFS, CFP®

ABOUT THE AUTHOR

Jeffrey B. Mershon, MBA, CPA/PFS, CFP® , is Chair for Financial Planning at the School of Continuing and Professional Studies at Kaplan University, a subsidiary of Kaplan Higher Education Corporation, which in turn is wholly-owned by Kaplan, Inc. Kaplan, Inc. is wholly-owned by The Washington Post Company. Mr. Mershon received his Bachelor of Arts degree in English Literature from Cornell University's College of Arts and Sciences and his Master of Business Administration degree in Accounting and Finance from Cornell University's Johnson Graduate School of Management. He developed Kaplan University's Insurance and Employee Benefits course, Income Tax Planning course, and a substantial portion of the Online Review course and Live Review materials.

Prior to joining Kaplan University, Mr. Mershon was Director of Curriculum Development at the College for Financial Planning, supervising the development and maintenance of the College's Certified Financial Planner™ and Master of Science in Financial Planning education courses and other education offerings. He served for five years as Assistant Executive Director and Director of Post-Certification at Certified Financial Planner Board of Standards in Denver, where he was instrumental in the development of CFP Board's *Code of Ethics and Professional Responsibility and Financial Planning Practice Standards*. He has practiced as a financial planner, consultant to various financial planning organizations, and as a partner in a local CPA firm, as well as in senior financial management in private industry. In addition to being a Certified Public Accountant, he has earned both the Certified Financial Planner™ certification and the Personal Financial Specialist designation. He is a member of the Financial Planning Association and the American Institute of CPAs.

Mr. Mershon is the author of *Fundamentals of Personal Financial Planning* (2nd edition) used in the introductory course of Kaplan University's Certificate in Financial Planning Online Education Program and Kaplan's accelerated classroom program, as well as by other educational institutions. He is co-author of *Insurance and Employee Benefits* (2nd edition) used in the Insurance and Employee Benefits course of Kaplan's Certificate in Financial Planning Online Education Program and Kaplan's accelerated classroom program. He is also co-author of *Individual Income Tax Planning* (2nd edition) used in the Income Tax Planning course of Kaplan's Certificate in Financial Planning Online Education Program and Kaplan's accelerated classroom program as well as by other educational institutions.

CHAPTER ONE

The Retirement Planning Process And Retirement Needs Analysis

• • •

The ability to retire at a particular age and at a comfortable standard of living is usually a primary goal of most financial planning clients. Normally, the amount of money necessary to achieve this goal is substantial and, just like the satisfaction of any other financial goal, requires significant planning. In order to provide comprehensive financial planning services, a financial planner needs to develop this specialized skill set.

Planning for retirement is a process, rather than a one-time event. The retirement planning process parallels that of the six-step personal financial planning process, beginning with establishing and defining the client-planner relationship and progressing through gathering client data, including goals; analyzing and evaluating the client's financial status; developing and presenting retirement planning recommendations and/or alternatives; implementing the retirement planning recommendations; and ending with monitoring the retirement planning recommendations. It should be understood that this is an ongoing process that perhaps will be performed several times for a given client (e.g., every 3 to 5 years). The primary reason for this is the long-term unpredictability of the various factors that enter into the retirement planning process, such as inflation, the after-tax investment return, life expectancy, and other unanticipated goals that may detract from retirement planning savings.

This chapter will acquaint the reader with the steps or stages in the retirement planning process and identify certain assumptions necessary not only in conducting such planning but also in determining the amount needed for a retirement fund and the most effective method of accumulating this fund. In addition, the reader will learn the several steps in determining the retirement savings need under both the capital utilization and capital preservation approaches. Determining the retirement savings need is not only one of the most important skills a financial planner must acquire and be able to employ effectively but is also one of the most challenging of the financial planning services.

Upon completing this chapter, you should be able to:

- Describe the basic stages in the retirement planning process
- Explain assumptions made in the retirement planning savings need analysis
- Determine financial needs during retirement and calculate their future value
- Determine the resources available to provide retirement income and calculate their future value
- Analyze a given situation to calculate the amount that needs to be saved for retirement on a present value basis, using time value of money concepts
- Compare taxable and tax-deferred savings alternatives

In-Depth: The Changing Face of Retirement

Retirement planning today is not your father's or grandfather's retirement planning. We used to think that retirees received pension benefits from their defined benefit pension plan (see chapter 13), representing a significant portion of their pre-retirement earned income; that they retired at age 65; and that they lived perhaps ten years or so after retirement. Moreover, what we used to understand as being "retired" meant being no longer gainfully employed and involved only in leisure activities.

Today's retirement planning realities are as follows:

1. Fewer businesses are offering company-funded pension plans thereby passing this obligation to employees at a time when the average savings rate has declined to less than 3 percent of total gross income.
2. Those relative few who receive company pension benefits replace only about one half of their pre-retirement income; even when Social Security benefits are figured in, total retirement income normally will not enable retirees to maintain their pre-retirement standard of living.
3. Due to great advances in health care, the average retiree can expect to live 20 to 25 years after retirement; however, the cost of health care during retirement has skyrocketed and retirees in poor health generally need to spend more of their income on their personal maintenance. Indeed, some people may experience a retirement life cycle that is longer than their working life cycle.
4. Over the last two decades, most workers had been retiring before reaching age 62, but now many are continuing to work longer or on a part-time basis or as independent contractors after reaching age 62.
5. Approximately three fourths of elderly retirees are forced to do without luxury items, including travel.
6. Inflation, while relatively low in recent years, causes the insidious erosion of one's retirement income.

(continued on next page)

(continued from previous page)

Retirement planning practitioners often speak of the "three-legged stool" of retirement security. Classically, these three legs have been (1) employer-sponsored retirement plans; (2) Social Security benefits; and (3) personal savings. But as discussed earlier, employer-sponsored retirement plans have gradually moved from defined benefit plans to defined contribution plans (see chapters 8 through 12) where the funding is provided in large part or wholly by the employee. Moreover, certain major employers (such as the airlines), have either suspended or terminated their retirement plans, thereby ceasing to make future employer contributions. Essentially *none* of the defined benefit pension plans provide a benefit of 100 percent of pre-retirement income. And since benefits from this type of plan are rarely adjusted for inflation, an inflation rate of 4 percent can reduce the purchasing power by 50 percent after 18 years of retirement.

With regard to Social Security benefits, the normal retirement age, which for many years has been age 65, is in the process of being gradually increased to age 67 over the years 2003-2027. In addition, the federal government is currently considering reform of the Social Security Retirement System to provide for its long-term viability. While this may involve the introduction of so-called "private accounts" which would permit younger employees to invest a portion of their Social Security contributions in limited types of mutual funds, it may also involve reduction of benefits and/or increase in the Social Security payroll or "FICA" tax.

Finally, with regard to the third leg of the retirement security stool, as mentioned previously, the average savings rate is currently at a very low level. Historically, workers have started too late, put away too little, and invested too conservatively. In order to provide for a reasonably comfortable retirement, younger workers will need to embark on an aggressive savings program through defined contribution plans, IRAs, and other methods to meet this substantial future need.

In the remainder of this chapter, we will discuss the retirement planning process, including one of the most important skills a financial planner must possess—calculation of a client's retirement savings need.

THE RETIREMENT PLANNING PROCESS

The gamut of retirement planning clients ranges from those who are many years away from retirement to those who are either just at the point of retirement or already retired. In addition, their circumstances may vary significantly. For instance, a business owner may be able to build his or her retirement funding through his or her business while a key executive may be in a position to negotiate meaningful retirement benefits. Other employees may not be able to influence the benefits provided by their employers. Further, certain clients may have considerable personal assets outside of their employer, while others will have very little other than company-provided retirement benefits and Social Security.

Moreover, retirement planning may not only involve the skills of a competent financial planner but may require the services of an attorney specializing in estate planning as well as an employee benefits expert and/or investment manager. However, it is usually the financial planner who will provide the major portion of the retirement planning services. To do this effectively, the financial planner follows a prescribed retirement planning process involving the following six general stages:

1. Establishing and defining the client-planner relationship
2. Gathering client data including retirement goals
3. Analyzing and evaluating the client's financial status
4. Developing and presenting retirement planning recommendations and/or alternatives

5. Implementing the retirement planning recommendations

6. Monitoring the retirement planning recommendations

In the following sections, we will discuss these six general stages of the retirement planning process.

Stage 1: Establishing and defining the client-planner relationship

In this first stage of the retirement planning process, the client and the planner identify the specific services to be provided by the planner. This involves educating the client as to his or her needs and the appropriateness of specific services to address those needs. This also requires that the client place a high degree of trust in the planner.

In the initial step, the planner and the client mutually define the "scope of the engagement". The **scope of the engagement** is the universe of services that the planner and the client agree is necessary and appropriate, and that the financial planner is qualified and willing to provide. The scope may include the entire array of retirement planning services or may be limited to specific activities. The process of mutual definition of the scope of the engagement is designed to provide realistic expectations for both parties. While there is no requirement that the scope of the engagement be in writing, it is normally a prudent practice for legal and ethics disclosure purposes. If an engagement letter is not executed by the parties, the financial planner should prepare file memoranda that document any oral understandings about the engagement objectives; the scope of the services provided; the roles and responsibilities of the financial planner, the client, and other advisors; compensation arrangements; and scope limitations and other constraints. Also, it is important for both the client and the financial planner to realize that the scope of the engagement may, after initial mutual definition, be revised by mutual agreement.

In mutually defining the scope of the engagement, the client and the financial planner may agree to so-called segmented (or modular) retirement planning rather than comprehensive retirement planning. In segmented retirement planning, the scope of the engagement is limited to a specific subject area or areas. For instance, a client who does not currently have nor is projected to accumulate significant assets, may not need the services of a separate estate planning attorney. On the other hand, a reasonably wealthy client who has never used the services of a financial planner may require comprehensive retirement planning in which all of the major aspects of retirement planning are evaluated.

Stage 2: Gathering client data including retirement goals

Having established and defined the client-planner relationship in Stage 1 and having determined that the scope of the engagement includes retirement planning services, the second stage of the retirement planning process is to determine a client's personal and financial goals, needs, and priorities and to gather appropriate quantitative information and documents relevant to the client's personal financial situation. In gathering client data, it is important to draw a distinction between **qualitative** and

quantitative information obtained from or about the client. Examples of *qualitative* data include the client's personal and financial goals, needs, priorities, time horizon, and risk tolerance. Such data are considered qualitative in that they are subjective and therefore require a judgment on the part of the client rather than constituting objective, factual data.

Examples of *quantitative* information include copies of wills, trust documents, recent income tax returns, employer's current statement of employee benefits, investment account statements, copies of insurance policies currently in force, statements of projected social insurance benefits, ages and current health of client family members, fair market value of assets owned, personal financial statements (including a statement of personal financial position and a personal cash flow statement), credit history, etc. All of these items constitute objective, factual data that can be expressed in quantitative terms. Depending upon the type of client engagement and its scope, the financial planner will need to make a determination as to what quantitative information is both sufficient and relevant to the particular engagement. This information may be obtained either directly from the client or through other sources by interview, questionnaire, data-gathering forms, client records, or other documents. Data-gathering forms may also be useful in garnering such qualitative information as the client's anticipated retirement date, where the client intends to reside during retirement, whether the client will work part-time during retirement, and whether the client anticipates significant changes in lifestyle during retirement.

Benefit Plan Information

In order to provide competent retirement planning, a planner needs to obtain complete information about all employee benefit plans in which the client and the client's spouse are currently participating *or have ever participated*. This includes not only qualified or nonqualified retirement plans but also other benefit plans such as health insurance, life insurance, or the use of employer athletic or health clubs during retirement. The planner should rely solely on the plan documents rather than on the client's understanding of the benefits provided by the plans involved. In that regard, plans subject to the provisions of the Employee Retirement Income Security Act of 1974 (ERISA) are required to provide each participant with a Summary Plan Description (SPD). This document contains much useful information about such topics as early retirement, normal retirement age, deferred retirement, payout options available at retirement, terms that may trigger a loss of benefits, and the procedures for filing claims against the plan.

As for qualified plans, the employer must provide an individual benefit statement at least annually. These statements must, at a minimum, show the employee/client his or her accrued benefit and vesting status; but other information, such as an estimate of the employee's Social Security benefit and death benefits payable to spouses or other beneficiaries, may also be included. For non-ERISA plans, documentation of the plan may be difficult or impossible to obtain. In these cases, the planner should refer to the employer's benefits manual or other similar information.

Finally, the planner needs to estimate the benefits the client will receive from government benefits such as Social Security, veterans' benefits, and the like.

Personal Financial Statements

In constructing or reviewing a statement of personal financial position (or personal balance sheet), the planner must ascertain that the included assets are stated at fair market value rather than at historical book value. This is especially true in the case of closely held businesses. Equally as important as determining a current value is the problem of determining whether the small business interest will continue as an income source during retirement.

It is essential that the planner not overlook the client's liabilities. The client's traditional debt obligations are usually easily determinable. However, some obligations may not appear on the statement of personal financial position, such as future alimony or child support or outstanding property settlement payments, state or federal tax liabilities, or legal judgments. Clients may also be reluctant, or even embarrassed, to offer information about some of these obligations.

The planner will then need to identify those client assets potentially available to generate retirement income. Generally, it is useful to categorize these assets as investment assets, investment real estate assets, tax-deferred savings, and before-tax savings. As a general rule, investment assets, including such items as securities, money market accounts, limited partnership interests, and mutual funds, are originally funded with after-tax dollars and are, therefore, presumed to be liquidated for retirement needs. Income earned on these assets is assumed to be taxable each year and such assets are assumed to be liquidated without the payment of income taxes, except to the extent that they have appreciated in value since acquisition.

Real estate assets that will be sold at retirement should be included in the available retirement resources at their estimated sale price less the income taxes and other expenses payable upon sale and any mortgage indebtedness at that time. Mortgage indebtedness amounts at retirement can be calculated on a financial function calculator.

The original invested amounts in tax-deferred savings vehicles funded with after-tax dollars will be recovered tax-free upon distribution but the earnings on the invested funds will be subject to income taxation. Examples of this type of asset are nondeductible IRAs, thrift plans, single or flexible premium annuities, and life insurance cash values.

Savings funded through income tax deductions (e.g. deductible IRAs) and/or by employer contributions to a retirement plan (e.g., 401(k) plans and 403(b) plans) are usually fully taxable upon distribution.

The amount of income needed in retirement is often determined by applying a ratio or percentage to the client's pre-retirement income. Typically these income replacement percentages have ranged from 70 to 80 percent. However, it can vary widely from one individual to another. While a planner may use typical income replacement ratios to weigh the reasonableness of a client's retirement income goal, a client's retirement income goal should not be determined based solely on such ratios. Rather, the planner needs to thoroughly analyze the client's personal cash flow statement to assess both current and expected retirement expenses. The accuracy of the retirement savings need calculation (discussed in Stage 3) depends on the accuracy of the estimated retirement expenditures that reflect the client's retirement goals and bear a reasonable relationship to pre-retirement expenditures. In determining the reasonableness of the estimated retirement expenditures, the planner should determine that the level of housing, health care, insurance, entertainment and travel, and pension expenses have been adjusted from the pre-retirement levels to reflect what is anticipated during retirement.

Retirement Planning Assumptions

Another part of the data gathering stage is the determination, by both the planner and the client, of the retirement planning assumptions. Key among these assumptions is the anticipated investment return on those assets earmarked for retirement. Most planners tend to use a flat average annual rate of return, which has the disadvantage of not taking into consideration the volatility of the return. Volatility can have a major impact on the actual average rate of return. For instance, if a planner were to use a 10 percent average annual return on a client's portfolio, each $1,000 would grow to about $1,611 in five years. If instead, the portfolio was to earn 20 percent in each of the first three years, 5 percent in the fourth, but then was to lose 15 percent in the fifth year, the average return is still 10 percent but each $1,000 has then grown only to about $1,542. One can construct other scenarios in which the average return over five years is 10 percent but yet the amount accumulated does not equal the amount that accumulates using a 10 percent year-over-year return.

Without much question, one of the greatest threats to a retiree's economic independence during retirement is inflation. Inflation gradually erodes a retiree's purchasing power over the retirement period. For instance, if we assume that the total of a retiree's pension income and Social Security benefit are exactly equal to the retiree's required retirement income in the first year of retirement, that inflation averages 4 percent per year, and that the retiree's pension income is not indexed for inflation (as is Social Security), after 10 years the retiree's retirement income will cover only about 75 percent of the retiree's retirement income requirement. After 25 years of retirement, his or her income will cover only 50 percent of the retiree's need.

Projecting future inflation rates is problematical; however, some general guidelines may be useful. For instance, from December 1950 to December 1992, the average compound increase in prices was 4.2 percent. Subsequent to 1992, inflation has averaged less than 3 percent. As a result, some planners may want to use 3-4 percent annual increase for the long term but other more cautious and conservative planners may choose a higher rate. Of course, another issue is that the consumer price index (CPI) is made up of a "market basket" of about 12 categories of goods and services purchased by the "average" consumer. Unfortunately, a specific client is not "average": His or her personal rate of inflation may vary significantly from the CPI due to regional variations from the national rate, the heavy weighting of housing prices in the CPI, and personal buying habits. Moreover, retirees generally purchase more services than goods, and services have escalated in price more quickly than have goods. Underestimating the actual inflation rate will cause a significant shortfall in retirement income.

In addition to the anticipated investment return and the rate of inflation, the planner and the client need to make a reasonable assumption about the client's age at retirement and life expectancy. While historically an individual's retirement age tended to be linked with the start of Social Security benefits (age 65, until recently), in recent years, a large percentage of individuals have instead retired early. In fact, today the average retirement age of American workers is age 62. Factors that have contributed to this earlier retirement age are health issues, job elimination, or corporate downsizing under early retirement incentive programs.

With regard to how long one can expect to live, even mortality-table data are at best only rough estimates in light of the fact that slightly more than one half of people of a given age will live *beyond* the life expectancy for their age. For instance, a couple in which the male is age 65 and the female is age 62, have individual life expectancies of about 15 and 21 years respectively. However, from a mathematical (or statistical) standpoint, these individuals have more than a 50 percent chance of living beyond their respective life expectancies. This is because the median age of death is the age when a person has exactly a 50/50 chance of surviving for his or her mortality-table life expectancy. For our 65 and 62 year-old couple, the *median* number of years until death is 15.7 and 22 years, respectively. This illustrates the inadvisability of using median ages of death. By reference to the same mortality table from which the foregoing life expectancies are derived, one can ascertain that the 65-year-old male has a 25 percent probability of surviving nearly 22 years to age 86.9 and a 10 percent chance of surviving almost 27 years to age 91.8. In comparison, the 62-year-old female has a 25 percent chance of surviving almost 28 years to age 90.9 and a 10 percent chance of surviving about 34 years to age 96.2. Consequently, the client needs to decide how much risk he or she is willing to incur that he or she will outlive his or her retirement income.

In the case of married couples, using the life expectancy of the spouse whose life expectancy is longer will result in underestimating the length of the couple's retirement income needs. Strangely enough, the average number of years until the second death of two persons is *longer* than the individual life expectancy of either person alone.[1] In fact, according to *National Vital Statistics Reports*, Vol. 51, No. 3, December 19, 2002, the average number of years until the second death of a husband and wife both age 65 is about 23.3 years, whereas the husband and wife have individual life expectancies of 16.3 years and 19.2 years, respectively. This is more than four years longer than the life expectancy of the wife, individually. Accordingly, planners should generally use *joint* (second-to-die) life expectancies (defined as the average number of years until both spouses will have died) rather than *joint-and-survivor* life expectancies in determining the average number of years of retirement income required for a married couple. In the case of the couple discussed earlier in which the male is 65 and the female is 62, use of joint-and-survivor life expectancies will result in half of such couples exhausting their retirement fund about one year early, one fourth depleting their funds about six years prematurely, and one in ten running out of money almost 11 years too soon. This also illustrates the necessity to use conservative estimates of life expectancy. Indeed, some people will likely be retired for more years than the number of years they actually worked.

A final key assumption is the client's anticipated effective income tax rate during retirement. This rate should be a blend of the client's federal and state income tax rates and should be based on only current income tax rates (since no one can hope to accurately predict future rates).

The data gathering stage of the retirement planning process is the one in which the client and the planner mutually identify retirement income needs as well as the resources or assets that are currently allocated and presumably available for meeting these needs.

---

[1] *Tools & Techniques of Financial Planning*, by Leimberg, Satinsky, Doyle, and Jackson, 7th edition, The National Underwriter Company, 2004, Chapter 29, page 397.

Stage 3: Analyzing and Evaluating the Client's Financial Status

Having gathered the client's qualitative and quantitative retirement data, the planner is now ready to move to the stage in which he or she analyzes and evaluates the client's financial status and degree of preparedness for retirement. This involves the calculation of the client's retirement savings need. This calculation involves the following six steps:

1. Develop an estimate of the value, at the time of retirement, of those assets designated as being available for retirement.
2. Develop an estimate of the after-tax value of the assets in step 1 by subtracting the estimated income taxes payable upon the anticipated sale or taxable distribution of such assets.
3. Determine if there is a first-year anticipated deficit or surplus of retirement income, based only on inflation-adjusted income sources.
4. Determine the amount of the retirement fund necessary to generate annual income, growing annually with inflation, that is adequate to offset any first-year retirement income deficit as determined in Step 3.
5. Calculate the additional amount of savings needed to create the retirement fund determined in Step 4.
6. Calculate the additional annual savings required to accumulate the necessary retirement fund.

Step 1: Develop an estimate of the value, at the time of retirement, of those assets designated as being available for retirement.

In this first step of the retirement savings need determination, the present value of the assets categorized in the data gathering stage (Stage 2) of the retirement planning process as investment assets, real estate assets, tax-deferred savings, and before-tax savings is converted to a future value. In order to make this conversion, we need to know the current market value of each of these assets, their assumed growth rates, and the number of years until retirement. Again, this information was obtained in Stage 2 of the retirement planning process. This step involves performing a future value calculation on a financial function calculator where the current market value is PV, the growth or appreciation rate is I/YR, and the number of years until retirement is N. For example, an asset having a current market value of $100,000 which is anticipated to grow in value at a compound rate of 5 percent per year for the next 10 years until retirement will have a future value at retirement of $162,889 calculated using the following keystrokes on the HP 10BII calculator:

100,000 +/- PV; 5 I/YR; 10 N; FV = 162,889

It is important to remember that the calculations to this point compute the future value of current asset balances only. It is assumed, for this purpose, that no further deposits/additions are made to these assets.

In those cases where the client has an *ongoing* savings/investment program, the value of such savings/investments at the time of retirement must be calculated and added to the future value of the assets that have already accumulated and calculated previously. In order to determine the future value of the client's future annual savings on a financial function calculator, the assumed annual level savings amount is treated as PMT, the assumed earnings rate on such annual savings amounts is treated as I/YR, and the number of years until retirement is treated as N. For example, $5,000 of level annual savings invested at 6 percent per year for 12 years will have a future value at retirement of $84,350 calculated using the following keystrokes on the HP 10BII calculator:

5,000 +/- PMT; 6 I/YR; 12 N; FV = 84,350

This amount would then be added to the amount determined as the future value of the already existing assets, calculated earlier.

Step 2: Develop an estimate of the after-tax value of the assets in Step 1 by subtracting the estimated income taxes payable upon the anticipated sale or taxable distribution of such assets.

Because of the impact of income taxation, the amounts calculated in Step 1 will most likely *not* be available in full at retirement. When these assets are distributed or sold at retirement, income tax will probably be due at that time. These anticipated income taxes must be subtracted from the future value of the assets calculated in Step 1 to arrive at the net amount of available resources (after taxes). Not all assets will necessarily be liquidated at retirement, especially those that are providing an acceptable return. However, for purposes of the retirement savings need calculation, it is assumed that all investment assets will indeed be liquidated at retirement. This assumption is made so that a later comparison may be made between total available retirement assets and total required retirement assets.

To determine the income taxes payable upon liquidation of each of the major categories of retirement assets, the following procedures should be employed:

- **Investment Assets:** Those investment assets that have earned only interest or dividends (have experienced no capital growth) will not be taxed at distribution; however, common stock and mutual funds will be taxed at capital gains rates to the extent they have increased in value since acquisition (anticipated future value less tax basis). The estimated capital gains taxes payable at retirement are then subtracted from the future before-tax value to arrive at the net proceeds at the date of retirement.

- **Real Estate Assets:** To determine the taxable portion of such assets sold at retirement, calculate the difference between the projected sales price and the property's income tax basis and subtract any projected selling expenses. Then apply the capital gains tax rate to determine the projected tax due. Subtract this from the projected before-tax future value to arrive at the net proceeds at date of retirement. If the asset involved is the retiree's personal residence, special tax rules apply and up to $500,000 (for a married couple filing jointly) of the taxable gain may be excluded from taxation, presuming the taxpayer meets the qualifying requirements. Where property is mortgaged, be sure to reduce the after-tax proceeds by any projected mortgage balance at retirement.

- **Tax-Deferred Savings:** Only the earnings that have accumulated tax-deferred are taxable at distribution. Subtract the cost basis (the total after-tax dollars invested) from the projected future value at retirement to determine the taxable gain and then apply the applicable regular income tax rate to this amount to arrive at the income tax due at retirement. Then subtract the estimated income taxes due from the projected future value to arrive at the net proceeds at date of retirement.

- **Before-Tax Savings:** Inasmuch as these assets were funded with before-tax dollars and have accumulated earnings on a tax-deferred basis, they will be fully taxable upon distribution. On the other hand, a lump-sum distribution from a qualified retirement plan may be rolled over into an IRA and withdrawn over the owner's lifetime, thus deferring taxation. However, as discussed earlier, the assumption here is that this distribution is still taxable at retirement. Step 2 includes only lump-sum distributions from retirement plans—not annual benefits. Annual benefits are included in income under Steps 3 and 5.

- **Future Savings/Investments:** To convert these amounts to an after-tax basis, use the procedures just described for the appropriate category of investment discussed in the previous bullets.

All of the assets that have been converted to an after-tax basis should now be totaled to arrive at the net future value of assets available to the client at his or her date of retirement.

Step 3: Determine if there is a first-year anticipated deficit or surplus of retirement income, based only on inflation-adjusted income sources.

In this step, only projected annual income (such as retirement plan benefits) that is adjusted annually during retirement for inflation is considered. Generally, retirement plan benefits are *not* adjusted annually for increases in the cost-of-living so such benefits will not be considered in this step. Level annual retirement plan benefits will be considered in Step 5.

To arrive at the retirement income shortfall, subtract any annual inflation-adjusted retirement income sources from the projected retirement income need as determined in Stage 2 of the retirement planning process. The amount remaining is the annual retirement income deficit that must be met either by income from the client's retirement funds or level (as opposed to inflation-adjusted) sources of retirement income (or both). In rare circumstances, a client will have a surplus (rather than a deficit) of annual retirement income over his or her retirement income needs. This means that the client does not need to use retirement assets to generate retirement income. Again, this is a situation that few planners will actually encounter.

Step 4: Determine the amount of the retirement fund necessary to generate annual income, growing annually with inflation, adequate to offset any first-year retirement income deficit as determined in Step 3.

In Step 4, the planner computes the lump-sum amount necessary to fund the projected annual income deficits over the entire retirement period. But before doing so, the planner must first adjust the projected first-year retirement income deficit, which at this point is expressed in today's dollars, to future dollars at the time of retirement. To make this calculation, let PV = the present value of the retirement income deficit (in today's dollars), let N = the number of years until retirement, and let I/YR = the assumed inflation rate. For example, if PV is $20,000 per year, N is 10 years, and I/YR is 4 percent, the calculation on the HP 10BII calculator is as follows:

20,000 +/- PV; 10 N; 4 I/YR; FV = 29,605

Having adjusted the projected first-year retirement income deficit to its value at the time of retirement, the planner is now ready to calculate the amount of the retirement fund needed to meet this projected income deficit. One complicating factor, however, is that this projected first-year retirement income deficit needs to increase annually with inflation. Consequently, the next calculation called for is what is known as "the present value of an annuity due" (PVAD). One of the key assumptions behind this calculation is that the amount of the fund calculated will be totally depleted at the end of the projected retirement period through the use of both principal and income to fund the annually-inflated income deficit. This is what is known as the **capital utilization** approach, as contrasted with the **capital preservation** approach where only income is used and principal is not consumed. We will discuss these alternative approaches in greater depth later in this chapter.

In order to perform the PVAD calculation, the planner first needs to determine the **inflation-adjusted yield**. While the planner is concerned with both the anticipated annual after-tax return on investments (i) and the expected annual inflation rate (r), unfortunately, the calculator will accommodate only one I/YR. Therefore these two rates must be incorporated into a single inflation-adjusted rate. Intuitively, one would simply subtract the inflation rate from the investment return rate and use the difference as the inflation-adjusted rate. However, from a theoretical standpoint, the inflation-adjusted rate must be calculated with use of the following formula:

I/YR (inflation-adjusted rate) = $[(1 + i)/(1 + r) - 1]$ x 100

For example, if the anticipated annual after-tax return on investments is 7 percent and the expected annual inflation rate is 3 percent, the inflation-adjusted rate is 3.88 percent calculated as follows:

$[(1 + .07)/(1 + .03) - 1]$ x 100 = [1.07/1.03 - 1] x 100 = [1.0388 - 1] x 100 = .0388 x 100 = 3.88

Having calculated the inflation-adjusted rate of return, the planner is now ready to perform the PVAD calculation to determine the retirement fund needed to meet the projected annual income deficit. Before doing so, however, the planner needs to recognize that a retiree will need to have access to his or her annual retirement income at the *beginning*, as opposed to the *end*, of each year during retirement. This is what makes the annual retirement income stream an annuity due rather than an "ordinary annuity" (where payments are made/received at the end of each year).

To perform this calculation, the planner needs to know the first-year retirement income deficit that will increase each year due to inflation (PMT), the inflation-adjusted rate of return (as described earlier) (I/YR), and the number of years of retirement (N). For example, if the first-year annual retirement deficit is $15,000, the inflation-adjusted rate of return is 3.88 (as calculated previously), and the number of years in actual retirement is 25, the retirement fund necessary to meet the inflation-adjusted retirement income deficit is $246,540 calculated as follows on the HP 10BII calculator:

> BEGIN mode; 15,000 +/- PMT; 3.88 I/YR; 25 N; PV = 246,540

Step 5: Calculate the additional amount of savings needed to create the retirement fund determined in Step 4.

Prior to completing this step, the planner needs to have a discussion with the client as to the client's feelings about his or her retirement funds. Is the client comfortable using both the principal and the income from those funds to meet his or her retirement income need or, alternatively, does the client wish to use only the income from those funds to provide his or her retirement income need, leaving the principal intact for possible transfer to his or her heirs or as a hedge against living beyond his or her life expectancy?

As discussed previously, these two approaches are known as **capital utilization** and **capital preservation.** The results of the calculations in Step 5 will vary significantly depending on which of these two approaches is used. As one would surmise, the capital utilization approach (in which capital is fully depleted) requires a much *smaller* retirement fund than that required under the capital preservation (use of fund earnings only) approach. On the other hand, as the retirement period increases, the gap between the size of the retirement fund required under these two approaches narrows.

Of course, everyone would like to be able to accumulate enough retirement assets so that he or she could live on the interest alone and never have to liquidate the principal amount. But for all but the very rich, this is not a realistic option. Most retirees will have to deplete their retirement funds to varying degrees.

Calculations Using the Capital Utilization Approach

To perform this calculation effectively, the planner begins with the amount of the retirement fund necessary to offset the projected retirement income deficit, as determined in Step 4. From this amount, the planner subtracts the total assets identified as available for retirement, which includes currently owned assets and the projected value of the client's existing savings program at the time of retirement, as determined in Step 2. Also subtracted is the present value of level (non-inflation-adjusted) retirement benefits referred to in Step 3. In order to calculate the present value of level retirement benefits, the benefits must first be adjusted for inflation between today and the assumed retirement date (unless already expressed in retirement period dollars). Then, to calculate the present value of these level retirement benefits, we use PMT to represent the level annual retirement benefit amount expressed in retirement period dollars; N to represent the number of years of retirement; and I/YR to represent the investment return rate. For example, if PMT is $15,000 per year, N is 25 years, and I/YR is 7 percent, we solve for PV by using the following HP 10BII keystrokes:

> BEGIN mode; 15,000 +/- PMT; 25 N; 7 I/YR; PV = 187,040

After reducing the retirement fund necessary to offset the projected retirement income deficit by both the total assets identified as being available for retirement and the present value of the anticipated level retirement benefits, the amount remaining is the additional savings need at retirement under the capital utilization approach.

One final adjustment is then to remove the effect of inflation from the additional savings need at retirement (we will perform this calculation in Step 6). This is accomplished by using FV as the additional savings need at retirement, N as the number of years until retirement, and I/YR as the inflation rate. For example, if we assume that FV is $100,000, N is 10 years, and I/YR is 7 percent per year, PV (the present value of the additional savings need at retirement) is $50,835 calculated on the HP 10BII as follows:

100,000 FV; 10 N; 7 I/YR; PV = 50,835

Calculations Using the Capital Preservation Approach

Again, in this calculation, the planner begins with the amount of the retirement fund necessary to offset the projected retirement income deficit, as determined in Step 4. However, the retirement resources available under the capital preservation approach are calculated a bit differently than under capital utilization. Accordingly, we again start with the total assets identified as available for retirement, which includes currently owned assets and the projected value of the client's existing savings program at the time of retirement, as determined in Step 2. However, from this amount, we then subtract the assets required to be preserved to determine the asset resources that are available. To this amount, we add two additional items: (1) the present value of the level annual income stream from the assets preserved, which is calculated by, first, multiplying the assets preserved by the investment return percentage to arrive at the level annual income stream and, then, calculating its present value over the retirement period using the after-tax investment return and (2) the present value of any level retirement benefits to be paid, as calculated under the capital utilization approach. The sum of these three items equals the total resources available.

Next, we subtract from the retirement fund, necessary to offset the projected retirement income deficit, the total resources available as calculated in the previous paragraph. The remainder is the additional savings need at retirement. Finally, as we did under the capital utilization approach, we must remove the effect of inflation from the additional savings need at retirement (again, we will perform this calculation in the upcoming Step 6). This is accomplished by using FV as the additional savings need at retirement, N as the number of years until retirement, and I/YR as the inflation rate. For example, if we assume that FV is $150,000, N is 10 years, and I/YR is 7 percent per year, PV (the present value of the additional savings need at retirement) is $76,252 calculated on the HP 10BII as follows:

150,000 FV; 10 N; 7 I/YR; PV = 76,252

Step 6: Calculate the additional annual savings required to accumulate the necessary retirement fund.

In this final step of the retirement savings need calculation, we need to, again, separately discuss the procedures employed under both the capital utilization and capital preservation approaches.

Calculations Using the Capital Utilization Approach

What we are attempting to do in this step is to calculate the annually-increasing serial savings amount required to accumulate the additional savings need at retirement, previously computed in Step 5. We will assume that the annual savings amounts will occur at the end of each year, meaning that we will be determining the present value of an ordinary annuity (PVOA), rather than an annuity due (PVAD). To perform this calculation, we need to begin with the amount of the additional savings need at retirement for the capital utilization approach as deflated for the effect of inflation, as computed in Step 5. Using this amount as FV, N as the number of years until retirement, and I/YR as the inflation-adjusted annual investment return (calculated in the manner described in Step 4), we calculate the PMT (or the annually-increasing serial savings amount required to accumulate the additional savings need at retirement). For example, if FV is $300,000, N is 10 years, and I/YR is 3.88 (using the same assumptions as we did in Step 4—an after-tax investment return of 7 percent and an inflation rate of 3 percent), then the PMT is $25,127 calculated as follows:

END mode; 300,000 FV; 10 N; 3.88 I/YR; PMT = 25,127

What we have just calculated is the first serial (increasing) savings payment *before* any adjustment for inflation. Since we will be making our savings payments at the *end* of each year, we need to, therefore, adjust this first payment to its value at the end of the first year by multiplying it by (1 + the inflation rate). This is the amount of the first-year serial savings payment to be made at the end of the year.

If instead of using annually-increasing savings amounts, the client prefers to make a fixed, level savings payment at the end of each year that will not increase annually, a different calculation is required. If you recall, in Step 5 we calculated the additional savings need required at retirement under both the capital utilization and capital preservation approaches and then deflated this amount to remove the effect of inflation. For purposes of this level payment calculation, however, we must not use the deflated amount, but rather the additional savings need at retirement unadjusted for inflation from Step 5. Letting this amount equal FV, letting N equal the number of years until retirement, and letting I/YR equal the after-tax investment return (rather than the inflation-adjusted return since we are no longer adjusting the annual savings amounts for inflation), we solve for PMT, the level savings payment invested at the end of each year. For example, if FV is $350,000, N is 10 years, and I/YR is 7 percent, PMT is $25,332 calculated as follows:

END mode; 350,000 FV; 10 N; 7 I/YR; PMT = 25,332

Calculations Using the Capital Preservation Approach

Under the capital preservation approach, the calculations for Step 6 are *identical* to those we just performed under the capital utilization approach. Accordingly, simply follow the instructions provided under the capital utilization approach using the amounts calculated under the capital preservation approach in previous steps.

Note: In Exhibit 1.1, starting on page 20, there is a comprehensive example of the calculation of the retirement savings need under both the capital utilization and capital preservation approaches, using the six steps of the process just described.

Stage 4: Developing and presenting retirement planning recommendations and/or alternatives

After having determined the retirement savings need in Stage 3 of the retirement planning process, using the 6-step retirement savings need calculation process, the planner is now in a position to evaluate alternative courses of action for the client and then develop definitive recommendations for a retirement savings program. In doing so, the planner may need to consider multiple assumptions and conduct research or consult with other professionals. The result of this analysis may be a single alternative, multiple alternatives, or no alternative to the client's current course of action. Clearly, the financial planner needs to evaluate such alternatives with a clear understanding of his or her level of competency and legal authority. The development and evaluation of alternatives is a highly subjective activity, and it is doubtful that any two financial planners will identify exactly the same alternatives.

After identifying and evaluating possible alternatives, the planner is now ready to develop recommendations that may be expected to reasonably achieve the client's goals, needs, and priorities. The planner must be satisfied that there is sufficient relevant information to form the basis for any recommendations made. Relevant information may include an understanding of the client's goals, existing financial situation, resources available for achieving the goals, non-financial factors, and external factors. Any resulting recommendations must, therefore, be consistent with and directly affected by the:

- Mutually-defined scope of the engagement
- Mutually-defined client goals, needs, and priorities
- Quantitative data provided by the client
- Personal and economic assumptions made
- Financial planner's analysis and evaluation of the client's current situation
- Alternatives selected by the financial planner

One possible result of the recommendations made is that the client may now need to revise one or more of his or her retirement lifestyle goals.

Where the Client is a Business Owner

If the client is the owner of a closely held business, it may be advantageous for the client to establish a qualified retirement plan, discussed in subsequent chapters. Some of the reasons for establishing such a plan include:

- The business obtains an income tax deduction for contributions made to the plan.
- The plan participant pays no income taxes when the employer makes the plan contributions but instead defers such taxation until plan benefits are distributed.
- The funds used for plan contributions come from the business, rather than from the owner's personal funds, and therefore do not affect his or her personal cash flow.
- If the plan permits employees to make pre-tax contributions, the amounts contributed by the employees avoid current taxation.

Use of a qualified retirement plan as a savings program option will necessitate upward adjustment of the retirement savings required at retirement age to add the taxes payable upon distribution from the plan at retirement. Another way to express this is that a larger before-tax amount must be accumulated so that the after-tax amount available to the client equals the retirement savings need. This adjustment is made by dividing the after-tax savings need calculated in Step 5 of the retirement planning process by (1 minus the client's effective tax rate) resulting in the before-tax retirement savings required at retirement age. Then, using this amount, the planner can recalculate the annual savings requirement necessary to accumulate the before-tax retirement savings required. This calculation was performed for the after-tax retirement savings required in Step 6 of the retirement planning process. In performing this recalculation, the planner needs to use the estimated before-tax savings need and a before-tax investment return (rather than an after-tax return) because of the fact that the return will be shielded from current taxation inside the qualified plan trust.

Of course, the amount recalculated as the annual savings requirement necessary to accumulate the before-tax retirement savings required at retirement age, as discussed in the previous paragraph, needs to be evaluated for feasibility. It may be that the closely held business does not currently have adequate cash flow to make plan contributions in this amount.

Where the Client is an Employee Rather Than a Business Owner

In this situation, the planner needs to refer to the information gathered about employer-provided qualified plans in Stage 2 of the retirement planning process. If the client is a married couple, such information must be obtained for both spouses. Then the planner needs to determine how much each spouse can contribute to his or her respective qualified plan. In addition, the planner needs to evaluate whether the spouses qualify to contribute to IRAs on either a deductible or non-deductible basis.

So much of making a recommendation regarding how to effectively take advantage of an employer's qualified retirement plan(s) is understanding the client's situation, including such information as the client's annual retirement savings need, the client's disposable income as reflected in the personal cash flow statement, the client's age, the client's budgeting and savings skills, salary, marginal income tax bracket, investment plan, and other client goals and objectives. The client's annual retirement savings need must be compared to the client's "disposable income" (excess of cash inflows over cash outflows) from the client's personal cash flow statement. The amount of the client's disposable income will, therefore, be an important factor in determining the type of plan that will fulfill the client's need. Moreover, tax-deductible contributions to a qualified retirement plan require less cash flow than do after-tax contributions. Clients who have difficulty saving on a regular basis may need a plan that automatically deducts, through a payroll deduction plan, contributions from their salaries.

The amount of a client's salary may also affect his or her ability to make the maximum contribution to specific types of plans. Likewise, clients in high marginal income tax brackets will benefit more from before-tax contributions and the tax deferral of annual earnings inside the fund. Finally, the planner needs to look at the client's other investments, outside of qualified retirement plans, to strike a reasonable portfolio balance. The investment options offered by certain plans may not be appropriate for the specific client. When making this determination, the planner also needs to consider penalties or fees associated with particular investment options, such as ongoing management fees, back-end loads on mutual funds, and deferred sales charges on annuities.

Client goals and objectives and the related time horizons for these goals may also drive the type of plan(s) recommended. For example, if client goals such as an extended vacation, college funding, home remodeling, or an automobile purchase will affect the client's future cash flow, it needs to be factored into the choice of retirement savings vehicle. In these instances, perhaps the client needs to consider installing or accessing a qualified plan that provides for "in-service distributions", such as a plan loan.

Presenting the Recommendations

After evaluating alternatives and developing recommendations, the financial planner must now communicate with the client and assist the client in making an informed decision. It is recommended that such communications be in writing and include a summary of the client's goals and significant assumptions, a description of any limitations on the work performed, the recommendations made, and a statement that projected results may not be achieved.

The financial planner is obligated to make a reasonable effort to assist the client in understanding his or her current situation, the recommendation(s) being made, the rationale for the recommendation(s), and the expected impact on the ability of the client to achieve his or her goals, needs, and priorities. Note that the financial planner is *not* responsible for making the client understand these issues, but he or she *is* required to make a reasonable effort in helping the client to understand them. Some of the factors the client needs to understand are:

- Material personal and economic assumptions
- Interdependence of recommendations
- Advantages and disadvantages of each recommendation
- Risks
- Time sensitivity

The client needs to appreciate the sensitivity of changes in personal and economic conditions on the results that may be achieved by the recommendation(s). New tax laws, a change in family status, loss of or change in job or career, actual versus anticipated investment returns, and the client's health could all have a significant effect on the degree of achievement of the client's goals, needs, and priorities under a particular recommendation.

The financial planner also has an obligation to disclose, if necessary, any conflicts of interest that may have resulted from the recommendation(s) made. For instance, if the financial planner is recommending the purchase of a large quantity of securities or mutual funds from which the financial planner will receive a material amount of compensation, this must be disclosed to the client before the client acts on the recommendation.

In summary, the planner needs to analyze the client's total financial and personal situation to determine how certain factors will be affected by the choice of particular qualified retirement plans or IRAs. The planner should also provide the client with the information just discussed so that the client can make an informed decision. The presentation of recommendations presents a good opportunity for the financial planner to determine whether his or her recommendations meet the expectations of the client, whether the client is motivated to act on the recommendations, and whether the recommendations may need revision.

Stage 5: Implementing the retirement planning recommendations

After the retirement planning recommendations have been developed, presented to the client, and accepted by the client, the planner and the client must mutually agree on the responsibilities for implementing the recommendations, consistent with the scope of the engagement. It is essential that the client take responsibility for accepting or rejecting the retirement planning recommendations and for either implementing them personally or delegating implementation to others. Regardless of the level of assistance, implementation decisions are made by the client, *not* by the planner. If the planner is to provide implementation services, the specific services must be mutually agreed upon by the client and the planner. This may involve revision of the scope of the engagement. Some of the responsibilities that may be assumed by the planner include:

- Identifying activities necessary for the plan's implementation
- Determining the division of activities between the planner and the client
- Establishing the selection criteria for selecting and referring to other professionals
- Coordinating with other professionals
- Sharing information as authorized
- Selecting and securing products and/or services

This is another time at which the planner may be obliged to disclose conflicts of interest, sources of compensation, or material relationships with other professionals or advisers that have not been disclosed previously. For instance, if the planner refers the client to other professionals or advisers, the planner is obligated to indicate the basis for the referral, including any direct or indirect compensation that he or she may receive as a result. This team of other professionals or advisers may include a financial planner, tax preparer, attorney, plan administration firm, and/or an actuary. The planner, however, should be the team leader in coordinating the efforts of each professional involved.

It is entirely possible that the planner may have been selected to implement the recommendations of another retirement planning professional (such as the tax preparer). This will require the planner to revert back to Step 1 in the retirement planning process to mutually define with the client the scope of the engagement, including such matters as the extent to which the planner will rely on any information, analysis, or recommendations provided by others.

In implementing the retirement planning recommendations, not only is the planner obligated to select any appropriate products and services consistent with the client's goals, needs, and priorities, but he or she also needs to reasonably investigate and evaluate those products and services. Different retirement planners might select different products or services for the same client, both of which may be suitable for the client and capable of achieving the client's goals, needs, and priorities. Clearly such a selection is subjective.

Stage 6: Monitoring the retirement planning recommendations

The final stage in the retirement planning process is the monitoring of retirement planning recommendations implemented in Stage 5. The planner needs to mutually define with the client the responsibilities for periodic monitoring of the implemented retirement planning recommendations. If the client wants the planner to monitor the progress and degree of success achieved by implementing the retirement planning recommendations, this needs to be agreed upon between the parties. Such an agreement should also specify exactly what is to be monitored, the frequency of monitoring, and how the results will be communicated to the client.

In determining a client's progress toward achieving established retirement planning goals, the planner should (1) ascertain whether all recommended actions to achieve the goals have been undertaken; (2) measure and evaluate the actual progress toward achievement of the goals; and (3) identify developments in the client's circumstances and in external factors that have affected the retirement planning recommendations. The client and planner also need to anticipate that the factors affecting the client's retirement savings program will change during the pre-retirement years. For example, the client may decide to revise his or her retirement planning goals, he or she may lose his or her job, or a second wage earner may enter the workforce. Moreover, interest rates, inflation, and other market factors may materially impact the client's retirement savings program. The planner should communicate to the client, typically in writing, an evaluation of progress toward achieving the client's retirement planning goals.

In certain cases, the results of monitoring may give rise to the re-initiation of earlier stages in the retirement planning process and modification of the scope of the engagement. This illustrates the point that retirement planning is an *ongoing process*, not a single transaction or series of transactions. Monitoring can, thereby, result in starting and restarting the process at various points in the process.

EXHIBIT 1.1 COMPREHENSIVE EXAMPLE OF THE RETIREMENT SAVINGS NEED CALCULATION

Dean and Cathy Graves, both age 40, have requested your help in planning for their retirement. Dean, who works for an investment advisory firm at a salary of $60,000 annually, is vested in his employer's qualified retirement plan. Cathy is an administrator for a large, local church at a salary of $50,000. The Graves have two sons: Tim, age 5 and Matt, age 8. The following information is available about the Graves:

- A personal cash flow statement for the prior calendar year
- A statement of personal financial position as of the end of the prior calendar year
- A summary of data gathered in Stage 2 of the retirement planning process

Dean and Cathy Graves
Personal Cash Flow Statement
For the Year Ending December 31, 20XX

CASH INFLOWS:

Cathy's salary	$50,000	
Dean's salary	60,000	
Rental income	7,200	
Interest income*	300	
Dividend/capital gain income**	3,800	
Total Cash Inflows		**$121,300**

CASH OUTFLOWS:

Savings and investment	$9,040	
Fixed Outflows:		
Auto loan payments (P&I)	$10,600	
Residence mortgage payments (PITI)	20,300	
Rental property mtg. pymts (PITI)	6,000	
Insurance premiums (auto, life)	860	
Total Fixed Outflows		**$37,760**
Variable Outflows:		
Food at home	$5,700	
Recreation/vacations	5,100	
Transportation	4,800	
Clothing/personal care	4,600	
Utilities/household expenses	4,400	
Medical/dental care	800	
IRA contributions	6,000	
Taxes (income, FICA)	39,000	
Miscellaneous	4,100	
Total Variable Outflows		**74,500**
TOTAL CASH OUTFLOWS		**$121,300**

*Interest earned on retirement assets only.
**Stock: $31,000 @ 4.9%; Mutual fund: $38,000 @ 6%.

Dean and Cathy Graves
Statement of Personal Financial Position
As of December 31, 20XX

Assets:		Liabilities and Net Worth:	
Cash/Cash Equivalents:		Liabilities:	
Checking account	$5,000	Credit card balance	$2,700
Money market fund		Margin a/c balance	5,800
(emergency fund)	18,000	Auto note balance	13,300
Certificate of deposit	6,100	Auto note balance	9,400
Total Cash/Cash Equivalents	**$29,100**	Rental property mtg. bal	81,600
		Residence mtg. balance	136,900
		Total Liabilities	**$249,700**
Invested Assets:			
Common stock	$31,000		
Mutual fund (college fund)	30,000		
Mutual fund	38,000		
Rental property	190,000		
IRAs	18,300		
Vested accrued pension			
benefits (Dean)	14,100		
Total Invested Assets	**$321,400**		
Use Assets:		**Net Worth**	**$496,100**
Art collection	$6,200		
Auto-Dean	23,000		
Auto-Cathy	17,000		
Household furnishings	12,500		
Clothing, jewelry, etc.	11,600		
Residence	325,000		
Total Use Assets	**$395,300**		
TOTAL ASSETS	**$745,800**	**TOTAL LIABILITIES & NET WORTH**	**$745,800**

**Dean and Cathy Graves
Summary of Data Gathered in Step 2
of the Retirement Planning Process**

Children:	Tim, age 5	Matt, age 8			
Retirement Income Need		$80,000			
Available Resources:			Growth Rate		
	Current Market Value	Capital Gains	Dividends & Interest	Total	Original Cost
Invested Assets:					
CD	$6,100		5%	5%	$6,100
Common stock	31,000	7%	2%	9%	31,000
Mutual fund	38,000		8%	8%	29,000
Real Estate Assets:					
		Appreciation Rate	Basis at Retirement	Mortgage at Retirement	Estimated Sales Costs
Rental property	190,000	5%	0	0	10%
Tax-Deferred Savings:	None				
Before-Tax Savings:		Growth Rate			
IRAs	18,300	8%			
Retirement income Sources:		Annual Benefit			
	Today's Dollars	Future Dollars	Duration (# of yrs.)	Inflation-Adjusted Payout?	
Dean's pension	20,000		Ret. 30 yrs	No	
Social Security	16,000		Ret. 30 yrs	Yes	
Future savings/investment program:		Annual Level Savings	Fund Earnings		
After-tax savings		3,600	5% after-tax		
Tax-deferred savings		6,000	8%		
Before-tax savings		-0-			
Other resources:	None				
Assumptions:					
Inflation rate—3%	Income Tax Rate 28%	Number of Years Until Retirement—27	After-Tax Return for Retirement Funds—7%	Length of Retirement—30 years	

Step 1: Develop an estimate of the value, at the time of retirement, of those assets designated as being available for retirement			

Number of years until retirement	27		

Estimate future value of available resources at retirement:

	Investment Assets:	**Current Market Value**	**Growth Rate**	**Future Value at Retirement**
	CD	$6,100	5%	$22,774
	Common stock	31,000	9%	317,598
	Mutual fund	38,000	8%	303,546
	Real Estate Assets:		**Appreciation Rate**	
	Rental property	190,000	5%	
	Tax-Deferred Savings:	-0-		709,357 -0-
	Before-Tax Savings:		**Growth Rate**	
	IRAs	18,300	8%	146,182

Estimate future value of future savings/investment program at retirement:

	Future Savings/ Investment Program	**Annual Level Savings**	**Fund Earnings**	
	After-tax savings	3,600	5% (after-tax)	196,809
	Tax-deferred savings	6,000	8%	524,105
	Before-Tax savings	-0-		-0-

Step 2: Develop an estimate of the after-tax value of the assets in Step 1 by deducting the estimated income taxes payable upon the anticipated sale or taxable distribution of such assets. (taxes estimated at 28%)

Investment Assets:	Future Value At Retirement	Less: Original Cost	Gain In Value	Taxable Portion Of Gain	Estimated Tax Payable	Future Value Minus Tax = Net Proceeds
CD	$22,774	$6,100	$16,674	0	0	$22,774
Common stock	317,598	31,000	286,598	233,685*	65,432	252,166
Mutual fund	303,546	29,000	274,546	0	0	303,546
Real Estate Assets:		Less: Basis and Sale Costs	Taxable Gain	Tax Payable	Mortgage Balance, Sale Costs	Future Value Minus Tax, Mortgage, & Sale Costs = Net Proceeds
Rental property	709,357	70,936	638,421	178,758	70,936	459,663
Tax-deferred savings	None					
Before-Tax Savings:						Future Value Minus Tax =Net Proceeds
IRAs	146,182			40,931		105,251
Future Savings/ Investment Program		Less: Cost Basis	Taxable Amount	Tax Payable		
After-Tax Savings	196,809	0	N/A	N/A		196,809
Tax-Deferred Savings	524,105	162,000	362,105	101,389		422,716
Other Resources:	None					
Net Asset Resources Available at Retirement						**$1,762,925**

*Reduced by dividends received at 2% per year on which income tax has already been paid (31,000 PV; 27 N; 2 I/YR; FV = 52,913; 286,598 – 52,913 = 233,685)

Step 3: Determine if there is a first-year anticipated deficit or surplus of retirement income, based only on inflation-adjusted income sources (in today's dollars).	
Annual retirement income need from Summary of Data Gathered in Stage 2 of the Retirement Planning Process	$80,000
Less: inflation-adjusted income from Summary of Data Gathered in Stage 2 of the Retirement Planning Process (Social Security)	16,000
Retirement income deficit (surplus) to be met by retirement fund and level income sources	$64,000

Step 4: Determine the amount of the retirement fund necessary to generate annual income, growing annually with inflation, adequate to offset any first-year retirement income deficit as determined in Step 3.

Adjust income deficit for inflation over pre-retirement period:
    $ 64,000—Present value of retirement income deficit (Step 3)
    27—Number of years until retirement
    3%—Inflation rate
    Future value of income deficit in first retirement year—$142,162

Determine retirement fund needed to meet income deficit:
    $142,162—Payment (FV of income deficit)
    30—Number of years of retirement
    3.8835%—Inflation-adjusted yield determined using:

                        7%   After-Tax Return
                        3%   Inflation Rate

Lump sum needed at **beginning** of retirement (PVAD) to fund annual income deficit that increases annually with inflation (i.e., a growing annuity)   **$2,590,253**

Step 5: Calculate the additional amount of savings needed to create the retirement fund determined in Step 4 using the CAPITAL UTILIZATION APPROACH.

Resources needed (Step 4)	$2,590,253

Resources available:

Asset resources (Step 2)	1,762,925

Present value of level benefits:

Adjust level benefits for inflation over pre-retirement period:

$20,000—Present value of level benefit

27—Number of years until retirement

3%—Inflation rate

$44,426—Future value of level benefit in first retirement year

Determine present value of level benefits at retirement:

$44,426—Payment (FV of level benefit)

30—Number of years of retirement

7%—After-tax investment return

$589,874—PVAD of level benefits

Total PVAD of level benefits	589,874
Total Resources Available	$2,352,799

Determine additional savings need at retirement using **Capital Utilization Approach**

$2,590,253—Resources needed

2,352,799—Less: resources available

Additional savings need at retirement using **Capital Utilization Approach**	$237,454

Deflation calculation:

27—Number of years until retirement

3%—Inflation rate

Deflated value of additional savings needed at retirement using

Capital Utilization Approach	**$106,899**

Step 6: Calculate the additional annual savings required to accumulate the necessary retirement fund using the CAPITAL UTILIZATION APPROACH

Serial (increasing) savings calculation (payments to be made at the end of the year, before adjustment for inflation):

$106,899—FV (deflated value of additional savings need from Step 5)

27—Number of years until retirement

3.8835%—Inflation-adjusted yield determined using:

7%—After-tax investment return

3%—Inflation rate

Calculate the first serial (increasing) savings payment before adjustment for inflation: $2,310

Inflation adjustment:

$2,310—Annual first-year unadjusted serial (increasing) savings required

3%—Inflation rate

Calculate the first serial (increasing) savings payment to be invested at the
end of the current year (adjusted for inflation) $2,379

Level savings calculation (payments to be made at the **end** of each year):

27—Number of years until retirement

7%—After-tax investment return

$ 237,454—Future value (FV) of additional savings needed at retirement from Step 5

Calculate the annual (level) savings payment to be invested at the **end** of each year   **$3,188**

Step 5: Calculate the additional amount of savings needed to create the retirement fund determined in Step 4 using the CAPITAL PRESERVATION APPROACH.	
Resources needed (Step 4)	$2,590,253
Resources available:	
Asset resources (Step 2)	
$1,762,925—Asset Resources Available (Step 2)	
303,546— Less: Assets to be preserved*	
Asset Resources Available using the **Capital Preservation Approach**	1,459,379
Determine present value of income from preserved assets:	
Calculate level income stream from preserved assets:	
$303,546—Assets to be preserved*	
18,213—Annual level income from preserved assets (6%)	
30—Number of years of retirement	
7%—After-tax investment return	
Present value (PVAD) of income from preserved assets	$241,826
Present value of level retirement benefits from Step 5 under Capital Utilization Approach	589,874
Total Resources Available	$2,291,079
Determine additional savings need at retirement using **Capital Preservation Approach:**	
$2,590,253—Resources needed (above)	
2,291,079—Less: Resources available (above)	
Additional savings need at retirement using **Capital Preservation Approach**	$299,174
Deflation calculation:	
27—Number of years until retirement	
3%—Inflation rate	
Deflated value of additional savings needed at retirement using **Capital Preservation Approach**	$134,685

*Assume mutual fund preserved as inheritance to children.

Step 6: Calculate the additional annual savings required to accumulate the necessary retirement fund using the CAPITAL PRESERVATION APPROACH

Serial (increasing) savings calculation (payments to be made at the **end** of the year, before adjustment for inflation):

   $134,685—Future value (deflated value of additional savings need from Step 5)
       27—Number of years until retirement
   3.8835%—Inflation-adjusted yield determined using:
           7%—After-tax investment return
           3%—Inflation rate
Calculate the first serial (increasing) savings payment before adjustment for inflation $2,910

Inflation adjustment:
       $2,910—Annual first-year unadjusted serial (increasing) savings required
           3%—Inflation rate
Calculate the first serial (increasing) savings payment to be invested at the **end** of
the current year (adjusted for inflation) $2,997

Level savings calculation (payments to be made at the **end** of each year):
           27—Number of years until retirement
           7%—After-tax investment return
       $299,174—Future value (FV) of additional savings needed at retirement from Step 5
Calculate the annual (level) savings payment to be invested at the **end** of each year   **$4,017**

IMPORTANT CONCEPTS

The six stages of the retirement planning process

Qualitative client retirement data

Quantitative client retirement data

Income replacement percentage

Joint (second-to-die) versus joint-and survivor life expectancies

The six steps of the retirement savings need analysis

Investment assets

Real estate assets

Tax-deferred savings

Before-tax savings

Future savings/investments

Inflation-adjusted yield

Capital utilization approach

Capital preservation approach

QUESTIONS FOR REVIEW

1. What are the stages of the retirement planning process and which do you consider the most critical?

2. What are some examples of qualitative client retirement data?

3. What are some examples of quantitative client retirement data?

4. How should a client's income replacement percentage be determined?

5. Why is it important for a planner to use joint (second-to-die) life expectancies for a couple rather than joint-and-survivor life expectancies?

6. What are the steps of the retirement savings need analysis?

7. What are some of the general categories of assets typically found on a client's statement of personal financial position?

8. What are the different methods by which a client can save for retirement?

9. What information about the client does the planner need to know before recommending how the client can effectively take advantage of an employer's qualified retirement plan(s)?

10. In what part of the retirement savings need analysis does the planner use the inflation-adjusted investment return and why?

11. How does the capital utilization approach differ from the capital preservation approach in calculating the retirement savings need?

SUGGESTIONS FOR ADDITIONAL READING

Tools & Techniques of Employee Benefit and Retirement Planning, 9th edition, Stephan R. Leimberg and John J. McFadden, The National Underwriter Company, 2005.

Tools & Techniques of Financial Planning, 7th edition, Stephan R. Leimberg, Martin J. Satinsky, Robert J. Doyle, Jr., and Michael Jackson, , The National Underwriter Company, 2004.

Personal Financial Planning, 10th edition, Lawrence J. Gitman and Michael D. Joehnk, Thomson/South-Western, 2005.

Retirement Planning, Carla Gordon, American Institute of Certified Public Accountants, 2002.

CHAPTER TWO

Social Security, Medicare and Medicaid

• • •

The identification of retirement income sources is often compared to a "three-legged stool," with the first leg consisting of government-sponsored retirement plans and the other legs consisting of personal savings and employer-sponsored plans. The most notable of the government-sponsored plans is Social Security, to which an individual and his or her employer contribute throughout the individual's working life. For most Americans, Social Security is the base of financial protection when earnings are lost due to retirement, disability, or death. This chapter discusses the provisions of Social Security coverage, eligibility requirements for the program, and types of benefits that are available. This chapter also discusses Medicare and Medicaid, which are primarily medical or long-term care programs that impact significantly upon the lifestyle that an individual may experience in retirement.

Upon completing this chapter, you should be able to:

- Identify basic provisions of Social Security (OASDI) coverage
- Analyze a situation to determine eligibility of an individual for Social Security benefits
- Identify basic provisions of Medicare coverage
- Analyze a situation to determine eligibility of an individual for Medicare benefits
- Explain the purpose and design of Medigap insurance
- Describe aspects of Medicaid or Medicaid planning

SOCIAL SECURITY

The original Social Security Act, as enacted by Congress in 1935, provided only retirement benefits that first became effective on January 1, 1937. In 1939, survivors benefits were added, followed in later years by disability benefits. The Social Security Act has been amended on several occasions and today provides coverage for retirement; survivors; disability; hospital and medical insurance for the aged, disabled, and those with end-stage renal disease; unemployment insurance; black lung benefits; Supplemental Security Income (SSI); and public assistance and welfare services (i.e., aid to needy families with children, medical assistance, maternal and child health services, child support enforcement, family and child welfare services, food stamps, and energy assistance).

The Social Security Administration administers the old age, survivors, and disability benefit programs as well as the Supplemental Security Income (SSI) program. The Centers for Medicare & Medicaid Services is the administrator for hospital and medical insurance for the aged and disabled.

Qualifying for Social Security Retirement Benefits

A person achieves qualification for retirement benefits under Social Security by becoming "fully insured." One becomes **fully insured** by meeting one of two tests: (1) having 40 quarters of coverage (10 years in covered work) or (2) having at least six quarters of coverage and at least as many quarters of coverage as there are years elapsing after 1950 (or, if later, *after* the year in which he reaches age 21) and *before* the year in which he or she dies, becomes disabled, or reaches, or will reach age 62, whichever occurs first. A quarter of coverage (in 2005) is credited to a worker's Social Security record for each $920 of earnings (up to four quarters per year). This amount of earnings is automatically increased each year to reflect increases in average wages. The method of calculating a quarter of coverage has changed over the years. For years prior to 1978, a worker received credit for a quarter of coverage for each quarter in which wages paid were $50 or more in covered employment. Moreover, each quarter of a year counted as a quarter of coverage if the employee's total wages for that calendar year equaled or exceeded the maximum Social Security earnings base for that year.

In addition to meeting the fully insured requirements, a person must also be at least age 62 throughout the first month of entitlement and must have filed an application for retirement benefits in order to qualify for such benefits. A person who is fully insured can elect to start receiving a reduced benefit at any time between age 62 and his or her normal retirement age (gradually increasing from 65 to 67), or wait until his or her normal retirement age to receive a full benefit. Normal retirement age is being increased by two months per year for those reaching age 62 in 2000-2005. It will be age 66 for workers reaching age 62 in 2006-2016 and will increase again by two months per year for workers reaching age 62 in 2017-2022. It will reach age 67 for workers attaining age 62 after 2022.

If a person has at least six quarters of coverage during the full 13-quarter period ending with the calendar quarter in which he or she (1) died, or (2) most recently became entitled to disability benefits, or (3) became entitled to retirement benefits, he or she is considered **currently insured**. The six quarters of coverage need not be consecutive, but they must be acquired during the 13-quarter period referred to earlier. If a person qualifies as currently insured at his or her death, child's benefits, mother's or father's benefits, and the lump sum death payment (discussed later) are available to the deceased person's survivor(s). However, benefits for a widow(er) age 60 or over, and benefits for a dependent parent, are payable only if the worker was fully insured at death.

Calculating the Social Security Retirement Benefit

In nearly every case, retirement benefits are based on the insured's Social Security earnings since 1950. In rare cases (i.e., where a person has little or no earnings since 1950), benefits may be computed based on earnings since 1937. Beginning in 1979, a wage indexing formula has been used to calculate the benefit. A retired worker whose retirement benefits start on his or her normal retirement age receives monthly benefits equal to his or her "primary insurance amount (PIA)." The PIA is based on "indexed" earnings over a fixed number of years after 1950. It is calculated by indexing the worker's earnings record for wage inflation, determining the Average Indexed Monthly Earnings (AIME), and then applying the PIA formula to the AIME. A person's AIME is based on Social Security earnings for years after 1950, including wages earned as an employee and/or self-employment income, up to the maximum earnings creditable for specific years. Indexing one's AIME results in an earnings history for each worker that is in line with national average wage levels at the time of eligibility. Earnings for each year are indexed up to the "indexing year," the second year before the worker reaches age 62. Indexing must be applied to earnings in each year beginning with 1951 up to, but not including, the indexing year. Actual earnings are used for the indexing year and all later years. The indexing year is related to the year of first eligibility and not to the year of entitlement. For example, a person filing for a retirement benefit in 2005 at age 64 is first eligible in 2003 (at age 62) and the earnings record will be indexed based on the indexing year 2001 (two years before first eligibility).

Having determined a worker's AIME, the final step in calculating the worker's primary insurance amount (PIA) is to apply a formula to the worker's AIME. For a worker reaching first eligibility in calendar year 2005, the PIA is the sum of the following three separate percentages of portions of the AIME: (1) 90 percent of the first $627 or less of the AIME; (2) 32 percent of the AIME in excess of $627 through $3,779, and (3) 15 percent of the AIME in excess of $3,779. While the foregoing percentages remain constant from year to year, the dollar amounts are adjusted for wage inflation each year. Moreover, a worker's PIA is subject to cost-of-living increases beginning with the year of first eligibility.

Reduced Benefit for Early Retirement

If a worker elects to begin receiving retirement benefits before his or her normal retirement age, the resulting benefits are reduced. This is accomplished by reducing the worker's PIA by 5/9ths of 1 percent (1/180) for each of the first 36 months that the worker is younger than normal retirement age when the benefits begin and 5/12ths of 1 percent (1/240) for each such month in excess of 36 months. Another effect of early retirement is that usually fewer years of higher earnings will be used in computing the worker's AIME.

Increased Benefit for Delayed Retirement

If a worker elects to work past his or her normal retirement age, his or her retirement benefit will be *increased* for each year he or she works between normal retirement age and age 70. Technically, the worker receives a retirement credit which began at 3 percent for those who attained age 62 in 1979 through 1986 and is scheduled to increase by one-half of 1 percent every other year until reaching 8 percent per year in 2009 or later. Another way in which the benefit is increased is that working past normal retirement age may result in a higher AIME. While the year in which the person reaches age 62 and succeeding years are not counted in the number of years used in the AIME calculation, if the earnings in those years are higher than those in the years counted, they may be substituted for earlier years and thereby increase AIME.

Loss of Benefits Due to "Excess" Earnings

If a person receiving Social Security retirement benefits has not yet attained his or her normal retirement age for an entire calendar year and earns $12,000 or less (in 2005), no benefits will be lost for that year. However, if that person were to earn over $12,000 (in 2005), he or she would generally lose $1 of benefits for each $2 of earnings over $12,000 (in 2005).

If in the year that a person receiving Social Security retirement benefits reaches his or her normal retirement age, he or she earns no more than $31,800 (in 2005), no benefits will be lost for that year. However, if that person were to earn over $31,800 (in 2005) before the month in which the person reaches normal retirement age, he or she would generally lose $1 for each $3 of earnings over $31,800 (in 2005).

When a person receiving Social Security retirement benefits is older than his or her normal retirement age, no benefits are lost because of his or her earnings.

A special rule applies in the initial year of retirement. Regardless of how much is earned in the initial year of retirement, no retirement benefits will be lost for any month in which the retiree neither (1) earns over $1,000 (for 2005) as an employee if retiring in a year prior to the year he reaches normal retirement age, nor (2) renders any substantial services in self-employment. The initial year of retirement is defined as the first year in which the retiree is both entitled to benefits and has a month in which he does not earn over the monthly exempt wage amount ($1,000 in 2005) and does not render substantial services in self-employment. In other words, the retiree gets full benefits for any month in which earnings do not exceed the monthly exempt amount and he or she does not perform substantial services in self-employment, regardless of his or her annual earnings. Substantial services in self-employment is determined by the actual services rendered in the month (i.e., how much was spent, the nature of the services, the activities performed both prior to retirement and after retirement, and the amount of capital the person has invested in the business). Generally, services of 45 hours or less in a month are not considered substantial. However, as few as 15 hours of service a month could be substantial if, for instance, they involved management of a sizeable business or were spent in a highly skilled occupation. Services of less than 15 hours a month are *never* considered substantial.

If a person is under the normal retirement age for the entire year and earns $12,000 or less (in 2005), there are no "excess earnings." If earnings for the year are more than $12,000 (in 2005), then one-half of the amount over $12,000 is "excess earnings." In the year a person reaches his or her normal retirement age, if he or she earns $31,800 (in 2005) or less, there are no "excess earnings." If, however, this person earns more than $31,800 before the month the person reaches his or her normal retirement age, then one-third of the amount over $31,800 (in 2005) is "excess earnings" (see previous discussion).

Excess earnings are offset first against retirement benefits payable on the worker's account for the first month of the year and then are offset in chronological order against subsequent months until all of the excess earnings are exhausted or no benefits remain for the year.

Wages, bonuses, commissions, fees, and earnings from all types of work, whether or not covered by Social Security, are treated as earnings for purposes of the retirement test, as are net earnings from self-employment. Even earnings from family employment and earnings in excess of the Social Security "taxable wage base" ($90,000 in 2005), while not covered by Social Security, are considered earnings for purposes of the retirement test. There is a long list of income items *not* counted as earnings for purposes of the retirement test. Some of these items include:

- Payments received on account of the employee's sickness or accident disability, medical or hospitalization expenses, or death
- Payments from certain trust funds that are exempt from income tax
- Payments from certain annuity plans that are exempt from income tax
- Pensions and retirement pay
- Sick pay if paid more than six months after the month the employee last worked
- Interest and dividends from stocks and bonds (unless received by a dealer in securities in the course of business)
- Gain or loss from the sale of capital assets, or sale, exchange, or conversion of other property which is not stock in trade nor includable in inventory
- Workers' compensation and unemployment compensation benefits
- Pay for jury duty
- Prize winnings from contests, unless the person enters contests as a trade or business
- Reimbursements by an employer for travel expenses
- Reimbursements or allowances by an employer for moving expenses, if they are not counted as wages for Social Security purposes
- Payments from IRAs and Keogh Plans

In general terms, a person may receive investment income or passive income *without* loss of benefits.

Qualifying for Social Security Survivor Benefits

Survivors of a deceased insured worker are entitled to various benefits. There are six types of benefits available to such survivors:

1. If the surviving spouse of a fully or currently insured worker is caring for a child of the deceased worker under age 16 or who has become disabled before age 22 and is entitled to a child's benefit on the deceased worker's account, the surviving spouse is eligible for a monthly **mother's or father's benefit** regardless of his or her age. However, the surviving spouse must not be married, must not be entitled to widow(er)'s benefits (discussed later), must not be entitled to a retirement benefit based on his or her own work record that is equal to or larger than the amount of the unadjusted mother's or father's benefit, and must have filed an application for benefits. In addition, the surviving spouse must have been married to the deceased worker for at least nine months before the worker died (unless the death was accidental or occurred in the line of duty while a member of a uniformed service serving on active duty); must have been the biological mother or father of the *worker's child* or legally adopted the worker's child during their marriage and before the child reached age 18; the *surviving spouse's child* was adopted by the worker during their marriage and before the child reached age 18; or the surviving spouse was entitled or potentially entitled to spouse's, widow(er)'s, father's, mother's, parent's, or childhood disability benefits in the month before the month the surviving spouse married the deceased worker.

2. The surviving child of a fully or currently insured deceased worker may qualify for a **child's benefit** if: (1) the child is under age 18, or over age 18 and disabled by a disability that began before age 22, or under age 19 and a full-time elementary or secondary school student; (2) not married; (3) dependent upon the deceased parent; and (4) an application is filed for such benefits. A child may receive benefits based on a deceased parent's Social Security account even though the other parent is still living and supporting the child. The surviving child's benefit is equal to 75 percent of the deceased parent's primary insurance amount (PIA) unless restricted due to the "family maximum" limit.

3. A widow(er) of a fully insured deceased worker may be entitled to a **widow(er)'s benefit** based on the deceased spouse's earnings if: (1) the widow(er) is age 60 or over, or is at least age 50 but not age 60 and is disabled; (2) the worker died fully insured; (3) the widow(er) is not entitled to a retirement benefit that is equal to or larger than the worker's PIA; (4) the widow(er) has filed an application for widow(er)'s benefits, and (5) the widow(er) is not married. The remarriage of a widow(er) or surviving divorced spouse after age 60, or the remarriage of a disabled widow(er) or disabled surviving divorced spouse after age 50 and after the date he or she became disabled, will not prevent that individual from becoming entitled to benefits on his or her prior deceased spouse's Social Security record.

4. A disabled widow(er) (or surviving divorced widow(er)) who otherwise qualifies for a widow(er)'s benefit may start receiving a **disabled widow(er)'s benefit** at any time after attaining age 50 and before attaining age 60. The monthly benefit is based on 100 percent of the deceased spouse's PIA, but is reduced by 28.5 percent so that the benefit equals 71.5

percent of the deceased spouse's PIA at age 60. A disabled widow(er) must meet the definition of disability used to determine if a worker is entitled to disability benefits. This means that the widow(er) must be unable to engage in *any* substantial gainful activity by reason of physical or mental impairment. The impairment must be medically determinable and expected to last for at least 12 months or result in death.

5. The parent of a deceased insured person is entitled to a **parent's benefit** if: (1) the insured person was fully insured at death; (2) the parent files an application for parent's benefits; (3) the parent has reached age 62; (4) the parent is not entitled to a retirement benefit that is equal to or larger than the amount of the unadjusted parent's benefit after any increase to the minimum benefit; (5) the parent was receiving at least one-half support from the insured person; (6) evidence that the support requirement was met has been filed with the Social Security Administration within the appropriate time limit, and (7) the parent has not remarried since the insured person's death. The parent must be a natural parent who is eligible under state law to share in the intestate property of the worker as the worker's father or mother; has legally adopted the insured person before the insured person attained age 16; or is a person eligible to claim benefits as the deceased's stepparent by a marriage entered into before the deceased had attained age 16. A parent's benefit is equal to 82.5 percent of the deceased worker's PIA, if there is only one eligible parent and 75 percent for each parent, if there are two parents entitled to benefits. A full benefit is payable at age 62, subject to the maximum family limit.

6. A **lump sum death benefit** of $255 is paid upon the death of a fully or currently insured worker, provided he or she is survived by a spouse who was living in the same household as the deceased at the time of death, or is survived by a spouse or dependent child eligible to receive Social Security benefits for the month of death based on his or her earnings record. If no surviving widow(er) or child (as defined above) survives, no lump sum is payable.

Where multiple family members are receiving Social Security benefits, they may be subject to a **Maximum Family Benefit**. In 2005, the Maximum Family Benefit for those reaching age 62 or dying before age 62 (adjusted for inflation annually) is calculated in the following manner:

1. 150 percent of the first $801 of PIA, plus
2. 272 percent of PIA over $801 through $1,156, plus
3. 134 percent of PIA over $1,156 through $1,508, plus
4. 175 percent of PIA over $1,508.

Qualifying for Social Security Disability Benefits

To qualify for Social Security disability benefits, a worker must: (1) be insured for disability benefits (defined later); (2) be under age 65; (3) have been disabled for 12 months, or is expected to be disabled for at least 12 months, or has a disability that is expected to result in death; (4) have filed an application for disability benefits; and (5) have completed a 5-month waiting period unless exempted from this requirement (discussed later). Determining whether a worker is disabled is performed by the

Disability Determination Services (DDS) agency of each individual state. However, DDS determinations of disability may be reviewed and reversed by the Social Security Administration's Office of Program and Integrity Reviews.

In deciding whether a worker is eligible for disability benefits, SSA uses the following 5-step process:

1. It determines whether the individual is engaging in substantial gainful activity. If so, the claim is denied at this point. If not, the process continues to the second step.

2. It determines whether the individual has a severe medically determinable physical or mental impairment. If not, the claim is denied at this point. If so, the process continues to the third step.

3. It determines whether the individual has an impairment included in its Listing of Impairments. If so, the claim is allowed. If not, the claim continues to the fourth step.

4. It determines whether the impairment prevents the individual from doing relevant work that was performed in the past. If not, the claim is denied at this point. If so, the claim continues to the fifth and final step.

5. It determines whether the impairment prevents the individual from doing any other work. If so, the claim is allowed. If not, the claim is denied.

A person is considered insured for disability benefits if he or she: (1) is fully insured under the Social Security system, and (2) has worked under Social Security for at least 5 of the 10 years (20-out-of-40 quarters) just before becoming disabled, or if the disability begins before age 31 but after age 24, for at least one-half of the quarters after reaching age 21 and before becoming disabled (but not less than six quarters). If a person becomes disabled before the quarter in which he attains age 24, he or she must have six quarters of coverage in the 12 quarter period ending with the quarter in which the disability began.

A person may receive disability benefits at any age before attaining his or her normal retirement age. If a person is receiving disability benefits when he or she attains normal retirement age, the disability benefit automatically ends and a retirement benefit begins.

A disabled worker may be exempted from the 5-month waiting period if he or she has had a prior period of disability and if the new disability arises within 5 years after the previous one ended and is expected to last for at least 12 months, or to result in death.

As is the case with retirement benefits, the family of a disabled worker may also qualify for a spouse's and/or child's benefit.

Calculating the Social Security Disability Benefit

A disabled worker's benefit is equal to his or her PIA, determined as if the worker were at normal retirement age and eligible for retirement benefits in the first month of his or her waiting period. However, the formula for determining a disabled worker's AIME and PIA differs from that used for a retiring worker. There are also different limits on the amount of family benefits that may be paid to a disabled worker and his or her family. A disabled worker's benefits may also be offset by a workers' compensation benefit or federal, state, or local public law disability benefit.

Moreover, a person's disability benefit has nothing to do with his or her personal wealth and whether or not the person's spouse is employed. However, a person will lose his or her disability benefit by refusing without good cause to accept vocational rehabilitation services. Finally, an individual will not be considered disabled if alcoholism or drug addiction is a contributing factor material to the SSA's determination that the individual is disabled.

A person's disability benefits end on the earliest of: (1) the second month after the month in which the disability ceases; (2) the month before the month the worker attains normal retirement age (at which point the benefits are automatically converted to retirement benefits); or (3) the month before the month in which the worker dies.

Income Taxation of Social Security Benefits

Social Security retirement, survivor, and disability benefits may be taxable in certain situations. For instance, if the beneficiary's sole income is Social Security benefits, most likely those benefits will *not* be taxable and a return need not be filed. However, if the beneficiary has income *in addition to* the Social Security benefits, a return will most likely be required even though the Social Security benefits are still not taxable.

In other situations, a portion of one's Social Security benefits *may* be taxable. Here, the amount that must be included in the beneficiary's gross income is the lesser of one-half of the annual benefits received or one-half of the excess of the beneficiary's "provisional income" over a specified **base amount** (used for lower provisional income levels). Provisional income is the beneficiary's modified adjusted gross income (MAGI) plus one-half of the Social Security or tier 1 railroad retirement benefits. In turn, MAGI is the beneficiary's adjusted gross income plus any tax-exempt interest, including interest earned on savings bonds used to finance higher education, and amounts excluded under an employer's adoption assistance program, deducted for interest on education loans, or as a qualified tuition expense.

For example, if a beneficiary's provisional income (MAGI plus one-half of his or her Social Security benefits) is more than a **base amount,** some portion of his or her benefits will be taxable. The base amount varies with a beneficiary's income tax filing status. Currently, it is $32,000 for a married couple filing jointly, $0 for married couples filing separately and who lived together at any time during the year, and $25,000 for other taxpayers. If a beneficiary's provisional income exceeds the applicable base amount, the lesser of one-half of the beneficiary's Social Security benefits or one-half of the excess of provisional income over the base amount is includible in gross income.

Here is an example to illustrate how the taxable portion of one's Social Security benefits is determined:

Fred and Judy Martin have adjusted gross income of $24,000 for 2005. Fred, who is retired, receives Social Security benefits of $7,200 per year. The couple also receives $6,000 per year from a mutual fund that invests solely in tax-exempt municipal bonds. On their joint return for 2005, the Martins' calculate the portion of Fred's Social Security benefits to be included in their gross income in the following manner:

1. Adjusted gross income	$24,000
2. Plus: All tax-exempt interest	6,000
3. Modified adjusted gross income (MAGI)	$30,000
4. Plus: One-half of Social Security benefits	3,600
5. "Provisional income"	$33,600
6. Less: Applicable base amount	32,000
7. Excess above base amount	$1,600
8. One-half of excess above base amount	$800
9. One-half of Social Security benefits	3,600
10. Amount includible in gross income (lesser of 8 or 9)	$800

Just to make things more confusing, if a beneficiary's provisional income is more than an **adjusted base amount**, the beneficiary must include in income the lesser of: (1) **85 percent** of the beneficiary's Social Security benefits or (2) 85 percent of the excess of provisional income over the applicable adjusted base amount, plus the sum of the smaller of (a) the amount that would otherwise be includible if the second threshold (adjusted base amount) did not apply or (b) $4,500 ($6,000 for joint filers). Like the base amount, this adjusted base amount also varies with a beneficiary's income tax filing status. Currently, it is $44,000 for married couples filing jointly, $0 for married couples filing separately and who lived together at any time during the year, and $34,000 for other taxpayers. If a person is married filing separately and lived with his or her spouse at any time during the year, up to 85 percent of his or her benefits is included in gross income.

Using the same facts as in the previous example, except that the Martins' provisional income now is increased from $33,600 to $53,600, the includible amount is determined in the following manner:

1. "Provisional income"	$53,600
2. Applicable adjusted base amount	44,000
3. Excess of 1. over 2.	$9,600
4. 85 percent of amount in 3.	$8,160
5. Amount otherwise includible (1/2 of Martins'benefits)	$3,600
6. Base amount for joint filers	$6,000
7. Lesser of 5. or 6.	$3,600
8. Sum of amounts in 4. and 7.	$11,760
9. 85 percent of Social Security benefits	6,120
10.Amount includible in gross income (lesser of 8. or 9.)	$6,120

A beneficiary may elect to have federal income tax withheld at 7, 10, 15, or 25 percent from his or her Social Security benefits. For tax purposes, the definition of Social Security benefits includes workers' compensation benefits to the extent they cause a reduction in Social Security and railroad retirement tier I disability benefits. Since, in this situation, workers' compensation benefits are paid in lieu of Social Security payments, this assures parallel treatment for tax purposes.

The Commissioner of Social Security files annual returns with the Secretary of the Treasury showing the benefits paid to each beneficiary in each year. Similarly, statements must also be provided to each recipient of benefits by January 31 of the year following the benefit payments.

Social Security Funding

Social Security is funded by a payroll tax of 6.2 percent of covered wages (up to $90,000 in 2005) imposed under the Federal Insurance Contributions Act (FICA) on both the employee and the employer. The employer may take an income tax deduction for its share of the tax. Self-employed persons are taxed under the Self-Employment Contributions Act at a current rate of 12.4 percent of their net earnings from self-employment (up to $90,000 in 2005). These persons are also permitted a tax deduction in arriving at adjusted gross income for 50 percent of the Social Security and Medicare (discussed later) self-employment tax paid. While many taxpayers focus on their federal income tax burden, a little recognized fact is that approximately 79 percent of Americans pay *more* in payroll taxes than they do in income taxes.

The Federal Old-Age and Survivors Insurance and Disability Insurance Trust Funds make any surplus revenues received under the system available to the federal government for general purposes. When the federal government taps these surplus payroll tax funds, it in effect guarantees repayment using its full faith and credit. There has been a surplus of payroll taxes since 1983. In 2003, the surplus was $160 billion but as indicated earlier, this surplus is projected to disappear and swing to a deficit unless Congress takes action to restore the program's financial integrity. Given the mechanics of the system, the so-called "trust funds," rather than having funds on hand available to pay benefits, have only IOUs from the federal government. These IOUs are special issue, non-marketable government bonds, which one part of the federal government owes to another. These claims on the U.S. Treasury, when redeemed, will have to be financed by raising taxes, borrowing from the public or reducing the benefits or other expenditures. Consequently, the existence of large Trust Fund balances does not, by itself, have any impact on the government's ability to pay benefits. Currently, the federal government owes the Social Security trust funds approximately $1.4 trillion. These bonds will continue to increase, with the interest paid in the form of additional bonds, unless some form of additional funding is found.

A recent estimate by the Social Security Trustees is that Social Security's cash flow will turn negative around 2018, at which point it will start cashing in bonds. It is estimated that between 2018 and 2042, the cost to redeem trust fund bonds will be about $5 trillion. When all of the IOUs have been redeemed, retiree benefits will need to be cut by 28 percent by about 2042. Absent Congressional action to address this issue, the SSA will then have authority to pay benefits only to the extent that payroll tax receipts may support them (projected to be about 72 percent of promised benefits).

A demographic issue that threatens the long-term financial stability of the Social Security program is the ratio of workers to retirees. In 1950, this ratio was 15 workers to 1 retiree; in 1960, it was 6:1 and currently it is about 3.4:1. It is projected that by 2030 it will be 2:1. Since today's workers pay the benefits of today's retirees, future retirees' benefits will have to be paid by younger workers. With the share of the U.S. population represented by the aged continuing to grow and the rate of growth of the younger labor force in decline, the Social Security program will be financially hard-pressed in future years unless some way is found to close the projected revenue gap.

An additional factor that places a great deal of pressure on the future ability to pay promised benefits is that not only are Social Security benefits adjusted annually for inflation after retirement, but initial benefits are indexed to generally increasing wages. This means that as long as wages grow faster than inflation, new retirees in the future will receive higher benefits than a new retiree today.

In spite of these dire forecasts, all experts agree that people who are today aged 55 or above will receive all promised benefits for the rest of their lives. However, unless the system is revised, younger workers will not receive benefits equal to what they have paid into Social Security during their working lives. Experts generally agree that there are only three ways to provide financial stability for Social Security- (1) raise taxes; (2) cut benefits; or (3) permit younger workers to invest a portion of their payroll tax dollars in either a governmental or individual private investment account. A plan has been put forth that would give younger workers the option to remain in the traditional Social Security program or participate in individual investment accounts. Under this proposed plan, those who elect to remain in the traditional system will receive the level of benefits that Social Security can pay with its existing revenues.

MEDICARE

Medicare is a federal health insurance program for persons 65 or older, persons of any age with permanent kidney failure, and certain disabled persons. As discussed in the section on Social Security, the Centers for Medicare & Medicaid Services (CMS) (a federal agency in the Department of Health and Human Services) administers the Medicare program. However, Social Security Administration (SSA) offices can take applications for Medicare, collect premiums, and provide general information about the program. CMS uses commercial insurance companies to process and pay Medicare claims and groups of doctors and other health care professionals to monitor the quality of care delivered to Medicare beneficiaries. CMS also has contractual relationships with hospitals, nursing homes, home health agencies, doctors, providers of medical equipment, clinical laboratories, and HMOs (as well as other managed care plans).

Medicare includes Hospital Insurance protection (Part A), Medical Insurance protection (Part B), Medicare Advantage (Part C) (formerly known as Medicare+Choice), and beginning in 2006, Prescription Drug Insurance (Part D). We will discuss each of these parts of Medicare in the following sections.

Medicare Hospital Insurance (Part A Coverage)

Part A of Medicare provides institutional care, including inpatient hospital care, skilled nursing home care, post-hospital home health care, and, under certain circumstances, hospice care.

Eligibility for Part A

Anyone receiving Social Security monthly benefits or a qualified railroad retirement beneficiary automatically qualifies for Part A Hospital Insurance coverage beginning with the first day of the month in which he or she becomes 65 years old. In fact, such a person need not even apply for Part A benefits. Moreover, even if such a person qualifies for Social Security or railroad retirement benefits but has not yet applied for them, he or she is eligible for Part A coverage.

Other persons who qualify for coverage include the following:

- A person who is age 65 or over, is otherwise qualified, and continues to work.
- A dependent or survivor of a person entitled to Part A benefits.
- A dependent of a person under age 65 who is entitled to retirement or disability benefits, if the dependent or survivor is at least 65 years old (e.g., a woman age 65 or over who is entitled to a spouse's or widow's Social Security benefit is eligible for benefits under Part A).
- A Social Security disability beneficiary after receiving disability benefits for 24 months or more. This includes disabled workers at any age, disabled widow(er)s age 50 or over, beneficiaries age 18 or older who receive benefits because of disability beginning before age 22, and disabled qualified railroad retirement annuitants.
- A person becoming re-entitled to disability benefits within five years after the end of a previous period of entitlement (within seven years in the case of disabled widow(er)s and

disabled children), without the need to wait another 24 months. The 5- or 7-year period is waived if the current reason for disability is the same as (or directly related to) that of the previous disability.

- A person age 65 or over who is otherwise ineligible for Part A coverage who enrolls voluntarily and pays a monthly premium, provided he or she also enrolls in Part B coverage, is a U.S. resident (either a citizen or a lawful alien with a green card and who has lived in the U.S. continuously during the five years immediately prior to applying for enrollment).

- An elderly or disabled Medicaid beneficiary with low income and very limited resources for whom the applicable state is required by federal law to pay Medicare costs. Such payments may be made under either the Qualified Medicare Beneficiary (QMB) program (for those at or below the national poverty level), the Special Low-Income Medicare Beneficiary (SLMB) program (for those with incomes no more than 20 percent higher than the national poverty level), or the Qualified Individual (QI) program (for those with incomes more than 20 percent higher than the national poverty level, but not more than 35 percent greater).

Special rules apply to those with permanent kidney failure, federal employees, and state and local government employees.

Part A Benefits

After paying an annual deductible and coinsurance, coverage is provided as follows:

1. **Inpatient hospital care** for up to 90 days in each "benefit period." The patient's deductible is $912 (in 2005) for the first 60 days and then he or she pays coinsurance of $228 (in 2005) per day for each additional day up to a maximum of 30 days. Moreover, each beneficiary has a one-time lifetime "reserve" of 60 additional hospital days with coinsurance of $456 (in 2005) per day.

2. **Post-hospital extended care in a "skilled nursing facility"** (defined later) for up to 100 days in each "benefit period." The patient pays nothing for the first 20 days (in 2005). After 20 days, the patient pays coinsurance of $114 per day (in 2005) for each additional day up to a maximum of 80 days.

3. The first 100 **post-hospital home health service visits** following a hospital or skilled nursing facility stay. The services must be made under a physician's plan of treatment, except that there is 20 percent cost-sharing payable by the patient for durable medical equipment (other than the purchase of certain used items).

4. **Hospice care** for terminally ill patients.

Inpatient hospital care is provided by Medicare if a doctor prescribes such care for the treatment of an illness or injury, the patient requires hospital care, the hospital participates in Medicare, and if the Utilization Review Committee of the hospital, a Quality Improvement Organization (QIO), or an intermediary, does not disapprove of the stay. Considering the deductible and coinsurance described in (1) above, a 90-day stay in a hospital could cost the patient $7,752 out-of-pocket. As discussed in (1), the patient is responsible for 100 percent of the hospital bill after 90 days, *unless* he or she chooses to utilize his or her lifetime reserve of 60 additional days (subject to daily coinsurance of $456). The

90-day benefit period begins anew with each spell of illness. However, the patient must be out of a hospital or skilled nursing or rehabilitative facility for 60 consecutive days before a benefit period ends. There is no limit on the number of 90-day benefit periods a person can have in his or her lifetime (except for mental illness); but the 60-day "lifetime reserve" is available only once.

Without going into the details of coverage for specific services, generally the following inpatient services are covered by Part A:

- Bed and board in a semi-private room or a ward; private room coverage only if medically necessary
- Meals, including special diets
- Nursing services (other than a private duty nurse or attendant)
- Medical social worker services
- Regular hospital equipment, supplies, and appliances
- Drugs and biologicals
- Diagnostic or therapeutic items and services ordinarily furnished by the hospital or by others
- Operating and recovery room costs, including hospital costs for anesthesia
- Services of interns and residents in training under an approved teaching program
- Blood transfusions, after the first three pints
- X-rays and other radiology services, including radiation therapy, billed by the hospital
- Lab tests
- Respiratory or inhalation therapy
- Independent clinical laboratory services under arrangement with the hospital
- Alcohol detoxification and rehabilitation services when furnished as inpatient hospital services (also covered under Part B when furnished as physician services)
- Dental services when hospitalization is required
- Cost of special care units, such as ICU, coronary care unit, etc.
- Rehabilitation services, such as physical therapy, occupational therapy, and speech pathology services
- Appliances (pacemakers, colostomy fittings, and artificial limbs) permanently installed at the hospital
- Lung and heart-lung transplants
- Psychiatric hospital care, subject to a lifetime limit of 190 days

Services that are *not* covered by Part A include:

- Services of physicians and surgeons
- Private duty nurse or attendant services, unless the patient's condition requires it and the provider is a bona fide employee of the hospital
- Personal convenience items requested by the patient (e.g., TV rental, radio rental, or telephone)

- The first three pints of whole blood received in a calendar year
- Supplies, appliances and equipment for use outside the hospital, unless continued use is required (e.g., a pacemaker)

A "skilled nursing facility" is a specially qualified facility (usually certified by the state), specializing in skilled care, and having the staff and equipment to provide skilled nursing care or skilled rehabilitative services and other related health services. Skilled nursing care is care that can *only* be performed by, or under the supervision of, licensed nursing personnel. It can take place in a skilled nursing home or a ward or wing of a hospital, or a section of an old-age home. A facility that provides only "custodial care" is *not* a skilled nursing facility. "Custodial care" is that primarily for the purpose of helping the patient with daily living or meeting personal needs, and may be provided safely and reasonably by people with professional skills or training (e.g., help with walking, getting in or out of bed, bathing, dressing, eating, and taking medication). Many residents of nursing homes do not qualify for Medicare coverage because coverage is restricted to patients in need of skilled nursing and rehabilitative services on a daily basis. An institution which is primarily for the care and treatment of mental diseases or tuberculosis is also not a skilled nursing facility. In fact, most nursing homes in the U.S. are *not* skilled nursing facilities and many skilled nursing facilities are *not* certified by Medicare.

To qualify for skilled nursing facility benefits, the patient must meet the following five conditions:

1. His or her condition requires daily skilled nursing or skilled rehabilitative services which can only be provided practically in a skilled nursing facility.

2. The patient has been in a hospital for three consecutive days prior to admission to the skilled nursing facility. If discharged from the skilled nursing facility and then readmitted within 30 days, he or she does not need to again satisfy the three-day hospital stay requirement.

3. The patient is admitted to the skilled nursing facility usually within 30 days after being discharged from the hospital.

4. The patient's care in the skilled nursing facility must be for a condition that was treated in the hospital, or for a condition that arose while receiving care in the skilled nursing facility for a condition which was treated in the hospital.

5. A medical professional certifies that the patient needs, and receives, skilled nursing or skilled rehabilitation services (post-hospital extended care) on a daily basis.

The types of services covered in a skilled nursing facility are similar to those covered in a hospital. Because of the required coinsurance payment by the patient, described earlier, a 100-day stay in a skilled nursing facility (during 2005) will cost the patient $9,120.

Post-hospital home health care is skilled health care in a patient's home for the treatment of an illness or injury. As discussed previously, Medicare covers the cost of 100 home health visits made on an "intermittent" basis during a home health spell of illness under a plan of treatment established by a physician. A home health agency may be a public agency or a private organization, licensed by state and local law, that also meets several other requirements established by Medicare.

Some of the types of services covered by Part A as post-hospital home health services include:

- Part-time or intermittent skilled nursing care
- Physical therapy
- Speech therapy
- If a patient needs any of the first three bulleted items, Medicare also pays for: (1) part-time or intermittent services of home health aides for personal care, simple dressing changes not requiring a licensed nurse, assistance with medications that are self-administered and do not required a licensed nurse, assistance with activities supportive of skilled therapy services, and routine care of prosthetic devices; (2) medical social services; (3) medical supplies; (4) durable medical equipment (20 percent coinsurance); and (5) occupational therapy.

Home health services that are *not* covered include:

- Home care services furnished primarily to assist people in meeting personal, family, and domestic needs (laundry, meal preparation, shopping, or assistance with bathing, dressing, or other personal needs)
- 24-hour-a-day nursing care at home
- Drugs and biologicals
- Blood transfusions
- Meals delivered to the home
- Homemaker services
- Venipuncture for blood samples

Hospice care is care provided for terminally ill patients that is focused on relieving the patient's pain and other uncomfortable symptoms rather than curing the disease. Such care works in an interdisciplinary manner by providing medical, social, psychological, emotional, and spiritual services through various caregivers. It also includes counseling and respite care for the family of the hospice patient as well as home care and inpatient care for the patient, when needed. The types of hospice care services covered by Part A include:

- Nursing care provided by or under the supervision of a registered professional nurse
- Medical social services provided by a social worker under a physician's direction
- Counseling for the patient's care and adjustment to his or her approaching death
- Short-term (up to 5 days) inpatient care
- Medical appliances and supplies
- Services of a home health aide and homemaker services
- Drugs, including outpatient drugs for pain relief and symptom management
- Physical therapy, occupational therapy, and speech-language pathology services to control symptoms or to enable the patient to maintain activities of daily living and basic functional skills

The benefit period for hospice care consists of two 90-day periods followed by an unlimited number of 60-day periods (requiring re-certification of terminal illness). There are no deductibles under the hospice benefit.

Financing of Part A Coverage

Part A Hospital Insurance is financed through a separate Hospital Insurance tax imposed on employers, employees, and the self-employed (currently 1.45 percent each for employees and employers and 2.90 percent for the self- employed). The tax is payable by all persons, regardless of age, who are subject to the regular Social Security tax or to the Railroad Retirement tax and by all federal employees as well as state and local government employees hired after March 1986 or not covered by a state retirement system in conjunction with their employment (beginning July 2, 1991). The tax is levied on *all* earnings, regardless of amount. As is the case with the Social Security tax, there is a special federal income tax deduction (in arriving at adjusted gross income) for 50 percent of the Hospital Insurance self-employment tax paid.

Medicare Medical Insurance (Part B Coverage)

For the most part, Part B of Medicare covers physicians' services (including surgery), home health services (other than post-hospital home health services), clinical laboratory services, durable medical equipment, and some other items and services not covered by Hospital Insurance, Part A.

Eligibility for Part B

Persons entitled to premium-free Hospital Insurance (Part A), or premium Hospital Insurance (Part A) for the working disabled under Medicare, have the option of enrolling in Medical Insurance (Part B). As a result, Social Security and Railroad Retirement beneficiaries, age 65 or over, are *automatically eligible*. As discussed earlier in this chapter, any person age 65 or over who is a U.S. resident and is either a U.S. citizen or an alien holding a green card and living in the U.S. continuously during the five years immediately prior to the month in which he or she applies for enrollment, may enroll in Part B.

Disabled workers under age 65, widow(er)s aged 50-64, and children aged 18 or over disabled before age 22 who have received disability benefits for at least two years are covered in the same manner as persons age 65 or over. A person who remains disabled may continue to buy either Part A only or both Parts A and B.

Also covered are persons with permanent kidney failure who require dialysis or a kidney transplant and are eligible for Part A coverage.

Social Security and Railroad Retirement beneficiaries are automatically enrolled at the time they become entitled to Part A coverage *unless* they opt out of Part B coverage by signing a form for that purpose. There is an initial enrollment period of seven full calendar months starting on the first day of the third month before the month a person becomes eligible to enroll and ends with the close of the last day of the third month following the month a person first becomes eligible to enroll. For example, if a person's 65th birthday is October 5, 2005, the initial enrollment period begins July 1, 2005 and ends January 31, 2006. However, if a person decides not to enroll during the initial enrollment period, he or she may enroll during a special enrollment period, as provided by statute.

In the situation where a person age 65 or older continues to work and is covered by an employer group health plan, he or she may apply for Part B coverage beginning with the month in which coverage under the private plan ends and for a total of seven months under the special enrollment period.

Those who fail to enroll during the initial enrollment period may enroll during a general enrollment period, which takes place each year from January 1 through March 31 with coverage being effective July 1 of that year. A person failing to enroll within 12 months or dropping Part B coverage and later re-enrolling is charged a higher premium (10 percent for each full 12 months during which he or she could have been enrolled, but was not).

Part B Benefits

Any person enrolled in premium-free Medicare Part A insurance, or premium Part A insurance for the working disabled, may enroll in Medical Insurance (Part B). This means that Social Security and Railroad Retirement beneficiaries, who are at least age 65, are eligible for Part B coverage. Other persons aged 65 or over may also enroll provided they are residents of the U.S. and are either: (1) a citizen of the U.S., or (2) an alien lawfully admitted for permanent residence and who has resided in the U.S. continuously during the five years immediately prior to the month in which he or she applies for coverage.

Social Security and Railroad Retirement beneficiaries are automatically enrolled in Part B at the time they become eligible for Part B insurance unless they elect not to be covered by signing a form which will be mailed to them. Others may enroll at their nearest Social Security office.

Under Part B, Medicare normally pays 80 percent of the approved charges for doctors' services and the cost of other covered services, after the patient pays his or her annual deductible. Part B pays for covered doctors' services no matter where delivered in the U.S. It includes the fees of physicians, surgeons, pathologists, radiologists, anesthesiologists, physiatrists, and osteopaths. Also included are the services of certain non-doctor specially qualified practitioners approved by Medicare, such as certified registered nurse anesthetists, certified nurse midwifes, clinical psychologists, clinical social workers (other than a hospital), physician assistants, and nurse practitioners and clinical nurse specialists in collaboration with a physician. The services of clinical psychologists, if they would otherwise be covered when furnished by a physician, are covered. The only services of licensed chiropractors that are covered are for manual manipulation of the spine to correct a subluxation. Podiatrists' fees are covered if for other than routine foot care. Plastic surgery for repair of an accidental injury, an impaired limb or a malformed part of the body is covered, but not plastic surgery for purely cosmetic reasons.

Also covered are diagnostic tests and procedures that are part of the patient's treatment, treatment of mental illness (coverage is limited), X-rays, services of the doctor's office nurse, drugs and biologicals that cannot be self-administered, transfusions of blood and blood components, medical supplies, and physical/occupational therapy and speech-language pathology services.

Part B *does not cover* most routine physical examinations and related tests (except some Pap smears and mammograms), most routine foot care and dental care, eye and ear examinations for fitting eyeglasses or hearing aids, immunizations (except annual flu shots, pneumonia vaccinations or immunizations required because of an injury or immediate risk of infection, and hepatitis B for certain persons at risk), cosmetic surgery, most prescription drugs, custodial care at home or in a nursing home, and orthopedic shoes.

Financing of Part B Coverage

Part B Medical Insurance is financed through monthly premiums paid by each enrollee and through contributions appropriated from federal general revenues. In 2005, the monthly premium for Part B coverage is $78.20. The premium is set at 25 percent of program costs each year, with the federal government absorbing the remaining 75 percent from general revenues. Part B premiums are deducted from the Social Security, Railroad Retirement, or federal civil service retirement benefit check of those so covered. Persons not receiving such benefits pay the premiums directly to the federal government. A person who enrolls after his or her initial open enrollment period or who re-enrolls after terminating coverage pays a premium that is 10 percent higher for each 12 full months the person could have been in the program but chose not to be. The monthly premium is *in addition to* the annual deductible ($110 for 2005) and 20 percent coinsurance amounts paid by each patient.

Elderly or disabled persons eligible for Medicare and who have a low income and very limited assets may qualify to have some or all of their Medicare expenses paid by Medicaid. Three programs are available to help those who qualify to pay their Medicare expenses. Under the Qualified Medicare Beneficiary (QMB) program, persons of limited resources whose income is at or below the national poverty level can have their Medicare Part B premiums, coinsurance (20 percent of Medicare-approved charges) and deductibles ($110 per year for 2005) paid for them. The Specified Low-Income Medicare Beneficiary (SLMB) program is designed for those whose incomes are slightly higher than the poverty level, but not more than 20 percent higher; SLMB, however, pays only the Part B premium. The third program is the Qualifying Individual (QI) program, designed for individuals and married couples whose income is more than 20 percent greater than the federal poverty level, but not more than 35 percent greater, and pays only a portion of the Part B premium.

Medical Insurance payments are made either directly to the doctor or other supplier or to the patient. When the doctor or other supplier agrees to accept the amount approved by the Medicare carrier as total payment for covered services, this is referred to as the assignment method of payment. It offers the convenience to the patient of not having to file claim forms. If a nonparticipating physician does not accept assignment, Medicare pays the patient 80 percent of the approved charge, after subtracting any part of the annual deductible the patient has not already paid. However, the doctor or other supplier may bill the patient for his or her actual charge even if it is more than the charge approved by the Medicare carrier. Utilizing a doctor who accepts assignment under Medicare may also have a significant impact on the patient's out-of-pocket costs. Even if a doctor does not accept assignment, he or she can bill the patient no more than 115 percent of what Medicare approves.

Medicare Advantage (Part C Coverage)

Medicare Advantage (formerly known as Medicare+Choice) provides beneficiaries with a choice as to whether to receive benefits through the original Medicare fee-for-service program or through (1) coordinated care plans, including HMOs, PPOs, and Provider-Sponsored Organizations (PSOs) or (2) private fee-for-service plans which reimburse providers on a fee-for-service basis, and are authorized to charge enrolled beneficiaries up to 115 percent of the plan's payment schedule.

An HMO has its own network of hospitals, skilled nursing facilities, home health agencies, doctors and other professionals and they usually provide service at one or more centrally located health facilities or in the private practice offices of the doctors and other health care professionals that are part of the plan. Generally, a beneficiary must receive all covered care through the plan or from health care professionals referred to by the plan. The beneficiary normally selects a primary care doctor from those participating in the plan.

A PSO is a public or private entity established by or organized by a health care provider, such as a hospital, or a group of affiliated health care providers, such as a geriatric unit of a hospital, that provides a substantial proportion of health care items and services directly through that provider or group.

A Medicare Advantage private fee-for-service plan is one that reimburses doctors, hospitals and other providers on a fee-for-service basis and does not restrict which doctor or hospital the member can use. The insurance plan, rather than Medicare, decides how much to reimburse for services provided. The beneficiary pays the Part B premium plus a monthly premium to the private fee-for-service plan and a co-pay for each visit or service.

Eligibility for Medicare Advantage (Part C)

Those who are entitled to Hospital Insurance (Part A) and enrolled in Medical Insurance (Part B) of Medicare are eligible to enroll in a plan that serves the geographic area in which they reside. Those enrolled only in Part B are *not* eligible. Beneficiaries can choose a Medicare Advantage plan at initial eligibility or during certain enrollment periods. Medicare Advantage plans are required to provide the current Medicare benefit package of services (excluding hospice services) available under Parts A and B.

Medicare Prescription Drug Insurance (Part D Coverage)

Part D, which becomes effective January 1, 2006, was added to Medicare by the Medicare Prescription Drug, Improvement, and Modernization Act of 2003. It is a voluntary program of health insurance that covers a portion of prescription drug costs not generally covered by other Medicare programs. It will be offered through private health plans and financed by premiums paid by participants. Participants will have the option of remaining with traditional Medicare in a drug-only plan or choosing a Medicare Advantage plan with comprehensive benefits. Until the plan becomes effective in 2006, participants may obtain a Medicare drug discount card for a small annual enrollment fee. These cards, which offer a discount of from 10 to 25 percent, become invalid after December 31, 2005.

Open enrollment for Part D will begin November 15, 2005 and run for a period of six months. Anyone entitled to participate in Part A or who is enrolled in Part B is eligible to participate in Part D. The monthly premium is estimated to be $35 and may be paid separately for a drug-only plan or as part of the premium for a comprehensive Medicare Advantage plan.

Beginning in 2006, Part D will provide the following standard benefit:

Prescription Drug Expenses	Beneficiary Costs	Medicare Pays
First $250	100% (up to $250)	Nothing
$251-$2,250	25% (up to $500)	75% (up to $1,500)
$2,251-$5,100	100% (up to $2,850)	Nothing
$5,100 and up	Up to 5% (based on income)	95% or more

Participants with low incomes will have lower cost sharing requirements than under the foregoing standard benefit.

Medigap Insurance Coverage

As you have discovered in our discussion of Parts A through D of Medicare, Medicare does *not* pay all medical expenses or most long-term care expenses. Beneficiaries must, therefore, absorb annual deductibles, coinsurance, and situations where particular services are not covered by Medicare. Medigap insurance, which is not provided by the federal government but rather by private insurance companies, is designed to pay for these "gaps" in Medicare coverage. However, Medigap will not pay for out-of-pocket expenses, such as copayments, in a managed care plan.

For a period of six months after the effective date of enrolling in Part B, a person age 65 or older cannot be denied Medigap insurance or charged higher premiums because of health problems. However, a Medigap policy purchased during the open enrollment period may exclude coverage for "pre-existing conditions" during the first six months that the policy is in effect. Moreover, Medigap policies are guaranteed renewable, meaning that they continue in force as long as the premium is paid.

Congress created federal standards for Medigap policies in 1990. In most states, there are no more than 10 standard policies available (denoted as coverages A through J). Coverage A is a basic policy providing only a "core package" of benefits. Each of the other coverages include the core package, but also offer additional benefits. In 1997, Congress added two more high deductible plans to the 10 standard plans. The core package covers (1) Part A coinsurance for the 61st through 90th day of hospitalization in any Medicare benefit period; (2) Part A coinsurance for the 91st through 150th day; (3) Part A expenses for an extra 365 days in the hospital; (4) Part A and Part B deductibles for the cost of the first three pints of blood; and (5) Part B coinsurance (20 percent of allowable charges).

Coverages B through J each offer a different mix of additional benefits above the core package, including (1) the entire $912 Part A deductible; (2) the $114 per day coinsurance for days 21-100 of Part A skilled nursing home care; (3) the $110 Part B deductible; (4) 80 percent or 100 percent of the amount paid by Part B beneficiaries whose doctors do not accept assignment; (5) 50 percent of outpatient prescription drug costs (subject to a $250 deductible and either a $1,250 or $3,000 annual maximum); (6) 80 percent of the Medicare-eligible costs of medically necessary emergency care when the insured is traveling outside the U.S.; (7) up to $120 per year for certain screening and preventive measures; (8) certain "short term, at-home assistance with activities of daily living" for people recovering from illness, injury, or surgery at home, in a relative's home, or in an institution (other than a hospital or skilled nursing facility), up to $1600 per year and subject to other dollar restrictions; and (9) "innovative benefits" that are appropriate, cost-effective, and consistent with the goal of simplifying Medigap insurance, with the prior approval of the state insurance commissioner.

The following table shows the benefits provided by the 10 standard Medigap policies:

Coverage	Basic core benefit-package	Part A Deducta-tible	Daily co-insurance for skilled nursing home care (days 21-100)	Part B Deduc-tible	Foreign Travel Emer-gencies	At-home recovery assistance	Preventive screening & care	80% of excess doctor charges under Part B	100% of excess doctor charges under Part B	50% of out patient drugs after $250 deduc., up to $1,250	50% of out-patient drugs after $250 deduc., up to $3,000
A	X										
B	X	X									
C	X	X	X	X							
D	X	X	X		X	X					
E	X	X	X		X		X				
F*	X	X	X	X	X				X		
G	X	X	X		X	X		X			
H	X	X	X		X					X	
I	X	X	X		X	X			X	X	
J*	X	X	X	X	X	X	X		X		X

*Each policy has a high deductible ($1,730 deductible in 2005) variation.

Prior to selecting a Medigap policy, the potential purchaser should make a reasonable estimate of the benefits he or she is likely to need. Not everyone needs the most comprehensive policy (Policy J).

It is *illegal* for Medigap policy sellers to sell or issue to an individual entitled to benefits under Part A or enrolled under Part B (1) a health insurance policy with knowledge that the policy duplicates health benefits the individual is otherwise entitled to under Medicare or Medicaid; (2) a Medigap policy with knowledge that the individual is entitled to benefits under another Medigap policy, or (3) a health insurance policy, other than a Medigap policy, with knowledge that the policy duplicates health benefits to which the individual is otherwise entitled. In addition, the application for such policies must include a statement, prominently displayed, disclosing the extent to which benefits payable under the policy or plan duplicate Medicare benefits. Moreover, sellers of Medigap policies are precluded from (1) telling a person that they are employees or agents of the Medicare program or of any government agency, (2) making a false statement that a policy meets legal standards for certification when it does not, (3) selling a person a Medigap policy that is not one of the 10 approved standard policies, (4) denying a person his or her Medigap open enrollment period by refusing to issue the person a policy, placing conditions on the policy, or discriminating in the price of a policy because of the person's health status, claim experience, receipt of health care, or the person's medical condition, or (5) using the U.S. mail in a state for advertising or delivering health insurance policies to supplement Medicare if the policies have not been approved for sale in that state.

MEDICAID

Medicaid is actually Title XIX of the Social Security Act and was established in 1965 as a federal-state matching entitlement program to pay the medical and custodial costs of individuals and families with low incomes and minimal resources. Under Title XIX of the Act, the federal government makes grants to the states for Medicaid coverage for qualified individuals. While both the federal government and the states share the cost of the program, it is administered solely by the states. The Centers for Medicare & Medicaid Services in the HHS Department have federal oversight responsibility for Medicaid.

States must provide mandatory Medicaid services to eligible recipients, including inpatient and outpatient hospital care, health screening, diagnosis and treatment to children, family planning, physician services and nursing facility services to individuals over age 21. The states may also provide any of over 30 specified optional services.

To qualify for Medicaid, applicants must have both incomes and assets below certain limits, which vary from state to state. Probably the most significant benefit of Medicaid is its coverage for extended nursing home care for elderly people who cannot afford to pay for it themselves. For those who do qualify, Medicaid even pays one's Medicare premiums, as well as Medicare coinsurance and deductibles. In some cases, it also pays the full cost of services not covered by Medicare. Of course, many applicants not in poverty have, in consultation with attorneys and financial planners, designed ways to qualify for Medicaid coverage of nursing home care in order to protect their wealth. However, the Omnibus Budget Reconciliation Act of 1993 (OBRA) increased the difficulty of upper and middle-class persons who attempt to qualify for Medicaid.

Medicaid Benefits

A state Medicaid program must offer certain basic services, generally including the following:

- Inpatient hospital services
- Outpatient hospital services
- Prenatal care
- Vaccines for children
- Physician services
- Nursing facility services for persons aged 21 or older
- Family planning services and supplies
- Rural health clinic services
- Home health care for persons eligible for skilled nursing services
- Laboratory and x-ray services
- Pediatric and family nurse practitioner services
- Nurse-midwife services
- Federally-qualified health-center (FQHC) services, and ambulatory services of an FQHC that would be available in other settings
- Early and periodic screening, diagnostic, and treatment services for children under age 21

States have the option to provide other services as well. Medicaid pays providers directly and the providers must accept Medicaid payment rates as payment in full.

Qualifying for Medicaid

A single individual will not qualify for Medicaid in most states *unless* he or she has less than $2,000 in "countable" assets-so-called "nonexempt" assets. Exempt or non-countable assets include:

- Cash value of permanent life insurance policies up to $1,500 of face value, and all life insurance policies with no cash value (term insurance)
- Household furnishings (furniture, paintings, appliances, etc.) only while used in the applicant's home
- Burial funds up to $1,500. There is no dollar limit if the burial plan is irrevocable
- Property used in a trade or business
- Burial space (grave site, crypt, mausoleum, urn, grave marker)
- One automobile of any value: (1) for a married couple where one spouse is institutionalized, (2) if equipped for a handicapped person, (3) if used to obtain medical treatment, or (4) if used for employment. This exemption is limited to $4,500 in all other cases.
- A home, regardless of value, provided it is the person's principal place of residence; this includes the land on which the home sits and any adjoining property

- Property owned with one or more other individuals if the other owners use the property as their principal place of residence and would be forced to move if the property were sold
- Personal effects, including clothing, photographs, jewelry, etc.

A person's home is treated as a resource after the individual has been institutionalized for six months, unless the individual's spouse or minor, disabled, or blind child continues to reside in the home, or it can be shown that the individual may be able to leave the institution and return home.

When a Medicaid recipient dies, exempt assets become countable and, accordingly, the state may claim reimbursement from the recipient's estate. In some cases, Medicaid authorities are granted a lien against the home, collectible after the death of the recipient (or the death of certain relatives living in the home) to compensate for Medicaid benefits paid to the homeowner.

Medicaid applicants also must meet income tests that vary by state. Some states have *no* upper income limit for persons in nursing homes and accordingly, they qualify for Medicaid as long as their income is less than the cost of nursing home care (and they have less than $2,000 in countable assets). Other states have what are referred to as "income caps" in determining eligibility for nursing home coverage. The income cap maximums are set by federal law, but states often use maximum income caps less than the amount permitted by federal law. If an applicant in an "income cap" state has income in excess of the income cap, he or she does *not* qualify for Medicaid.

Spousal Impoverishment

In the case of a married couple, where one spouse is in a nursing facility or medical institution and is expected to remain there for at least 30 days, the so-called "spousal impoverishment" provisions come into play. These provisions serve to protect the couple's income and resources for the non-institutionalized spouse. Upon application for Medicaid, the couple's resources are combined and appropriate exemptions are deducted for the home, household goods, an automobile, and burial funds. The remainder is the "spousal resource amount." Depending on the state involved, the spousal resource amount may be either the state's minimum resource standard ($19,020 in 2005) or the spousal share, which is one-half of the couple's combined resources, not to exceed the maximum permitted by the state ($95,100 in 2005).

To determine whether the spouse residing in a medical facility is eligible for Medicaid, the couple's total countable resources must be aggregated. This amount is considered to be available to the institutionalized spouse, except for what is referred to as the protected resource amount (PRA). The PRA is the greatest of (1) the spousal resource amount; (2) the state spousal resource standard (the amount determined by the state as being protected for the community spouse); (3) an amount transferred to the community spouse for his/her support as directed by a court order; or (4) an amount designated by a state hearing officer to raise the community spouse's protected resources up to the minimum monthly maintenance needs standard.

If there is any amount remaining after deducting the PRA from the couple's total countable resources, it is considered attributable to the institutionalized spouse. If this amount of resources is below the state's resource standard, the individual is eligible for Medicaid. After the institutionalized spouse qualifies for Medicaid, resources of the community spouse are no longer attributed to the institutionalized spouse. Finally, a determination is made as to (1) how much the institutionalized spouse must contribute toward the cost of nursing facility/institutional care and (2) how much of the institutionalized spouse's income is protected for use by the community spouse. From the total income of the institutionalized spouse, deductions are then made in the following order:

- A personal needs allowance of at least $30
- The community spouse's monthly income allowance (between $1,562 and $2,378 in 2005), as long as the income is actually made available to the spouse
- A family monthly income allowance
- An amount for medical expenses incurred by the institutionalized spouse

Any balance remaining is the amount the institutionalized spouse must contribute to the cost of care.

Transferring Assets to Qualify for Medicaid

If a person transfers property for less than its fair market value prior to applying for Medicaid, he or she may be denied benefits. If such a transfer takes place within 36 months of applying for Medicaid, the applicable state may delay eligibility for Medicaid. This period of ineligibility begins either in the month when the resources were transferred or the month following the transfer, depending on the rules of the state involved, and subsequently continues for the number of months equal to the total value of transferred property divided by the average cost of nursing home care to a private patient in the applicant's state or community. The length of the penalty period is unlimited. The following example explains how the penalty period is calculated:

> If Frank, a Medicaid applicant, gifts his house worth $300,000 to his daughter in a state with an average cost of nursing home care of $3,000 per month, he will be penalized for 100 months of ineligibility for Medicaid ($300,000 ÷ $3,000 = 100). Alternatively, if Frank had gifted the house to his daughter and then waited more than 36 months before applying for Medicaid, the transfer would not have been reportable and there would have been no penalty period.

While the Medicaid law includes a criminal provision for aiding and abetting such transfers, the Department of Justice has elected *not* to enforce it and has even been enjoined by a federal district court from doing so.

Some transfers may be made during the 36 months prior to applying for Medicaid without the imposition of a penalty period. For instance, an applicant's family home may be transferred to (1) the community spouse, (2) a child under age 21, blind, or permanently and totally disabled, (3) an adult son or daughter residing in the home and providing care that delayed the applicant's need for care in a medical institution or nursing facility for at least two years, (4) a trust created solely for the benefit of disabled children of the applicant, (5) certain trusts created for a disabled child or grandchild under

CHAPTER TWO

age 65, and (6) a brother or sister who has an ownership interest in the house and who has been living in the home for at least one year immediately before the person's admission for care. Also, if the applicant proves that the transfer was made at fair market value or for other valuable consideration, or that the transfer was not made with the purpose of qualifying for Medicaid, no penalty period will be imposed. Each state also may waive the penalty period when it results in undue hardship to the applicant and his or her family.

In light of these rules, an applicant should transfer assets to family members more than 36 months before applying for Medicaid or, if already living in a nursing home or about to enter one, retain enough assets to pay for 36 months of care, transfer the balance, and then wait 36 months after the last transfer before applying for Medicaid.

Use of Trusts to Shelter Assets

In limited circumstances, trusts may also be used to shelter a Medicaid applicant's assets. The basic rule is that if the Medicaid applicant or his or her spouse derives any benefit from the trust, the trust assets are considered available to the applicant to the extent of the benefits derived. The look-back period for trusts is 60 months rather than 36 months, as is the case with other transfers. However, the penalty period is calculated in the same way by dividing the total value of assets transferred during the 60-month look-back period by the average monthly cost to a private patient of nursing facility services in the applicable state at the time of application.

If the applicant uses a *revocable* trust, the trust corpus is considered a resource available to the individual, with payments from the trust to or for the benefit of the applicant considered income of the applicant. Any other payments from the trust are also counted against the applicant during the 60-month "look-back" period.

The rules are different for an *irrevocable* trust. If payments may be made from the irrevocable trust to or for the benefit of the applicant, the portion of the trust corpus from which, or the income on the corpus from which, payments to the applicant may be made is considered an available resource to the applicant. Payments from that portion of the corpus or income to or for the benefit of the applicant are considered income of the applicant and payments for any other purpose are considered a transfer of assets by the applicant. Also, any portion of the trust from which, or any income on the corpus from which, no payment could be made under any circumstances to the applicant, is considered (as of the date of the establishment of the trust) to be assets disposed of by the applicant.

Three types of trusts are *exempt* from the Medicaid trust rules:
- A trust established by a parent, grandparent, guardian, or court for the benefit of an applicant who is disabled and under age 65, using the applicant's own funds
- A trust composed only of pension, Social Security, and other income of the applicant, in states which make applicants eligible for institutional care under a special income level, but do not cover institutional care for the medically needy

- A trust established by a disabled applicant, parent, grandparent, guardian, or court for the disabled applicant, using the applicant's own funds, where the trust is made up of pooled funds and managed by a nonprofit organization for the sole benefit of each individual included in the trust

In each of these three cases, the trust must provide that the state receives reimbursement for the amount of Medicaid benefits paid on behalf of the applicant, to the extent of funds remaining in the trust when the applicant dies.

As indicated previously, states are required to recover the cost of nursing facility and other long-term care services furnished to a Medicaid beneficiary from his or her estate, except in the case of undue hardship. However, these estate recovery rules apply only to the estates of Medicaid beneficiaries dying on or after October 1, 1993, only to benefits paid on or after that date, and only for costs for a Medicaid recipient who was age 55 or older at the time the costs were incurred. Further, such recovery may not occur while the surviving spouse is still alive.

IMPORTANT CONCEPTS

The "three-legged stool" of retirement income sources

Fully insured

Currently insured

Primary insurance amount (PIA)

Average indexed monthly earnings (AIME)

"Excess" earnings

Mother's or father's survivor benefit

Child's survivor benefit

Widow(er)'s survivor benefit

Disabled widow(er)'s survivor benefit

Parent's survivor benefit

Lump sum death benefit

Maximum family benefit

Social Security definition of disability

Base amount

Adjusted base amount

Federal Insurance Contributions Act (FICA)

OASDI

Centers for Medicare & Medicaid Services (CMS)

Medicare Hospital Insurance (Part A)

Medicare Medical Insurance (Part B)

Medicare Advantage (Part C)

Medicare Prescription Drug Insurance (Part D)

Qualified Medicare Beneficiary (QMB) program

Special Low-Income Medicare Beneficiary (SLMB) program

Qualified Individual (QI) program

Part A deductible

Part A coinsurance

Skilled nursing care

Custodial care

Home health care

Hospice care

Hospital insurance tax

Part B deductible

Part B coinsurance

Accepting assignment

Medigap insurance

Policies A through J

Medicaid

Countable assets

Exempt assets

"Income cap" states

Spousal impoverishment

Protected resource amount (PRA)

Asset transfers to qualify for Medicaid

Look-back period

Penalty period

Use of trusts to shelter assets

QUESTIONS FOR REVIEW

1. What are the three legs of the "three-legged stool" of retirement income sources?

2. What types of coverage are provided by the Social Security Act, as amended?

3. What does it mean to be fully insured under Social Security?

4. What constitutes a quarter of coverage under Social Security?

5. What is meant by an individual's normal retirement age under Social Security?

6. How does being currently insured under Social Security differ from being fully insured?

7. What is the significance of an insured's primary insurance amount (PIA)?

8. How does an insured's PIA differ from his or her AIME and how are they interrelated?

9. In what way, if any, is a worker's benefit adjusted if he or she elects to receive Social Security benefits prior to his or her normal retirement age?

10. In what way, if any, is a worker's benefit adjusted if he or she elects to receive Social Security benefits after his or her normal retirement age?

11. In what way, if any, is a Social Security beneficiary's monthly benefits adjusted if he or she continues to work?

12. What are some of the items not counted as earnings for purposes of the Social Security retirement test?

13. What are the various types of Social Security survivor benefits and to whom are they paid?

14. What limitations, if any, are placed on multiple family members receiving Social Security benefits?

15. What is the definition of disability for Social Security disability benefit purposes?

16. What is the 5-step process used by the SSA to decide whether a worker is eligible for disability benefits?

17. In what way, if any, is a person's Social Security disability benefit affected by his or her personal wealth and whether or not the person's spouse is employed?

18. How does the base amount differ from the adjusted base amount in determining the income taxation of Social Security benefits?

19. How are Social Security benefits funded?

20. How are Social Security payroll taxes invested by the Federal Old-Age and Survivors Insurance and Disability Insurance Trust Funds?

21. What demographic issue threatens the long-term financial stability of the Social Security program?

22. What types of persons may potentially receive benefits from Medicare?

23. What are the four basic parts of Medicare and what benefits are provided by each part?

24. What are the current deductibles and required coinsurance payments under Parts A and B of Medicare?

25. What services are *not* covered by Part A of Medicare?

26. What types of services are included in hospice care?

27. How are Parts A and B of Medicare financed?

28. What is the effect on his or her future coverage if a person elects not to enroll in Medicare Part B during his or her initial enrollment period?

29. What are some of the items *not* covered by Part B of Medicare?

30. What programs are available to help pay the Medicare expenses of elderly or disabled persons who have low incomes and very limited assets?

31. How does Medicare Advantage differ from Parts A and B of Medicare?

32. What Medicare benefit becomes effective January 1, 2006?

33. What is the purpose of Medigap insurance?

34. What general requirements must a person meet to become eligible for Medicaid?

35. What potentially major expense is covered by Medicaid but not by Medicare?

36. What are the rules surrounding the transfer of assets to qualify for Medicaid?

37. Under the Medicaid rules, what is the difference in the "look-back period" for transfers to trusts versus transfers to others in attempting to qualify for Medicaid?

SUGGESTIONS FOR ADDITIONAL READING

2005 Social Security Manual, The National Underwriter Company, 2005.

2005 All About Medicare, The National Underwriter Company, 2005

Traditional IRAs

• • •

As discussed in chapter 1, one of the three legs of the retirement security stool is personal savings. Beginning in 1974 with the introduction of the original IRA, the federal government has created several income tax and other incentives for individuals to save for their own retirement. By permitting individuals to claim income tax deductions for contributing a limited portion of their earnings to an IRA and to defer taxation on the earnings in such accounts until withdrawal, the IRA has contributed significantly to their ability to achieve retirement income goals. While certain types of IRAs (discussed later in this chapter) also permit employer contributions, IRAs are primarily plans of individual savings, rather than employee benefits.

While the Internal Revenue Service uses the term "traditional IRA" to refer to either an original IRA (deductible or nondeductible) or a SEP/IRA (discussed in chapter 6), the discussion in this chapter will be confined to the initial type of IRA originally created by the Employee Retirement Income Security Act of 1974 (ERISA).

Upon completing this chapter, you should be able to:
- Describe the basic qualification requirements of the original (traditional) individual retirement arrangement
- Describe the so-called prohibited transactions
- Explain the rules governing contributions to traditional IRAs and their tax-deductibility
- Analyze a given situation to calculate the amount of deductible IRA contributions
- Describe the rules governing distributions from traditional IRAs
- Identify the rules governing rollovers into and out of traditional IRAs
- Describe the special rules applicable to inherited IRAs

TERMINOLOGY ISSUES

Under IRC Section 408, an individual who receives compensation (including compensation earned as an employee, alimony received, and, in the case of a self-employed person, earned income) that is includible in gross income may establish and make contributions to his or her own **individual retirement arrangement** (IRA). If such an arrangement is funded through a trust or custodial account, it is called an **individual retirement account** (IRA). Similarly, if such an arrangement is funded through the purchase of an annuity contract or contracts, it is referred to as an **individual retirement annuity** (IRA). Technically, when we speak of an IRA, we are referring to an individual retirement arrangement funded in either of these two ways. In this book, we will simply refer to an individual retirement arrangement, no matter how funded, as an IRA.

TYPES OF INDIVIDUAL RETIREMENT ARRANGEMENTS

There are basically four types of individual retirement arrangements. The original IRA, authorized by ERISA in 1974, is referred to as a "traditional IRA." As mentioned previously, this type of IRA will be the subject of this chapter. Contributions to a traditional IRA may be made *only* by the individual for whom the IRA is maintained or his or her spouse and not by the individual's employer. Annual contributions to such an IRA are limited in amount and, if they meet other requirements (discussed later in this chapter), are deductible from gross income. Generally, a distribution from a traditional IRA is taxable to the extent it exceeds any nondeductible contributions made by the owner.

Another type of IRA enacted in 1978 as part of the Revenue Act of 1978 is the SEP/IRA. SEP stands for "simplified employee pension." The SEP/IRA is essentially the same as a traditional IRA, except that only the owner's employer may make contributions to it (unless it is the now defunct Salary Reduction SEP (SARSEP) that did permit employee salary reduction contributions). Employer contributions and the related income tax deductions are subject to limitations that are essentially the same as those that apply to qualified profit-sharing plans (discussed in chapter 9). On the other hand, owner contributions and tax deductions are subject to the same limitations that apply to traditional IRAs. Again, a distribution from a SEP/IRA is taxable to the extent it exceeds the owner's basis (nondeductible contributions). We will discuss SEP/IRAs in chapter 6.

A third type of IRA, referred to as a SIMPLE IRA, was established by the Small Business Job Protection Act of 1996. SIMPLE is an acronym for Savings Incentive Match Plan. Only the owner's employer may contribute to a SIMPLE IRA. The owner is not permitted to make either deductible or nondeductible contributions but the owner may authorize salary reduction contributions, which are treated as contributions of the employer for tax purposes. The employer is required to match such salary reduction contributions. Annual amount limitations apply to salary reduction contributions and to matching contributions. Since the owner can never have a basis in such an account, distributions are taxable in their entirety. We will discuss SIMPLE IRAs in chapter 6.

Congress created a fourth type of IRA in the Taxpayer Relief Act of 1997. It is known as the Roth IRA which prohibits employer contributions and permits limited nondeductible contributions by the owner. "Qualified distributions" from a Roth IRA are *never* taxable. Nonqualified distributions are taxable to the extent they exceed the owner's nondeductible contributions. We will discuss Roth IRAs in chapter 4.

Just to further confuse the issue, there are two other types of IRAs. One was formerly known as an education IRA, created by the same act as the Roth IRA-the Taxpayer Relief Act of 1997. These accounts were created to encourage savings for higher education and actually have nothing to do with one's retirement. They have been renamed Coverdell Education Savings Accounts (CESAs). This type of IRA account is not discussed in this book.

A final type of IRA, initiated in 2003, is known as a "deemed IRA." Under the authorizing legislation, a qualified plan (chapter 8), tax-sheltered annuity arrangement (chapter 6), or nonqualified government plan (chapter 6) may elect to accept voluntary employee contributions and treat them as contributions to a conventional IRA or Roth IRA, as the employee chooses.

QUALIFICATION REQUIREMENTS

Each method of funding an individual retirement arrangement (i.e., individual retirement account or individual retirement annuity) is subject to specific requirements.

Individual Retirement Accounts

As mentioned earlier, an individual retirement account is a trust or custodial account created and organized under a written instrument for the exclusive benefit of an individual or his or her beneficiaries. The written document creating the IRA must meet the following requirements:

1. The trustee or custodian may be a bank, a federally insured credit union, a savings and loan association, or other entity approved by the IRS to act as trustee or custodian. The IRS has issued a list of approved non-bank trustees. However, the account owner may not serve as trustee or custodian.

2. The trustee or custodian generally cannot accept contributions of more than the applicable dollar limit (discussed later in this chapter) with these contributions consisting of cash, except for rollover contributions (discussed later in this chapter), which are also not subject to the dollar limitation.

3. The owner's right to the amount in the account must be fully vested at all times.

4. Funds in the account may not be used to purchase a life insurance policy. However, such funds may be used to purchase an endowment policy, under certain conditions.

5. The funds in the account cannot be commingled with other property, except in a common trust fund or common investment fund (e.g., as offered by a bank trust department).

6. The owner must begin to receive distributions from his or her account not later than April 1 of the year following the year in which he or she reaches age 70 1/2. A penalty tax is imposed on excess accumulations after the owner reaches 70 1/2.

Individual Retirement Annuities

One creates an individual retirement annuity by purchasing an annuity contract or an endowment contract from a life insurance company. The contract must be issued in the name of the owner and must be for the exclusive benefit of the owner and his or her surviving beneficiaries. Only the owner or his or her surviving beneficiaries may receive benefits under the contract. An individual retirement annuity must meet all of the following requirements:

1. The contract must be nontransferable and the owner's interest must be nonforfeitable.
2. The contract must provide for premiums that are adjusted for any change in owner compensation.
3. The contribution limit (discussed later in this chapter) must not exceed that amount also permitted for individual retirement accounts.
4. The owner must use any refunded premiums either to pay for future premiums or to purchase additional benefits.
5. Distributions must meet the same requirements as those for individual retirement accounts (i.e., they must begin by April 1 of the year following the year in which the owner reaches age 70 1/2.

Finally, the owner of an individual retirement annuity may not borrow against the annuity, either directly from the issuing insurance company or from third parties using the annuity as security. Violation of this prohibition causes the individual retirement annuity to terminate, resulting in its entire value being included in the owner's income at that time.

CONTRIBUTION AND DEDUCTION LIMITS

Being permitted to make a contribution to a traditional IRA does not necessarily mean that such contribution may be deductible for income tax purposes. And even though a deduction may not be permitted, an individual may still make a nondeductible contribution to an IRA within the contribution limits described below. A nondeductible traditional IRA contribution is the excess of the maximum annual contribution amount over the amount deductible (discussed later). Nondeductible contributions are not taxable when they are distributed but the income earned on those contributions is taxable. Accordingly, amounts withdrawn are partly taxable and partly nontaxable. In the following sections we will describe the separate limitations for the amounts that may be contributed to an IRA and the amounts contributed that are tax-deductible.

Contribution Limits

Only contributions made by or on behalf of the IRA owner or the owner's surviving spouse, who acquired the IRA by reason of the owner's death, qualify for deduction and tax-free buildup. Any other person succeeding to an owner's IRA because of the owner's death (other than the owner's surviving spouse) may *not* make a qualifying contribution to the IRA. A qualifying contribution must be in cash (unless it is a rollover contribution) within the limitations established by law and made in a tax year that ends before the IRA owner has reached age 70 1/2. It does not matter where the contributed funds come from. They may be contributed by a non-owner; however the contribution and deduction limits are determined with reference to the owner's compensation, adjusted gross income (including that of his or her spouse in the case of a joint return), and status as a qualified retirement plan participant.

In 2005, the contribution limit is the smaller of $4,000 (or $4,500 if the owner is 50 or older) or the owner's taxable compensation. See the Supplement to this text for the limitations in later years. Taxable compensation includes amounts received for providing personal services, such as wages, salaries, tips, professional fees, bonuses, and other similar receipts. It also includes any amounts received that are calculated as a percentage of profits or sales price (commissions) as well as net earnings from self-employment derived from a trade or business (reduced by contributions on behalf of the IRA owner to retirement plans and by the deduction permitted for one-half of the self-employment tax paid). For IRA contribution purposes, compensation also includes taxable alimony and separate maintenance payments received under a decree of divorce or separate maintenance. Rental income, interest income, dividend income, pension or annuity income, deferred compensation payments, income from a limited partnership or where the IRA owner's services are not a material income-producing factor, and foreign earned income and housing costs excluded from income do not constitute taxable compensation for this purpose. The foregoing limitation applies to the total of all IRAs owned by the same individual.

Generally, one's income tax filing status has *no* effect on the amount of allowable contributions to one's traditional IRA. However, a taxpayer who files a joint return with his or her spouse and has taxable compensation less than that of the spouse, is subject to the following contribution limit:

- $4,000 ($4,500 if 50 or older) for 2005 (see the Supplement to this text for the limits for later years) or
- the total compensation includible in the gross income of both the taxpayer and his or her spouse for the year, reduced by: (1) the spouse's IRA contribution for the year to a traditional IRA and (2) any contributions for the year to a Roth IRA on behalf of the spouse.

If a taxpayer makes contributions to his or her IRA for a particular year that were less than the limits described above, he or she cannot make additional contributions after the due date of the tax return for that same tax year. Likewise, if a taxpayer contributes more than the allowable limit for a particular tax year, the excess contributions may only be applied to a later tax year if the contributions for that later year are less than the maximum allowed for that year. However, a penalty or additional tax may then be applicable, as discussed later in this chapter.

Also, if a taxpayer has no taxable compensation in a given tax year, he or she may not make a contribution unless he or she received alimony or filed a joint return with a spouse who had taxable compensation in that year.

Contributions for a particular year may be made at any time during that year, or even after the year, until the due date for filing the tax return for that year, not including extensions of time to file. When making a contribution between January 1 and April 15, it is important that the IRA owner clearly specifies to the IRA sponsor for which tax year he or she is making contributions (the current or prior year). Moreover, a taxpayer may file his or her tax return without having actually made a traditional IRA contribution for that year as long as the contribution is made by the due date of the return.

Deduction Limits

Generally, the maximum amount that may be deducted from gross income for contributions to IRAs in any tax year is the same as the limit on contributions. However, in the case where the owner is an "active participant" in an employer-sponsored retirement plan or is a non-active participant filing a joint return with a spouse who is an active participant, the dollar limitation on the deduction may be *reduced*. As mentioned previously, however, even though no deduction may be allowed, an individual may still make a nondeductible contribution to an IRA equal to the IRA contribution limit for the current year.

The deduction rules are as follows:

1. In the case of a married couple, if neither spouse was an "active participant" (defined later) in an employer-maintained retirement plan during any part of a particular year, each spouse may claim a deduction for total contributions to one or more of his or her traditional IRAs of up to the lesser of :

    - $4,000 or $4,500, if 50 or older, (for 2005)(see the Supplement to this text for the limits for later years) or
    - 100 percent of each spouse's compensation

2. Where a married couple has unequal compensation and files a joint return, the deduction for contributions to the traditional IRA of the spouse with less compensation is limited to the lesser of:

    - $4,000 or $4,500, if 50 or older, (for 2005) (see the Supplement to this text for the limits for later years) or
    - The total compensation includible in the gross income of both spouses for the year reduced by the following three amounts.
        - The IRA deduction for the year of the spouse with the greater compensation
        - Any designated nondeductible contribution for the year made on behalf of the spouse with the greater compensation
        - Any contributions for the year to a Roth IRA on behalf of the spouse with the greater compensation

3. If either spouse was covered by an employer-maintained retirement plan, each spouse may be entitled to only a partial (reduced) deduction or no deduction at all, depending on their income and filing status, as discussed later.

Active Participation in an Employer-Maintained Retirement Plan

An active participant is an individual who is an active participant in (1) a qualified pension, profit-sharing, or stock bonus plan (including a 401(k) plan or union plan), (2) a simplified employee pension (SEP), (3) a plan (other than a Sec. 457 plan, discussed later), established for employees by the United States, a state or political subdivision of a state, or by a federal or state instrumentality, or (4) a SIMPLE retirement account. An individual who is retired and receiving pension annuity payments from any one of the foregoing plans or arrangements is *not* an active participant. Nor is an individual who is covered only by Social Security or by a railroad retirement program. The determination of status as an active participant is made without regard to whether an individual's rights under an employer-maintained plan are forfeitable or nonforfeitable. In fact, the U.S. Tax Court has ruled that an employee's active participation in his employer's retirement plans prevented him from taking a deduction on his federal taxes for contributions to an IRA, even though his interest in the funds was forfeited upon his termination of employment.

An individual is considered to be an active participant in a defined contribution plan (discussed in chapters 9 through 12) if amounts are contributed or allocated to his or her account for the plan year that ends with or within a particular tax year. In the case of a defined benefit plan (discussed in chapter 13), if an individual is eligible to participate in his or her employer's defined benefit plan for the plan year that ends within his or her tax year, he or she is covered by the plan. This is true even if the individual declines to participate in the plan, did not make a required contribution, or did not perform the minimum service required to accrue a benefit for the year. If an individual receives retirement benefits from a previous employer's plan, he or she is not covered by that plan.

Effect of Active Participation in an Employer-Maintained Retirement Plan

If a married individual is *not* an active participant but his or her spouse *is* an active participant, and the couple files a joint return, the deduction for the non-participant is gradually phased out when the couple has modified adjusted gross income (MAGI) of more than $150,000 (in 2005) and completely eliminated when their MAGI exceeds $160,000 (in 2005). See the Supplement to this text for the phaseout range for later years. If a married individual is *not* an active participant but his or her spouse *is* an active participant, and the individual files a separate return, the deduction for the non-participant is phased out between MAGI of zero and $9,999. If MAGI is $10,000 or more, no deduction is permitted.

MAGI is defined as adjusted gross income (AGI) without taking into consideration (1) the IRA deduction; (2) the student loan interest deduction; (3) the tuition and fees deduction; (4) the foreign earned income exclusion; (5) the foreign housing exclusion or deduction; (6) the qualified savings bond interest exclusion; and (7) the employer-provided adoption benefits exclusion.

If a single or head of household filer is an active participant, he or she may claim a full deduction if his or her MAGI is $50,000 or less (in 2005) (see the Supplement to this text for the amounts in later years). If his or her MAGI is more than $50,000 but less than $60,000, he or she may claim a partial deduction under the phaseout provisions. If his or her MAGI is $60,000 or more, no deduction is permitted.

If one's filing status is married filing jointly or qualifying widow(er) and he or she is an active participant, a full deduction may be claimed if MAGI is $70,000 or less (in 2005) (see the Supplement to this text for the amounts in later years). If MAGI is more than $70,000 but less than $80,000, he or she may claim a partial deduction under the phaseout provisions. If MAGI is $80,000 or more, no deduction is permitted.

If one's filing status is married filing separate return and he or she is an active participant, a partial deduction may be claimed under the phaseout provisions if MAGI is less than $10,000. If MAGI is $10,000 or more, no deduction is permitted.

Special rules apply (not discussed in this text) if the individual received Social Security benefits during the year, received taxable compensation, made contributions to his or her traditional IRA, and either the individual or his or her spouse was an active participant.

In those cases where a reduced deduction applies, the allowable deduction is calculated by subtracting the amount by which MAGI exceeds the phaseout threshold (or point at which the phaseout begins) from $10,000, dividing the remainder by $10,000, and then multiplying the product by the maximum allowable deduction. For example, if an individual is married filing jointly and is an active participant with MAGI of $77,000 (in 2005), the amount by which MAGI exceeds the phaseout threshold is $7,000 ($77,000 - $70,000). This amount is then subtracted from $10,000 yielding $3,000 which in turn is divided by $10,000 resulting in a factor of 0.3. Then multiplying the 0.3 by the maximum allowable deduction of $4,000 (if less than 50 years of age) yields an allowable deduction of $1,200.

See IRS Tables 1-2 and 1-3 to determine the amount of a traditional IRA contribution that is deductible.

Table 1-2. **Effect of Modified AGI[1] on Deduction If You Are Covered by a Retirement Plan at Work***

If you are covered by a retirement plan at work, use this table to determine if your modified AGI affects the amount of your deduction.

IF you filing status is…	AND your modified adjusted gross income (modified AGI is…)	THEN you can take…
single or head of household	$45,000 or less	a full deduction
	more than $45,000 but less than $55,000	a partial deduction
	$55,000 or more	no deduction
married filing jointly or qualifying widow(er)	$65,000 or less	a full deduction
	more than $65,000 but less than $75,000	a partial deduction
	$75,000 or more	no deduction
married filing separetely[2]	less than $10,000	a partial deduction
	$10,000 or more	no deduction

[1] Modified AGI (adjusted gross income). *See Modified adjusted gross income (AGI)*, later.
[2] If you did not live with your spouse at any time during the year, your filing status is considered Single for this purpose (therefore, your IRA deduction is determined under the "Single" filing status).

*This table is from IRS Publication 590.

Table 1-3. **Effect of Modified AGI[1] on Deduction If You Are NOT Covered by a Retirement Plan at Work***

If you are NOT covered by a retirement plan at work, use this table to determine if your modified AGI affects the amount of your deduction.

IF you filing status is…	AND your modified adjusted gross income (modified AGI is…)	THEN you can take…
single, head of household, or qualifying widow(er)	any amount	a full deduction
married filing jointly or separately with a spouse who is not covered by a plan at work	any amount	a full deduction
married filing jointly with a spouse who is covered by a plan at work	$150,000 or less	a full deduction
	more than $150,000 but less than $160,000	a partial deduction
	$160,000 or more	no deduction
married filing separately with a spouse who is covered by a plan at work[2]	less than $10,000	a partial deduction
	$10,000 or more	no deduction

[1] Modified AGI (adjusted gross income). *See Modified adjusted gross income (AGI)*, later.
[2] You are entitled to the full deduction if you did not live with with your spouse at any time during the year.

*This table is from IRS Publication 590.

Finally, instead of an income tax deduction, certain lower income taxpayers who make contributions to a traditional IRA may qualify for a limited nonrefundable tax credit.

TRANSFER OF RETIREMENT PLAN ASSETS

Money or property residing in retirement programs (including traditional IRAs) may be transferred to a traditional IRA on a tax-free basis without limitation as to amount. There are three types of such transfers:

1. A transfer from one trustee to another
2. A "rollover" (as defined below)

3. A transfer incident to a divorce

If an IRA owner decides to move his or her IRA funds from an existing traditional IRA to another either existing or new traditional IRA, he or she may do so by transferring the funds directly from the trustee of the existing IRA to the trustee of the other IRA. Such a transfer is *not* considered a rollover and because the IRA owner never has access to the transferred funds, it is *not* taxable to the owner. Also, such a transfer is not subject to 20 percent withholding tax (discussed later), the 10 percent additional tax (where the recipient is under age 59 1/2, or the one-year waiting period required between rollovers (discussed later).

A "rollover" is a tax-free distribution to the IRA owner of cash or other assets from one retirement plan that is deposited (called a "rollover contribution") in another retirement plan. Rollovers may be made into a traditional IRA from the following sources:

- A traditional IRA
- An employer's qualified retirement plan
- A deferred compensation plan of a state or local government (Section 457 plan discussed in chapter 6), or
- A tax-sheltered annuity plan (Section 403(b) plan discussed in chapter 6)

A rollover distribution is not deductible and must be reported on the account owner's tax return for the year distributed.

A rollover may also be made from a traditional IRA into a qualified plan, including the Federal Thrift Savings Fund (for federal employees), Section 457 plans, and Section 403(b) annuity plans. However, qualified plans do not have to accept such transfers from traditional IRAs. A traditional IRA owner may also roll over his interest in one traditional IRA to another traditional IRA.

Generally, a rollover contribution must be made by the 60th day after the day the owner receives a distribution from his or her traditional IRA or employer's plan. If such distributions are not rolled over within the 60-day period, they do not qualify for tax-free rollover treatment. Instead they are treated as a taxable distribution. Also, the owner may have to pay a 10 percent additional tax on early distribution (discussed later) of his or her interest. However, the 60-day rollover period may be waived by the IRS under specific circumstances.

Normally, if an IRA owner makes a tax-free rollover of any part of a distribution from a traditional IRA, he or she cannot, within a 1-year period, make a tax-free rollover of any later distribution from that same IRA. In addition, the owner cannot make a tax-free rollover of any amount distributed, within the same 1-year period, from the IRA into which he or she made the tax-free rollover. The 1-year period begins on the date the owner receives the IRA distribution, not on the date he or she rolled it over into an IRA. However, the once-a-year limit on IRA-to-IRA rollovers does not apply to eligible rollover distributions (defined next) from an employer plan. This means that an owner may roll over more than one distribution from the same employer plan within a year.

An "eligible rollover distribution" from an owner's (or owner's deceased spouse's) qualified pension, profit-sharing, or stock bonus plan, annuity plan, Section 403(b) plan, or Section 457 plan may be rolled over into a traditional IRA. An "eligible rollover distribution" is any distribution of all or part of the balance to an owner's credit in a qualified retirement plan, with the following eight exceptions:

1. A required minimum distribution (explained later in this chapter)

2. A hardship distribution (explained later in this chapter)

3. Any of a series of substantially equal periodic distributions paid at least once a year over the owner's life expectancy, the lifetimes or life expectancies of the owner and his or her beneficiary, or a period of 10 years or more

4. Corrective distributions of excess contributions or excess deferrals, and any income allocable to the excess, or of excess annual additions and any allocable gains

5. A loan treated as a distribution because it does not satisfy certain requirements either when made or later (such as upon default), unless the participant's accrued benefits are reduced (offset) to repay the loan

6. Dividends on employer securities

7. The cost of life insurance coverage

8. Generally, a distribution to the plan participant's beneficiary

To the extent the distribution is rolled over into a traditional IRA, it is not includible in the owner's income. However, if an eligible rollover distribution is paid directly to the account owner, the payer must withhold 20 percent of the distribution amount. This is true even if the owner plans to roll over the distribution to a traditional IRA. The key here is whether the check is made out to the account owner or to the custodian of the transferee IRA (on behalf of the owner). The payer does not have to withhold income tax if all distributions from the same plan (or, at the payer's option, from all of the payee's employer's plans) total less than $200 or the distribution consists solely of employer securities, plus cash of $200 or less in lieu of fractional shares.

Conduit IRAs

An individual receiving an eligible rollover distribution from his or her employer's plan may roll over part or all of it into one or more conduit IRAs. Subsequently, these assets may be rolled over into a new employer's plan. A traditional IRA may be used as a conduit IRA, even if the owner continues to make regular contributions to it or adds funds from sources other than his or her employer's plan. However, if the owner does so, the qualified plan into which the funds are eventually transferred will not be eligible for any optional tax treatment for which it otherwise might have qualified.

Where an individual receives property (other than cash) in an eligible rollover distribution from a qualified retirement plan, he or she cannot keep the property and contribute cash to a traditional IRA instead of the property. He or she must then either roll over the property or sell it and roll over the proceeds. If the individual elects to sell the property and roll over all the proceeds into a traditional IRA, no gain or loss is recognized. One additional limitation is that a life insurance contract distributed from a qualified plan may not be rolled over into a traditional IRA.

The third type of transfer that may be made tax-free is a transfer incident to divorce. An interest in a traditional IRA transferred to an individual from his or her spouse or former spouse pursuant to a divorce or separate maintenance decree or a written document related to such a decree, is treated as the transferee's own IRA. Such a tax-free transfer may be accomplished by either changing the name on the IRA or by making a direct transfer of the IRA assets.

A final type of transfer of traditional IRA assets is a conversion of such assets into a Roth IRA. This type of transfer will be discussed in chapter 4.

DISTRIBUTIONS OF IRA ASSETS

A traditional IRA owner can withdraw or use his or her IRA assets at any time. However, if the owner is less than 59 1/2 years of age at the time of the withdrawal, such a withdrawal is considered to be an early distribution and he or she will generally be subject to a 10 percent additional tax. However, an IRA owner may make a tax-free and penalty-free withdrawal of contributions if he or she does so *before* the due date for filing his or her tax return for the year in which the contributions were made (even if the owner is under age 59 1/2). The IRA owner must not have taken a deduction for the contribution and he or she must withdraw any interest or other income earned on the contribution. The earnings on withdrawn contributions must also be included in gross income for the year in which the contributions were made—not the year in which they were withdrawn. Withdrawals of contributions after the due date (or extended due date) of the owner's return are treated as taxable distributions.

Funds contributed to a traditional IRA must eventually be distributed. If the owner does not take distributions or if the distributions taken are not large enough, the owner may be subject to a 50 percent excise tax on the amount not distributed as required. The requirements for distributing IRA funds vary, depending on whether the recipient is the IRA owner or the beneficiary of a decedent's IRA.

The amount that must be distributed each year is referred to as the "required minimum distribution" (RMD). Such amounts are *not* eligible for rollover treatment.

IRA Owner's Required Minimum Distribution

An IRA owner must start receiving distributions from his or her IRA by April 1 (known as the "required beginning date") of the year following the year in which he or she reaches age 70 1/2. A minimum amount must be distributed each year starting with the year the owner reaches 70 1/2. If the first minimum distribution is not received in the year in which the owner turns 70 1/2, then it must be made by April 1 of the subsequent year. However, the required minimum distribution for any year after the year the owner turns 70 1/2 must be made by December 31 of that later year. If an owner dies after reaching 70 1/2, but before April 1 of the following year, no minimum distribution is required because his or her death occurred before the required beginning date.

Example: John attains age 70 1/2 during calendar year 2006. If John does not take his first required minimum distribution for 2006 on or before December 31, 2006, he has until April 1, 2007 to take that distribution. However, if John does not take the 2006 RMD during 2006, he will have to take both the RMD for 2006 (by April 1, 2007) and the RMD for 2007 by December 31, 2007, resulting in two RMDs in the same tax year.

In the case of an individual retirement account, either the owner or the trustee must calculate the required minimum distribution (RMD) for each year. For individual retirement annuities, special rules apply to figuring the required minimum distribution.

In order to calculate the amount of the RMD for a specific year, one divides the IRA account balance as of the close of business on December 31 of the preceding year by the applicable *distribution period* or *life expectancy*. The IRA account balance as of December 31 of the preceding year must be adjusted for rollovers and recharacterizations of Roth IRA conversions (discussed in chapter 4) that were not in the account at the end of the preceding year. The distribution period is the maximum number of years over which an IRA owner is permitted to take distributions from his or her IRA. This period is derived from the IRS Uniform Lifetime Table (Table III) which is for unmarried IRA owners, married owners whose spouses are the sole beneficiaries of their IRAs and are not more than 10 years younger than the IRA owner, and married owners whose spouses are not the sole beneficiaries of their IRAs.

In the situation where the sole beneficiary of an owner's IRA is his or her spouse who is more than 10 years younger than the owner, the owner must use the IRS Joint Life and Last Survivor Expectancy Tables (Table II) to determine the life expectancy for purposes of the required minimum distribution calculation.

The beneficiary of an IRA who is an individual must use the IRS Single Life Expectancy Table (Table I) to determine the required minimum distribution. If the IRA owner's spouse is the sole designated beneficiary, the life expectancy of the spouse is used from Table I. If the owner died before the year in which he or she reached age 70 1/2, distributions to the spouse do not need to begin until the year in which the owner would have reached age 70 1/2. Where the beneficiary is someone *other than the owner's spouse*, such beneficiary must use the life expectancy listed in the table next to the beneficiary's age as of his or her birthday in the year following the year the owner died, reduced by the number of years since the year following the owner's death. For example, if a father died in 2005 and his son is the designated beneficiary of his traditional IRA, the son must use Table I (based on his age in 2006) to determine his life expectancy. If the son is 53 years old in 2006, his life expectancy is 31.4 years. If the IRA was worth $100,000 at the end of 2005, the required minimum distribution for 2006 is $3,185 ($100,000/31.4). If the value of the IRA at the end of 2006 was again $100,000, the required minimum distribution for 2007 would be $3,289 ($100,000/30.4).

Where the beneficiary of an IRA is *not* an individual (e.g., the owner's estate) and the owner died on or after the required beginning date, the required minimum distribution is determined from Table I using the owner's age as of his or her birthday in the year of death, reduced by the number of years since the year of death. If the owner died before the required beginning date, the entire account balance must be distributed by the end of the fifth year following the year of the owner's death. No distribution is required for any year before that fifth year.

In summary, the IRS tables should be used as follows:

- Table I: use for years after the year of the owner's death if the beneficiary is either (1) an individual and a designated beneficiary but not both the owner's surviving spouse and sole designated beneficiary, or (2) not an individual and the owner died on or after the required beginning date. If the beneficiary is the owner's surviving spouse and sole designated beneficiary and the owner had not reached age 70 1/2 when he or she died, and the beneficiary does not elect to be treated as the owner of the IRA, the beneficiary does not have to take distributions (using Table I) until the year in which the owner would have reached 70 1/2.

- Table II: use if the IRA owner's spouse is both the sole designated beneficiary and more than 10 years younger than the IRA owner. This table is also used in the year of the owner's death if he or she died after the required beginning date and would have been used had he or she not died.

- Table III: use if the IRA owner's spouse is *not* both the sole designated beneficiary and more than 10 years younger than the owner. This table is also used in the year of the owner's death if he or she died after the required beginning date and would have been used had he or she not died.

- Do not use *any* of the tables if the designated beneficiary is *not* an individual and the owner died *before* the required beginning date. In this case, the entire account balance must be distributed by the end of the fifth year following the year of the IRA owner's death. In addition, an individual may elect to take the entire account by the end of the fifth year following the year of the owner's death.

Taxation of IRA Distributions

In general, a distribution from a traditional IRA is taxable as ordinary income in the year received, except to the extent that the distribution constitutes a rollover, contributions withdrawn by the due date of the tax return (where a tax deduction was not taken for the contributions), or a return of nondeductible contributions. If the IRA(s) from which the distribution(s) was (were) made contained only deductible contributions, the IRA owner has no tax basis in such accounts and therefore the entire amount withdrawn is fully taxable. On the other hand, if the IRA(s) from which the distribution(s) was (were) made included nondeductible contributions, the IRA owner has a tax basis and he or she can receive them free of tax as a return of his or her investment. In this latter case, distributions received will consist partially of nondeductible contributions (tax basis) and partially of deductible contributions, earnings, and gains (if any). Until the entire tax basis is recovered, each distribution is partly nontaxable and partly taxable. The calculation of the portion considered taxable is made on IRS Form 8606 using Worksheet 1-5.

PROHIBITED TRANSACTIONS

Any improper use of a traditional IRA account or annuity by the IRA owner, his or her beneficiary, or any "disqualified person" constitutes a **prohibited transaction**. A disqualified person includes the IRA owner's fiduciary (IRA custodian or trustee) and members of the account owner's family (spouse, ancestor, lineal descendant, and any spouse of a lineal descendant). A fiduciary, for these purposes, is anyone who exercises any discretionary authority or discretionary control in managing the IRA or exercises any authority or control in managing or disposing of its assets, provides investment advice to the IRA for a fee or has any authority or responsibility to do so, or has any discretionary authority or discretionary responsibility in administering the IRA. Prohibited transactions with a traditional IRA include:

1. the sale, exchange, or lease of any property between an IRA and a disqualified person;
2. the lending of money or other extension of credit between an IRA and a disqualified person;
3. the furnishing of goods, services, or facilities between an IRA and a disqualified person;
4. the transfer to, or use by or for the benefit of, a disqualified person of the income or assets of an IRA;
5. an act by a disqualified person who is a fiduciary whereby he or she deals with the income or assets of an IRA in his or her own interest or his or her own account; and
6. the receipt of any consideration for his or her own personal account by a disqualified person who is a fiduciary from any party dealing with the IRA in connection with a transaction involving the income or assets of the plan.

The Code exempts certain transactions that might otherwise be prohibited under the above rules but none of these exemptions apply to transactions in which an IRA directly or indirectly lends any part of the corpus or income to, pays any compensation for personal services rendered to the plan to, or acquires for the plan any property from, or sells any property to, the owner or beneficiary of an IRA.

Engaging in a prohibited transaction has very severe consequences. If any of the above-described persons (including the owner or his or her beneficiary) engages in such a transaction at any time during the year, the account stops being an IRA as of the first day of that year. The result is that the assets in the account are treated as being distributed to the owner at their fair market values on the first day of the year. If the total of these values exceeds the owner's basis, the excess will constitute a taxable gain.

If someone other than the owner or beneficiary of a traditional IRA engages in a prohibited transaction, that person may be liable for certain taxes, including a 15 percent tax on the amount of the prohibited transaction and a 100 percent additional tax if the transaction is not corrected. If the owner or beneficiary engages in a prohibited transaction, they are not liable for these excise taxes but they may be subject to both income tax and the 10 percent early distribution penalty.

Other Transactions Treated as Distributions

Certain other transactions are not considered disqualifying transactions but treated as distributions to the owner. These transactions include:

- Pledging any portion of an individual retirement account as security for a loan
- Borrowing money against an individual retirement annuity either from the issuing insurance company or from third parties using the contract as security

- Investing in collectibles (e.g., art works, rugs, antiques, metals, gems, stamps, coins, alcoholic beverages, and certain other tangible personal property specified by the U.S. Treasury Department) by an individual retirement account. Certain types of U.S.-minted (not foreign-minted) gold, silver, and platinum coins, coins issued under the laws of any state, and any gold, silver, platinum, or palladium bullion meeting certain quality requirements are excepted.

Early Distributions

Distributions from a traditional IRA account or annuity are those distributed *before* the IRA owner is age 59 1/2. Such distributions are subject to a 10 percent tax which is in addition to the regular income tax payable on such distributions. The 10 percent tax is applicable to the portion of the distribution that must be included in gross income.

There are several exceptions to the age 59 1/2 rule as follows:

- The owner has unreimbursed medical expenses that are more than 7.5 percent of his or her adjusted gross income (AGI).

- The distributions are not more than the cost of the owner's medical insurance. The owner must have lost his or her job; he or she must have collected unemployment compensation for 12 consecutive weeks because of losing his or her job; he or she must also have received the distributions during either the year the unemployment compensation was received or the following year; and the distributions must have been received no later than 60 days after the owner becomes reemployed.

- The owner is disabled, meaning that the owner furnishes proof that he or she cannot do any substantial gainful activity because of a physical or mental condition. A physician must determine that the owner's condition may be expected to result in death or to be of long, continued, and indefinite duration.

- The recipient of the distribution is the beneficiary of a deceased IRA owner.

- The owner is receiving distributions in the form of an annuity which are part of a series of substantially equal payments over the owner's life (or life expectancy) or over the lives (or the joint life expectancies) of the owner and his or her beneficiary (commonly known as "72(t) payments" after the Internal Revenue Code Section of the same number).

- The distributions are not more than the qualified higher education expenses of the owner, the owner's spouse, or the children or grandchildren of the owner or of his or her spouse. Not included in such expenses are those paid with tax-free distributions from a Coverdell education savings account, the tax-free portion of scholarships and fellowships, Pell grants, employer-provided educational assistance, veterans' educational assistance, or any other tax-free payment (other than a gift or inheritance) received as educational assistance.

- The owner uses the distributions to buy, build, or rebuild a first home, if the qualified acquisition costs were paid within 120 days of receiving the distributions, they do not exceed $10,000, and they were paid for the main home of a first-time homebuyer (including the owner, the owner's spouse, the owner's or spouse's child, grandchild, parent, or other ancestor). A first-time homebuyer is someone who did not own a main home during the 2-year period ending on the date of acquisition of the home for which the distribution is being used to buy, build, or rebuild. The date of acquisition is either the date that the owner entered into a binding contract to buy the main home or the building or rebuilding of the main home begins

- The distribution is due to an IRS assessment imposed on the qualified plan.

EXCESS CONTRIBUTIONS

An excess contribution is the amount contributed (whether deductible or nondeductible) to a traditional IRA for the year that is *more than* the amount allowable for that year (usually the smaller of $4,000 [for 2005] [or $4,500 if 50 or older] or the owner's taxable compensation for the year. As discussed previously in this chapter, if a taxpayer makes contributions to his or her IRA for a particular year that were less than the limits, he or she cannot make additional contributions after the due date of the tax return for that same tax year. Likewise, if a taxpayer contributes more than the allowable limit for a particular tax year, the excess contributions may be applied to a later tax year if the contributions for that later year are less than the maximum allowed for that year. However, a penalty or additional tax may be applicable.

Generally, excess contributions not withdrawn by the due date are subject to a 6 percent penalty tax. If such excess contributions remain in an owner's traditional IRA at the end of the owner's tax year, the owner must continue to pay the 6 percent tax for each year the excess contributions remain there. The tax is limited to 6 percent of the year-end value of the IRA. The tax is calculated and reported on IRS Form 5329.

If the owner withdraws an excess contribution made during a tax year, including any interest or other income earned on the excess contribution, by the due date (including extensions) of the tax return for that year, the 6 percent tax does not have to be paid. This assumes that no deduction was allowed for the excess contribution and that the interest or other income earned on the excess contribution was also withdrawn. The interest or other income that was earned on the excess contribution must be included in the owner's gross income for the year in which the excess contribution was made. The withdrawal of interest or other income earned may be subject to the additional 10 percent tax on early distributions.

If the owner withdraws excess contributions *after* the due date of his or her tax return for the year in which the excess contributions were made, they need not be included in the owner's gross income if:

- Total contributions (other than rollover contributions) for 2005 to the owner's IRA were not more than $4,000 ($4,500 if 50 or older) and
- The owner did not take a deduction for the excess contributions being withdrawn

INHERITED AND SPOUSAL IRAS

When a traditional IRA owner dies and his or her IRA is acquired by an individual who is not the decedent's surviving spouse, the IRA is referred to as an "inherited IRA" and the person acquiring it is called a "beneficiary." As a beneficiary, he or she must include in his or her gross income any taxable distributions received from the inherited IRA. In fact, the assets of an inherited IRA will not be taxed until they are distributed. If the IRA owner dies before minimum distributions are required to begin, the beneficiary may receive the interest of the deceased owner under one of two methods: (1) the so-called five-year rule, under which the deceased owner's interest in the IRA must be distributed within five years of the owner's death; or (2) the life expectancy rule, under which the deceased owner's interest is distributed, beginning within one year of the owner's death, over the life of the beneficiary or over a period not extending beyond the beneficiary's life expectancy. Clearly, in most cases, it will be advantageous to the beneficiary to opt for the life expectancy rule to extend the payout period and resulting tax on inherited amounts.

While an inherited IRA may be treated like any other traditional IRA for some purposes, under IRC Section 219(d)(4) no deduction may be taken for contributions to an inherited IRA. Likewise, under IRC Section 408(d)(3)(C), no rollover may be made to or from an inherited IRA.

If the individual inherits the traditional IRA from anyone other than his or her deceased spouse, the inherited IRA may not be treated as his or her own (discussed later). Accordingly, as mentioned previously, this individual cannot make any contributions to the IRA nor roll over any amounts into or out of the inherited IRA. However, a trustee-to-trustee transfer is permissible as long as the IRA into which amounts are moved is established and maintained in the name of the deceased IRA owner for the benefit of the beneficiary.

The tax basis of an inherited traditional IRA carries over to the beneficiary. Only the surviving spouse of a deceased IRA owner who elects to treat the IRA acquired from his or her deceased spouse as his or her own (discussed later) may combine the carried over tax basis with any basis he or she has in his or her own traditional IRA(s).

> **Example: Inherited IRA**-if Fred is 70 years old and his son, Jake, is 49 years old and Fred dies before minimum distributions from Fred's IRA are required to begin, Jake may receive Fred's interest in the IRA under one of two methods: (1) the so-called five-year rule, under which Fred's interest in the IRA must be distributed within five years of Fred's death; or (2) the life expectancy rule, under which Fred's interest is distributed, beginning within one year of the employee's death, over the life of the beneficiary (Jake) or over a period not extending beyond Jake's life expectancy. Most likely, Jake will opt for the life expectancy rule to extend the payouts over a longer period and minimize income tax in the long run.

On the other hand, if the individual who acquires an IRA from a decedent is the decedent's surviving spouse, the IRA is *not* an inherited IRA-it is referred to as a "spousal IRA." A surviving spouse who inherits a traditional IRA from his or her spouse has basically three options available:

- Treat the IRA as his or her own by designating him- or herself as the account owner;

- Treat the IRA as his or her own by rolling it over into his or her traditional IRA, or to the extent it is taxable, into a qualified plan; qualified employee annuity plan (Section 403(a) plan); tax-sheltered annuity plan (Section 403(b) plan); deferred compensation plan of a state or local government (Section 457 plan); or
- Treat him- or herself as the beneficiary rather than treating the IRA as his or her own.

Example: **Spousal IRA**-if Fred is 70 years old and his wife, Alice, is 62 years old and Fred dies, Alice (as the beneficiary) can treat Fred's IRA as her own and take RMDs based on *her* life expectancy. Alice can also roll Fred's IRA into her own traditional IRA, or roll the taxable portion of Fred's IRA into a qualified plan, Section 403(a), Section 403(b), or Section 457 plan. Alice can also treat herself as the *beneficiary* of Fred's IRA (rather than the new owner), in which case she will be required to take the minimum distributions that Fred would have had to take after attaining the age of 70 1/2.

If the surviving spouse makes contributions (including rollover contributions) to the IRA acquired as a result of the death of his or her spouse or fails to take the required minimum distribution for a year as a beneficiary of the IRA, he or she will be considered to have elected to treat the IRA as his or her own.

IMPORTANT CONCEPTS

Individual retirement arrangement	Trustee-to-trustee transfer
Individual retirement account	Rollover
Individual retirement annuity	Transfer incident to divorce
Traditional IRA	Conduit IRA
SEP/IRA	Required minimum distribution
SIMPLE IRA	IRS Tables I, II, and III
Roth IRA	Taxation of traditional IRA distributions
Deemed IRA	Prohibited Transactions
Contribution limits	Other transactions treated as distributions
Deduction limits and phaseout	Early distribution penalty and exceptions thereto
Taxable compensation	Excess contributions
Active participant in an employer-sponsored retirement plan	Inherited IRA

QUESTIONS FOR REVIEW

1. How does an individual retirement account differ from an individual retirement annuity?

2. What are the other types of IRAs besides a traditional IRA?

3. What requirements must be met by the written document creating a traditional individal retirement account?

4. What requirements must be met by an individual retirement annuity?

5. What are the factors that affect the amount that can be contributed annually to a traditional IRA?

6. What is the permissible timing for making an annual contribution to an IRA?

7. How does an IRA owner's or his or her spouse's active participation in an employer-maintained retirement plan affect the ability of the owner to claim an income tax deduction for an annual contribution to a traditional IRA?

8. What constitutes active participation?

9. How does a trustee-to-trustee transfer of IRA funds differ from a rollover?

10. What types of distributions from a traditional IRA are not considered an "eligible rollover distribution?"

11. What is the function of a conduit IRA?

12. How should the three IRS life expectancy or uniform lifetime tables be used to calculate the required minimum distribution for various types of beneficiaries?

13. What is the purpose of IRS Form 8606?

14. What is a "prohibited transaction" and what are some examples of a prohibited transaction?

15. What transactions, other than prohibited transactions, are treated as distributions to the IRA owner?

16. What is meant by an early distribution and what is the effect of taking one?

17. What is meant by an excess contribution and what is the penalty for not withdrawing such contributions by the deadline for doing so?

18. What is meant by an inherited IRA?

SUGGESTIONS FOR ADDITIONAL READING

Tools & Techniques of Employee Benefit and Retirement Planning, 9th edition, Stephan R. Leimberg and John J. McFadden, The National Underwriter Company, 2005.

Internal Revenue Service Publication 590, Individual Retirement Arrangements (IRAs).

Retirement Planning, Carla Gordon, American Institute of Certified Public Accountants, 2002.

Retirement Benefits Tax Guide, Thomas F. Rutherford, CCH Incorporated.

U.S. Master Tax Guide, current edition, CCH Incorporated.

CHAPTER FOUR

Roth IRAs

• • •

In chapter 3, we learned that there may be various restrictions placed on the ability of a traditional IRA owner to claim an income tax deduction for contributions to his or her IRA. Of course, the IRA owner may still be able to make nondeductible contributions to his or her traditional IRA and not be taxed on these nondeductible contributions when they are eventually distributed. However, the earnings on these contributions, while tax-deferred until distributed, are not tax-free at that time. Partially to overcome this latter shortcoming of a traditional IRA and to further encourage individuals to save for their retirement, Congress created the Roth IRA, named after William V. Roth, Jr., Chairman of the Senate Finance Committee at the time of enactment as part of the Taxpayer Relief Act of 1997 (TRA '97). Beginning in 1998, contributions could be made to a Roth IRA within certain statutory limits on a nondeductible basis with 100 percent of withdrawals tax-free if certain requirements are met.

In general, except as will be discussed in this chapter, the tax rules concerning Roth IRAs are the *same* as for traditional IRAs discussed in Chapter 3. In this chapter we will attempt to point out the rules governing Roth IRAs that are different from those concerning traditional IRAs.

Upon completing this chapter, you should be able to:
- Compare the attributes of a Roth IRA to those of a traditional IRA
- Apply the Roth IRA contribution limits to a given client situation
- Describe the procedure for converting a traditional IRA to a Roth IRA
- Identify what is meant by a failed conversion of a traditional IRA to a Roth IRA
- Describe what is meant by a recharacterization of the conversion of a traditional IRA to a Roth IRA
- Describe the rules governing the rollover of Roth IRA funds
- Explain the rules governing the distribution of Roth IRA funds

CREATING A ROTH IRA

Since the creation of the traditional IRA in 1974, the number of two-income couples, high-income individuals, and active participants in employer-sponsored retirement plans has increased. This trend resulted in a reduction in the number of traditional IRAs established because of the inability of such persons to claim a tax deduction for contributions to this type of IRA. To address this problem, Congress created the Roth IRA in 1997 to permit not only nondeductible contributions (as are permissible with a traditional IRA) but also tax-free distributions from such IRAs (if certain requirements are met) and contributions by active participants in employer-sponsored retirement plans. Like traditional IRAs, Roth IRAs are primarily plans of individual savings and an alternative form of tax-favored individual retirement plan.

An individual may establish a Roth IRA by designating it as such at the time and manner prescribed by the IRS. The document creating the Roth IRA must clearly designate the IRA as a Roth IRA, and such designation is irrevocable. Accordingly, a Roth IRA cannot later be treated as a non-Roth IRA. However, the reverse is permissible; that is, a non-Roth IRA may be converted to a Roth IRA (discussed later in this chapter). Moreover, a contribution to a Roth IRA may be recharacterized as a contribution to a non-Roth IRA and vice versa (discussed later in this chapter). A "deemed IRA" (discussed in chapter 3 and later in this chapter) may also be a Roth IRA; however, neither a SIMPLE/IRA nor a SEP/IRA may be designated as a Roth IRA (discussed in chapter 6).

Financial institutions may use any of three model Roth IRA forms (for trusteed accounts, custodial accounts, and annuity contracts) released by the IRS for the purpose of creating a Roth IRA. However, a Roth IRA must be funded using one of these three options.

CONTRIBUTION LIMITS

Except for rollovers (discussed later in this chapter), contributions to a Roth IRA must be in cash and are limited in amount. Generally, an individual may contribute to a Roth IRA if he or she has taxable compensation (as previously defined in chapter 3) and his or her modified AGI (as defined in chapter 3 less conversion income, if applicable, as discussed later in this chapter) is less than (1) $160,000 for a taxpayer who is married filing jointly or a qualifying widow(er); (2) $10,000 for a taxpayer who is married filing separately and lived with his or her spouse at any time during the year; and (3) $110,000 for a single, head of household, or married filing separately taxpayer who did not live with his or her spouse at any time during the year.

For a taxpayer who is married filing jointly or a qualifying widow(er), he or she may contribute up to $4,000 in 2005 ($4,500, if age 50 or older) (see the Supplement to this text for limits for later years), assuming his or her taxable compensation is at least that amount, if his or her modified AGI is less than $150,000. If such a taxpayer's modified AGI is $150,000 to $159,999, his or her contribution is subject to a gradual phaseout.

For a taxpayer who is married filing separately and lived with his or her spouse at any time during the year, he or she may contribute up to $4,000 in 2005 ($4,500, if age 50 or older) (see the Supplement to this text for limits for later years), assuming his or her taxable compensation is at least that amount, if his or her AGI is zero. If such a taxpayer's modified AGI is greater than zero but less than $10,000, his or her contribution is subject to a gradual phaseout.

For a taxpayer who is single, head of household, or married filing separately who did not live with his or her spouse at any time during the year, he or she may contribute up to $4,000 in 2005 ($4,500, if age 50 or older) (see the Supplement to this text for limits for later years), assuming his or her taxable compensation is at least that amount, if his or her modified AGI is less than $95,000. If such a taxpayer's modified AGI is $95,000 to $109,999, his or her contribution is subject to a gradual phaseout.

To determine whether or not an individual's Roth IRA contribution limit is reduced, he or she must first determine his or her modified AGI. If the contribution limit is reduced based on the individual's modified AGI, use IRS Worksheet 2.2 on this page to determine by how much it is reduced.

Contributions are limited to $4,000 per year (in 2005) ($4,500 if 50 or over) (see the Supplement to this text for later years) or 100 percent of

IRS Worksheet 2.2. Determining Your Reduced Roth IRA Contribution Limit

1. Enter your modified AGI for Roth IRA purposes . . . . 1. _____
2. Enter
   - $150,000 if filing a joint return or qualifying widow(er)
   - $0 if married filing a separate return and you lived with your spouse at any time in 2004
   - $95,000 for all others . . . . 2. _____
3. Subtract line 2 from line 1 . . . . 3. _____
4. Enter
   - $10,000 if filing a joint return or qualifying widow(er) or married filing a separate return and you lived with your spouse at any time during the year
   - $15,000 for all others . . . . 4. _____
5. Divide line 3 by line 4 and enter the result as a decimal (rounded to at least three places). If the result is 1.000 or more, enter 1.000 . . . . . . 5. _____
6. Enter the lesser of:
   - $3,000 ($3,500 if 50 or older; for 2005, $4,000 or $4,500, if 50 or older), or
   - Your taxable compensation . . . 6. _____
7. Multiply line 5 by line 6 . . . . 7. _____
8. Subtract line 7 from line 6. Round the result up to the nearest $10. If the result is less than $200, enter $200 . . . . 8. _____
9. Enter contributions for the year to other IRAs . . . . 9. _____
10. Subtract line 9 from line 6 . . . . 10. _____
11. Enter the lesser of line 8 or line 10. This is your **reduced Roth IRA contribution limit** . . . . 11. _____

taxable compensation, whichever is *less*. This limit includes contributions made to both traditional IRAs and Roth IRAs. If contributions are made only to Roth IRAs, the contribution limit is generally the lesser of $4,000 (in 2005) ($4,500 if 50 or older) or the Roth IRA owner's taxable compensation subject, of course, to the modified AGI phaseout ranges. However, if an individual makes contributions to both Roth IRAs and traditional IRAs, the contribution limit for Roth IRAs is generally the same as the limit would be if contributions were made only to Roth IRAs, but this limit is then reduced by all contributions (other than employer contributions under a SEP or SIMPLE IRA plan) for the year to all IRAs other than Roth IRAs. And, of course, the modified AGI phaseout ranges may still apply.

Here is an example of how the limitations described in the previous paragraph work in actual practice.

Example: Doug Smith, age 42, is married and files a joint return with his wife. He is an active participant in an employer-sponsored retirement plan. For the tax year 2005, he maintains both a traditional IRA and a Roth IRA. For that year, he has modified AGI of $158,000 and compensation that exceeds $4,000. The limit on the amount that Doug may contribute to his Roth IRA for the year is $800 ($4,000 less ($8,000/$10,000 x $4,000)). If he contributes that amount, he may also contribute $3,200 to his traditional nondeductible IRA. If he contributes $400 to his Roth IRA, he may contribute $3,600 to his traditional nondeductible IRA in 2005, because his deduction limit is zero. That is, the $4,000 deduction limitation has been completely phased out. If the calculation of the reduction produces a contribution limit that is not a multiple of $10, it is rounded to the next lowest multiple of $10. However, if the calculation produces a reduced limit that is less than $200 but more than zero, the limit is a flat $200.

Unlike traditional IRAs, contributions to Roth IRAs may be made *regardless of age* and therefore can be made *after* reaching age 70 1/2. Furthermore, eligibility is *not* affected by the individual's (or his or her spouse's) active participation in an employer-sponsored retirement plan. Moreover, as is the case with a traditional IRA, a non-working spouse may also contribute to a Roth IRA provided the contributions satisfy the spousal IRA limit, the married couple files jointly, and their modified AGI is less than $160,000.

Modified AGI is as defined in chapter 3 except for one additional item that must be subtracted. This item is any conversion income resulting from the conversion of a non-Roth IRA to a Roth IRA, discussed later in this chapter.

Contributions to a Roth IRA for a specific year may be made anytime during that year or by the due date of the tax return for that year (not including extensions of time to file).

As with traditional IRAs, "excess contributions" (amounts contributed for the tax year to a Roth IRA that are more than the contribution limit for the year plus any excess contributions for the preceding year, reduced by the total of any distributions out of the Roth IRA for the year, plus the contribution limit for the year minus contributions made to all IRAs for the year) are subject to a 6 percent excise tax. Excess contributions withdrawn on or before the due date (including extensions) for filing the owner's tax return for the year are treated as an amount not contributed, provided any earnings on the contributions are also withdrawn. If contributions to a Roth IRA for a year are more than the applicable limit, the owner may apply the excess contribution in one year to a later year *if* the contributions for that later year are less than the maximum allowed for that year.

CONVERSION OF A NON-ROTH IRA TO A ROTH IRA

Under certain conditions, an IRA owner may be able to convert amounts from either a traditional, SEP, or SIMPLE IRA into a Roth IRA. In addition, contributions made to a particular type of IRA may be recharacterized as having been made directly to a different IRA.

Probably the most common type of conversion is from a traditional IRA to a Roth IRA. Such a conversion may be accomplished in any of the following three ways:

- Rollover—a distribution from a traditional IRA is rolled over (contributed to) a Roth IRA within 60 days of the distribution.
- Trustee-to-trustee transfer—transfer of an amount from the trustee of a traditional IRA to the trustee of a Roth IRA.
- Same trustee transfer—transfer of an amount from a traditional IRA to a Roth IRA when both IRAs are maintained by the same trustee. The trustee may be directed by the IRA owner to redesignate the traditional IRA as a Roth IRA, thus avoiding creation of a new account and the issuance of a new contract.

In order to convert amounts from a traditional IRA into a Roth IRA in the year the owner withdraws the funds from the traditional IRA, the owner's modified AGI for Roth IRA purposes must *not* be more than $100,000 and the owner must *not* be a married individual filing a separate return. If the owner did not live with his or her spouse at any time during the year and he or she files a separate return, his or her filing status, for this purpose, is single. If the same property that is withdrawn from the traditional IRA is contributed (converted) to the Roth IRA within the permissible 60-day rollover period, the 10 percent additional tax on early distributions (discussed in chapter 3) is not applicable.

Required minimum distributions from a traditional IRA for a particular year may not be converted to a Roth IRA. Likewise, a traditional IRA inherited from someone other than one's spouse may not be converted to a Roth IRA.

Failed Conversions

If the account owner who converted a traditional or SIMPLE IRA into a Roth IRA anticipated, prior to the conversion, that his or her modified AGI would be less than $100,000 and that his or her filing status would be other than married filing separately, and one or both assumptions did not in fact occur, the conversion is considered a "failed conversion."

Accordingly, if the converted amount is not recharacterized (discussed in the next section), the contribution will be treated as a regular contribution to the Roth IRA and subject to: (1) the 6 percent excise tax per year for any excess contribution not withdrawn from the Roth IRA; (2) taxation of the taxable portion of the distribution from the traditional IRA; and (3) imposition of the 10 percent additional tax on early distributions, if applicable.

Recharacterization of IRA Contributions

Sometimes an individual may make a contribution to one type of IRA and then decide later that he or she should have made the contribution to another type of IRA. Changing the IRA to which a contribution is being made is known as "recharacterizing the contribution." In order to accomplish a recharacterization, the funds deposited in the first IRA must be transferred to the second IRA through the use of a trustee-to-trustee transfer by the due date (including extensions) of the tax return for the year during which the contribution was made. The effect of recharacterizing a contribution is, therefore, to treat the contribution as if it had been made originally to the second IRA instead of to the first IRA. In addition, after the transfer has taken place, the election to recharacterize is irrevocable. A recharacterization is reported on IRS Form 8606 attached to the IRA owner's tax return.

Before a recharacterization may be considered effective, the IRA owner must do all of the following:

- Include in the transfer any net income allocable to the contribution. Accordingly, if there was a loss, the net income that must be transferred may be a negative amount.
- Report the recharacterization on his or her tax return for the year during which the contribution was made.
- Treat the contribution as having been made to the second IRA on the date that it was actually made to the first IRA.

The IRA owner is required to notify both the trustee of the first IRA (the one to which the contribution was actually made) and the trustee of the second IRA (the one to which the contribution is being moved) that the owner has elected to treat the contribution as having been made to the second IRA rather than the first. The required notifications must be made by the date of the transfer and must include: (1) the type and amount of the contribution to the first IRA that is to be recharacterized; (2) the date on which the contribution was made to the first IRA and the year for which it was made; (3) an instruction to the trustee of the first IRA as to how to make a trustee-to-trustee transfer of the amount of the contribution and any net income (or loss) allocable to the contribution to the trustee of the second IRA; (4) the names of both trustees; and (5) any additional information necessary to make the transfer.

In addition, a recharacterized contribution will *not* be treated as having been made to the second IRA to the extent an IRA owner has taken an income tax deduction for the contribution to the first IRA. If an IRA owner receives a distribution from a traditional IRA in one tax year and rolls it over into a Roth IRA in the next tax year, but is still within the 60-day rollover period, it is treated as a contribution to the Roth IRA in the year he or she received the distribution from the traditional IRA. Finally, the recharacterization of a contribution is *not* treated as a rollover for purposes of the 1-year waiting period.

Reconversions

It is not permissible to convert one type of IRA to a different type of IRA and then reconvert back to the first type of IRA during the same tax year. However, even if a reconversion takes place in a year subsequent to the original conversion, the reconversion cannot take place during the 30-day period following a recharacterization. If a reconversion takes place during either of these periods of time, it is treated as a failed conversion. For example, if an IRA owner converted an amount from a traditional IRA to a Roth IRA and then transferred that amount back to a traditional IRA in a recharacterization in the same year, the IRA owner could not reconvert that amount from the traditional IRA to a Roth

IRA until the tax year *after* the year in which the original conversion took place or, if later, not until waiting at least 30 days after the amount was recharacterized back to a traditional IRA.

ROLLOVERS

The owner of a Roth IRA may withdraw, tax free, all or part of the assets from his or her Roth IRA if they are contributed within 60 days to another Roth IRA. Most of the rollover rules for traditional IRAs are applicable to Roth rollovers. If the owner receives a rollover from a retirement plan other than a Roth IRA, it is disregarded for purposes of the 1-year waiting period between rollovers. Moreover, a rollover from a Roth IRA to an employer retirement plan is *not* permitted.

DISTRIBUTIONS

While it is intuitive to think that all distributions from a Roth IRA are nontaxable, it is only "qualified distributions" that enjoy this tax treatment. Other nonqualified distributions are treated as a nontaxable return of the owner's contributions to the Roth IRA until those contributions are exhausted, as discussed below.

Qualified (Nontaxable) Distributions

Only a distribution that meets *both* of the following requirements is considered a qualified distribution and is therefore nontaxable:

1. It must be made after the five consecutive tax years beginning with the tax year for which a contribution was first made to any Roth IRA owned by the IRA owner. Such an initial contribution may include an ordinary cash contribution, a rollover contribution from a non-Roth IRA or, after 2005, a rollover contribution from a designated Roth account.

2. It is made (a) on or after the date when the owner reaches age 59 1/2; (b) because the owner is disabled; (c) because the owner has died and the distribution is then made to either a beneficiary or to the deceased's estate; or (d) because it meets the requirements of a first-time home buyer distribution ($10,000 lifetime limit), discussed in chapter 3.

Because of the five-year requirement, no qualified distribution could have been made by any Roth IRA before a taxable year beginning in 2003 (inasmuch as 1998 was the first year that a Roth IRA could have been created). In addition, the five-year period does not start over when the owner of a Roth IRA dies. The period during which the Roth IRA is held in the name of a beneficiary or in the name of a surviving spouse who treats the decedent's Roth IRA as his or her own, includes the period during which it was held by the decedent.

The five-year period for a Roth IRA held by an individual who is a beneficiary of a deceased Roth IRA owner is determined independently of the five-year period for the beneficiary's own Roth IRA. If a surviving spouse treats her deceased spouse's Roth IRA as his or her own, the five-year period with respect to any of the surviving spouse's Roth IRAs (including the one that the surviving spouse treats as his or her own) ends with the termination of the five-year period for the decedent or the termination of the five-year period applicable to the spouse's own Roth IRAs, whichever is earlier.

Nonqualified (Taxable) Distributions

Distributions that do not meet the foregoing requirements as qualified distributions, unless rolled over or constituting a corrective distribution, are first considered to be a nontaxable return of the owner's contributions to the Roth IRA. After the owner's contributions in all of his or her Roth IRAs have then been recovered, any additional amounts distributed to the owner are taxable to him or her. Such nonqualified distributions may also be subject to the 10 percent additional tax on early distributions. For example, if an IRA owner converts an amount from a traditional IRA to a Roth IRA and then takes a distribution from the Roth IRA within the 5-year period starting with the first day of the tax year in which the conversion took place, he or she may have to pay the 10 percent additional tax on early distributions. This 10 percent early distribution penalty is payable, however, only on the portion of the amount converted that the owner had to include in income.

One significant difference between distributions from traditional IRAs and Roth IRAs is that the mandatory minimum distribution rules that apply to IRA owners who are at least age 70 1/2 do *not* apply to Roth IRAs. Moreover, in determining the tax consequences of distributions from Roth IRAs, *all* Roth IRAs are to be treated as one contract, *all* distributions from Roth IRAs are to be treated as one distribution, and the value of the contract, income on the contract, and investment in the contract are to be computed as of the close of the tax year.

Ordering Rules for Nonqualified Roth IRA Distributions

As explained earlier, a Roth IRA owner who receives a distribution from his or her Roth IRA that is not a qualified distribution, will be taxed on a portion of the distribution. Such distributions are treated as made in the following order (determined as of the end of the taxable year and exhausting each category before moving to the following category):

- Regular contributions.
- Conversion contributions, on a first-in-first-out basis (generally, total conversions from the earliest year first). The taxable portion of any conversion contributions are taken into account before any nontaxable portion.
- Earnings on the Roth IRA contributions.

Rollover contributions from other Roth IRAs are disregarded for this purpose.

A second set of ordering rules (known as the aggregation, or grouping and adding, rules) are then applied to determine the taxable amounts withdrawn (distributed) as follows:

- Add together all distributions from all the owner's Roth IRAs during the year.

- Add together all regular contributions made for the year (including those made after the close of the year, but before the due date of the tax return). This total is then added to the total undistributed regular contributions made in prior years.

- Add together all conversion contributions made during the year.

For the purpose of these ordering rules, in the case of any conversion in which the conversion distribution is made in 2005 and the conversion contribution is made in 2006, treat the conversion contribution as contributed before any other conversion contributions made in 2006.

Finally, in applying these aggregation rules, add any recharacterized contributions that end up in a Roth IRA to the appropriate contribution group for the year that the original contribution would have been taken into account if it had been made directly to the Roth IRA. In this respect, also disregard any recharacterized contribution that ends up in an IRA other than a Roth IRA. Any amount withdrawn to correct an excess contribution (including the earnings withdrawn) is also disregarded for this purpose.

See IRS Worksheet 2-3 to calculate the taxable part of a distribution that is *not* a qualified distribution.

IRS Worksheet 2.3. Figuring the Taxable Part of a Distribution(Other Than a Qualified Distribution) From a Roth IRA

1. Enter the total of all distributions made from your Roth IRA(s) during the year . . . . 1. _____

2. Enter the amount of qualified distributions made during the year 2. _____

3. Subtract line 2 from line 1 . . . . . . 3. _____

4. Enter the amount of distributions made during the year to correct excess contributions made during the year. (Do not include earnings.) . . . . 4. _____

5. Subtract line 4 from line 3 . . . . . . 5. _____

6. Enter the amount of distributions made during the year that were contributed to another Roth IRA in a qualified rollover contribution . . 6. _____

7. Subtract line 6 from line 5 . . . . . . 7. _____

8. Enter the amount of *all* prior distributions from your Roth IRA(s) (whether or not they were qualified distributions) . . . . 8. _____

9. Add lines 1 and 8 . . . . 9. _____

10. Enter the amount of the distributions included on line 8 that were previously includible in your income . . . . 10. _____

11. Subtract line 10 from line 9 . . . . . 11. _____

12. Enter the total of all your contributions to all of your Roth IRAs . . . . 12. _____

13. Enter the total of all distributions made (this year and in prior years) to correct excess contributions. (Include earnings.) . . . . 13. _____

14. Subtract line 13 from line 12. (If the result is less than 0, enter 0.) 14. _____

15. Subtract line 14 from line 11. (If the result is less than 0, enter 0.) 15. _____

16. Enter the smaller of the amount on line 7 or the amount on line 15. This is the taxable part of your distribution . . . . 16. _____

Minimum Distribution Rules After the Death of the Roth IRA Owner

As discussed previously, the minimum distribution rules do not apply during the lifetime of an owner of a Roth IRA who reaches age 70 1/2. This means that a Roth IRA owner is not required to take distributions from his or her Roth IRA at any age. However, when a Roth IRA owner dies, the minimum distribution rules that apply to traditional IRAs (discussed in chapter 3) apply to Roth IRAs as though the Roth IRA owner died *before* his or her required beginning date (RBD).

Ordinarily, the entire interest in the Roth IRA of a deceased Roth IRA owner must be distributed by the end of the fifth calendar year after the year in which the owner died, unless the interest is payable to a designated beneficiary over the life or life expectancy of the designated beneficiary (as an annuity). Where the interest is distributed as an annuity, the entire interest must then be payable over a period not greater than the designated beneficiary's life expectancy and distributions must begin before the end of the calendar year following the year of death. If the sole beneficiary of the Roth IRA is the decedent's spouse, he or she may delay distributions until the decedent would have attained age 70 1/2 or he or she may treat the Roth IRA as his or her own. If the beneficiary/surviving spouse elects to treat the Roth IRA as his or her own, that individual's five-year holding period is then used to determine whether a distribution is qualified with no minimum lifetime distributions required to be taken.

If a distribution to a beneficiary is not a qualified distribution, it is generally taxable to the beneficiary in the same manner as it would have been taxable to the owner had it been distributed to the IRA owner when he or she was alive.

Treatment of Losses on Roth IRA Investments

When all of the amounts in all of an individual's Roth IRAs have been distributed to the owner and the total of such distributions is less than the owner's unrecovered basis (total cumulative contributions), the owner may claim the loss as a miscellaneous itemized deduction, subject to the 2 percent-of-AGI limitation.

COMPARISON OF TRADITIONAL AND ROTH IRAS

Whether a traditional or Roth IRA is more beneficial for a particular individual is highly subjective and depends on the person's individual goals, needs, and objectives. By using the attached Figure 4.1, the reader may make a side-by-side comparison of the two types of IRAs.

Figure 4.1*

COMPARISON OF TRADITIONAL AND ROTH IRA		
	TRADITIONAL IRA	**ROTH IRA**
Contributions must be made out of earned income, not investment income	Yes	Yes
Annual dollar limit	Yes (before-tax) [total for sum of Roth and traditional IRA contributions]	Yes (after-tax) [total for sum of Roth and traditional IRA contributions}
Restrictions based on AGI	No, unless active participant in tax-favored employer plan	Yes, contribution limit phased out between $95,000 and $110,000 (single); $150,000 and $160,000 (joint)
Restrictions on deduction or contribution if active participant in tax-favored employer plan	Yes, deduction limited based on AGI	No
Tax-free buildup during accumulation period	Yes	Yes
Withdrawals tax-free	No	Yes, after waiting period
10% penalty on early withdrawals	Yes	Yes
Required minimum distributions	Yes, begining at earlier of age 70 1/2 or death	Yes, begining at death
Can rollover to (another) regular IRA	Yes (once annually)	No
Can rollover to (another) Roth IRA	Yes, if joint AGI $100,000 or less; must pay tax	Yes
Can rollover to qualified plan, TDA or Section 457 governmental plan	Yes	No

**Tools & Techniques of Employee Benefit and Retirement Planning*, 9th ed., Stephan R. Leimberg and John J. McFadden, The National Underwriter Company, 2005. Used with permission.

IMPORTANT CONCEPTS

Roth contribution limits

Modified AGI

Excise tax on excess contributions

Conversion to a Roth IRA

Rollover

Trustee-to-trustee transfer

Failed conversion

Recharacterization

Reconversion

Qualified distribution from a Roth IRA

Five-year requirement

Nonqualified distribution

Ordering rules for nonqualified distributions

Minimum distribution rules after the death of the Roth IRA owner

Traditional IRAs versus Roth IRAs

QUESTIONS FOR REVIEW

1. What are some of the reasons why Congress considered it necessary to create the Roth IRA in 1997?

2. What are the requirements for making a contribution to a Roth IRA?

3. How does the definition of modified adjusted gross income (MAGI) for purposes of making a contribution to a traditional IRA differ from the definition used for purposes of making a contribution to a Roth IRA?

4. How, if at all, are the contribution limits integrated where an IRA owner makes contributions to both Roth and non-Roth IRAs?

5. What is the age limit for making contributions to a traditional IRA versus making contributions to a Roth IRA?

6. In what way does being an active participant in an employer-sponsored retirement plan affect one's ability to contribute to a traditional IRA versus a Roth IRA?

7. In what three ways can a conversion of a non-Roth IRA into a Roth IRA be accomplished?

8. What requirements must be met by a non-Roth IRA owner to convert an amount in his or her IRA to a Roth IRA?

9. What is meant by a failed conversion?

10. What does it mean to recharacterize an IRA contribution?

11. What actions must be taken by an IRA owner before a recharacterization can be considered effective?

12. How does a reconversion of a Roth IRA differ from a recharacterization?

13. What types of rollovers involving Roth IRAs are permissible?

14. What constitutes a qualified distribution from a Roth IRA?

15. What is the income tax treatment of nonqualified distributions from a Roth IRA?

16. How, if at all, are traditional IRAs and Roth IRAs affected by the required minimum distribution rules?

17. To what extent, if any, do the required minimum distribution rules apply to the beneficiary of a Roth IRA after the death of the Roth IRA owner?

18. How are losses on Roth IRA investments treated for income tax purposes?

19. In what ways do traditional IRAs differ from Roth IRAs?

SUGGESTIONS FOR ADDITIONAL READING

Tools & Techniques of Employee Benefit and Retirement Planning, 9th edition, Stephan R. Leimberg and John J. McFadden, The National Underwriter Company, 2005.

Internal Revenue Service Publication 590, *Individual Retirement Arrangements (IRAs).*

Retirement Planning, Carla Gordon, American Institute of Certified Public Accountants, 2002.

Retirement Benefits Tax Guide, current edition, Thomas F. Rutherford, CCH Incorporated.

U.S. Master Tax Guide, current edition, CCH Incorporated.

CHAPTER FIVE

The Use of Annuities in Retirement Planning

• • •

Created and marketed by life insurance companies, annuities are another common component of retirement planning. While considered by many only as investments, annuities are primarily designed for the management of risk. These contracts, while providing for the systematic liquidation of principal and interest through the use of a series of payments over time, provide protection against interest rate risk, reinvestment risk, superannuation (outliving one's assets), and certain market volatility risks. An annuity's many benefits include tax-deferral, monthly income for the life of the annuitant, avoidance of probate, possible freedom of responsibility for investment decisions, retirement income to supplement that from IRAs and other sources, guaranteed death benefits, and guaranteed living benefits.

Annuities can be thought of as the *reverse* of life insurance. Life insurance is primarily designed to systematically accumulate an estate that can be used to protect against financial losses resulting from premature death. An annuity, on the other hand, employs the systematic liquidation of an estate to protect against the risk of outliving one's assets. Annuities come in several flavors and varieties designed for different purposes. In this chapter we will discuss the many ways in which annuities are categorized and how annuities are used in planning for an individual's retirement.

Upon completing this chapter, you should be able to:

- Define what is meant by an annuity
- Describe the many ways in which annuities are categorized
- Compare how an annuity differs from life insurance
- Discuss the accumulation phase of an annuity
- Discuss the distribution or annuitization phase of an annuity
- Describe the income taxation of annuities

DEFINITION AND CHARACTERISTICS OF AN ANNUITY

An annuity is an insurance contract under which a regular series of payments (referred to as "distributions") is made over a specific period of time in return for a set purchase price or premium. If the distributions constitute a "life annuity," the life insurance company promises that payouts will continue for as long as the annuitant (or annuitants) live. If the payouts are to continue for a fixed or guaranteed period of time, regardless of the annuitant's survival, the annuity is known as a "fixed period annuity" (or "term-certain annuity"). It is even possible to purchase an annuity under which the payouts utilize a combination of the life and fixed period options (e.g., for the greater of 15 years or the life of the annuitant(s)). Modern individual annuity contracts permit the payout of accumulated funds in a variety of ways. Relatively few individual annuities today are taken as a life income (annuitized).

The parties to an annuity contract are the **annuity owner**, the **annuitant**, the **beneficiary**, and the **issuing life insurance company**. In the majority of cases, the annuity owner and the annuitant are the same person. The annuity owner is the person or entity who owns the rights under an annuity contract. The annuitant is the person whose life generally determines the timing and amount of any payout affected by life expectancy. On the other hand, the beneficiary is the person or entity named in the contract to receive the death benefit under the annuity in the event that the owner dies before the benefits are paid from the annuity. In the event that the beneficiary is the deceased owner's surviving spouse, he or she is allowed by the tax law to treat the annuity as his or her own and to continue it as the new owner. The issuing life insurance company is the life insurance company issuing the contract.

The monthly payments received from an annuity are made up of three parts: principal, interest, and survivorship benefits. The principal is the premium amounts paid in by the annuitant before the distributions begin. The interest is the amount earned on the principal between the time the premiums are paid and the time when the benefits begin. Any amount of principal and interest not returned to the annuitant prior to his or her death is known as the "survivorship benefit."

Accumulation Phase

An investor purchases an annuity by making a cash payment or a series of periodic payments (premiums) over time to a life insurance company. The insurance company invests the premiums and the cumulative amount deposited is periodically credited with earnings. There is no legal or tax limit on the amount of annual contributions (or single premiums) that an annuity owner can make. However, contributions are not tax-deductible (that is, they are made with "after-tax dollars.")

Distribution or Annuitization Phase

The distribution phase is the period during which the owner receives benefits or payouts from the annuity. The distributions may be adjusted to suit the needs of the owner, except for certain limiting factors, including surrender charges payable during the early years of the contract and the 10 percent penalty tax on distributions taken before age 59 1/2 (subject to certain exceptions). In addition, annuity contracts usually specify an age by which benefits must commence, but this may be as late as age 85. Fortunately, the tax laws set *no* required beginning date for the most popular type of annuity—the so-called "nonqualified annuity" (discussed in the next section).

ADVANTAGES OF ANNUITIES

The principal advantages of annuities include the following:

1. The opportunity to own a safe investment with a guaranteed lifelong income (if selected) and (in the case of a fixed annuity) guaranteed principal and interest. This makes it ideal for retirees seeking fixed monthly income and lifetime guarantees.

2. The opportunity (through the purchase of a variable annuity) to invest in the securities market while at the same time reducing one's risk (compared to investing directly in the underlying investments) through the availability of guaranteed death proceeds or a specific annuitization amount.

3. The ability to plan the timing of income receipt to take advantage of lower tax bracket years.

4. The ability to achieve a higher effective yield due to an annuity's tax deferral.

5. The ability to reduce one's adjusted gross income (AGI) by choosing not to take withdrawals and as a result of the manner in which annuities are taxed (partial recovery of basis associated with each payment, discussed later in this chapter). Lowering one's AGI may help increase medical and miscellaneous itemized deductions and avoid or minimize the phaseout of exemptions and itemized deductions.

DISADVANTAGES OF ANNUITIES

The principal disadvantages of annuities include the following:

1. The inability of annuitized payments to keep up with inflation.

2. The imposition of the 10 percent penalty tax on the earnings portion of withdrawals taken prior to age 59 1/2 (subject to certain exceptions).

3. The lack of annuity contract treatment for a corporate or other entity owner that is not a natural person, resulting in the taxation of the income of an annuity contract (whether or not distributed to the owner).

4. The inability to receive income averaging treatment on the receipt of a lump sum at retirement or by a beneficiary at the owner's death.

5. The imposition of management fees, sales costs, and possible surrender charges upon liquidation of the annuity in the early years of ownership. These costs may include a one percent or more insurance fee plus annual management fees of perhaps 1 to 2 percent plus a contract charge of perhaps $30 to $60 per year. Back-end surrender fees range from 5 to 10 percent of the account balance in the first year and then taper off to zero over 5 to 7 years.

6. The unavailability of capital gains or dividend taxation treatment of investment earnings included in distributions.

USING ANNUITIES IN RETIREMENT PLANNING

In the retirement planning process, generally an annuity should be considered when the client seeks:

- Tax-deferred growth of invested funds
- Retirement income or an income stream for another person that cannot be outlived and he or she is willing to liquidate capital to do so
- Freedom from investing and managing retirement assets (except in the case of a variable annuity)
- An alternative or supplement to an IRA, permitting unlimited contributions
- To avoid probate and perhaps avoid a will contest
- Safety of principal, minimum interest guarantees, and guaranteed death benefits

If safety of the underlying principal is paramount and /or the retiree is an extremely conservative investor, the *fixed annuity* type of investment should be considered. If the investor wants more control of the investment decisions and is willing to bear greater market risk to purchase the potential of a greater annuity payout, a *variable annuity* is probably appropriate.

CATEGORIZATION OF ANNUITIES

Annuities are categorized in several ways, including the following:

1. By how the premiums are paid
2. By what residual values, if any, remain at the death of the annuitant
3. By the starting date of the distributions
4. By the number of lives covered by the contract
5. By the investment options available to the annuity contract owner
6. By how the benefits are calculated
7. By the reason for which they were purchased

Premium Payment Method

There are basically three options for paying the required premiums under an annuity. An investor who has a large sum of cash may purchase a **single premium annuity** without any continuing premium obligation. For many years, investors without a large cash sum upfront have instead made fixed annual, semiannual, quarterly, or monthly premium payments until the distributions begin. In more recent times, **fixed-premium annuities** have been replaced by **flexible-premium annuities**. Flexible-premium annuities permit the owner to make premium contributions at any time and in any amount he or she wishes. Some insurance companies also impose minimum annual contributions in the early years of such an annuity contract but, generally, there are no restrictions or requirements on the timing or amount of these future contributions.

Disposition of Proceeds at Death of the Annuitant

Under the common **life annuity**, annuity payouts continue as long as the annuitant (or one of the annuitants) survives, without a final payment or refund at the death of the last annuitant. This is true even if the total amount paid out is *less than* the amount invested in the contract. Under the terms of such an annuity, a single annuitant dying soon after purchase of such a contract would forfeit almost the entire amount invested in the contract. As a result, purchasers of life annuities usually select some sort of guarantee so that their beneficiary(ies) will obtain at least the investment in the contract if the purchaser dies soon after its purchase. This guarantee may take one of two forms: (1) a **refund annuity** that promises to pay (either in a lump sum or in installments) the difference between the amount invested in the contract and the annuity payouts actually received before the death of the annuitant; or (2) a **period certain annuity** that promises to make payments for an agreed-upon period of time (e.g., 5, 10, or 20 years), or for the life of the annuitant, whichever is longer. Of course, these guarantees do *not* compensate the annuitant's beneficiary for the time value of money. Indeed, if the investment in the contract had been invested at a reasonable rate of return, it likely would have accumulated to much more than the original investment.

An investor may also purchase a **term-certain annuity** which promises to make payments for a specific period of time, irrespective of how long the annuitant lives. Another variation on this theme is a **temporary annuity** which, instead of making payments for the *longer* of the annuitant's life or a specified period (as does a period-certain annuity), makes payments for the *shorter* of the annuitant's life or the specified period.

Starting Date of the Distributions

Annuities are also categorized by when the distributions begin. If the payments under an annuity start within one year after all of the premiums are paid, it is referred to as an **immediate annuity**. For instance, if someone just received a large lump-sum distribution from a qualified pension or profit-sharing plan, the proceeds of a lawsuit, or already had accumulated a significant amount of cash, and wants to convert it into an immediate income stream, he or she may purchase an immediate annuity. Annuities which do not begin making payouts until a particular period of time after the end of the accumulation phase are known as **deferred annuities**. A person having cash available for investment prior to retirement who wants to postpone the commencement of annuity payouts until he or she retires, would purchase such a contract.

Number of Lives Covered by the Contract

The annuity payout period may depend on one or more lives. If the contract covers only one annuitant and it makes payments until the death of the sole annuitant, it is referred to as a **single life annuity**. Depending on the contract terms, an annuity involving more than one life may provide payments until the death of the last annuitant or only until the first annuitant dies. An annuity that continues until the death of the last annuitant is known as a **joint and last survivor annuity**, or alternatively, a joint and survivor annuity. A less common type is an annuity whose payments stop at the time of the first death, referred to as a **joint life annuity**.

Under a joint and last survivor annuity, the owner selects a survivor benefit ratio which is applied to the survivor's benefit after the death of the first annuitant. Typically, the percentage payable to a survivor may vary from 50 percent to 100 percent. The survivor's benefit may also be affected by which annuitant dies first. Typically, there is a primary annuitant and a secondary annuitant. The survivor benefit ratio applies only to the benefit payable to the surviving secondary annuitant after the principal annuitant's death. If the secondary annuitant dies first, the benefit payments to the primary annuitant are not reduced. A newer form of joint and survivor annuity, known as the **contemporary joint and survivor annuity**, makes reduced payments to the surviving annuitant regardless of which dies first.

Investment Options

There are essentially two types of annuities that offer different investment options. A **fixed rate annuity** credits the annuity value with the insurance company's initial credited interest rate for a specified period of time (anywhere from one month to as long as 10 years). The life insurance company then determines the initial credited interest rate based on the performance of the bonds and mortgages in its general investment portfolio or general account. At the end of the initial credited rate guarantee period, the insurer can revise the rate it will pay in the future (usually subject to a minimum guaranteed interest rate). Therefore, in this instance, the life insurance company, rather than the investor, bears the investment risk.

Variable annuities offer the investor the ability to invest in a wide but limited array of investment options or separate accounts. The cash value of a variable annuity depends on the market value of the underlying investments in the investment options selected by the investor. Because of this method of valuation, a variable annuity owner bears the market risk and normally does *not* receive any minimum interest rate guarantees as is the case with a fixed rate annuity. In fact, not even the principal is guaranteed. A variable annuity owner has the potential to achieve higher returns than those available from a fixed rate annuity and the ability to structure his or her portfolio as he or she sees fit. The amount ultimately paid out to the annuitant varies with the investment results obtained by the insurance company. Accordingly, the annuitant takes a chance that his or her monthly income will be less than anticipated. In fact, during the 2000-02 bear market, variable annuity returns fell well below the returns on corresponding fixed rate annuities. However, a strategy that has worked for many investors is to own a variable annuity during the accumulation stage and then switch to a fixed rate annuity at the beginning of the distribution stage. Variable annuities are securities and may be sold only through a prospectus by registered security representatives who are licensed and authorized to sell this particular product.

In recent years, a new type of annuity called an **equity-index annuity** (EIA) has been developed as a cross between a fixed rate annuity and a variable annuity. The rate of return on an EIA is tied to a particular equity index, such as the S&P 500 index. The EIA shares in a certain percentage (the participation rate) of the change in the reference equity index with the investor guaranteed a minimum amount in the event of a decline in the reference equity index. This design provides the investor with some of the upside potential of a variable annuity and the downside protection of a fixed rate annuity.

Benefit Calculation Method

A fixed benefit annuity guarantees a minimum benefit tied to the amount in the account at the time of annuitization of the annuity. A variable benefit annuity does not provide a guaranteed benefit but instead offers a benefit based on the market value of the investments in the separate accounts at the time distributions begin.

The reader is referred to Figure 5.1 for a diagram of how annuities are classified as discussed in the foregoing sections.

Figure 5.1*

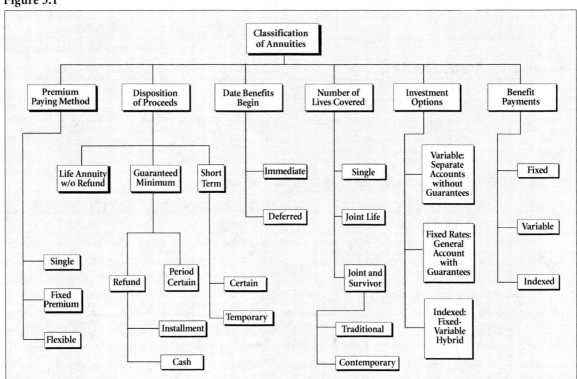

**Tools & Techniques of Life Insurance Planning*, 3rd ed., Stephan R. Leimberg and Robert J. Doyle, Jr., The National Underwriter Company, 2004. Used with permission.

Reason for Which the Annuity Is Purchased

All annuities fall within one of two general categories for tax purposes—they are either qualified or nonqualified. A **qualified annuity** is purchased as a part of, or in conjunction with, an employer-provided qualified retirement plan or within an individual IRA. If certain requirements are met, contributions to qualified annuities are made with *before-tax dollars* and both the investment and earnings on the investment are not taxed until subsequent distribution. However, upon distribution, payments from such an annuity are then fully taxable at ordinary income rates.

In contrast, a **nonqualified annuity**, which includes a commercial annuity, a private annuity, and a charitable gift annuity, is *not* part of an employer-provided retirement plan and is purchased by an individual or other entity. Contributions are made with *after-tax dollars* and do not receive an income tax deduction. Commercial annuities are purchased from a life insurance company for cash with the value determined by standard actuarial tables and the general investment climate. A "private annuity" is an unsecured agreement between two persons for one of them to pay an annuity to the other in return for a consideration, usually a transfer of property. It must be unsecured and the distributions must not be tied to the income generated by the transferred property. In many cases, the property transferor using a private annuity wishes to make a partial gift to the transferee. Accordingly, it tends to occur most often between family members. A charitable gift annuity is an arrangement in which an individual transfers money or property to a charitable organization in exchange for a promise by the charity to pay an annuity to the donor or another person. Typically, the donor wants to secure a fixed income stream for the annuity period and wishes to make a gift to the charitable organization of the remainder interest.

TAXATION OF ANNUITIES

There are several income tax rules applicable to annuities (some of which we will discuss below); however, the most important tax concept is that of the "exclusion ratio" discussed next.

Annuity Distribution Exclusion Ratio

Regular fixed annuities are taxed upon distribution by application of what is known as an **exclusion ratio**. Each distribution is basically divided into two parts—the first representing return of the investor's investment in the contract (which is nontaxable) and the second constituting income earned on the contract over its life which has been deferred for tax purposes (and which is currently taxable). The exclusion ratio is the percentage obtained by dividing the investor's unrecovered "investment in the contract" (usually the total premiums paid less any dividends received in cash or used to reduce premiums and minus the cumulative amount already received and excluded from taxation) by the "expected return." The expected return is the total amount that the owner is anticipated to receive over his or her life expectancy. For instance, if a 70-year-old sole annuitant will receive $500 per month over his or her life expectancy of 16 years (according to government tables for this purpose), he or she can expect to receive total payments of $96,000 ($500 x 12 x 16). If the annuitant has an unrecovered investment in the contract of $60,000, the exclusion ratio is, therefore, 62.5 percent ($60,000/$96,000). This ratio is applied to each distribution with the resulting monthly amount being treated as nontaxable. Hence, if we continue with the 70-year-old annuitant in our example, of each $500 monthly payment received, $312.50 will be treated as a return of the annuitant's investment in the contract. The remaining $187.50 per month will be includable in the annuitant's gross income. At the point when the annuitant has recovered his or her entire $60,000 investment, each subsequent payment, if any, will be fully taxable to the annuitant.

Other Tax Rules Applicable to Annuities

The following are some of the additional rules applicable to the taxation of annuities:

1. If an annuitant owns a refund or period certain type of annuity, and the annuitant dies before receiving all of the guaranteed payments, the surviving owner or beneficiary receiving the remaining guaranteed payments has no taxable income until the annuitant's investment in the contract has been fully recovered (both by the annuitant and the survivor). In some cases, the surviving owner or beneficiary may elect to apply the present value of the remaining installments to the purchase of a new annuity. If this option is elected, the payments received will be taxed under the normal annuity rules described in the previous paragraph, with the surviving owner or beneficiary using the refund amount as his or her investment in the contract and a new exclusion ratio being calculated. This option is beneficial where the refund amount exceeds the unrecovered investment in the contract and would result in a partially taxable lump sum payment.

2. If the surviving owner of a joint and survivor annuity was a joint owner of the annuity, he or she uses the same exclusion ratio used by the first annuitant. The survivor owner/annuitant may be entitled to an income tax deduction if the first annuitant was required to include the annuity in his or her estate.

3. If an owner/annuitant elects to take a partial withdrawal from his or her annuity and accordingly elects to receive lower future distributions, he or she will be taxed on a portion of the partial withdrawal.

4. Similarly, if an owner/annuitant elects to take a partial withdrawal from his or her annuity but elects to receive distributions in the same amount as prior to the partial withdrawal, but for a reduced period of time, he or she will realize taxable gain to the extent the cash surrender value of the contract exceeds the investment in the contract.

5. Income on a variable annuity is not taxed until either the contract is surrendered, a withdrawal is made from the contract, or at the time the annuity is annuitized (payments begin). However, to receive annuity treatment for tax purposes, IRS regulations require the underlying investments in the separate accounts to be "adequately diversified." Moreover, because of the inability to determine the expected return under a variable annuity, the exclusion ratio is calculated in a different way than that for a regular fixed annuity, as discussed earlier. Instead of dividing the investment in the contract by the expected return

(as is the case with a fixed annuity), the investment in the contract is divided by the number of years of expected return. This number of years will vary depending upon the length of the guaranteed period. For example, payments may be guaranteed for a specific number of years regardless of life expectancy or, alternatively, may be tied to a specific single life or joint and survivor lives, thus requiring use of either IRS Table V or VI.

6. For annuities that started after July 1, 1986, if an annuitant dies before recovering all of his or her investment in the contract, an itemized loss deduction may be claimed by the decedent on his or her final income tax return. Since the loss deduction is not considered a miscellaneous itemized deduction for income tax purposes, it is not subject to the 2 percent of AGI limitation. This deduction also extends to the decedent's estate or other beneficiary receiving subsequent distributions.

7. In the situation where an annuity owner takes dividends or cash withdrawals (including loans) from his or her annuity before the beginning of the annuitization phase, these amounts are taxable to the extent that the contract cash value exceeds the investment in the contract. In order to discourage use of annuities as short-term investments, such amounts withdrawn are treated first as income or growth and are therefore fully taxable (until the excess of contract cash value over investment in the contract has been withdrawn). This is known as "last-in-first out" or LIFO tax treatment.

8. Distributions made prior to certain dates discussed below are considered "premature" distributions and accordingly are subject to both ordinary income tax rates and the 10 percent penalty tax. However, the 10 percent penalty tax does *not* apply in any of the following typical situations:

    a) Annuitized payments made over the life (or life expectancy) of the taxpayer or the joint lives (or joint life expectancies) of the taxpayer and his or her beneficiary

    b) Payments made after the contract owner reaches age 59 1/2

    c) Payments made due to the contract owner's disability

    d) Payments made from qualified retirement plans and IRAs (which are already subject to a similar penalty)

    e) Payments made to a beneficiary (or annuitant's estate) on or after the death of an annuitant

    f) Distribution payments made under an immediate annuity

9. When an owner dies before the annuity distributions begin, the cash value of the contract is required to be distributed to the beneficiary within 5 years of the owner's death. Alternatively, the cash value may be used within one year of the owner's death to provide a life annuity or installment payments payable over a period not longer than the beneficiary's life expectancy. However, as we learned with respect to IRAs in chapters 3 and 4, if the beneficiary is the owner's surviving spouse, the spouse may elect to treat the contract as his or her own.

10. A separate tax rule, known as the "Simplified Rule," applies to annuity payments from a qualified retirement plan. It is discussed in greater depth in IRS Publication 575, Pension

and Annuity Income. This rule permits the annuity payment recipient to calculate the nontaxable portion of each distribution from his or her qualified annuity using a single table. The total amount of after-tax contributions to the qualified plan is then divided by the number of expected monthly payments to determine the nontaxable amount included in each payment.

FINANCIAL STRENGTH OF THE LIFE INSURANCE COMPANY

While an investor should carefully read a proposed annuity contract to determine the guaranteed interest rates, how long they apply, and if the contract contains a "bailout provision," it is even more important to determine the financial strength of the life insurance company that issued the contract. A bailout provision permits the annuity owner to withdraw his or her investment, free of any surrender charges, if the rate of return earned on the annuity falls below a certain level (e.g., a point or more below the starting rate). However, the bailout clause often applies only for a *limited period*. The bailout provision will not, of course, avoid the premature distribution penalty unless the funds are transferred to another annuity through what is known as a "Section 1035 exchange" (after the Internal Revenue Code section of the same number).

The investor should also check the rating of the issuing life insurance company as determined by A.M. Best, Standard & Poor's, or Moody's. Unlike bank deposit accounts, annuities are *not* insured by the FDIC or any other federal agency. It is recommended by most experts that only insurers carrying a rating of A ++ or A + from Best's; AAA or AA from S&P; and Aaa or Aa from Moody's be considered.

In this regard, it is important to remember that the separate accounts of a variable annuity are *not* subject to the claims of the insurance company's creditors. Therefore, an investor would not lose his or her investment in such a contract. However, the assets supporting fixed annuities *are* invested in the general assets of the insurance company. If the insurer becomes insolvent, fixed annuity owners would, therefore, become general creditors of the insurer. Accordingly, the investor must perform even greater due diligence on the issuer of a fixed annuity than on the issuer of a variable annuity.

IMPORTANT CONCEPTS

Life annuity	Joint life annuity
Fixed-period or term-certain annuity	Contemporary joint and survivor annuity
Annuitant	Fixed rate annuity
Beneficiary	Variable annuity
Survivorship benefit	Equity-index annuity (EIA)
Accumulation phase	Fixed benefit annuity
Distribution or annuitization phase	Variable benefit annuity
Surrender charges	Qualified annuity
Single-premium annuity	Nonqualified annuity
Fixed-premium annuity	Commercial annuity
Flexible-premium annuity	Private annuity
Refund annuity	Charitable gift annuity
Term-certain annuity	Exclusion ratio
Temporary annuity	Premature distribution
Immediate annuity	Income-first rule
Deferred annuity	Bailout provision
Single life annuity	Variable annuity separate accounts
Joint and last survivor annuity	

QUESTIONS FOR REVIEW

1. In what way is an annuity the reverse of life insurance?

2. How does a life annuity differ from a fixed period or term-certain annuity?

3. Who are the main parties to an annuity contract?

4. What are the three parts of the monthly payments received from an annuity during the distribution phase?

5. What is meant by the accumulation phase of an annuity?

6. What is meant by the distribution or annuitization phase of an annuity?

7. What are the principal advantages of an annuity?

8. What are the principal disadvantages of an annuity?

9. What benefits do annuities provide in retirement planning?

10. What are the many ways in which annuities are categorized?

11. What are the differences between a single-premium annuity, a fixed-premium annuity, and a flexible-premium annuity?

12. How does a refund annuity differ from a period-certain annuity?

13. How does a term-certain annuity differ from a temporary annuity?

14. How does an immediate annuity differ from a deferred annuity?

15. In what ways does a joint and last survivor annuity differ from a joint life annuity?

16. How does a fixed rate annuity differ from a variable annuity and who bears the investment risk in each type of annuity?

17. What are the characteristics of an equity-index annuity?

18. What is the difference between a qualified and a nonqualified annuity?

19. How is the exclusion ratio calculated for a regular fixed annuity versus a variable annuity?

20. When an annuity owner dies before the annuity distribution phase, within what time period must the cash value of the contract be distributed to the beneficiary? How, if at all, is this period affected if the beneficiary is the owner's surviving spouse?

21. What is meant by a bailout provision in an annuity?

22. In the event of the insolvency of the issuing life insurance company, in what way would the owner of a fixed annuity be affected versus the owner of a variable annuity?

SUGGESTIONS FOR ADDITIONAL READING

The Tools & Techniques of Life Insurance Planning, 3rd edition, Stephan R. Leimberg and Robert J. Doyle, Jr., The National Underwriter Company, 2004.

The Tools & Techniques of Employee Benefit and Retirement Planning, 9th edition, Stephan R. Leimberg and John J. McFadden, The National Underwriter Company, 2005.

Personal Financial Planning, 10th edition, Lawrence J. Gitman and Michael D. Joehnk, Thomson/South-Western, 2005.

Personal Financial Planning, 7th edition, G. Victor Hallman and Jerry S. Rosenbloom, McGraw-Hill, 2003.

Internal Revenue Service, Publication 575, Pension and Annuity Income.

Internal Revenue Service, Publication 939, General Rule for Pensions and Annuities.

CHAPTER SIX

Employer-Sponsored Tax-Advantaged Plans

• • •

In this chapter we will begin our discussion of the third leg of the retirement income "three-legged stool"—an employer-sponsored retirement plan. This term is difficult to define, since employer-sponsored plans encompass not only what are referred to as tax-qualified corporate plans for employees, but also plans where employers contribute to an IRA established on behalf of an employee, such as in a Simplified Employee Pension (SEP) or a Savings Incentive Match Plan for Employees (SIMPLE). This chapter investigates all of these types of employer-sponsored plans as well as those retirement plans offered by tax-exempt organizations and state and local governments. This chapter describes the basic provisions of all of these various types of plans where an employer assists the employee in saving for his or her own retirement. These plans are to be distinguished from the standard form of corporate pension or profit-sharing qualified plan where the employer takes the initiative in ensuring a comfortable employee retirement.

Upon completing this chapter, you should be able to:
- Describe the basic provisions of a Simplified Employee Pension (SEP) used by for-profit small businesses
- Describe the basic provisions of a Savings Incentive Match Plan for Employees (SIMPLE) used by for-profit small businesses
- Compare a Section 403(b) plan to a Section 457 plan
- Describe the basic provisions of a tax-sheltered annuity (TSA) (403(b)) plan used by nonprofit entities
- Describe the basic provisions of a Section 457 plan used for state or local government employees or nonprofit entities.

DEFINITIONS

Before we begin our discussion of SEPs, SIMPLEs, 403(b), and 457 plans, we will first define some terms that will be used throughout this chapter and in other chapters.

Annual additions

Annual additions are the total of: (1) all the employer's contributions in a year; (2) employee contributions (not including rollovers); and (3) forfeitures of non-vested employees who are leaving the employer allocated to a participant's account.

Annual benefits

Annual benefits are the benefits to be paid yearly in the form of a straight life annuity (with no extra benefits) under a plan to which employees do not contribute and under which no rollover contributions are made.

Business

A business is an activity in which a profit motive is present and economic activity is involved.

Common-law employee

A common-law employee is any individual who, under common law, would have the status of an employee. A leased employee can also be a common-law employee. A common-law employee is a person who performs services for an employer who has the right to control and direct the results of the work and the way in which it is done. For example, the employer provides the employee's tools, materials, and workplace, and can fire the employee.

Common-law employees are *not* self-employed and *may not* set up retirement plans for income from their work, even if that income is treated as self-employment income for social security tax purposes. For example, common-law employees who are ministers, members of religious orders, full-time insurance salespeople, and U.S. citizens employed in the United States by foreign governments cannot set up retirement plans for their earnings from those employments, even though their earnings are treated as self-employment income.

However, an individual may be a common-law employee and a self-employed person at the same time. For example, an attorney may be a corporate common-law employee during regular working hours and also practice law in the evening as a self-employed person.

Compensation

Compensation for plan allocations is the pay a participant receives from the employer for personal services for a year. Compensation generally includes (1) wages and salaries; (2) fees for professional services; and (3) other amounts received (cash or noncash) for personal services actually rendered by an employee, including, but not limited to, commissions and tips, fringe benefits, and bonuses.

For a self-employed person, compensation means the earned income of that individual. However, compensation also includes amounts deferred in the following employee benefit plans as before-tax "elective deferrals": (1) a qualified cash or deferred arrangement (Section 401(k) plan) (discussed in chapter 11); (2) salary reduction agreement to contribute to a Section 403(b) plan, a SIMPLE IRA plan, or a SARSEP; (3) Section 457 nonqualified deferred compensation plan (discussed later in this chapter); and (4) a Section 125 cafeteria plan.

Finally, an employer may choose to exclude elective deferrals under the above plans from the definition of compensation.

Contribution

A contribution is an amount the employer pays into a plan for all those participating in the plan, including self-employed individuals. Plan limits may apply to the amount that may be contributed each year for a participant.

Deduction

A deduction is the plan contributions the employer may subtract from gross income on the employer's federal income tax return. Statutory limits apply to the amount deductible.

Earned Income

Earned income is net earnings from self-employment, from a business in which the employee materially helped to produce the income. An individual may also have earned income from property that his or her personal efforts helped create, such as royalties from his or her books or inventions.

Employer

An employer is generally any person for whom an individual performs or did perform any service, of whatever nature, as an employee. A sole proprietor is treated as his or her own employer for retirement plan purposes. However, a partner is *not* an employer for retirement plan purposes. Instead, the partnership is treated as the employer of each partner.

Highly compensated employee

A highly compensated employee is an individual who:

- Owned more than 5 percent of the interest in the employer's business at any time during the year or the preceding year, or
- For the preceding year, received compensation from the employer of more than $95,000 (in 2005) and, if the employer so chooses, was in the top 20 percent of employees when ranked by compensation.

Leased employee

A leased employee who is not the common-law employee of an employer must generally be treated as the employer's employee for retirement plan purposes if he or she does all of the following:

- Provides services to the employer under an agreement between the employer and a leasing organization
- Has performed services for the employer (or for the employer and related persons) substantially full time for at least one year
- Performs services under the employer's primary direction or control

However, a leased employee is *not* treated as the employer's employee if all the following conditions are met:

- Leased employees are not more than 20 percent of the employer's non-highly compensated work force
- The employee is covered under the leasing corporation's qualified pension plan
- The leasing organization's plan is a money purchase pension plan that has immediate participation, full and immediate vesting, and a nonintegrated employer contribution rate of at least 10 percent of compensation for each participant

Moreover, if the leased employee is the employer's common-law employee, that employee will be the employer's employee for all purposes, regardless of any pension plan of the leasing organization.

Net earnings from self-employment

For SEP and qualified plans, net earnings from self-employment is an individual's gross income from his or her trade or business (provided his or her personal services are a material income-producing factor) minus allowable business deductions (including contributions to SEP and qualified plans for common-law employees and the deduction allowed for one-half of the individual's self-employment tax).

Participant

A participant is an eligible employee who is covered by the employer's retirement plan. Different types of retirement plans have different definitions of an employee eligible to participate in each type of plan.

Partner

A partner is an individual who shares ownership of an unincorporated trade or business with one or more persons. For retirement plans, a partner is treated as an employee of the partnership.

Self-employed individual

An individual in business for himself or herself is self-employed. Sole proprietors and partners are self-employed. Self-employment may also include part-time work.

Not everyone who has net earnings from self-employment for social security tax purposes is self-employed for qualified plan purposes, as discussed previously under **Common-law employee** and **Net earnings from self-employment**.

Sole proprietor

A sole proprietor is an individual who owns an unincorporated business by himself or herself. For retirement plans, a sole proprietor is treated as both an employer and an employee.

SIMPLIFIED EMPLOYEE PENSION (SEP)

A simplified employee pension (SEP) is a written plan that allows an employer to make contributions toward his or her own retirement (if he or she is self-employed) and toward that of his or her employees' retirement without getting involved in a more complex qualified plan. By adopting a SEP agreement, an employer may make contributions directly to a traditional individual retirement account or a traditional individual retirement annuity (SEP-IRA) set up for each eligible employee. A SEP-IRA is owned and controlled by the employee, and only the employer makes contributions to the financial institution where the SEP-IRA is maintained.

SEP-IRAs are established, at a minimum, for each eligible employee and may have to be set up for a leased employee but do not have to be set up for excludable employees, defined later. An eligible employee is an individual who is at least 21 years of age, has worked for the employer in at least 3 of the last 5 years, and has received at least $450 in compensation from the employer (in 2005). The participation requirements established by the employer can be less restrictive than those just described, but cannot be more restrictive.

Certain employees may be excluded from coverage under a SEP. They include (1) employees covered by a union agreement and whose retirement benefits were bargained for in good faith by the employees' union and the employer, and (2) nonresident alien employees who have received no U.S. source wages, salaries, or other personal services compensation from the employer.

Reasons to Adopt a SEP

Probably the major reason why small employers (say, 10 employees or less) would consider adopting a SEP is that they are easier and less expensive to both install and administer than a qualified profit-sharing plan. Another significant reason why a small employer would consider adopting a SEP is if the employer has had very good financial results for the tax year just ended and wants to shelter some of its high profits from taxation. While qualified plans must be adopted before the end of the year in which they are to be effective, a SEP may be established as late as the due date (including extensions) of the tax return for the year in which the high profits occurred. In effect, this permits the employer to wait until the financial results are available and then decide whether to create a SEP rather than having to hurry to create a qualified plan before the end of the tax year without having final financial results available.

Some advantages of SEPs include (1) total portability of benefits for employees; (2) employer discretion to make no contribution to the plan in any given year; and (3) transfer of investment risk to the employee.

SEPS also have certain disadvantages, including: (1) it will not guarantee an adequate retirement benefit for employees since the employer is not required to make substantial and regular contributions and older employees entering the plan have a limited number of years to fund their retirement; (2) allowable annual contributions may not be as large as would be permitted under a qualified plan; and (3) SEP distributions do not receive special income averaging tax treatment as do certain qualified plan distributions.

Establishing a SEP

An employer needs to observe three steps in establishing a SEP. First, the employer must execute a formal written agreement to provide benefits to all eligible employees. Second, the employer must give each eligible employee certain information about the SEP. Finally, a SEP-IRA must be established by or for each eligible employee.

To satisfy the formal written agreement requirement, an employer may adopt an IRS model SEP using IRS Form 5305-SEP. One main advantage of using this model SEP is that the employer does not need prior IRS approval or an IRS determination letter. An additional advantage is that the employer will not have to file annual retirement plan information returns with the IRS and the Department of Labor.

In the following situations, however, an employer is not allowed to use Form 5305-SEP if any of the following applies:

- The employer maintains any other qualified retirement plan. However, if the employer already maintains another SEP, the employer may establish a second one.
- The employer has eligible employees for whom IRAs have not been established.
- The employer uses the services of leased employees.
- The employer is a member of any of the following unless all eligible employees of all the members of these groups, trades, or businesses participate under the SEP: (1) an affiliated service group described in IRS Section 414(m); (2) a controlled group of corporations described in IRS Section 414(b); or (3) trades or businesses under common control described in IRS Section 414(c).

Upon establishing a SEP, the employer must give to each eligible employee a copy of Form 5305-SEP, its instructions, and the other information listed in the Form 5305-SEP instructions. An IRS model SEP is *not* considered adopted until the employer gives each employee this information.

A SEP-IRA must be established by or for each eligible employee with a bank, insurance company, or other qualified financial institution. A SEP may be established for a particular calendar year as late as the due date (including extensions) of the employer's income tax return for that year. An employer adopting a plan may be eligible for a business tax credit of up to $500 per year for each of the first three years of the plan for the "qualified startup costs" of starting a SEP.

Contribution Limitations

A limited amount of money may be contributed each year to each employee's SEP-IRA. For those employers who are self-employed, the employer may contribute to his or her own SEP-IRA. Contributions must be in the form of money (cash, check, or money order) and not property. However, participants may be able to transfer or roll over certain property from one retirement plan to another.

An employer does *not* have to make contributions every year. However, contributions made must be based on a written allocation formula and must not discriminate in favor of highly compensated employees (defined previously). In a year that contributions are made, the employer must contribute to the SEP-IRAs of all participants who actually performed personal services during the year for which the contributions are made, even those employees who die or terminate employment before the contributions are made.

The contributions made under a SEP are treated as if made to a qualified pension, stock bonus, profit-sharing, or annuity plan. As a result, SEP contributions are deductible within limits, discussed later in this chapter, and are not taxable to the plan participants.

A SEP-IRA cannot be designated as a Roth IRA; however, employer contributions to a SEP-IRA will not affect the amount an individual can contribute to a Roth IRA.

In order for the employer to obtain a tax deduction, contributions to a SEP must be made by the due date (including extensions) of the employer's tax return for the year.

Contributions made to a common-law employee's SEP-IRA cannot exceed **the lesser of 25 percent of the employee's compensation or $42,000 (for 2005)**. Compensation, however, generally does *not* include the employer's contributions to the SEP. The annual limits on an employer's contributions to a common-law employee's SEP-IRA also apply to contributions the employer makes to his or her own SEP-IRA, except that special rules apply when calculating the employer's maximum deductible contribution. This calculation is discussed in the next section on deduction limitations.

In calculating the annual compensation limit, the employer may *not* take into consideration the portion of an employee's compensation that exceeds $210,000 (in 2005). However, this is somewhat academic since $42,000 (in 2005) is the maximum contribution for an eligible employee.

If the employer also contributes to a defined contribution plan (discussed in chapter 12), annual additions to an account are limited to the lesser of $42,000 (in 2005) or 100 percent of the participant's compensation. In calculating this limit, the employer must add employer contributions to all defined contribution plans. Because a SEP is considered a defined contribution plan for this limit, the employer's contributions to a SEP must also be added to the employer's contributions to other defined contribution plans.

Employer contributions to an employee's SEP-IRA (or to the employer's own SEP-IRA) that exceed the contribution limits defined earlier are included in the employee's income for the year and are treated as contributions by the employee to his or her SEP-IRA. Unlike employee "elective deferrals" generally, employer contributions to a SEP are *not* subject to social security (FICA) or federal unemployment (FUTA) taxes.

Finally, each participating employee is always 100 percent vested in *all* contributions to his or her SEP-IRA and must receive an annual statement stating the amount contributed to his or her account for the year.

Deduction Limitations

Generally, an employer may deduct the contributions the employer makes each year to each employee's SEP-IRA and, if the employer is self-employed, the contributions made each year to the employer's own SEP-IRA. The maximum deduction for contributions (other than elective deferrals, discussed later in this chapter) for participants is the *lesser of* the following amounts:

- The employer's contributions (including any excess contributions carryover)
- 25 percent of the compensation (limited to $210,000 per participant, in 2005) paid to the participants during the year from the business that maintains the plan, not to exceed $42,000 per participant (in 2005). Compensation here includes elective deferrals (discussed later in this chapter under Salary Reduction Simplified Employee Pension (SARSEP)). Elective deferrals to a SARSEP are no longer subject to this deduction limit. However, the combined deduction for a participant's elective deferrals and other SEP contributions cannot exceed $42,000 (in 2005).

In the case of a self-employed individual who contributes to his or her own SEP-IRA, he or she must make a special computation (as mentioned earlier) to figure his or her maximum deduction for these contributions. The compensation of such an individual is his or her "net earnings from self-employment" (defined earlier in this chapter), which takes into account both the deduction for one-half of his or her self-employment tax and the deduction for contributions to his or her own SEP-IRA. As a result of this method of calculation, the deduction for contributions to a self-employed employer's own SEP-IRA and his or her net earnings depend on each other. Consequently, to determine the deduction for contributions to a self-employed employer's own SEP-IRA, one must reduce the contribution rate called for in the SEP plan. This requires the use of the IRS Rate Table for Self-Employed or the IRS Rate Worksheet for Self-Employed, whichever is appropriate for the plan's contribution rate. Finally, the maximum deduction is calculated using the IRS Deduction Worksheet for Self-Employed.

As alluded to earlier, when calculating the deduction limitation, treat all of the employer's qualified defined contribution plans as a single plan and all of the employer's defined benefit plans (discussed in chapter 13) as a single plan. If the employer has both kinds of plans, a SEP is treated as a separate profit-sharing (defined contribution) plan. In addition, if the employer also contributes to a qualified defined contribution plan, the employer must reduce the 25 percent deduction limit for that plan by the allowable deductions for contributions to the SEP-IRAs of those participating in both the SEP plan and the defined contribution plan.

If an employer made SEP contributions that are more than the deduction limit (nondeductible contributions), the employer may carry over and deduct the difference in later years. However, the carryover, when combined with the contribution for the later year, is subject to the deduction limit for that year. Finally, if an employer made nondeductible (excess) contributions to a SEP, the employer may also be subject to a 10 percent excise tax.

Contributions made for common-law employees are deducted on the employer's tax return. For example, a sole proprietor deducts such contributions on Schedule C of Form 1040, Profit or Loss From Business, or Schedule F of Form 1040, Profit or Loss From Farming. A partnership deducts them on Form 1065, U.S. Return of Partnership Income, and a corporation deducts them on Form 1120, U.S. Corporation Income Tax Return, Form 1120-A, U.S. Corporation Short-Form Income Tax Return, or Form 1120S, U.S. Income Tax Return for an S Corporation. Sole proprietors and partners deduct contributions for themselves on line 32 of Form 1040.

Distributions from SEPs

SEP contributions and earnings may be withdrawn at any time; but, like traditional IRAs, withdrawals are taxable in the year received and subject to the 10 percent additional tax if withdrawn before age 59 1/2. SEP contributions and earnings may be rolled over tax free to other IRAs and retirement plans and, like traditional IRAs, they are subject to the required minimum distribution rules discussed in chapter 3.

A loan to a SEP participant is considered a prohibited transaction (thus disqualifying the SEP-IRA as an IRA) and while in-service withdrawals are permitted, they are includible in income and subject to a 10 percent additional tax if the participant is under age 59 1/2.

SALARY REDUCTION SIMPLIFIED EMPLOYEE PENSION (SARSEP)

As discussed in the previous section, only *employer* contributions are permitted to a SEP. However, there is a different type of SEP, known as a SARSEP, which permits *employees* to make what are referred to as "elective deferrals" to their SEP-IRA instead of receiving the amount contributed as cash compensation. SARSEPs had to have been established prior to 1997 and may no longer be established. However, if a SARSEP is "grandfathered," the employees elect to have the employer contribute a portion of their compensation to their SARSEP rather than receive it in cash. By making this election, employees defer income taxation on a portion of their compensation until it is distributed to them. Nevertheless, such elective deferrals are included in wages for social security, Medicare, and federal unemployment (FUTA) tax. A limited nonrefundable tax credit, known as the "saver's credit," is available to certain lower income taxpayers who make elective deferrals to a SARSEP.

A SARSEP established before 1997 may continue to be maintained by an employer if all of the following conditions are met:

1. At least 50 percent of the employees eligible to participate choose to make elective deferrals

2. The employer has 25 or fewer employees who were eligible to participate in the SEP at any time during the preceding year

3. The elective deferrals of the highly compensated employees meet the "SARSEP ADP test." Under this test, the amount deferred each year by each eligible highly compensated employee as a percentage of pay (the deferral percentage) cannot be more than 125 percent of the average deferral percentage (ADP) of all non-highly compensated employees eligible to participate. See the definition of highly compensated employee in the Definitions section of this chapter. To calculate the deferral percentage for an employee for a year, simply divide the elective employer contributions (excluding certain catch-up contributions) paid to the SEP for the employee for the year by the employee's includible compensation (limited to $210,000 in 2005). In determining the employee's compensation, elective deferrals under the SARSEP (unless elected otherwise by the employer) are included in calculating the employee's deferral percentage, even though they are not included in the employee's income for income tax purposes.

The maximum amount a participant in a SARSEP meeting all of the foregoing conditions can elect to defer is the *lesser of*:
- 25 percent of the participant's compensation (limited to $210,000 in 2005)
- $14,000 in 2005

The $14,000 limit in 2005 applies to the total elective deferrals the employee makes for the year to a SEP and is aggregated with any of the following: a 401(k) plan, a 403(b) plan, or a SIMPLE IRA plan (discussed later in this chapter).

Another advantage of a SARSEP is that it allows participants who are age 50 or over at the end of the calendar year to also make "catch-up" contributions. The catch-up contribution limit for 2005 is $4,000. Elective deferrals are not treated as catch-up contributions for 2005 until they exceed: (1) the elective deferral limit (the lesser of 25 percent of compensation or $14,000, in 2005); (2) the SARSEP ADP test limit discussed earlier in this chapter; or (3) the plan limit (if any). Moreover, the maximum permissible catch-up contribution a participant may make for a year cannot exceed the *lesser of* (1) the catch-up contribution limit or (2) the excess of the participant's compensation over the elective deferrals that are not catch-up contributions. Catch-up contributions are not subject to the elective deferral limit (the lesser of 25 percent of compensation or $14,000, in 2005).

If an employer makes what are referred to as "excess SEP contributions," the employer must notify its highly compensated employees within 2 1/2 months after the end of the plan year of their excess SEP contributions. Excess SEP contributions are elective deferrals of highly compensated employees that are more than the amount permitted under the SARSEP ADP test, discussed earlier. Failure to notify the highly compensated employees involved within the 2 1/2-month time limit may result in the employer having to pay a 10 percent tax on the excess.

Distributions from a SARSEP are subject to the same IRA distribution rules discussed in chapter 3.

SAVINGS INCENTIVE MATCH PLAN FOR EMPLOYEES (SIMPLE)

A SIMPLE plan is a written arrangement that provides an employer and its employees with a simplified way to make contributions for the purpose of funding retirement income. Just like a SARSEP, an employee may elect to make salary reduction contributions (elective deferrals) to the plan rather than receiving these amounts as part of their regular compensation. The employer may then make matching or nonelective contributions. SIMPLE plans may only be maintained on a calendar-year basis and may only be established in either of two ways-using SIMPLE IRAs (SIMPLE IRA plan) or as part of a 401(k) plan (SIMPLE 401(k) plan).

SIMPLE IRA Plan

A SIMPLE IRA plan is a retirement plan that maintains SIMPLE IRAs for each eligible employee. An employer may establish a SIMPLE IRA plan if it meets the employee limit and does not maintain another qualified plan, except plans for collective bargaining employees. An employer must have 100 or fewer employees who received $5,000 or more in compensation from the employer for the preceding year. In addition, an employer must take into account all employees employed at any time during the calendar year regardless of whether they are eligible to participate. This includes self-employed individuals who received earned income from the employer and leased employees (discussed under Definitions in this chapter). After the plan has been established, the employer must then continue to meet the 100-employee limit each year the plan is maintained. Special rules apply in the case of an employer who maintains the plan for at least one year and then fails to meet the 100-employee limit in a later year and in the case of an acquisition, disposition, or similar transaction.

Another important provision of a SIMPLE IRA plan is that it must be the *only* retirement plan to which the employer makes contributions, or to which benefits accrue, for service in any year beginning with the year the SIMPLE IRA plan becomes effective. However, as mentioned earlier, a qualified plan for collective bargaining employees is generally permitted.

Eligible Employee

For purposes of participation in a SIMPLE IRA, an "eligible employee" is any employee who receives a minimum of $5,000 in compensation during any two years preceding the current calendar year and is reasonably expected to receive at least $5,000 during the current calendar year. The term also includes a self-employed individual who received earned income from the employer. An employer has the option to waive or reduce (but not increase) these compensation requirements, but may not add other participation requirements. As with SEPs, union employees and nonresident aliens receiving no U.S. source compensation from the employer may be excluded from participation.

Compensation

Employee compensation that may be considered for purposes of SIMPLE IRA contributions includes their W-2 income plus any salary reduction contributions made under the SIMPLE IRA plan, compensation deferred under a Section 457 plan, and the employees' elective deferrals under a Section 401(k) plan, a SARSEP, or a Section 403(b) annuity contract. Compensation for a self-employed person is his or her net earnings from self-employment before subtracting any contributions made to the SIMPLE IRA plan for him- or herself.

Reasons to Adopt a SIMPLE IRA Plan

Probably the major reason why small employers (say, 100 employees or less) would consider adopting a SIMPLE IRA plan is that, like SEPs, they are easier and less expensive to both install and administer than a qualified profit- sharing plan. Another significant reason why a small employer would consider adopting a SIMPLE IRA plan is if the employer wants to fund the plan through salary reductions. Moreover, in the employer's particular situation, the SIMPLE IRA contribution limit may be higher than those permitted under either a Keogh plan or SEP.

Some advantages of SIMPLE IRA plans include (1) ease of establishment by using standard IRS forms (5304-SIMPLE or 5305-SIMPLE); (2) total portability and 100 percent employee vesting; (3) the transfer of investment risk to the employee; and (4) the availability of salary reduction contributions, if IRS requirements are met.

SIMPLE IRA plans also have certain *disadvantages*, including: (1) no guarantee of an adequate retirement benefit for employees unless they make meaningful and consistent annual salary reduction contributions over many years (older employees entering the plan have a limited number of years to fund their retirement); (2) allowable annual contributions may not be as large as would be permitted under a qualified plan (such as a 401(k)); (3) SIMPLE IRA distributions do not receive special income averaging tax treatment as do certain qualified plan distributions; and (4) the employer may not also maintain a qualified plan, a SEP, a 403(a) annuity, a 403(b) tax-sheltered annuity (discussed in the next section), or a Section 457 plan. A union plan, however, may coexist with a SIMPLE IRA plan.

Certain lower income employees making salary deferrals may qualify for the "saver's credit" (as discussed under SARSEPs) and employers adopting a new SIMPLE IRA plan may qualify for a business tax credit of up to $500 for the "qualified startup costs" of the plan (as discussed under SEPs).

Establishing a SIMPLE IRA Plan

Just as with a SEP, an employer may establish a SIMPLE IRA plan by using a model SIMPLE plan document found on Forms 5304-SIMPLE or 5305-SIMPLE. If the employer wishes to permit each employee to select the financial institution to receive his or her contributions, the employer uses Form 5304-SIMPLE. If the employer wants to select the financial institution where all contributions will initially be deposited, the employer uses Form 5305-SIMPLE. When the appropriate form has been fully completed and signed by both the employer and the financial institution, if any, the SIMPLE plan is considered to be adopted. As with a SEP, using the standard form avoids having to file the paperwork with the IRS. Also, page 3 of this form may be used to satisfy the employer notification requirements to plan participants.

Just as with a SEP, the employer may be able to claim a tax credit for part of the startup costs of establishing a SIMPLE IRA plan.

If an employer establishes a SIMPLE IRA plan, it must notify each employee of the following four items of information before the beginning of what is known as the election period:

1. The employee's opportunity to make or change a salary reduction choice under a SIMPLE IRA plan
2. The employer's choice to make either matching contributions or nonelective contributions (discussed later in this chapter)
3. A summary description provided by the financial institution
4. Written notice that an employee's balance may be transferred without cost or penalty if the employer uses a designated financial institution

The election period is generally the 60-day period immediately preceding January 1 of a calendar year (November 2 through December 31 of the preceding calendar year). These dates are modified if the SIMPLE IRA plan is established in mid-year or if the 60-day period falls before the first day an employee becomes eligible to participate in the SIMPLE IRA plan. The plan document may provide a longer period to enter into any salary reduction agreement or to modify a prior agreement.

Contribution Limitations

Contributions to SIMPLE IRAs include both salary reduction contributions (by employees) and employer contributions (either matching or nonelective contributions). No other contributions may be made to a SIMPLE IRA plan (other than rollover contributions).

An employee may elect to have the employer contribute, on his or her behalf, to his or her SIMPLE IRA up to $10,000 (in 2005). The amount of a salary reduction contribution must be determined as a percentage of the employee's compensation unless the employer permits the employee to contribute a flat amount of money up to the $10,000 limit (in 2005). If an employee participates during the year in any other employer plan and has either salary reductions or deferred compensation under that plan, the salary reduction contributions under the SIMPLE IRA plan are also considered elective deferrals and accordingly must be included in determining the overall limit ($14,000 in 2005) for exclusion of salary reduction contributions and other elective deferrals.

In addition to the foregoing salary reduction contributions, participants who are age 50 or over at the end of the calendar year may also be permitted by a SIMPLE IRA plan to make catch-up contributions of up to $2,000 (in 2005). As with SARSEPs, salary reduction contributions are *not* treated as catch-up contributions until they exceed $10,000 (for 2005). Finally, a participant's compensation must be greater than the total contributions elected.

An employer must also match each employee's salary reduction contributions on a dollar-for-dollar basis up to 3 percent of the employee's compensation. For example, if an employee's salary is $40,000 and he or she elects to defer 5 percent of his or her salary, the total contribution the employer can make for this employee is $3,200, calculated as follows:

Salary reduction contributions ($40,000 x .05)	$2,000
Employer matching contribution ($40,000 x .03)	1,200
	$3,200

However, if the employer elects a matching contribution less than 3 percent, the percentage must be at least 1 percent. The employees must be notified of the lower match within a reasonable period of time before the 60-day election period (discussed earlier in this chapter) for the calendar year. The matching contribution requirements just described do *not* apply if the employer instead elects to make nonelective contributions of 2 percent of compensation on behalf of each eligible employee who has at least $5,000 (or a lower amount selected by the employer) of compensation from the employer for the year. One downside for the employer of choosing nonelective contributions versus matching contributions is that the employer must then make the nonelective contributions each year, even if the employee elects *not* to make salary reduction contributions. And as we learned earlier, no more than $210,000 (in 2005) of the employee's compensation may be taken into account in calculating this contribution limit.

Salary reduction contributions to a SIMPLE IRA generally must be made within 30 days after the end of the month in which the amounts would otherwise have been payable to the employee in cash. However, matching or nonelective contributions may be made by the due date (including extensions) for filing the employer's federal income tax return for the year.

Deduction Limitations

SIMPLE IRA contributions are deductible in the tax year within which the calendar year for which contributions were made ends. Contributions are deductible for a particular tax year if they are made for that tax year by the due date (including extensions) of the employer's income tax return for that year. For example, if the employer has a fiscal year ending June 30, contributions under a SIMPLE IRA plan for the calendar year 2005 (including those contributions made during the first six months of 2005 (before July 1, 2005) are deductible in the tax year ending June 30, 2006. Alternatively, if the employer is a sole proprietor whose tax year is the calendar year, contributions under a SIMPLE IRA for calendar year 2005 (including contributions made in 2006 by April 15, 2006) are deductible in the 2005 tax year.

A sole proprietor deducts SIMPLE IRA contributions on Schedule C of IRS Form 1040, Profit or Loss From Business, or on Schedule F, if a farmer. Partnerships deduct such contributions on IRS Form 1065, U.S. Return of Partnership Income, and corporations deduct them on IRS Form 1120, U.S. Corporation Income Tax Return, Form 1120-A, or IRS Form 1120S, if an S Corporation. Sole proprietors and partners deduct contributions for themselves on line 32 of IRS Form 1040.

Qualifying contributions made on behalf of employees are deductible by the employer and not taxable to the employees. However, salary reduction contributions are subject to social security, Medicare, and FUTA taxes. Matching and nonelective contributions are not subject to these taxes.

Distributions from SIMPLE IRAs

Distributions from SIMPLE IRAs are taxed under the same rates applicable to traditional IRAs. Also, rollovers may be made from one SIMPLE IRA to another but rollovers from a SIMPLE IRA to a non-SIMPLE IRA may be made tax-free only *after* two years of participation in the SIMPLE IRA plan. Early withdrawals made before fulfilling this 2-year participation requirement are subject to a 25 percent additional tax, rather than the normal 10 percent tax.

SIMPLE 401(k) Plan

An employer interested in developing a SIMPLE plan also has the option of creating a SIMPLE 401(k) plan instead of a SIMPLE IRA plan. Of course, doing so involves somewhat more complexity since a SIMPLE 401(k) plan is a *qualified* retirement plan subject to most of the rules applicable to such plans. The only rules that do not apply to a SIMPLE 401(k) plan are the general nondiscrimination and top-heavy rules, assuming the plan satisfies the following conditions:

1. An employee may elect to have the employer make salary reduction contributions for the year to a trust in an amount expressed as a percentage of the employee's compensation, up to $10,000 (for 2005) plus up to $2,000 (for 2005) additional if the employee is age 50 or over.

2. The employer must make either:

   • matching contributions up to 3 percent of compensation for the year, or

   • nonelective contributions of 2 percent of compensation on behalf of each eligible employee who has at least $5,000 of compensation from the employer for the year (as discussed earlier under Contribution Limitations).

3. No other contributions are made to the trust.

4. No contributions are made, and no benefits accrue, for services during the year under any other employer qualified retirement plan on behalf of any employee eligible to participate in the SIMPLE 401(k) plan.

5. The employee's rights to any contributions are fully vested at all times.

Finally, just as is the case with a SIMPLE IRA plan, no more than $210,000 (in 2005) in compensation may be taken into account in figuring salary reduction contributions, matching contributions, and nonelective contributions.

IRS Revenue Procedure 97-9 in Cumulative Bulletin 1997-1 provides a model amendment that an employer may use to adopt a plan with SIMPLE 401(k) provisions or to incorporate 401(k) provisions in plans containing cash or deferred arrangements.

TAX-SHELTERED ANNUITY PLANS (403(B) PLANS)

A tax-sheltered annuity (TSA) plan, authorized by Section 403(b) of the Internal Revenue Code, is a retirement plan designed for certain employees of public schools, employees of certain tax-exempt organizations, and certain ministers. There are three types of individual accounts in a 403(b) plan:

• An annuity contract provided by an insurance company

• A custodial account invested in mutual funds

• A retirement income account, invested in either annuities or mutual funds, set up for church employees

To be eligible to participate in a 403(b) plan, an individual must be an employee of: (1) a tax-exempt organization established under IRC Section 501(c)(3); (2) a public school system (the employee must be involved in the day-to-day operations of the school); (3) a public school system organized by Indian tribal governments; (4) a cooperative hospital service organization; or (5) the Uniformed Services University of the Health Sciences (USUHS). Individuals who are ministers may also participate in a 403(b) plan if they meet any of the following requirements: (1) they are employed by a Section 501(c)(3) organization; (2) they are self-employed and perform services for a qualified employer and, accordingly, are treated as employed by a tax-exempt organization that is a qualified employer; or (3) they are employed by non-501(c)(3) organizations and function as ministers in their day-to-day professional responsibilities with their employers (including chaplains in a state-run prison and chaplains in the U.S. Armed Forces).

A 501(c)(3) organization is one that is "organized and operated exclusively for religious, charitable, scientific, testing for public safety, literary, or educational purposes, or to foster national or international amateur sport competition...or for the prevention of cruelty to children or animals." In addition, the organization must benefit the public, rather than any private owner or individual, and it must not engage in lobbying activities for political purposes or to influence legislation. Prime examples include churches, hospitals, public schools and colleges, and charitable institutions. Educational organizations must have a regular faculty and curriculum and regularly enrolled students in attendance, operated by a state or municipal agency.

Only the qualified employer may establish the 403(b) account—not the employee. This is true even for self-employed ministers.

Reasons to Adopt a 403(b) Plan

From the standpoint of employees, a 403(b) plan permits employees of qualifying organizations to not pay tax on allowable contributions in the year that they are made, to defer taxation of earnings and gains on amounts in the 403(b) account until withdrawn, and (for lower income employees) to qualify for a "saver's credit" for elective deferrals contributed to their 403(b) accounts.

From an employer's standpoint, if the employer has a small budget to provide retirement benefits beyond basic salary and other benefits, a 403(b) plan may be funded (except for the installation and administration costs) through the use of employee salary reductions. The employer also has the flexibility of making additional contributions from employer funds. Generally, a TSA plan works best with a young work force that enjoys the advantage of a substantial amount of time to accumulate retirement funds and that is willing to incur some degree of investment risk to accomplish its goals. Moreover, a 403(b) plan functions well as a supplement to the employer's existing defined benefit or other qualified plan.

Probably the primary advantage of establishing a TSA plan is the tax deferral achieved just as in a qualified retirement plan. In addition, employees enjoy the flexibility of deciding how much to contribute to the plan and the employer does not need to (but has the flexibility to) contribute its own funds to the plan. Finally, TSA plans also offer employee in-service withdrawals.

Some of the downside of establishing a TSA plan are: (1) they do not necessarily provide an adequate retirement benefit for employees, especially those who joined the plan when relatively near retirement; (2) the annual salary reduction is subject to the elective deferral limit, as described later in this chapter; (3) the plan is subject to the sometimes onerous nondiscrimination tests, described later in this chapter; and (4) the investment risk is incurred by the employees (although, oftentimes, they have a choice of investments to minimize this risk).

Contribution Limitations

Generally, except for after-tax contributions described later, only an employer may make contributions to a 403(b) account. This includes before-tax elective deferrals made under a salary reduction agreement, employer nonelective contributions (including matching contributions, discretionary contributions, and mandatory contributions) not made under a salary reduction agreement, after-tax contributions (provided from employee funds), and a combination of any of these three types of contributions.

A self-employed minister is considered both an employee and an employer and can contribute to a retirement income account for his or her own benefit, deducting the contributions on his or her income tax return.

The limit on the amount that can be contributed to an employee's 403(b) account for any year is called the "maximum amount contributable (MAC)." An employee's MAC consists of the limit on annual additions (discussed later in this chapter) and the limit on elective deferrals (also discussed later in this chapter). Contributions to an employee's 403(b) account are limited to the lesser of the limit on annual additions or the limit on elective deferrals. The type of contributions made to an employee's 403(b) account determines whether both, or only one, of these limits apply to that employee. For example, if elective deferrals are the only contributions made, the employee needs to calculate both limits and then select the lesser amount as his or her MAC. In the case of nonelective contributions, only the limit on annual additions must be calculated to determine the employee's MAC. Where there is a combination of both elective deferrals and nonelective contributions, both limits will then need to be calculated. In order to avoid penalties and additional taxes, an employee should calculate his or her MAC at the beginning of each tax year by reviewing his or her actual compensation for the prior year and determining whether the amount contributed for the prior year is within the allowable limits.

Limitation on Annual Additions

The total annual additions that may be made to an employee's 403(b) account is the sum of elective deferrals, nonelective contributions, and after-tax contributions. This limit is the *lesser of*: (1) $42,000 (in 2005), or (2) 100 percent of the employee's "includible compensation for his or her most recent year of service." An employee must combine the contributions made to all of his or her 403(b) accounts (even if with different employers) and if the employee participates in both a 403(b) plan and a qualified plan, he or she must combine contributions made to the 403(b) account, the qualified plan, and, if applicable, SEP accounts of all corporations, partnerships, and sole proprietorships in which the employee has more than 50 percent control.

An employee's includible compensation for his or her most recent year of service is the total of taxable wages and benefits he or she received from the employer that maintained a 403(b) account for the employee's benefit during his or her most recent year of service. If the employee's tax year is not the same as the employer's annual work period, the employee's most recent year of service may be a different period of time than that of the employer. Also, compensation of different employers cannot be mixed.

In order to calculate one's most recent year of service, the employee must first determine what constitutes a full year of service for his or her particular position. An employee who works less than full time or only seasonally may also need to add several previous years of service to arrive at one year of full time service.

Having identified the most recent year of service, the employee must then determine the includible compensation that corresponds with that most recent year of service. Unfortunately, includible compensation is *not* the same as the income appearing on one's W-2 form and which is reported on one's income tax return. The term "compensation" refers to the combination of income and benefits received for services provided to the employer. Alternatively, includible compensation means the following:

- Elective deferrals
- Amounts contributed or deferred by the employer under a Section 125 cafeteria plan
- Amounts contributed or deferred, at the employee's election, under an eligible Section 457 nonqualified deferred compensation plan (state or local government or tax-exempt organization plan, discussed later in this chapter)
- Wages, salaries, and fees for personal services earned with the employer maintaining the employee's 403(b) account
- Income otherwise excluded under the foreign earned income exclusion
- The value of qualified transportation fringe benefits (including transit passes, certain parking, and transportation in a commuter highway vehicle between the employee's home and work)

Not included in "includible compensation" are the following:

- The employer's contributions to the employee's 403(b) account
- Compensation earned while the employer was not an eligible employer
- The employer's contributions to a qualified plan that are on the employee's behalf and are excludable from income
- The cost of incidental life insurance as determined by reference to the IRS table for Uniform One-Year Term Premiums for $1,000 Life Insurance Protection

An employee may use worksheets developed by the IRS to calculate his or her includible compensation for his or her most recent year of service. (See Figure 6.1)

IRS Worksheet 6.1 Includible Compensation for Your Most Recent Year of Service*

Note. *Use this worksheet to figure includible compensation for your most recent year of service.*

1. Enter your includible wages from the employer maintaining your 403(b) account for your most recent year of service . . . . 1._____

2. Enter elective deferrals for your most recent year of service . . . . 2._____

3. Enter amounts contributed or deferred by your employer under a cafeteria plan for your most recent year of service . . . . 3._____

4. Enter amounts contributed or deferred by your employer to your 457 account (a nonqualified plan of a state or local government or of a tax-exempt organization) for your most recent year of service . . 4._____

5. Enter the value of qualified transportation fringe benefits you received from your employer for your most recent year of service . . . . 5._____

6. Enter your foreign earned income exclusion for your most recent year of service . . . . 6._____

7. Add lines 1, 2, 3, 4, 5, and 6 . . . . 7._____

8. Enter the cost of incidental life insurance that is part of your annuity contract for your most recent year of service . . . . 8._____

9. Enter compensation that was both:
   • Earned during your most recent year of service, and
   • Earned while your employer was not qualified to maintain a 403(b) plan . . . . 9._____

10. Add lines 8 and 9 . . . . 10._____

11. Subtract line 10 from line 7. This is your includible compensation for your most recent year of service . . .11._____

* *Use estimated amounts if figuring includible compensation before the end of the year.*

Finally, an employer may make nonelective contributions for an employee for up to five years after the employee retires, based on the employee's includible compensation for the last year of service before retirement.

Limitation on Elective Deferrals

As indicated previously, the second component of MAC is the limit on elective deferrals (the amount that may be contributed to an employee's 403(b) account through a salary reduction agreement). Therefore, the limit on elective deferrals applies to amounts contributed to:

- 401(k) plans, to the extent excluded from income
- Section 501(c)(18) plans, to the extent excluded from income
- SIMPLE plans
- Simplified employee pension (SEP) plans
- All 403(b) plans

For 2005, the general limit on annual elective deferrals to a 403(b) account is $14,000. A special "catch-up" rule applies to employees of public school systems, hospitals, home health service agencies, health and welfare service agencies, churches, or conventions or associations of churches (or associated organizations) who have at least 15 years of service. An employee qualifying for this 15-year rule may have annual elective deferrals of as much as $17,000 (for 2005). An employee's "years of service" are the total number of years he or she has worked for the employer maintaining his or her 403(b) account as of the end of the year.

Here is an example to illustrate how the limitation on elective deferrals works. Let us assume that Frank has already calculated his limit on annual additions to be $42,000 (for 2005) and now needs to determine his limit on elective deferrals before being able to compute his maximum amount contributable (MAC). Assume that Frank has been employed with his current employer for less than 15 years and, as a result, does *not* qualify under the special 15-year rule for an increase in his elective deferrals. Therefore, his limit on elective deferrals for 2005 is $14,000. Further assume that Frank's employer does not make either nonelective contributions or after-tax contributions to Frank's 403(b) account. Because elective deferrals are the only contributions made to Frank's account, the maximum amount that may be contributed to a 403(b) account on Frank's behalf in 2005 is $14,000, the lesser of the elective deferral on annual additions ($42,000) limit.

Alternative Limit Option for Ministers and Church Employees

For the most part, self-employed ministers and church employees participating in 403(b) plans are subject to the same rules as other 403(b) plan participants. Accordingly, the MAC of such a person is the lesser of his or her limit on annual additions or his or her limit on elective deferrals. As discussed earlier in this chapter, the limit on annual additions is ordinarily the lesser of $42,000 (in 2005) or the minister's or church employee's includible compensation for his or her most recent year of service.

However, church employees may elect an alternative limit and method of calculating their includible compensation for the most recent year of service. A church employee is anyone who is an employee of a church or a convention or association of churches, including an employee of a tax-exempt organization controlled by or associated with a convention or association of churches. Accordingly, such an employee may elect an alternative limit on annual additions of $10,000 per year, subject to a lifetime limit of $40,000.

In calculating includible compensation for the most recent year of service, foreign missionaries and self-employed ministers do so in a different way than do other 403(b) plan participants. For example, a foreign missionary does not include in his or her compensation the contributions to his or her 403(b) account made by the church during the year. Contributions to the 403(b) account of a foreign missionary are not considered to exceed the limit of annual additions if the contributions are not more than the greater of $3,000 or 100 percent of his or her includible compensation. A foreign missionary includes a layperson or a duly ordained, commissioned, or licensed minister of a church who is an employee of a church or convention or association of churches and who performs services for the church outside of the U.S.

A self-employed minister is considered to be an employee of a tax-exempt organization that is a qualified employer. His or her includible compensation is his or her net earnings from his or her ministry minus the contributions made to the retirement plan on his or her behalf and the deduction for one-half of the self-employment tax.

Catch-Up Contributions

For employees who will be age 50 or older by the end of the year, they may make additional catch-up contributions (other than after-tax contributions), as discussed earlier in this chapter. In order to qualify for these additional catch-up contributions, such employees must have already made the maximum elective deferrals permissible for the plan year. The maximum amount of catch-up contributions is the lesser of $4,000 (in 2005) or the employee's includible compensation minus his or her elective deferrals for the year. In determining the maximum allowable catch-up contribution for an employee, the employee must combine all catch-up contributions made by his or her employer on the employee's behalf to (1) qualified retirement plans; (2) 403(b) plans; (3) SEP plans; and (4) SIMPLE plans. Catch-up contributions have no effect on an employee's MAC. Therefore, an employee can have contributions made on his or her behalf equal to his or her MAC *plus* allowable catch-up contributions.

Excess Contributions

Contributions to a 403(b) that are greater than an employee's MAC are considered to be "excess contributions." Such contributions may result in income tax, additional taxes, and penalties. In order to avoid these potential taxes and penalties, it is therefore important for an employee to monitor his or her MAC as the year progresses. At the beginning of the subsequent year, an employee should recalculate his or her MAC based on the actual compensation received during the prior year and the actual contributions made for that year to determine if excess contributions have been made for the prior year. Once it has been determined that excess contributions have indeed been made, it must then be determined whether they are excess annual additions or excess elective deferrals.

In a year in which an employee's contributions are more than his or her limit on annual additions, the excess amount is included in his or her income. Any portion of the excess due to elective deferrals may be distributed if the excess contributions were made for any of several reasons, including: (1) a reasonable error in determining the amount of elective deferrals that could be made under the limit on annual additions; or (2) a reasonable error in projecting the amount of an employee's compensation.

A 403(b) account investing in mutual funds that exceeds the limit on annual additions, may be subject to a nondeductible 6 percent excise tax on the excess contributions. These contributions may be corrected by contributing less than the applicable limit in later years or by making permissible distributions. A permissible distribution may be made upon the occurrence of one of the following events:

- The employee reaches age 59 1/2
- The employee's employment is severed
- The employee dies
- The employee becomes disabled
- The employee suffers financial hardship because of making salary reduction contributions

If the excess contributions are the result of an excess over the limit on elective deferrals (rather than an excess over the limit on annual additions), the 403(b) plan document may permit distribution of such deferrals. A corrective distribution may be made only if the employee or employer designates the distribution as an excess deferral (to the extent there are excess deferrals for the year) and the corrective distribution is made after the date on which the excess deferral was made. Such corrective distributions may be made up to April 15 of the subsequent year and are includible in the employee's income for the year in which the excess deferral was made. Income on the excess deferral distributed is then taxable in the year received.

Distributions and Rollovers From 403(b) Accounts

As discussed in the previous section on Excess Contributions, a distribution may not be made from a 403(b) account until the employee (1) reaches age 59 1/2; (2) leaves the employ of the employer; (3) dies; (4) becomes disabled; or (5) in the case of salary reduction contributions, incurs financial hardship. Such distributions are fully taxable to the employee as ordinary income. The rules surrounding such distributions are generally the same as those applicable to distributions from other retirement plans.

Minimum distributions of a participant's account must be made by April 1 of the calendar year following the later of the calendar year in which the employee becomes age 70 1/2 or the calendar year in which he or she retires. Failure to take a required minimum distribution may result in a 50 percent excise tax on the difference between the required minimum distribution and the amount actually distributed.

From an income taxation standpoint, a distribution from a 403(b) plan does not qualify as a lump-sum distribution subject to the special 10-year averaging treatment.

Transfer of all or part of an employee's interest in his or her 403(b) account to another 403(b) account is a tax-free transfer, known as a "90-24 transfer." One requirement is that the transferred interest must be subject to the same or stricter distribution restrictions. In addition, an employee may make a direct trustee-to-trustee transfer from his or her governmental 403(b) account to a defined benefit governmental plan for the purpose of purchasing service credits.

Finally, an employee may roll over tax free all of or any part of a distribution from a 403(b) plan to a traditional IRA or an eligible retirement plan. As is generally true with such rollovers, they must be completed by the 60th day following the day on which the employee receives the distribution. The IRS may waive this 60-day rollover period if the distribution was made because of a genuine employee hardship (e.g., casualty, disaster, or other events beyond the reasonable control of the employee). An employee seeking such a hardship exception must apply to the IRS for such a waiver and pay a user fee with the application. In deciding whether to grant the exception, the IRS will consider whether errors were made by the financial institution involved; whether the employee could not complete the rollover because of death, disability, hospitalization, incarceration, restrictions imposed by a foreign country or postal error; whether the employee cashed the distribution check and used the proceeds; and how much time has elapsed since the date of distribution.

Rollovers to and from 403(b) plans and eligible retirement plans (i.e., IRAs, qualified retirement plans, 403(b) plans, and government eligible 457 plans, discussed next) may be made tax free. However, an employee may not rollover tax free a required minimum distribution, substantially equal payments over the employee's life or life expectancy or over the joint lives or life expectancies of the employee's beneficiary and the employee, substantially equal payments for a period of 10 years or more, and corrective distributions of excess contributions or excess deferrals nor the income allocable to such excesses, or excess annual additions and the related gains.

So-called "direct rollovers" (trustee-to-trustee transfers) are *not* subject to the 20 percent required withholding tax as are distributions made to the employee. Where a distribution is received by the employee, the employee has the option of rolling over the 80 percent of the distribution actually received or replacing the 20 percent that was withheld with other funds (within the 60-day period) in order to make a 100 percent rollover.

Retirement Savings Contributions Credit (Saver's Credit)

Certain lower income eligible participants may claim a nonrefundable tax credit through 2006 for their contributions to certain specified elective deferral plans or IRAs. The credit amount, limited to a maximum of $1,000, is calculated based on the participant's "applicable percentage," determined by filing status and adjusted gross income, times the total qualified retirement savings contributions (not to exceed $2,000) in the tax year to certain specified retirement plans. Eligible contributions are those made to either a traditional or Roth IRA, and salary reduction contributions to a 401(k) plan (including a SIMPLE 401(k) plan), a 403(b) annuity, a 457 plan, a SIMPLE IRA plan, or a SARSEP. To be eligible for the credit, a participant must be at least 18 years of age at the close of the tax year, must *not* be claimed as a dependent by someone else, and must *not* be a student as defined in IRC Section 151(c)(4). The maximum applicable percentage is 50 percent and is completely phased out when AGI exceeds $50,000 for joint return filers, $37,500 for head of household filers, and $25,000 for single and married filing separately filers.

GOVERNMENTAL AND TAX-EXEMPT EMPLOYER DEFERRED COMPENSATION (SECTION 457) PLANS

Non-qualified plans of deferred compensation described in IRC Section 457 are available for certain state and local governments, governmental agencies or instrumentalities of a state or local government (such as a school district or sewage authority), and non-governmental, non-church controlled entities tax exempt under IRC Section 501. Accordingly, 457 plans may be further categorized as an eligible plan under IRC Section 457(b), which permit employees of sponsoring organizations to defer income taxation on retirement savings into future years, and ineligible plans under IRC Section 457(f). An eligible 457 plan is one that imposes limits on the amounts deferred while an ineligible 457 plan is one that permits greater deferral usually targeted at top executives.

Reasons to Adopt a 457 Plan

One primary reason to adopt a 457 plan is that there are *no* specific coverage requirements. In the case of a *governmental* organization, the plan may be made available to all employees, to a specific group of employees, or even to a single employee. Alternatively, *private non-governmental* tax-exempt organizations are required to comply with ERISA, including its eligibility rules, unless these plans are structured to take advantage of certain specific ERISA exemptions (i.e., unfunded plans covering only top management). Private tax-exempt plans may be "financed" with insurance or annuities, whereas governmental organization plans are required to be "funded" by placing plan assets in trusts or custodial accounts.

Since the entities that may establish a 457 plan are not subject to income taxation, tax-deductibility is not an issue.

Contribution Limitations

The limit on the amount that may be deferred each year by an eligible plan is the *lesser of*: (1) 100 percent of the participant's compensation (i.e., gross compensation before salary reductions), or (2) $14,000 (for 2005). When calculating the limit, all Section 457 plans in which an employee participates must be included. One of the principal advantages of 457 plans is that salary reduction contributions to such plans do *not* affect the amount that can be contributed to other types of salary reduction plans (e.g., 403(b) plans or 401(k) plans).

Catch-Up Contributions

A complicating factor with regard to 457 plans is that participants in a *governmental employer* plan aged 50 or over may be able to make *additional* salary reduction contributions. This is *not* the case with private tax-exempt organization 457 plans. Participants in governmental employer plans aged 50 or over may contribute catch-up contributions of $4,000 (in 2005) provided the amount does not exceed the excess of the participant's compensation over all of their regular elective deferrals. For example, if a participant over age 50 in 2005 has total compensation of $15,000 and makes regular salary reductions of $14,000, he or she may not contribute more than an additional $1,000 in catch-up contributions.

The IRC Section 415 limitation on annual additions ($42,000 or 100 percent of compensation) has no effect on the ability of a participant to make 50-or-over catch-up contributions. Therefore, if a participant age 50 or over qualifies for $42,000 of regular annual additions (in 2005) to the employer's defined contribution plans, he or she may still make a $4,000 catch-up contribution (in 2005). However, this general catch-up contribution rule does not apply to a participant who qualifies under an earlier 3-year catch-up rule. This earlier catch-up rule applies to the three years directly prior to the plan's normal retirement age. During this 3-year period, a participant may defer the lesser of (1) double the regular dollar limit or (2) the sum of the regular dollar limit plus the amount by which the limit in prior years exceeded the amount actually deferred by the participant in those years. This 3-year catch-up rule applies to both governmental employer plans and to private tax-exempt organization 457 plans—not just to governmental employer plans.

Distributions From a 457 Plan

A participant in a 457 plan may not take a distribution before the year in which the participant reaches age 70 1/2, leaves the employ of the employer, or has an "unforeseen emergency" (severe financial hardship resulting from a sudden and unexpected illness or accident of the participant or a dependent, a casualty loss to his or her property, or other similar extraordinary and unforeseeable circumstances beyond the control of the participant). However, a participant in a tax-exempt nongovernmental organization's plan may take an involuntary distribution up to $5,000 from his or her account if there has been no deferral by him or her for the last two years, and no prior distributions have been taken.

Moreover, a participant may defer the start of distributions (if the amounts are otherwise available and before the beginning of distributions) by making a one-time election to do so.

Required minimum distributions must be taken under the same rules applicable to qualified plans.

Participants in governmental 457 plans report distributions as income when received. Participants in non-governmental, tax-exempt plans report distributions as income either when received or when they are made available (meaning at the time there is no longer a substantial risk of forfeiture). Just as with 403(b) plans, distributions from 457 plans do *not* qualify for the favorable lump sum 10-year averaging treatment available to qualified plans.

Comparison of Employer-Sponsored Tax-Advantaged Plans

Type of Plan	Who Can Establish	How Established	Eligible Employee	Contribution Limit	Catch-Up Contributions	Deduction Limit	Treatment of Distributions	Rollovers	Advantages	Disadvantages
Simplified Employee Pension (SEP)	Typically small employers, usually 10 employees or less	1. execute formal written agreement 2. provide employees with information about plan 3. must establish a SEP-IRA for each eligible employee	At least Age 21; worked for employer 3 of last 5 years; at least $450 in compensation from employer	Only employer contributions. Lesser of 25 percent of employee's compensation or $42,000 (for 2005). Compensation does not include employer's contributions to SEP; maximum compensation of $210,000 in 2005	No	Same as contribution limit; special computation for self-employed participant	Can make withdrawals at any time but subject to income tax & 10 percent additional tax if before age 59 1/2.; subject to required minimum distribution rules	Contributions and earnings can be rolled over tax-free to other IRAs and retirement plans.	1. easier and less expensive to install & administer 2. can create retroactively 3. no required contribution by employer 4. employee bears investment risk	1. will not guarantee adequate retirement benefit 2. annual contributions less than qualified plan 3. no 10-year averaging
Salary Reduction Simplified Employee Pension (SARSEP)	Must have been established prior to 1997.	Employer can continue to maintain plan if: 50% or more of employees make elective deferrals; 25 or fewer employees eligible to participate at any time in prior year; HCEs must meet SARSEP ADP test.	Participants in plans established prior to 1997 can continue to make elective deferrals	Employees can make elective deferrals; lesser of 25% of employee's compensation or $14,000 (in 2005)	Yes. $4,000 for 2005 not subject to elective deferral limit	Same as contribution limit	Same rules as traditional IRAs.	OK.	1. limits on elective deferrals greater than those for SIMPLE IRAs and SIMPLE 401(k) plans	1. Must meet SARSEP ADP test for HCEs.

(continued on next page)

(continued from previous page)

Type of Plan	Who Can Establish	How Established	Eligible Employee	Contribution Limit	Catch-Up Contributions	Deduction Limit	Treatment of Distributions	Rollovers	Advantages	Disadvantages
Savings Incentive Match Plan for Employees (SIMPLE)	100 or fewer employees who received $5,000 or more in compensation from employer in prior 2 yrs.	Calendar-year basis only; IRAs or 401(k) options; must be only retirement plan except union plan.	Must include self-employed & leased employees; can exclude union & non-resident aliens with no U.S. source income from employer	Employees can make elective deferrals; employer can make matching or nonelective contributions; up to $10,000 (in 2005) as % of comp. or as flat amount; employer must match up to 3% of comp unless elects less than 3%--then % must be at least 1%; or employer can make nonelective contributions of 2%	Yes. $2,000 for 2005	Same as contribution limit	Same as contribution limit	OK from one SIMPLE-IRA to another; if from SIMPLE-IRA to non-SIMPLE-IRA, must have 2 yrs. participation in SIMPLE-IRA plan to be tax-free; 25% additional tax, rather than 10%, if fail to wait 2 yrs.	1. easier and less expensive to install & administer 2. can fund plan through salary reductions 3. limits may be higher than Keogh or SEP 4. employee bears investment risk	1. will not guarantee adequate retirement benefit 2. contributions may be smaller than qualified plan 3. No 10-yr averaging 4. cannot also have qualified plan, SEP, 403(a) annuity, 403(b) plan, or 457 plan
Tax-Sheltered Annuity (403(b)) Plan	Public schools; tax-exempt organizations; certain ministers	Only the employer can do so; self-employed minister cannot do so—only the organization with which he or she is associated can do so.	Employee of 501(c)(3) org, public school system;cooperative hospital service org, or USUHS, and ministers employed by 501(c)(3) org, self-employed & perform services for qualified employer, or employed by non-501(c)(3) org & functions as minister with employer.	Maximum amount contributable (MAC)-lesser of limit on annual additions or limit on elective deferrals; annual additions limit- lesser of $42,000 (in 2005) or 100% of includible compensation for most recent year of service; elective deferral limit-$14,000 (in 2005) unless have 15 yrs. of service.-$17,000 (in 2005). Alternative limit for ministers & church employees.	Yes. $4,000 for 2005	Same as contribution limit.	No distribution until employee reaches age 59 1/2, leaves employ of employer, dies, becomes disabled, or incurs financial hardship (salary reduction contributions only); generally same rules as other retirement plans	Can make 90-24 transfer to another 403(b) account; trustee-to-trustee transfer to a defined benefit govt plan to purchase service credits; can roll to traditional IRA or eligible retirement plan	1. tax deferral for employees 2. employer can fund thru employee salary reductions 3. employer can also make contributions, if desired 4. in-service withdrawals as in profit-sharing plans 5. employee bears investment risk.	1.will not guarantee adequate retirement benefit 2. salary reductions subject to elective deferral limit 3. subject to non-discrimination tests 4. employees have choice of investments 5. no 10-yr. averaging
Governmental and Tax-Exempt Employer Deferred Compensation (Section 457) Plan	Certain state & local governments, governmental agencies or instrumentalities of a state or local govt (such as a school district or sewage authority); also non-governmental, non-church controlled entities tax exempt under IRC Section 501	Employer must adopt plan containing required provisions; forms must be furnished to employees to make salary reduction elections	Employees of eligible organizations.	Lesser of 100% of participant's compensation (gross before salary reductions) or $14,000 (in 2005). All 457 plans in which employee participates must be included.	Participants in govt plans may contribute up to $4,000 (in 2005) provided income is adequate; general rule not applicable to participant who qualifies for earlier 3-yr catch-up rule (3-yr rule applies to both govt & private tax-exempt orgs)	Employers not subject to income taxation	Cannot take distribution before year in which participant reaches age 70 1/2, leaves employer, or has "unforeseen emergency"; participant in tax-exempt non-govt org plan can take distribution up to $5,000 if no deferral for last 2 yrs, & no prior distribution taken; may defer start of distributions	Automatic rollover to IRA rule for distribution in excess of $1,000 and less than or equal to $5,000 unless participant elects to have distribution transferred to another eligible retirement plan or to take distribution in cash. Final safe harbor rules not yet issued by DOL.	1. no specific coverage requirements 2. govt entities can make available to any employee or employees 3. salary reduction contributions do not affect the amount that can be contributed to other types of salary reduction plans (403(b) or 401(k))	1. may not be funded but may be "financed" with insurance or annuities 2. Govt org plans required to be funded by placing plan assets in trusts or custodial accounts. 3. No 10-yr averaging

IMPORTANT CONCEPTS

Annual additions

Annual benefits

Common-law employee

Compensation

Contribution

Deduction

Earned income

Highly compensated employee

Leased employee

Net earnings from self-employment

Participant

Self-employed individual

Simplified Employee Pension (SEP)

Salary Reduction Simplified Employee Pension (SARSEP)

Distribution

Elective deferrals

Savings Incentive Match Plan for Employees (SIMPLE) IRA or 401(k)

Eligible employee

Tax-sheltered annuity (403(b)) plan

501(c)(3) organization

Maximum amount contributable (MAC)

Catch-up contributions

Excess contributions

Rollovers

Saver's credit

Section 457 plan

QUESTIONS FOR REVIEW

1. What items are included in annual additions?

2. What is meant by a common-law employee and what is the significance of the term with regard to retirement plans?

3. What items are included in an employee's compensation for retirement plan allocation purposes?

4. What items constitute earned income?

5. Who is considered a highly compensated employee for employee benefit purposes?

6. What is the significance of a leased employee for retirement plan purposes?

7. How are net earnings from self-employment determined?

8. For purposes of a SEP plan, who is an eligible employee and which employees are excludable from coverage?

9. What are two main reasons why a qualifying employer would adopt a SEP plan?

10. What are the three requirements for establishing a SEP plan?

11. What are the contribution limitations for a SEP-IRA plan?

12. To what extent is a participant in a SEP-IRA plan vested in the contributions to his or her account?

13. How does a self-employed individual who contributes to his or her own SEP-IRA calculate the maximum deduction for his or her contributions?

14. What is the tax treatment of a loan to a SEP participant from his or her SEP-IRA?

15. How does a SEP differ from a SARSEP?

16. What is the SARSEP ADP test?

17. In what ways are SEP and SIMPLE plans similar and in what ways do they differ?

18. What are the contribution limits for a SIMPLE IRA plan and how much additional may participants age 50 or over contribute to such a plan

19. What types of entities may establish a tax-sheltered annuity (403(b)) plan?

20. If a qualified employer has a small budget to provide retirement benefits beyond basic salary and other benefits, what is a principal advantage of adopting a 403(b) plan for its employees?

21. In a 403(b) plan, how is an employee's MAC determined?

22. Which items make up an employee's includible compensation for purposes of determining the total annual additions to his or her 403(b) account?

23. What is the general limit on elective deferrals to a 403(b) account in 2005? What is the effect on this limit if an employee of a public school system, hospital, home health service agency, health and welfare service agency, church, or convention or association of churches has at least 15 years of service?

24. What is the treatment of excess contributions (greater than an employee's MAC) to a 403(b) account?

25. What types of entities may establish a Section 457 plan?

26. What coverage requirements are applicable to a governmental organization establishing a Section 457 plan?

27. What is the contribution limit for a Section 457 plan?

28. When can a participant take a distribution from a Section 457 plan?

SUGGESTIONS FOR ADDITIONAL READING

IRS Publication 571, *Tax-Sheltered Annuity Plans (403(b) Plans)*

IRS Publication 590, *Individual Retirement Arrangements (IRAs)*

IRS Publication 560, *Retirement Plans for Small Business (SEP, SIMPLE, and Qualified Plans)*

IRS Publication 4406, *403(b) and 457 Retirement Plans*

IRS Publication 575, *Pension and Annuity Income*

IRS Publication 525, *Taxable and Nontaxable Income*

The Tools & Techniques of Employee Benefit and Retirement Planning, 9th edition, Stephan R. Leimberg and John J. McFadden, The National Underwriter Company, 2005.

CHAPTER SEVEN

Qualified Plans: Rules for Qualification

• • •

In order to provide effective client services, a financial planner needs to understand how retirement plans are structured, the benefits they can provide to clients, and the rules governing their tax qualification. Internal Revenue Code Section 401(a) specifies the numerous requirements for qualification as a retirement plan. Because this topic is so highly complex, we will provide in this chapter only a summary of the more important requirements for retirement plan qualification with which a financial planner should be familiar.

Upon completing this chapter, you should be able to:

- Describe the minimum participation standards of a qualified retirement plan
- Distinguish between the ratio percentage test and the average benefit test with regard to plan coverage and participation
- Apply the safe harbor test to determine if a retirement plan meets the nondiscriminatory classification requirement under the average benefit test
- Describe the 50/40 test that must be met by defined benefit plans
- Define the term "highly compensated employee" as described in IRC Section 414(q)
- Identify which plan participants are included in the "top-paid group" of employees
- Describe the general minimum vesting standards applicable to qualified retirement plans and the standards that apply to employer matching contributions and top-heavy plans
- Discuss the treatment of plan forfeitures by qualified retirement plans
- Identify the general required minimum distribution rules applicable to qualified retirement plans

- Define the term *top-heavy plan*
- Distinguish between a highly compensated employee and a key employee as those terms are used in connection with qualified retirement plans
- Explain the rules applicable to assignment or alienation of qualified retirement plan accrued benefits
- Compare the excess method to the offset method used by defined benefit plans to integrate plan benefit formulas with Social Security benefits
- Describe the limit to which a defined benefit plan's integration level is subject
- Explain the limits imposed by the "maximum offset allowance" in integrating a defined benefit plan's benefit formula with Social Security benefits
- Discuss the method used by a defined contribution plan in integrating its plan benefits formula with Social Security benefits
- Identify the benefit and contribution limitations for qualified retirement plans
- Describe the elective deferral limitations

EXCLUSIVE BENEFIT RULE

One of the basic requirements for tax-qualification of a retirement plan is that it be established for the exclusive benefit of the employer's employees or their beneficiaries (not just corporate executives and business owners). In fact, none of the plan's trust corpus or income may be used for, or diverted to, purposes other than for the exclusive benefit of employees or their beneficiaries.

MINIMUM PARTICIPATION STANDARDS

Another set of requirements that qualified retirement plans must meet is the minimum participation standards of IRC Section 410. These include the "age and service" requirements that the plan establishes as conditions of participation in the plan and the "overall coverage" and "participation" requirements. Section 410 does not permit a plan to require an employee to complete a period of service with the employer (or employers) maintaining the plan extending beyond the *later of*: (1) the date on which the employee attains age 21 or (2) the date on which the employee completes one year of service. Certain plans are subject to special rules. For example, a plan that provides 100 percent vesting (discussed later in this chapter), after meeting a requirement of not more than two years of service, is considered to satisfy the minimum participation standards. Also, a plan maintained exclusively for employees of a tax-exempt educational institution, that provides 100 percent vesting after meeting a requirement of at least one year of service, may substitute age 26 for age 21 in the foregoing requirements.

A qualified plan must provide that any employee who has satisfied the minimum age and service requirements specified in the previous paragraph, and who is otherwise entitled to participate in the plan, must commence participation in the plan no later than the *earlier of*: (1) the first day of the first plan year beginning after the date on which such employee satisfied such requirements, or (2) the date 6 months after the date on which the employee satisfied such requirements.

A "year of service" means a 12-month period during which the employee has not less than 1,000 hours of service.

In addition to the age and service requirement, a qualified retirement plan must meet one of three alternative overall coverage and participation tests under IRC Section 410(b):

- **Ratio percentage test**—the plan must benefit at least 70 percent of the nonhighly compensated employees *or* the plan must benefit a percentage of nonhighly compensated employees that is at least 70 percent of the percentage of highly compensated employees benefiting under the plan.

- **Average benefit test**—the plan must benefit a nondiscriminatory classification of employees and the average benefit, as a percentage of compensation, for all nonhighly compensated employees of the employer must be at least 70 percent of the average benefit for highly compensated employees. Note that the average benefit test is a two-part test. Not only must the plan meet the nondiscriminatory classification part of the test but it must also meet the 70 percent average benefit test.

IRC Section 410(b) explains what is meant by a nondiscriminatory classification of employees. Plans that meet a "safe harbor" test in a table (see Table 7.1) included in the related regulations are statutorily deemed to meet the nondiscriminatory classification requirement.

Table 7.1 (Duplicated from Reg. §1.410(b)-4(c)(4)(iv))

Nonhighly compensated employee concentration percentage	Safe harbor percentage	Unsafe harbor percentage	Nonhighly compensated employee concentration percentage	Safe harbor percentage	Unsafe harbor percentage
0-60	50.00	40.00	80	35.00	25.00
61	49.25	39.25	81	34.25	24.25
62	48.50	38.50	82	33.50	23.50
63	47.75	37.75	83	32.75	22.75
64	47.00	37.00	84	32.00	22.00
65	46.25	36.25	85	31.25	21.25
66	45.50	35.50	86	30.50	20.50
67	44.75	34.75	87	29.75	20.00
68	44.00	34.00	88	29.00	20.00
69	43.25	33.25	89	28.25	20.00
70	42.50	32.50	90	27.50	20.00
71	41.75	31.75	91	26.75	20.00
72	41.00	31.00	92	26.00	20.00
73	40.25	30.25	93	25.25	20.00
74	39.50	29.50	94	24.50	20.00
75	38.75	28.75	95	23.75	20.00
76	38.00	28.00	96	23.00	20.00
77	37.25	27.25	97	22.25	20.00
78	36.50	26.50	98	21.50	20.00
79	35.75	25.75	99	20.75	20.00

In the foregoing table, the nonhighly compensated employee concentration percentage is the percentage of all the employees who are nonhighly compensated employees. Employees who are excludable employees for purposes of the average benefit test are not taken into account. The safe harbor percentage of an employer is 50 percent, reduced by 3/4 of a percentage point for each whole percentage point by which the nonhighly compensated employee concentration percentage exceeds 60 percent. The unsafe harbor percentage of an employer is 40 percent, reduced by 3/4 of a percentage point for each whole percentage point by which the nonhighly compensated employee concentration percentage exceeds 60 percent. However, as the table illustrates, in no case is the unsafe harbor percentage less than 20 percent.

Here is an example using Table 7.1.

> **Example:** Assume Crays Co. has 800 salaried office employees, including 150 highly compensated employees, and 10,200 production employees, of whom 450 are highly compensated. Crays Co. wants to have a qualified plan only for the office employees. However, the office plan does not meet the ratio percentage test since its ratio percentage is 25 percent [(650/10,400)/(150/600)]. Accordingly, we now need to determine whether the plan meets the average benefit test. The plan's nonhighly compensated concentration percentage is 10,400/11,000 or 94.55% (rounded down to 94%). Looking in the table under 94 percent nonhighly compensated employee concentration percentage, we see that the safe harbor percentage is 24.50. Since the plan has an actual ratio percentage of 25 percent, it is deemed to meet the nondiscriminatory classification test. However, before it can be considered to have met the average benefit test, the plan's average benefit, as a percentage of compensation, for all nonhighly compensated employees must be at least 70 percent of that for highly compensated employees (the second part of the average benefit test). Here, that percentage is 94.55 percent, so it is acceptable.

In the situation where a plan's ratio percentage falls between the safe and unsafe harbor percentages in Table 7.1, the IRS will determine, through an examination of the plan specifics, whether the classification is discriminatory. When the ratio percentage is less than the unsafe harbor percentage, the plan is presumed to be discriminatory.

In the previous example, if any of the production employees had been included in a collective bargaining unit (union), they could be excluded from the plan (assuming there was good faith bargaining on retirement benefits). Moreover, employers that are related through common ownership are treated as one employer. If Crays Co., in our example, had bona fide "separate lines of business," the coverage test could have been applied separately to each line of business.

Just to make an already complex set of rules even more complex, a *defined benefit plan* (discussed in chapter 13) must meet an additional coverage requirement known as the 50/40 test in order to be qualified. On each day of the plan year, the defined benefit plan must cover the *lesser of*: (1) 50 employees or (2) the *greater of*: (a) 40 percent or more of all employees, or (b) two employees (or, if there is only one employee, that employee).

OTHER NONDISCRIMINATION REQUIREMENTS

Contributions to or benefits from a qualified plan must *not* discriminate in favor of "highly compensated employees," as that term is defined in IRC Section 414(q). Section 414(q) defines a "highly compensated employee" as any employee who (1) was a 5-percent owner (defined in IRC Section 416(i)(1)) at any time during the year or the preceding year, or (2) for the preceding year, had compensation from the employer in excess of $95,000 (in 2005), and, if the employer so elects, was in the "top-paid group" of employees for such preceding year. An employee is in the top-paid group of employees for any year if such employee is in the group consisting of the top 20 percent of the employees when ranked on the basis of "compensation" paid during such year. The following employees may be excluded in determining the top-paid group:

- Employees with less than six months of service
- Employees who normally work less than 17 1/2 hours per week
- Seasonal employees who normally work during not more than six months in any year
- Employees under the age of 21
- Except as provided by regulations, union employees
- Nonresident aliens with no U.S. earned income

Compensation, as defined in IRC Section 415(c)(3), is the compensation of the participant from the employer for the year and includes elective deferrals and other amounts contributed or deferred by the employer at the election of the employee, which is not includable in the gross income of the employee. As discussed previously, if there is evidence that retirement benefits were the subject of good faith bargaining between employee representatives and the employer (or employers), union employees covered by a collective bargaining agreement are excluded for this purpose. Also excluded are employees who are nonresident aliens and who receive no earned income from the employer which constitutes income from U.S. sources.

In classifying employees for retirement plan purposes, a classification is not considered discriminatory merely because it is limited to salaried or clerical employees. In addition, contributions or benefits of, or on behalf of, the employees under the plan are permitted to bear a uniform relationship to the compensation of such employees. For example, if an employee receives a benefit of 8 percent of his or her compensation, regardless of the amount of his or her compensation, such a benefit formula is not considered to discriminate against low-paid employees. Moreover, a plan is not considered discriminatory merely because the contributions or benefits of, or on behalf of, the employees under the plan favor highly compensated employees.

In testing for nondiscrimination, defined contribution plans (discussed later in this chapter) are normally tested under the "contributions" test but may be tested using the "benefits" test. This is known as "cross testing" of a plan. Defined benefit plans must meet a "general" test or a uniformity requirement and one of three safe harbors. These tests will be discussed in more detail in chapter 13. The defined benefit tests compare the rate at which benefits accrue for highly compensated employees to the rate benefits accrue for other employees.

VESTING REQUIREMENTS

A qualified plan must meet the requirements of IRC Section 411 relating to minimum vesting standards. Generally, this means that an employee's right to his or her normal retirement benefit is nonforfeitable upon the attainment of his or her normal retirement age. At all times, an employee's accrued benefit in his or her *own* contributions is nonforfeitable (100 percent vested). With regard to *employer* contributions, a plan must provide for either 5-year vesting (100 percent vesting after completing 5 years of service, otherwise known as "cliff vesting") or 3 to 7-year vesting (20 percent vesting with 3 years of service; 40 percent vesting with 4 years of service; 60 percent vesting with 5 years of service; 80 percent vesting with 6 years of service; and 100 percent vesting with 7 or more years of service, otherwise known as "graded vesting").

In counting years of service for purposes of determining an employee's vested rights, the plan may disregard, among other years of service, years of service before age 18, years of service during a period for which the employee elected not to contribute to a plan requiring employee contributions, years of service during any period for which the employer did not maintain the plan (or predecessor plan), or years of service during which there was a "break in service." A one-year break in service is a calendar year, plan year, or other 12-consecutive-month period designated by the plan during which a participant has not completed more than 500 hours of service. The significance of a one-year break in service is that the employer is *not* required to take into account years of service before the break in service until an employee has completed a year of service *after* his or her return to work. Also, if a participant has five consecutive one-year breaks in service, the employer is *not* required to take into account years of service *after* the 5-year period for purposes of determining the nonforfeitable percentage of his or her accrued benefit derived from employer contributions that accrued before the 5-year period.

Normal retirement age is defined in Section 411 as the time a plan participant attains normal retirement age under the plan, or the later of (1) the time a plan participant attains age 65, or (2) the 5th anniversary of the time a plan participant commenced participation in the plan.

Accelerated vesting rules apply to employer matching contributions, which are contributions made by an employer on account of employee contributions or elective deferrals or forfeitures allocated on the basis of employee contributions, matching contributions, or elective deferrals. With regard to these contributions, a plan must provide for either 3-year vesting (100 percent vesting after completing 3 years of service, otherwise known as "cliff vesting") or 2 to 6-year vesting (20 percent vesting with 2 years of service; 40 percent vesting with 3 years of service; 60 percent vesting with 4 years of service; 80 percent vesting with 5 years of service; and 100 percent vesting with 6 or more years of service, otherwise known as "graded vesting"). This same accelerated vesting schedule also applies to top-heavy plans, discussed later in this chapter.

FORFEITURES

In the situation where a plan participant terminates employment before becoming 100 percent vested, the employee may be entitled to some benefits, usually depending on the number of years the employee worked for the employer. For example, if at the time of termination, a participant's account balance in a defined contribution plan is $10,000 and he or she is 60 percent vested, his or her vested benefit is $6,000 (60 % x $10,000). The balance in the account that is not vested at the time of termination ($4,000 in this example) will be forfeited at the *earlier of*: (1) when the participant receives a distribution or (2) after the employee incurs five consecutive one-year breaks in service. Accordingly, forfeitures are benefits in which a plan participant did not vest (under the minimum vesting standards discussed in the previous section) prior to his or her death or termination of employment from his or her employer, and therefore are forfeited. Generally, each plan determines how it will allocate forfeitures to the remaining participants.

However, a defined benefit plan *must* use forfeitures to reduce future employer contributions and may *not* apply forfeitures to increase the benefits remaining participants would otherwise receive under the plan. Alternatively, defined contribution plans may provide that forfeitures may be used either to reduce contributions or to increase benefits provided under the plan.

REQUIRED MINIMUM DISTRIBUTIONS (RMDs)

A qualified plan must provide that the entire interest of each participant is to be distributed in accordance with the required distribution rules of IRC Section 401(a)(9). These rules will be discussed in detail in chapter 15, but generally they provide that a participant's entire interest in the plan must be distributed to him or her not later than his or her "required beginning date" or over the life of the participant or over the lives of the participant and a designated beneficiary (or over a period not extending beyond the life expectancy of the participant or the life expectancy of the participant and a designated beneficiary). A participant's required beginning date is April 1 of the calendar year following the *later of*: (1) the calendar year in which the participant attains age 70 1/2, or (2) the calendar year in which the participant retires. However, in the case of a 5-percent business owner, the required beginning date is April 1 of the calendar year following the calendar year in which the participant attains age 70 1/2 , *not* the calendar year in which he or she retires.

If a participant dies before his or her entire interest is distributed and his or her required distributions had already begun at the time of death, the remaining portion of his or her interest must be distributed at least as rapidly as under the method of distributions being used as of the date of death. Alternatively, if a participant dies before the distribution of his or her interest has begun, the entire interest of the participant must be distributed within 5 years after the participant's death. There is an exception to this 5-year rule in the situation in which benefits are payable over the life of a designated beneficiary (or over a period not extending beyond the life expectancy of such beneficiary), if such distributions begin not later than 1 year after the date of the participant's death. In addition, if the designated beneficiary is the *surviving spouse* of the participant, the date on which the distributions are required to begin is not earlier than the date on which the participant would have attained age 70 1/2. If the surviving spouse dies before the distributions to him or her have begun, he or she is treated the same as the participant (i.e., the entire interest must be distributed within 5 years of his or her death).

For purposes of the required minimum distribution rules, the life expectancy of a participant and the participant's spouse may be redetermined not more frequently than annually.

PLANS COVERING OWNER-EMPLOYEES AND TOP-HEAVY PLANS

If a plan provides contributions or benefits for employees some or all of whom are owner-employees, the plan must provide that contributions on behalf of any owner-employee may be made only with respect to the earned income of such owner-employee that is derived from the trade or business with respect to which such plan is established. For this purpose, an "owner-employee" is an employee who either owns the entire interest in an unincorporated trade or business or, in the case of a partnership, is a partner who owns more than 10 percent of either the capital interest or the profits interest in such partnership.

Special rules apply to so-called "top-heavy" plans. A top-heavy defined benefit plan is one in which, as of the determination date for a plan year, the present value of the cumulative accrued benefits under the plan for "key employees" exceeds 60 percent of the present value of the cumulative accrued benefits under the plan for all employees. A top-heavy defined contribution plan is one in which the aggregate of the accounts of key employees under the plan exceeds 60 percent of the aggregate of the accounts of all employees under the plan. The definition of a "key employee" is *not* the same as that of a "highly-compensated employee," discussed under Other Nondiscrimination Requirements earlier in this chapter. Instead, Section 416(i) defines a "key employee" as an employee who, at any time during the plan year, is one of the following:

- An officer of the employer having an annual compensation greater than $135,000 (in 2005)
- A 5-percent owner of the employer
- A 1-percent owner of the employer having an annual compensation from the employer of more than $150,000

A "top-heavy plan" or a plan which may become top-heavy must meet the requirements of IRC Section 416. Section 416 requires top-heavy plans to meet either 3-year, 100 percent vesting (cliff vesting) or 6-year graded vesting, both of which were described previously in this chapter. In addition, top-heavy plans must meet the minimum benefits or contribution requirements of Section 416. For defined benefit plans, the accrued benefit derived from employer contributions of each participant who is a non-key employee, when expressed as an annual retirement benefit, must not be less than the "applicable percentage" of the participant's average compensation for years in the "testing period." The applicable percentage is the *lesser of* (1) 2 percent multiplied by the number of years of service with the employer, or (2) 20 percent. A participant's testing period is the period of consecutive years (not exceeding five) during which the participant had the greatest aggregate compensation from the employer.

In the case of defined contribution plans, the employer contribution for a year for each participant who is a non-key employee in a top-heavy plan must be not less than 3 percent of such participant's compensation.

JOINT AND SURVIVOR ANNUITY AND PRERETIREMENT SURVIVOR ANNUITY REQUIREMENTS

IRC Section 401(a)(11) requires that a qualified plan provide the accrued benefit payable to a participant, who does not die before the annuity starting date, in the form of a qualified joint and survivor annuity (QJSA). If the participant dies before the annuity starting date and has a surviving spouse, a qualified preretirement survivor annuity (QPSA) must be provided to the participant's surviving spouse. It is permissible for a plan to provide that benefits will not be payable to the participant's surviving spouse unless the participant and his or her spouse had been married throughout the 1-year period ending on the earlier of the participant's annuity starting date or the date of the participant's death.

MERGER, CONSOLIDATION, OR TRANSFER OF ASSETS OR LIABILITIES TO ANOTHER PLAN

A qualified plan must provide that in the event of any merger or consolidation with, or transfer of assets or liabilities to, any other plan, each participant in the plan would, if the plan then terminated, receive a benefit immediately after the merger, consolidation, or transfer that is equal to or greater than the benefit he or she would have been entitled to receive immediately before the merger, consolidation, or transfer.

ASSIGNMENT AND ALIENATION

A qualified plan must provide that benefits provided under the plan may *not* be assigned or alienated. The major exception to this general rule is that a voluntary and revocable assignment of not more than 10 percent of any benefit payment is permitted. A loan to a participant is not treated as an assignment or alienation, provided the loan is secured by the participant's accrued nonforfeitable benefit. This prohibition against assignment or alienation of a participant's accrued benefit also does not apply in the case of a qualified domestic relations order (QDRO), as a result of a divorce settlement.

BENEFIT PAYMENT TRIGGER EVENTS

A qualified plan must provide that unless a participant elects otherwise, the payment of benefits to the participant under the plan must begin not later than the 60th day after the latest of the close of the plan year in which:

- The date on which the participant attains the earlier of age 65 or the normal retirement age specified under the plan;
- Occurs the 10th anniversary of the year in which the participant commenced participation in the plan; or
- The participant terminates his or her service with the employer.

If a plan provides for the payment of an early retirement benefit, the plan must provide that a participant who satisfies the service requirements for such early retirement benefits, but then separates from service before satisfying the age requirement for such early retirement benefit, is entitled to receive a benefit not less than the benefit to which he or she would have been entitled at the normal retirement age, actuarially reduced under applicable regulations.

INTEGRATION WITH SOCIAL SECURITY

A qualified plan must provide, in the case of a participant or beneficiary who is receiving benefits under the plan or a participant who is separated from the service and has nonforfeitable rights to benefits, that such benefits are *not* decreased by reason of any increase in Social Security benefit levels or any increase in the Social Security wage base. However, it *is* permissible to integrate a plan's benefit or contribution formula with Social Security. A plan that is integrated with Social Security normally provides greater contributions or benefits for higher paid employees whose compensation is greater than the Social Security taxable wage base. This is because lower paid employees receive a higher percentage of their total retirement benefit from Social Security than do higher paid employees. As a result, a disparity exists between lower paid employees and higher paid employees with regard to the contributions or benefits provided by the plan. The allowable size of this difference in contributions or benefits between those for highly compensated employees and those for nonhighly compensated employees is known as the "permitted disparity" and it cannot exceed certain statutory limits.

For defined benefit plans, there are two methods of integrating plan benefit formulas with Social Security—the "excess" method and the "offset" method. In the case of the excess method, the plan establishes a level of compensation known as the "integration level" and then provides benefits for compensation in excess of the integration level that are *greater than* those provided for compensation below the integration level. The integration level may be established at either a certain dollar amount or by use of a formula. However, a plan's integration level may not exceed an amount known as "covered compensation," determined from an IRS covered compensation table or, alternatively, from an IRS rounded covered compensation table. In addition to limiting the integration level, the Internal Revenue Code and related regulations limit the size of the disparity between the benefit as a percentage of compensation above and below the integration level. A plan's "base benefit percentage" is the percentage of compensation provided for compensation below the integration level, while the "excess benefit percentage" is the percentage of compensation above the integration level. Under IRC Section 401(l)(4)(A), the excess benefit percentage cannot exceed the base benefit percentage by more than the "maximum excess allowance." The maximum excess allowance, with respect to any single year of service with the employer taken into account under the plan is 3/4 of a percentage point (0.75 percent). With respect to total benefits, the maximum excess allowance is 3/4 of a percentage point multiplied by the participant's years of service (not to exceed 35 years) with the employer taken into account under the plan. In addition, the maximum excess allowance may never exceed the base benefit percentage.

Here are some examples to illustrate how the defined benefit plan *excess method* of Social Security integration works:

> **Example 1:** Franks Manufacturing Company's defined benefit plan has an integrated formula providing an annual benefit of 28 percent of final average annual compensation plus 24 percent of compensation above the plan's integration level. Jason Martin, born in 1940, is a participant in the plan who retires in 2005. Jason's final average compensation is $60,000. The integration level (using rounded covered compensation from Table 7.3) is $48,000. To determine Jason's annual retirement benefit, we make the following calculations:

> - 28% of final average compensation of $60,000, or $16,800.
> - 24% of $12,000 ($60,000 - $48,000) or $2,880
> - The total benefit is, therefore, $19,680 ($16,800 + $2,880)

> **Example 2:** Now assume that a defined benefit plan provides a benefit of 1.25% of compensation below the integration level for each year of service. Applying what we just learned about the maximum excess allowance, the excess benefit percentage cannot exceed 2 percent (1.25% + 0.75%). So for a participant with 35 years of service, if the plan provides a benefit of 28% of final average compensation below the integration level, it cannot provide more than 54.25% of compensation above the integration level (0.75% x 35 years = 26.25% + 28% = 54.25%). We then need to check for the other limitation (that the maximum excess allowance may be no greater than the base percentage). In the case of the Franks plan from Example 1, the maximum excess allowance (the difference between the excess and base percentage) cannot exceed 28%. Therefore, the maximum excess allowance is 56% (28% + 28%). Franks plan uses 28% as its base percentage and 24% as its excess percentage for a maximum excess allowance of 52% (which meets both tests just discussed).

A defined benefit plan that uses the *offset method* reduces the benefit attributable to employer contributions for each participant by an amount specified in the plan. Under the offset method of Social Security integration, a defined benefit plan's benefit formula is reduced either by a fixed amount or a formula amount (limited by the Code and regulations) that takes into account a participant's Social Security benefits. However, the offset method does not employ an integration level as does the excess method. Instead, the plan must provide that a participant's accrued benefit attributable to employer contributions may not be reduced (by reason of the offset) by more than the "maximum offset allowance," with benefits based on average annual compensation. The maximum offset allowance for any year of service with the employer taken into account under the plan is 3/4 of a percentage point and for total benefits, 3/4 of a percentage point multiplied by a participant's years of service (not to exceed 35 years). Moreover, in no event may the maximum offset allowance exceed 50 percent of the benefit which would have accrued without regard to the offset reduction. This means, for example, that a plan formula of 50 percent of final average compensation using an offset for Social Security must provide at least 25 percent of final average compensation to even the lowest paid participant.

Table 7.2   2005 Covered Compensation Table

Calendar Year of Birth	Calendar Year of Social Security Normal Retirement Age	2005 Covered Compensation	Calendar Year of Birth	Calendar Year of Social Security Normal Retirement Age	2005 Covered Compensation
1907	1972	$4,488	1940	2006	48,696
1908	1973	4,704	1941	2007	51,012
1909	1974	5,004	1942	2008	53,268
1910	1975	5,316	1943	2009	55,464
1911	1976	5,664	1944	2010	57,636
1912	1977	6,060	1945	2011	59,772
1913	1978	6,480	1946	2012	61,872
1914	1979	7,044	1947	2013	63,936
1915	1980	7,692	1948	2014	65,856
1916	1981	8,460	1949	2015	67,680
1917	1982	9,300	1950	2016	69,408
1918	1983	10,236	1951	2017	71,052
1919	1984	11,232	1952	2018	72,600
1920	1985	12,276	1953	2019	74,100
1921	1986	13,368	1954	2020	75,540
1922	1987	14,520	1955	2022	78,228
1923	1988	15,708	1956	2023	79,512
1924	1989	16,968	1957	2024	80,712
1925	1990	18,312	1958	2025	81,816
1926	1991	19,728	1959	2026	82,860
1927	1992	21,192	1960	2027	83,844
1928	1993	22,716	1961	2028	84,780
1929	1994	24,312	1962	2029	85,620
1930	1995	25,920	1963	2030	86,436
1931	1996	27,576	1964	2031	87,216
1932	1997	29,304	1965	2032	87,924
1933	1998	31,128	1966	2033	88,536
1934	1999	33,060	1967	2034	89,040
1935	2000	35,100	1968	2035	89,424
1936	2001	37,212	1969	2036	89,700
1937	2002	39,444	1970	2037	89,844
1938	2004	43,992	1971	2038	89,940
1939	2005	46,344	1972 and later	2039	90,000

Table 7.3 2005 Rounded Covered Compensation Table

Year of Birth1	Covered Compensation
1937	39,000
1938-1939	45,000
1940	48,000
1941	51,000
1942-1943	54,000
1944	57,000
1945	60,000
1946-1947	63,000
1948	66,000
1949-1950	69,000
1951-1952	72,000
1953-1954	75,000
1955	78,000
1956-1958	81,000
1959-1961	84,000
1962-1965	87,000
1966 and later	90,000

A defined contribution plan may use *only* the excess method in integrating for Social Security benefits. In such a plan, the excess contribution percentage may *not* exceed the base contribution percentage by more than the *lesser of*: (1) the base contribution percentage, or (2) 5.7 percentage points or the old-age insurance portion of the Social Security tax, as may be adjusted from time to time, whichever is greater. Accordingly, an integrated plan, for a plan year beginning in 2005, having an integration level of $90,000, and allocating employer contributions plus forfeitures at the rate of 15.7 percent of compensation above the integration level, would have to provide at least a 10 percent (15.7 - 5.7) allocation for compensation below the integration level. Defined contribution plans, however, go to great lengths to determine the actual optimum integration level to maximize benefits for higher paid employees and stay within the limitations imposed by law.

BENEFIT AND CONTRIBUTION LIMITATIONS

IRC Section 415 establishes the limits on benefits and contributions for qualified plans. For defined benefit plans, a participant's "annual benefit" may not exceed the *lesser of*:

- $170,000 (for 2005) or
- 100 percent of the participant's average compensation (not exceeding $210,000, for 2005) for the participant's three consecutive years of highest compensation.

This maximum annual benefit is actuarially reduced when retirement benefits are paid before age 62 and increased when paid after age 65. However, if certain requirements are met, a minimum annual benefit of $10,000 may be provided by the plan. The benefit limit and the compensation limit are reduced in the case of participants with less than 10 years of service with the employer. A participant's annual benefit is defined as a benefit payable annually in the form of a straight life annuity (with no ancillary benefits) under a plan to which employees do not contribute and under which no rollover contributions are made.

For defined contribution plans, "annual additions" (contributions and other additions) with respect to a participant may not exceed the *lesser of*:

- $42,000 (for 2005), or
- 100 percent of the participant's compensation (not exceeding $210,000, for 2005)

The term "annual additions" is the sum for any year of (1) employer contributions; (2) employee contributions; and (3) forfeitures. Participants who will be at least 50 years of age by the end of the tax year are also permitted to make "catch-up" contributions to most employer-sponsored defined contribution plans, including a 401(k) plan, a SEP, a SIMPLE plan, a 403(b) plan, and a 457 plan. The maximum amount of the catch-up contributions, however, depends on the type of plan established by the employer.

VOTING RIGHTS IN EMPLOYER SECURITIES

Defined contribution plans (other than profit-sharing plans) established by an employer whose stock is not readily tradable on an established securities market and, after acquiring securities of the employer, more than 10 percent of the total assets of the plan are securities of the employer, must meet the requirements of IRC Section 409(e). Section 409(e) requires that a plan investing in employer securities that are of a registration type provide voting rights to participants or beneficiaries in the plan. If the employer's securities are not registration-type securities, the participants or beneficiaries must be provided with voting rights with respect to approval or disapproval of any corporate merger or consolidation, recapitalization, reclassification, liquidation, dissolution, sale of substantially all assets of a trade or business, or such similar transaction. "Registration-type" securities is a class of securities required to be registered under section 12 of the Securities Exchange Act of 1934 or exempted from registration under section 12.

LIMITATIONS ON ELECTIVE DEFERRALS

A plan that permits elective deferrals must limit the amount of such annual deferrals to the limitation specified in IRC Section 402(g)(1)(A). This limitation is $14,000 in 2005 and $15,000 in 2006 or thereafter. Of course, as discussed previously, there is a greater limitation for plan participants age 50 or over by the end of the taxable year (known as "catch-up" contributions). Such participants (other than 401(k) plan participants) may contribute an additional $4,000 in 2005 and $5,000 in 2006 or thereafter. 401(k) plan participants may contribute an additional $2,000 in 2005 and $2,500 in 2006 or thereafter. The $5,000 and $2,500 amounts are adjusted annually for inflation beginning in 2007.

MINIMUM FUNDING STANDARDS

Qualified plans (other than profit-sharing plans) must make minimum annual contributions to avoid having to pay a penalty for underpayment. However, even a profit-sharing plan must make what the IRS refers to as "recurring and substantial" contributions, generally defined as contributions for every five years that the plan is in effect.

A defined benefit plan uses an "actuarial cost method" to determine the employer's annual plan contribution. The theory behind such method is to determine how much the employer should deposit each year so that each retiring employee's benefit is fully funded. The two general actuarial cost methods are the **projected benefit** and the **accrued benefit** methods. The *projected benefit method* uses the value of each participant's retirement benefit and the period of time until each employee retires to calculate the total cost of participant benefits. It then divides this total cost into equal annual contributions necessary to fund this cost. This may be calculated either on an individual participant basis or on an aggregate basis. Under the aggregate basis, the annual cost is determined as a percentage of the employer's total payroll, rather than by individual participant.

Under the *accrued benefit method*, the annual contributions are increased each year as each participant approaches retirement. It makes sense that these annual deposits would need to be increased, since each participant accrues another year of benefits each year he or she remains in the plan, while the amount of time remaining until his or her retirement is constantly decreasing. However, the accrued benefit method does not necessarily result in a higher overall plan cost than the projected benefit method since the number of plan participants usually varies significantly from one year to the next.

A defined benefit plan may also provide benefits for service with the employer occurring prior to the establishment of the plan. The costs of providing this additional benefit may be included in the annual deposits under either the projected benefit or accrued benefit methods or, alternatively, may be funded separately through creation of an **unfunded past service liability**, also known as a **supplemental liability**. Normally, this liability is retired through annual payments over a fixed period of time as long as 30 years in duration.

In order to use any actuarial cost method, the actuary must make certain reasonable actuarial assumptions. Some of the key assumptions that need to be made include:

- The assumed investment return on the plan's funds
- The future level of participants' salaries
- The number of participants that are projected to die before retirement and the corresponding benefits that will not have to be paid
- The funds needed at retirement to provide an annuity for each retiring participant in the amount specified in the plan
- The level of employee turnover resulting in either a reduced or no benefit paid to terminated participants

CONTRIBUTION DEDUCTION LIMITS

In the case of a defined benefit plan, an employer may claim an income tax deduction for contributions to the plan to the extent of the *greater of*: (1) an amount determined actuarially as provided in IRC Section 404(a), or (2) the amount required to satisfy the "minimum funding standards" of IRC Section 412.

Employers may deduct contributions to profit-sharing and stock bonus types of defined contribution plans to the extent of 25 percent of total aggregate compensation or payroll. Compensation includes elective deferrals to a qualified plan, 403(b) plan, 457 plan, SEP, SIMPLE, or a Section 125 flexible spending account plan. Also, in determining the total amount that the employer has contributed to a plan, elective deferrals are *not* required to be included. Here is an example to illustrate the deduction limitation for a plan that allows for employee elective deferrals.

> **Example:** Assume that Marshall Manufacturing's participating employees make elective deferrals to Marshall's 401(k) plan in the amount of $15,000. The total annual payroll cost for all plan participants in the current plan year is $150,000. Accordingly, Marshall may claim an income tax deduction for $37,500 (25 percent of $150,000). Note that the gross payroll cost does *not* need to be reduced by the $15,000 of elective deferrals before applying the 25 percent limitation. Also note that the $37,500 income tax deduction calculated above does *not* need to be reduced by the $15,000 of elective deferrals. Accordingly, Marshall may contribute and deduct an employer contribution of $37,500 plus the $15,000 of elective deferrals made by its employees for a total deduction of $52,500.

Some employers offer both defined benefit and defined contribution plans. In such event, the employer deduction limit is the *greater of*: (1) 25 percent of the compensation of all participants; or (2) the amount necessary to satisfy the minimum funding standards for the defined benefit plan.

In the situation where an employer contributes to a plan an amount greater than the deduction limits, the excess contributions are subject to a 10 percent penalty.

TIME LIMIT FOR MAKING PLAN CONTRIBUTIONS

Defined benefit plan contributions must be paid within 8 1/2 months after the end of the plan year. If the defined benefit plan fails to meet the funding requirements for a particular plan year, it must pay the deficiency in quarterly payments during the next plan year. Defined contribution pension plan contributions are due within 2 1/2 months of the end of the plan year. This deadline, however, may be extended up to six months. If an employer fails to meet the minimum funding requirements, it is subject to penalties. As discussed earlier, however, profit-sharing plans are not subject to the minimum funding requirements and are, therefore, extremely flexible in this regard.

FIDUCIARY OBLIGATIONS

An employer must tread carefully when sponsoring a qualified retirement plan. While an employer's officers or shareholders may serve as plan trustees, they must function in the legal capacity of a *fiduciary* and meet strict requirements that protect the interest of the plan participants and beneficiaries. Unlike employees, the employer is subject to penalties for borrowing from the plan as a breach of its fiduciary duty to the plan participants and beneficiaries.

IMPORTANT CONCEPTS

Minimum participation standards

Ratio percentage test

Average benefit test

Defined benefit plan 50/40 test

Highly compensated employee

Top-paid group of employees

Minimum vesting standards

Plan forfeitures

Minimum distribution rules

Top-heavy plan

Key employee

Assignment or alienation of plan benefits

Integration of plan benefit formulas with Social Security benefits

Excess method

Offset method

Integration level

Maximum offset allowance

Elective deferral limitations

Minimum funding standards

Projected benefit actuarial cost method

Accrued benefit actuarial cost method

QUESTIONS FOR REVIEW

1. What are the "age and service" requirements that qualified retirement plans must meet?

2. For purposes of satisfying a qualified plan's service requirement, what is meant by a "year of service?"

3. What are the two alternative overall coverage and participation tests under IRC Section 410(b)?

4. How does the ratio percentage test differ from the average benefit test?

5. How does one determine whether a retirement plan meets the nondiscriminatory classification test?

6. What is meant by the 50/40 coverage test for defined benefit plans?

7. What constitutes a highly compensated employee under IRC Section 414(q)?

8. What is meant by the "top-paid group" of employees?

9. What is the required vesting schedule for an employee's own contributions to a qualified plan?

10. What is the difference between cliff vesting and graded vesting?

11. What types of service may be disregarded for purposes of determining an employee's vesting rights in a qualified plan?

12. What are the minimum vesting standards for employer matching contributions and for top-heavy plans?

13. What is meant by a qualified plan forfeiture?

14. What is the difference in treatment between defined benefit plan forfeitures and defined contribution plan forfeitures?

15. What is meant by a plan participant's required beginning date for plan distributions?

16. How must a plan participant's interest be distributed if he or she has already begun taking plan distributions at the time of his or her death?

17. How must a plan participant's interest be distributed if he or she had not yet begun to take plan distributions at the time of his or her death?

18. If a plan participant's designated beneficiary is his or her surviving spouse and the participant dies, what is the latest date that plan distributions are required to begin?

19. Under the required minimum distribution rules, how often may the life expectancy of a participant and the participant's spouse be redetermined?

20. How is an "owner-employee" defined?

21. What is a "top-heavy" plan?

22. How is a "key employee" defined under IRC Section 416(i)?

23. How must a qualified plan provide the accrued benefits payable to a participant who dies before the annuity starting date and how does it differ from the manner in which it must provide benefits if the participant does not die before the annuity starting date?

24. What is meant by assignment or alienation of plan benefits and why is it important for a qualified plan?

25. What does it mean for a qualified plan to be integrated with Social Security?

26. What is the difference between the "excess method" and the "offset method" of integrating a defined benefit plan's benefit formula with Social Security benefits?

27. What is meant by "covered compensation?"

28. How does the "base benefit percentage" differ from the "excess benefit percentage" and what is meant by the "maximum excess allowance" and the "permitted disparity?"

29. By what percentage may a defined contribution plan's excess contribution percentage exceed the base contribution percentage?

30. What are the benefits and contribution limitations under IRC Section 415?

31. What are the limitations on elective deferrals under a qualified plan?

32. How does the projected benefit actuarial cost method differ from the accrued benefit actuarial cost method in determining annual plan funding?

33. What is meant by "unfunded past service liability?"

34. What are some of the key actuarial assumptions that an actuary must make in determining the funding of a defined benefit plan?

35. What are the current contribution deduction limits for profit-sharing and stock bonus plans?

36. What are the time limits for making contributions to both a defined benefit plan and a defined contribution plan?

SUGGESTIONS FOR ADDITIONAL READING

The Tools & Techniques of Employee Benefit and Retirement Planning, 9th edition, Stephen R. Leimberg and John J. McFadden, The National Underwriter Company, 2005.

U.S. Master Tax Guide, Current Edition, CCH Editorial Staff Publication, CCH Incorporated.

CHAPTER EIGHT

Keogh Plans/Retirement Plans for the Self-Employed

• • •

In chapter 6, we discussed employer-sponsored tax-advantaged plans, including SEP, SIMPLE, 403(b), and 457 plans designed to provide benefits to employees. In this chapter, you will be introduced to a type of "qualified plan" designed to provide benefits for one or more self-employed individuals-a Keogh or HR 10 plan. Technically, self-employed individuals such as sole proprietors or partners are not considered employees and accordingly are subject to somewhat different rules than those applicable to employees. In chapter 7, we explored in depth the concept of a qualified plan and you learned that in order to achieve a tax-qualified status a retirement plan must comply with the numerous provisions of Internal Revenue Code (IRC) Section 401(a) concerning plan coverage, eligibility, vesting, contribution limitations, benefit limitations, and many other requirements. Also, as you learned in chapter 7, compliance with these provisions permits the plan sponsor to take an income tax deduction at the time contributions are made to the plan, to have investment income grow tax-deferred in the plan, and to have plan participants incur income taxation only upon withdrawal of benefits from the plan. We discussed the fact that qualified plans come in two general categories—defined benefit and defined contribution plans. Keogh plans are usually designed as defined contribution plans. As you will recall, under this type of plan, no specific benefit is promised to the participant; instead the plan sponsor makes contributions to the plan as provided in the plan document, invests them in each participant's separate account as decided by the participant (with the investment risk assumed by the participant), and turns over to the participant, at a time or times specified in the plan document, his or her vested interest in the accumulated funds.

Upon completing this chapter, you should be able to:

- Differentiate among the provisions of a retirement plan for the self-employed individual (Keogh or HR 10 plan)
- Determine the maximum permissible deduction on behalf of a self-employed business owner to his or her Keogh plan
- Determine the maximum permissible deduction on behalf of an employee of a self-employed business owner to the Keogh plan of the business
- Describe those factors that distinguish a Keogh plan from other types of qualified plans
- Describe the advantages of a Keogh plan over other qualified plans
- Discuss the reasons why Keogh plans normally adopt the defined contribution profit-sharing form
- Identify the steps involved in establishing a Keogh plan
- Compare the rules governing Keogh plan contributions for employees versus plan contributions for self-employed owners
- Describe the income tax treatment of a cash value life insurance policy included in a Keogh plan

KEOGH PLAN DEFINITION, PURPOSE, AND PROS AND CONS

As indicated previously, a Keogh plan is a qualified retirement plan established by an unincorporated business (sole proprietor or partnership) covering one or more self-employed individuals (usually the owner(s)) as well as employees. Except for the contribution limits applicable to self-employed persons (discussed later) versus those applicable to employees, the rules governing a Keogh plan are essentially the same as for any other qualified plan. In the past, the terms "Keogh Plan" or "H.R. 10 Plan" were used to distinguish a retirement plan established by a self-employed individual from a plan established by a corporation or other entity. However, self-employed retirement plans are now generally referred to by the name that is used for the particular type of plan (e.g., SEP IRA, SIMPLE 401(k), or self-employed 401(k)).

Generally, a Keogh plan makes sense for a self-employed business owner who wants to both provide a benefit for his or her employees and accumulate funds for his or her own account on a tax-qualified basis. In some cases, the owner's earned income is substantial and there is a need to shelter a portion from current taxation. Another situation in which a Keogh plan may be beneficial is where a relatively highly-compensated employee also has self-employment income from an outside business, does not need his or her self-employment income to meet immediate needs, and desires to invest as much as possible of the self-employment income on a tax-deferred basis.

Probably the greatest advantages of a Keogh plan are the tax-deductibility of contributions, tax-deferral of the income on the plan's investments, and the deferral of taxation to the participant until such time as the funds are distributed. The impact of the deferral of taxation of the income on the plan's investments is cumulatively quite substantial. In fact, after a period of 15 years or more (depending upon the investment rate earned), the cumulative tax-deferred earnings will usually exceed the cumulative contributions to the plan.

Other advantages include the availability of plan loans to owners and employees (if certain specific requirements are met), the availability of 10-year income tax averaging for participants born before 1936, substantially higher contribution limits than for IRAs, participation by the majority of employees under the qualified plan coverage requirements, and the possible availability of a business tax credit for qualified plan startup costs.

Of course, these advantages are offset by some Keogh Plan disadvantages. First, while it can be costly and administratively burdensome to establish and operate a Keogh plan, these effects may be minimized through the use of prototype plans. This cost factor may be compounded by the need to comply with the plan coverage requirements, in the case where the employer has several employees. In addition, there is the potential of the 10 percent penalty applicable to premature withdrawals of plan funds and the negative impact of the required minimum distribution rules for more-than-5 percent owners (i.e., required commencement of distributions by April 1 of the year after attainment of age 70 1/2 rather than when the participant retires).

WHO CAN ESTABLISH A KEOGH PLAN

As indicated previously, a Keogh plan sponsor must be an unincorporated business (e.g., sole proprietorship or partnership). Neither an employee nor a partner can establish a Keogh plan. While taxpayers may have more than one Keogh plan, their contributions to all the plans must not exceed the overall limits (discussed later in this chapter).

TYPES OF KEOGH PLANS

Self-employed individuals may be covered by any type of qualified plan but Keogh plans generally opt for the defined contribution plan where there is *not* a fixed contribution requirement. As you learned in chapter 7, one of the distinguishing features of a defined contribution plan is that it includes an individual account, to which the employer contributes, for each plan participant. While there is no specific promised benefit to each participant in a defined contribution plan, a participant receives contributions to his or her account as provided in the plan, earnings (or losses) on those contributions, and possible forfeitures of other accounts. In addition, the *participant* (rather than the employer) bears the investment risk of the underlying investments in his or her account.

Also, as you learned in chapter 7, a defined contribution plan may be either a profit-sharing plan or a money purchase pension plan. As discussed previously, Keogh plans tend to adopt the profit-sharing form because of the greater flexibility in making annual contributions. While such a plan does not have to provide a definite formula for the sharing of profits, if it fails to do so, it is still required to make "recurring and substantial" contributions. Moreover, the plan must have a definite formula for allocating contributions among the participants and for eventually distributing the accumulated funds to the participants. Money purchase pension plans, on the other hand, require *fixed* contributions not based on business profits.

In chapter 7, you learned that a defined benefit plan is any plan that is *not* a defined contribution plan. The contributions are those required to provide definitely determinable benefits to plan participants. Actuarial assumptions and computations are required to calculate these contributions. As a result, this type of plan is generally expensive to establish and administer and suffers from the same disadvantage as a money purchase pension plan—required contributions not based on business profits. For these reasons, Keogh plans generally do *not* adopt the defined benefit option.

ESTABLISHING A KEOGH PLAN

The first action an employer must take in establishing a Keogh plan is to adopt a written plan. This may take the form of an IRS-approved master or prototype plan or an individually designed plan. The plan must then be communicated to employees. A master plan is offered by various plan providers (including banks, trade or professional organizations, insurance companies, mutual funds, federally insured credit unions, and certain savings and loan associations) and involves the creation of a single trust or custodial account which is shared by all employers that adopt the plan. With a prototype plan, a separate trust or custodial account is set up for each employer. An employer electing to establish an individually designed plan typically needs to engage a professional with expertise in this area, pay a fee, if applicable, and seek IRS approval, in the form of a determination letter.

Next, the employer must decide how to invest the plan's funds. This may be accomplished by creating a trust or custodial account, purchasing an annuity contract from an insurance company, or purchasing face-amount certificates (treated like annuity contracts) from an insurance company. Setting up a trust normally involves procuring the services of an attorney, while a custodial account may be created by a bank, savings and loan association, credit union, or other qualified financial institution, with that institution then acting as the plan trustee.

If the employer opts for a money purchase pension plan or defined benefit plan, minimum funding standards must be satisfied each year the plan is in existence.

To qualify for an income tax deduction for contributions for a tax year, a Keogh plan must be established (adopted) by the last day of that year (December 31 for calendar year employers).

CONTRIBUTIONS

Normally, a qualified plan is funded by the employer. However, plan participants may also be allowed to make contributions. Contributions for a tax year are due by the deadline for filing the tax return (including extensions) for that year.

Employer Contributions

Self-employed owners may make deductible contributions for themselves *only* if they have net earnings (their "compensation") from self-employment. Thus, if they have a net loss from self-employment, they cannot make contributions for themselves for the year, even if they contribute for employees based on employee compensation. Compensation for the self-employed is referred to as "earned income" and consists of the taxpayer's net earnings from self-employment from the trade or business, net of two deductions: (1) the self-employment tax deduction (one-half of the self-employment tax) permitted under IRC Section 164(f), and (2) the deduction allowed for plan contributions on the individual's own behalf. Because a self-employed owner's earned income is the amount remaining after taking into account these two deductions, the calculation of his or her maximum deductible contribution to a Keogh plan becomes mathematically somewhat complex and requires, in effect, an algebraic solution. (See "Deduction Worksheet for Self-Employed" later in this chapter).

As you learned in chapter 7, a defined benefit plan may provide a benefit that does not exceed the lesser of: (1) 100 percent of the participant's average compensation for his or her highest three consecutive calendar years, or (2) $170,000 (in 2005). A defined contribution plan may make annual contributions and other additions (excluding earnings) to the account of a participant up to the lesser of: (1) 100 percent of the participant's compensation, or (2) $42,000 (in 2005). These limits do not include catch-up contributions.

Employee Contributions

In addition to the employer contributions, limited as described in the previous section, nondeductible contributions may also be made by participants. The earnings on participant contributions are tax-deferred until distributed. Moreover, these contributions must meet the nondiscrimination test of IRC Section 401(m).

EMPLOYER DEDUCTION

Generally, an employer may deduct, within limits, contributions made to a qualified plan, including those made on behalf of a self-employed owner. As you learned in chapter 7, the contributions and earnings and gains on the contributions are normally tax-deferred until distributed from the plan.

Employer's Deduction Limit for an Employee

In the case of a defined contribution plan (either a profit-sharing plan or money purchase pension plan), which is the most common type of Keogh plan, the deduction is limited to 25 percent of the compensation paid (or accrued) during the year to participating employees. In determining the deduction limit, elective deferrals are *not* subject to the limit but compensation does include any elective deferrals that are made. The maximum compensation that may be taken into account for each employee is $210,000 (in 2005).

With regard to a defined benefit plan, the deduction is based on actuarial assumptions and computations and is limited to the plan's "unfunded current liability", as discussed in chapter 7.

Employer's Deduction Limit for a Self-Employed Owner

A self-employed owner is subject to a percentage limit *lower than* 25 percent for contributions made to his or her own account. Therefore, to determine the maximum permissible deduction a special computation is required. As discussed previously in this chapter, a self-employed owner's compensation equals his or her net earnings from self-employment *after* deducting one-half of his or her self-employment tax and the deduction for contributions to the plan on his or her behalf. Since the self-employed owner's net earnings from self-employment and his or her deduction for his or her own contributions are dependent upon each other, the self-employed owner must, therefore, reduce the contribution rate specified in the plan document. The IRS provides both a *Rate Table for Self-Employed* and a *Rate Worksheet for Self-Employed* for the purpose of determining the lower contribution rate. After consulting that Table, the self-employed owner may then calculate the maximum deduction by using the IRS *Deduction Worksheet for Self-Employed*. These IRS forms are applicable *only* to a self-employed owner who has only one defined contribution plan (usually a profit-sharing plan).

The *Rate Table for Self-Employed* is designed for plans that have a contribution rate that is a whole percentage (e.g., 10 percent, rather than 10 1/2 percent). The *Rate Worksheet for Self-Employed* is used where the plan contribution rate is not a whole percentage. The *Rate Table for Self-Employed* is as follows:

Rate Table for Self Employeed

| Column A
If the plan contri-
bution rate is:
(shown as %) | Column B
Your
rate is:
(shown as decimal) |
|---|---|
| 1 | .009901 |
| 2 | .019608 |
| 3 | .029126 |
| 4 | .038462 |
| 5 | .047619 |
| 6 | .056604 |
| 7 | .065421 |
| 8 | .074074 |
| 9 | .082569 |
| 10 | .090909 |
| 11 | .099099 |
| 12 | .107143 |
| 13 | .115044 |
| 14 | .122807 |
| 15 | .130435 |
| 16 | .137931 |
| 17 | .145299 |
| 18 | .152542 |
| 19 | .159664 |
| 20 | .166667 |
| 21 | .173554 |
| 22 | .180328 |
| 23 | .186992 |
| 24 | .193548 |
| 25 | .200000* |

*The deduction for annual employer contributions (other than elective deferrals) to a SEP plan, a profit-sharing plan, or a money purchase plan, cannot be more than 20% of the net earnings of the self-employed owner (figured without deducting contributions for the self-employed owner) from the business that has the plan.

Here is an example of how to use this table.

> **Example:** Assume a sole proprietor does not have any employees. If the retirement plan has a contribution rate of 10 percent of a participant's compensation, the rate applicable to the self-employed sole proprietor is, therefore, 0.090909. This rate should be entered in Step 4 of the *Deduction Worksheet for Self-Employed* to calculate the maximum deductible contribution for the sole proprietor.

As discussed previously, if the plan's contribution rate is not a whole percentage, the self-employed owner must use the following *Rate Worksheet for Self-Employed.*

Rate Worksheet for Self-Employed

1) Plan contribution rate as a decimal
   (for example, 10 1/2% = 0.105   _____

2) Rate in line 1 plus 1 (for example,
   0.105 + 1 = 1.105)   _____

3) Self-employed rate as a decimal
   rounded to at least 3 decimal places
   (line 1 ÷ line 2)   **_____**

The amount calculated on line 3 should then be entered in step 4 of the following *Deduction Worksheet for Self-Employed.*

Deduction Worksheet for Self-Employed

Step 1: Enter your net profit from line 31, Schedule C (Form 1040); line 3, Schedule C-EZ (Form 1040); line 36, Schedule F (Form 1040); or box 14, code A*, Schedule K-1 (Form 1065) *General partners should reduce this amount by the same additional expenses subtracted from box 14, code A to determine the amount on line 1 or 2 of Schedule SE	
Step 2: Enter your deduction for self-employment tax from line 30, Form 1040	
Step 3: Net earnings from self-employment. Subtract step 2 from step 1	
Step 4: Enter your rate from the *Rate Table for Self-Employed* or *Rate Worksheet for Self-Employed*	
Step 5: Multiply step 3 by step 4	
Step 6: Multiply $210,000 (for 2005) by your plan contribution rate (not the reduced rate)	
Step 7: Enter the **smaller** of step 5 or step 6	

Step 8: Contribution dollar limit
    • **If you made any elective deferrals, go to step 9.**
    • **Otherwise, skip steps 9 through 18 and enter the smaller of step 7 or step 8 on step 19.**
	$42,000 (2005)

Step 9: Enter your allowable elective deferrals made during 2005. Do not enter more than $14,000 (for 2005)	
Step 10: Subtract step 9 from step 8	
Step 11: Subtract step 9 from step 3	
Step 12: Enter one-half of step 11	
Step 13: Enter the **smallest** of step 7, 10, or 12	
Step 14: Subtract step 13 from step 3	

Step 15: Enter the **smaller** of step 9 or step 14
    • **If you made catch-up contributions, go to step 16.**
    • **Otherwise, skip steps 16 through 18 and go to step 19.**	

Step 16: Subtract step 15 from step 14	
Step 17: Enter your catch-up contributions, if any. Do not enter more than $4,000 (for 2005)	
Step 18: Enter the smaller of step 16 or step 17	
Step 19: Add steps 13, 15, and 18. This is your **maximum deductible contribution.**	
Next: Enter this amount on line 32, Form 1040	

Here is an example of how to calculate the maximum deductible contribution for a self-employed owner.

> **Example:** Assume a sole proprietor does not have any employees and the plan's contribution rate is 8 1/2% (.085) of the sole proprietor's compensation. Also assume the sole proprietor's net profit from line 31, Schedule C (Form 1040) is $200,000. Finally, also assume that the sole proprietor has not made any elective deferrals or catch-up contributions. His or her self-employment tax deduction on line 30 of Form 1040 is $9,563. This amount is entered in step 2 of the *Deduction Worksheet for Self-Employed*. The sole proprietor must then use the *Rate Worksheet for Self-Employed*, since the plan's contribution rate is not a whole percentage. The calculation is to divide .085 by 1.085, resulting in a self-employed contribution rate of 0.078. This rate is then entered in step 4 of the *Deduction Worksheet for Self-Employed*. The sole proprietor's net profit is then entered in step 1 of the worksheet. In order to arrive at step 3, step 2 is subtracted from step 1 ($200,000 - $9,563) resulting in net earnings from self-employment of $190,437. This amount is multiplied by the reduced self-employed contribution rate of 0.078 to arrive at step 5, or $14,854. In step 6, the maximum amount of compensation that may be taken into account ($210,000, for 2005) is multiplied by the plan's contribution rate (before reduction), 8.5%, resulting in the amount of $17,850. Finally, in step 7, the sole proprietor selects the smaller of step 5 or step 6, which is $14,854, the maximum deductible contribution.

USE OF LIFE INSURANCE IN A KEOGH PLAN

If an employer provides life insurance coverage to employee participants in a Keogh plan, the employer deducts those premiums as a plan contribution. The employees are subsequently charged with the value of the pure life insurance element as additional compensation using IRS Table 2001 (replacing the former P.S. 58 table previously used to compute this amount).

However, the pure life insurance element of premiums paid for a self-employed owner is *not* deductible by the employer. The remaining portion of premiums paid is deductible by the employer as a plan contribution. Unlike the situation with an employee, in which the compensation element is specifically charged to the employee, a self-employed owner is taxed indirectly in that the nondeductible portion of the premium flows through to the owner as additional profit subject to taxation.

At the time of distribution from the plan, an employee is able to offset against his or her distribution the cumulative amount of Table 2001 costs previously included in income (provided the distribution is made from the same life insurance policy on which the Table 2001 costs were paid). However, in spite of the fact that the self-employed owner indirectly paid tax on the Table 2001 costs applicable to his or her account, he or she is *not* able to offset such cumulative costs against distributions made from the plan insurance policy. In effect, an employee has a cost basis in his or her insurance policy that may be used to reduce the amount of any policy distributions subject to taxation. However, the self-employed owner is *not* considered to have this same cost basis in the plan insurance policy.

OTHER CONSIDERATIONS

In the situation where there is only one self-employed owner and no employees, it may make more sense to adopt a SEP or SIMPLE IRA (as discussed in chapter 6) since they are probably easier to adopt than a Keogh plan and may be established as late as the individual's tax return filing date for the previous year, rather than having to be created by the last day of the tax year, as is the case with a Keogh plan.

Some would recommend simply contributing to either a traditional or Roth IRA rather than setting up a Keogh plan. However, as you learned in chapters 3 and 4, there are many limitations on the amount that may be contributed to an IRA and generally the Keogh plan offers the opportunity to contribute a substantially greater amount.

Finally, if a business owner having a Keogh plan elects to incorporate his or her business, the Keogh status of the underlying qualified plan is removed. This offers no overriding advantage inasmuch as corporate plans and Keogh plans receive essentially the same treatment.

REPORTING REQUIREMENTS

The annual reporting requirements applicable to qualified plans are somewhat less onerous for many Keogh plans and other small plans. For instance, if the only persons covered by a plan are the business owner(s) and spouse or spouses, the plan may file simplified IRS Form 5500-EZ, instead of the voluminous IRS Form 5500.

IMPORTANT CONCEPTS

Types of Keogh plans

Master plan

Prototype plan

Individually designed plan

Trust or custodial account

Earned income of a self-employed owner

Employer's deduction limit for an employee

Employer's deduction limit for a self-employed owner

Rate Table for Self-Employed

Rate Worksheet for Self-Employed

Deduction Worksheet for Self-Employed

Life insurance policies in a Keogh plan

IRS Form 5500-EZ

QUESTIONS FOR REVIEW

1. Why are Keogh plans usually designed as defined contribution profit-sharing plans?

2. What types of organizations may establish a Keogh plan?

3. What are some of the advantages and disadvantages of a Keogh plan?

4. In the typical Keogh plan, who bears the investment risk?

5. Under a money purchase pension plan type of Keogh plan, what is the effect on plan contributions if the employer has no profits in a given plan year?

6. What are the three ways in which an employer can adopt a written Keogh plan?

7. In order to be able to deduct contributions to a Keogh plan for a plan year, by what date must the plan be established?

8. What is the deadline for making contributions to a Keogh plan for a particular plan year?

9. Before a self-employed owner can make deductible contributions for him- or herself to a Keogh plan, what requirement must first be satisfied?

10. What is the limit on deduction of employee contributions to a defined contribution type of Keogh plan?

11. How, if at all, do elective deferrals affect an employee's compensation for purposes of his or her employer making a contribution to a defined contribution Keogh plan on behalf of the employee?

12. Why is it necessary to reduce the contribution rate specified in the Keogh plan document in the case of self-employed owners?

13. If a Keogh plan's contribution rate is not a whole percentage, how is the contribution rate for a self-employed owner calculated?

14. A self-employed owner's "earned income" is his or her net earnings from self-employment net of what two deductions?

15. What is the difference, if any, in the income tax treatment of premiums paid on cash value life insurance contracts in a Keogh plan for employees versus self-employed owners?

16. What advantages does a SEP or SIMPLE IRA offer over a Keogh plan?

SUGGESTIONS FOR ADDITIONAL READING

The Tools & Techniques of Employee Benefit and Retirement Planning, 9th edition, Stephan R. Leimberg and John J. McFadden, The National Underwriter Company, 2005.

U.S. Master Tax Guide, Current Edition, CCH Editorial Staff Publication, CCH Incorporated.

Internal Revenue Service Publication 560, *Retirement Plans for Small Business (SEP, SIMPLE, and Qualified Plans),* Current Edition.

CHAPTER NINE

Profit-Sharing Plans

• • •

Many small businesses experience significant volatility in annual profits and cash flow. In adopting a qualified retirement plan, such businesses run the risk that they will not be able to fund the plan's required annual contributions on a consistent basis. In addition, young businesses may have just completed two or three high-profit years and are looking for income tax deductions to shelter these profits from current taxation. Often, such businesses adopt a qualified retirement plan for this purpose and then experience a few low profit or loss years when they are unable to fund the plan's contributions.

A qualified retirement plan that typically addresses the needs of these types of small businesses is the profit-sharing plan. Profit-sharing plan contributions need *not* be made each year, provided the contributions made are "recurring and substantial." In fact, it is not even necessary that the employer have profits in order to make contributions into profit-sharing plans. Accordingly, even a tax-exempt organization may maintain a profit-sharing plan. Under a profit-sharing plan, employers may base contributions on profits, but the existence of profits is not a prerequisite in calculating contributions.

In this chapter, we will discuss the profit-sharing plan and the benefits it offers compared to other qualified retirement plans.

Upon completing this chapter, you should be able to:

- Describe the basic characteristics of a profit-sharing plan
- Identify the current limitation on annual additions to a profit-sharing plan
- Describe how highly compensated employees can receive a greater allocation of profit-sharing plan contributions through the use of integration with Social Security benefits

- Describe how highly compensated employees can receive a greater allocation of profit-sharing plan contributions through the use of either an age-weighted or cross-tested benefit formula
- Identify the two general types of contribution provisions under a profit-sharing plan
- Differentiate between age-weighted and cross-tested profit-sharing plans
- Identify the types of vesting schedules permissible in profit-sharing plans
- Describe what is meant by an "in service distribution" from a profit-sharing plan
- Identify the two safe-harbor tests and the general test for nondiscrimination that defined contribution plans must meet in order to remain tax-qualified
- Compare profit-sharing plans to other retirement plan options

DEFINITION, PURPOSE, AND PROS AND CONS

Under IRS Regulation 1.401-1(b)(1)(ii), a "profit-sharing plan is a plan established and maintained by an employer to provide for the participation in his profits by his employees or their beneficiaries. The plan must provide a definite predetermined formula for allocating the contributions made to the plan among the participants and for distributing the funds accumulated under the plan after a fixed number of years, the attainment of a stated age, or upon the prior occurrence of some event such as layoff, illness, disability, retirement, death, or severance of employment. A formula for allocating the contributions among the participants is definite if, for example, it provides for an allocation in proportion to the basic compensation of each participant. A plan (whether or not it contains a definite predetermined formula for determining the profits to be shared with the employees) does not qualify under section 401(a) if the contributions to the plan are made at such times or in such amounts that the plan in operation discriminates in favor of officers, shareholders, persons whose principal duties consist in supervising the work of other employees, or highly compensated employees."

A profit-sharing plan is a qualified defined contribution plan under which the employer makes contributions on behalf of participating employees using a definite predetermined formula that may, in part, be based upon profits. The main advantage of such a plan is its flexible contributions for employers whose profits vary significantly from year to year. The benefits receivable by the participants (or beneficiaries) depend upon the amounts contributed (in a nondiscriminatory manner), any earnings on the contributed amounts, and forfeitures allocated to the participants' individual accounts. Normally, a participant's account balance is distributed as a lump sum under the plan when the employee terminates his or her employment.

A profit-sharing plan not only provides flexibility in annual contributions but may also function as an incentive for employees to increase both employer profits and ultimately their own account balances. Such plans are best suited to an employer whose employees are relatively young and therefore tend to earn less, have many years before retirement to accumulate a retirement fund, and have a long time horizon over which they can afford to take increased investment risk. A profit-sharing plan sometimes works well in tandem with a defined benefit plan to balance out the overall investment risk to which participants are subject.

In addition to contribution flexibility (even when there are no current or accumulated profits), a profit-sharing plan offers ease and lower cost of design and administration as compared to defined benefit and some other types of plans. On the other hand, older participants entering such a plan may not accrue meaningful benefits before retirement, particularly in light of the employer's ability to reduce or eliminate contributions (within limits). In fact, *all* participants in such plans are *not guaranteed* any particular benefit. Moreover, the accounts of highly compensated employees, such as owners or key employees, are allocated contributions that represent a relatively smaller proportion of their compensation than those allocated to lower paid employees. Finally, participants bear the investment risk in such plans.

PLAN CONTRIBUTIONS

As a defined contribution plan, a profit-sharing plan may make annual additions (employer contributions, employee contributions, and forfeitures) with respect to a participant that do not exceed the *lesser of*:

- $42,000 (for 2005), or
- 100 percent of the participant's compensation (not exceeding $210,000, for 2005)

As a result, an employee earning $42,000 (in 2005) could conceivably receive a contribution to his or her account of that same amount. However, it is doubtful that an employer would contribute 100 percent of an employee's salary to a qualified retirement plan. On the other hand, the contribution for an employee earning $300,000 cannot exceed $42,000 (in 2005), which is only 14 percent of his or her compensation. Highly compensated employees, therefore, may receive a greater allocation through the use of either integration with Social Security benefits (as discussed in chapter 7) or an age-weighted or cross-tested benefit formula (discussed later in this chapter).

There are two general types of employer contribution provisions under a profit-sharing plan—discretionary or formula. A *discretionary* provision permits an employer to contribute annually, if the employer so elects, any amount up to the maximum deductible limit. An employer may elect to make no contribution in a particular year, as long as it meets the somewhat vague "recurring and substantial" requirements of Treasury Regulation 1.401-1(b)(2). However, if too many plan year contributions are missed, the plan will be treated by the IRS as "terminated," causing all nonvested amounts in participants' accounts to become immediately 100 percent vested.

A *formula* provision requires the employer to legally make a specific contribution to the extent of profits earned. Formula provisions may be drafted to permit the omission of a contribution in certain specified financial hardship situations.

After adopting either a discretionary or formula provision to determine the total amount of employer contributions to a profit-sharing plan, a formula must be in place to determine how to allocate contributions to individual employee accounts. As we have discussed previously, such allocations must *not* discriminate in favor of highly compensated employees. Typically, such participant allocation formulas use a participant's compensation as a percentage of the compensation of all participants multiplied by the total employer contribution for the year. An equitable method of defining what is meant by "compensation" is necessary so that the formula does not discriminate in favor of highly compensated employees. As discussed earlier, under qualified plan law, a participant's compensation that may be taken into account in the compensation formula is limited to $210,000 in 2005.

A profit-sharing allocation formula that also factors in a participant's years of service has to meet one of the various safe harbors of Treasury Regulation 1.401(a)(4)-2 or use "cross-testing" (testing defined contribution plans on the basis of benefits, discussed later in this chapter).

As long as a profit-sharing plan continues to meet the "tax-qualification" requirements discussed in chapter 7, employer contributions are tax-deductible as made, up to 25 percent of the total compensation of covered employees. Contributions in excess of this limit are normally subject to a 10 percent penalty. As discussed previously, only the first $210,000 (in 2005) of each participant's compensation may be taken into account in determining this limit.

Plan participants are not taxed until their account balances are withdrawn. Participants born before 1936 may qualify for special 10-year averaging for lump sum distributions. Employers establishing a profit-sharing plan may also qualify for a business tax credit of up to $500 for "qualified startup costs."

Finally, plan participants may be able to direct the investment of their account balances through a limited number of investment options that, if meeting Department of Labor (DOL) requirements (e.g., minimum of three diversified investment choices), usually relieve the plan trustee of any fiduciary responsibility for account losses resulting from participant-selected investments.

VESTING

Profit-sharing plans may use any vesting schedule permitted by the IRC, with graded "3-to-7 year" being the norm (i.e., 20 percent after 3 years, increasing by 20 percent annually to year 7 when it reaches 100 percent). Plans that provide for matching contributions, however, must use "2-to-6 year" (so-called accelerated) vesting for such contributions. Nonvested balances left by employees separating from the employer's service (i.e., forfeitures) are typically added to the account balances of remaining participants; but this must be done in a nondiscriminatory manner by allocating forfeitures on the basis of compensation rather than on existing account balances.

DISTRIBUTIONS

Typically a participant in a profit-sharing plan receives either a lump sum or installment payments (subject to the minimum distribution rules) of his or her account balance either at termination of his or her employment or at the normal retirement age specified in the plan.

Profit-sharing plans frequently offer the benefit of "in service distributions" (i.e., benefits payable prior to termination of employment). Such distributions may be limited to so-called "hardship" circumstances, such as medical emergencies, home repair, or educational expenses, with the amount further limited only to a participant's vested account balance. The IRS generally requires employer contributions to be in the plan for at least two years prior to making in service distributions. Some plans penalize participants for taking in service distributions by temporarily suspending them from the plan; but such penalties cannot affect a participant's vested benefits under the plan.

As with other qualified plans, there is a 10 percent early distribution penalty for certain distributions made to participants prior to attainment of age 59 1/2. This penalty may be avoided through the use of a plan loan provision.

AGE-WEIGHTED PROFIT-SHARING PLANS

In many cases, an employer sponsoring a profit-sharing plan would like to allocate a greater percentage of contributions to older owners and other key employees. Using only the normal compensation-based allocation formulas, this may not be possible. An age-weighted profit-sharing plan, however, takes into account the participants' ages in addition to their compensation. Thus, allocations of contributions to *older* employees may be maximized, while allocations to younger employees are minimized. Consider the following example:

> **Example:** Raybon Company's profit-sharing plan covers the highly compensated, older owner and four nonhighly compensated, younger employees. Contributions to the plan are set at 10 percent of total compensation per year. The employee profile is as follows:

Name	Age	Compensation	Contribution
DR	50	$150,000	$15,000
A	40	40,000	4,000
B	35	40,000	4,000
C	30	40,000	4,000
D	30	30,000	3,000
Totals		**$300,000**	**$30,000**

Under an age-weighted plan, each participant's compensation is weighted by an age factor. A simple method of calculating age-weighted compensation is to discount each participant's compensation from the normal retirement age under the plan to his or her current age at an allowable interest rate (typically a rate between 7.5 percent and 8.5 percent). Using a normal retirement age of 65 and a discount rate of 8.5 percent, the age-weighted compensation levels and contribution levels in the above example are:

Name	Age	Age-Weighted Compensation	Contribution
DR	50	$44,121	$23,298
A	40	5,204	2,748
B	35	3,461	1,828
C	30	2,302	1,215
D	30	1,726	911
Totals		**$56,814**	**$30,000**

The contributions are allocated proportionately, but based on the age-weighted compensation levels. In this example, the owner (DR) is allocated nearly 78 percent of the total allocation under age-weighting, compared to 50 percent under the traditional profit-sharing allocation. While the uniform age-weighted formula in this plan is nondiscriminatory, the allocation rate for the highly compensated owner exceeds the average allocation rate for the nonhighly compensated employees by a considerable amount. In fact, if contributions were to be tested (discussed later in this chapter), the plan would not meet the nondiscrimination requirements, but if the contributions were to be converted to equivalent benefits, the plan would meet the "cross-testing" provisions (discussed later in this chapter). Of course, this outcome is the direct result of this particular employee profile (older highly compensated owner and younger nonhighly compensated employees).

When using an age-weighted profit-sharing formula to allocate contributions, it may be necessary to adjust participants' accounts to reflect the various limits applicable to qualified plans. For instance, if any participant's allocation exceeds the annual additions limitation (100 percent of compensation or $42,000 (in 2005)), such excess must be reallocated to other employees in a nondiscriminatory manner. Inasmuch as age-weighted profit-sharing plans are used primarily by smaller employers, such plans often run afoul of the top-heavy rules discussed in chapter 7. In fact, the plan in the previous example would be treated as top-heavy. While the minimum contribution of 3 percent of salary was met, the plan would nevertheless have to comply with the remaining restrictions of top-heavy plans.

CROSS-TESTED PROFIT-SHARING PLANS

Probably the most popular age-weighted profit-sharing plan is a cross-tested plan, sometimes referred to as a **new comparability plan**. This type of plan makes it easier to satisfy the nondiscrimination requirement applying generally to all types of qualified plans. Cross-testing permits a defined contribution plan to be tested on a benefits basis (known as an "equivalent accrual") under the general nondiscrimination test for defined benefit plans. These tests are discussed later in this chapter. Age-weighted profit-sharing plans and new comparability plans (also usually profit-sharing plans) are the most common types of plans that rely on cross-testing.

A defined contribution plan is nondiscriminatory with respect to benefits for a plan year if the plan's equivalent accrual rates were substituted for each employee's allocation (contribution) rate and the plan either:

1. Provides broadly available allocation rates;
2. Uses certain age-based allocation rates; or
3. Satisfies a minimum allocation gateway.

A plan is said to provide broadly available allocation rates if each allocation rate under the plan is currently available to a nondiscriminatory group of employees. Plans that use gradual age or service schedules, or provide allocation rates based on a uniform target benefit allocation also meet the conditions for cross-testing. If the plan does not meet the first two conditions, it must satisfy a minimum allocation gateway. This gateway test requires that the allocation rate for each nonhighly compensated employee (NHCE) be at least the lesser of: (1) one-third of the allocation rate of the highly compensated employee (HCE) with the highest allocation rate; or (2) 5 percent of the NHCE's compensation.

New comparability plans also have built-in disparities between the allocation rates for HCEs and the allocation rates for NHCEs. In the typical new comparability plan, HCEs (typically older) receive high allocation rates, while NHCEs, regardless of their age or years of service, receive comparatively low allocation rates. For example, HCEs in such a plan might receive allocations of 20 percent of compensation, while NHCEs receive allocations of 3 percent of compensation. Therefore, the manner whereby these plans demonstrate compliance with the nondiscrimination rules is by comparing the actuarially projected value of the employer contributions for the younger NHCEs with the actuarial projections of the HCEs. As a result, these plans are generally able to provide higher rates of employer contributions to HCEs, while NHCEs are not allowed to earn the higher allocation rates as they work additional years for the employer or grow older.

TESTING FOR DISCRIMINATION IN DEFINED CONTRIBUTION PLANS

Generally, defined contribution plans demonstrate nondiscrimination with respect to contributions. However, as we discussed in the previous section, any plan may be tested for nondiscrimination on the basis of contributions or benefits without regard to whether it is a defined benefit or a defined contribution plan (i.e., cross-testing).

For defined contribution plans, there are two "safe-harbor tests" that are available in determining whether contributions under a plan are nondiscriminatory. If a plan does not satisfy one of these two safe harbors, it must satisfy a general test for nondiscrimination.

If a plan has a uniform allocation formula it automatically satisfies the first safe harbor. Such a plan allocates all contributions and forfeitures under a formula that allocates the same percentage of plan year compensation, the same dollar amount, or the same dollar amount for each uniform unit of service (not to exceed one week) performed by a participant during the plan year. A plan that meets the Social Security integration rules does not fail to have a uniform formula because of the differences in employee's allocations attributable to uniform disparities permitted under the integration rules, discussed in chapter 7.

The second safe harbor is a uniform points plan under which each employee's allocation for the plan year equals the product determined by multiplying all amounts allocated to all employees in the plan for the plan year by a fraction, the numerator of which is the employee's points for the plan year and the denominator of which is the sum of the points of all employees in the plan for the plan year. An employee's points equal the sum of the employee's points for age, service, and units of compensation for the plan year. Each employee must receive the same number of points for age, service, and unit of compensation. The plan must also grant points for either age or service. A unit of compensation is not required to be used, but if it is, it must be a single dollar amount not in excess of $200. In addition, the average of the allocation rates for HCEs in the plan may not exceed the average of the allocation rates for the NHCEs in the plan.

If neither of these two safe-harbor tests is met, contributions will still be considered nondiscriminatory if they satisfy the general test for contributions. This general test is met if each rate group under the plan satisfies the minimum coverage requirements of IRC Section 410(b). A rate group exists for each HCE in the plan and consists of that HCE and all other employees in the plan who have an allocation rate greater than or equal to the HCE's allocation rate. Accordingly, an employee is in the rate group for each HCE in the plan who has an allocation rate less than or equal to that employee's allocation rate. The allocation rate of an employee under this test is the sum of the allocations to the employee's account for the plan year, expressed either as a percentage of compensation or as a dollar amount. Amounts taken into consideration for this purpose include employer contributions and forfeitures but exclude income, expenses, gains, and losses attributable to the employee's account. An employer may group employees' allocation rates within a range of no more than 5 percent (not 5 percentage points) above and below a midpoint rate chosen by the employer. If allocation rates are determined as a percentage of compensation, such rates may be grouped within a range of no more than a quarter of a percentage point. Here is an example:

> **Example:** Employer XYZ has only seven employees, all of whom benefit under Plan S. The HCEs are H1 and H2, and the NHCEs are N1 through N5. For the plan year, H1 and N1 through N3 have allocation rates of 5.0 percent of plan year compensation. For the same plan year, H2, N4, and N5 have allocation rates of 7.5 percent of plan year compensation.

> Given this employee profile, there are two rate groups in Plan S. Rate group 1 consists of H1 and all those employees who have an allocation rate greater than or equal to H1's allocation rate (5.0 percent). Thus, rate group 1 consists of H1, H2, and N1 through N5. Rate group 2 consists of H2, and all those employees who have an allocation rate greater than or equal to H2's allocation rate (7.5 percent). Thus, rate group 2 consists of H2, N4, and N5. Rate group 1 satisfies the ratio percentage test, because the ratio percentage of the rate group is 100 percent (the percentage of all NHCEs who are in the rate group). Rate group 2 also satisfies the ratio percentage test, because the ratio percentage of the rate group is 80 percent—i.e., 40 percent (the percentage of all NHCEs who are in the rate group) divided by 50 percent (the percentage of all HCEs who are in the rate group).

PROFIT-SHARING PLANS VERSUS OTHER PLANS

Another type of defined contribution plan that is similar to a profit-sharing plan is a money purchase plan (discussed in chapter 12). While both plans offer a contribution and tax deduction of up to 25 percent of each participant's compensation, a money purchase plan involves *compulsory* (rather than flexible) annual plan contributions.

An age-weighted profit-sharing plan has some of the attributes of a defined benefit plan (see chapter 13 of this text). The age-weighted plan permits the employer to base contribution percentages on the employee's age at the time of plan entry, thereby favoring older owners, HCEs, or key employees. Regular defined benefit plans provide a more secure retirement benefit and allow the employer to make greater contributions for older participants but suffer from increased complexity and cost of design and administration.

While nonqualified deferred compensation plans allow the employer to discriminate in favor of HCEs or key employees, they do not provide a current tax deduction for contributions, as do profit-sharing plans.

Finally, the use of individual retirement savings plans, such as IRAs, is at best only a supplement to an employer plan and permits only very limited, if any, tax deductions for contributions.

IMPORTANT CONCEPTS

"Recurring and substantial" contributions

Flexible employer contributions

Limit on annual additions

Age-weighted profit-sharing plan

Cross-tested profit-sharing plan

Discretionary employer contribution provision

Formula employer contribution provision

3-to-7 year vesting

2-to-6 year vesting

Forfeitures

In service distributions

New comparability plan

Equivalent accrual

Broadly available allocation rates

Gradual age or service schedules

Minimum allocation gateway

HCE

NHCE

Safe-harbor tests for defined contribution plans

Uniform allocation formula

Uniform points plan

General test for contributions

Rate group

QUESTIONS FOR REVIEW

1. What is the main advantage to an employer of a profit-sharing plan over other qualified retirement plans?

2. What factors determine the benefits receivable by a participant (or beneficiary) in a profit-sharing plan?

3. It what ways can a profit-sharing plan be revised to provide in a nondiscriminatory manner greater contributions to the accounts of highly compensated employees?

4. What is the current limitation on annual additions to the account of a participant in a profit-sharing plan?

5. What are the two general types of employer contribution provisions under a profit-sharing plan?

6. Under a discretionary employer contribution provision, what contribution options are available to the sponsor of a profit-sharing plan?

7. Under a formula employer contribution provision, what is the employer's legal obligation with regard to contributions to a profit-sharing plan?

8. What is the typical participant allocation formula used in a profit-sharing plan?

9. What is the current dollar limit on a participant's compensation that can be taken into account in a profit-sharing plan's compensation formula?

10. When is a participant in a profit-sharing plan taxed?

11. Under a profit-sharing plan, who bears the investment risk?

12. What vesting schedule is required for a profit-sharing plan that provides for matching contributions?

13. What is meant by an "in service distribution"?

14. How is a participant's age taken into account (in addition to his or her compensation) in an age-weighted profit-sharing plan?

15. What is meant by the term "cross-tested" with regard to an age-weighted profit-sharing plan?

16. What is another term for a cross-tested, age-weighted profit-sharing plan?

17. What does it mean for a profit-sharing plan to provide "broadly available allocation rates"?

18. What does it mean for a profit-sharing plan to provide "age-based allocation rates"?

19. What is meant by the "minimum allocation gateway" with regard to testing for nondiscrimination in a profit-sharing plan?

20. What are the two safe-harbor tests for determining whether contributions to a defined contribution plan are nondiscriminatory?

21. What is the general test for nondiscrimination in contributions in a defined contribution plan?

22. What constitutes a "rate group" under the general test for nondiscrimination in contributions in a defined contribution plan?

23. How does a profit-sharing plan differ from a money purchase plan?

24. In what ways does a defined benefit plan differ from an age-weighted profit-sharing plan?

SUGGESTIONS FOR ADDITIONAL READING

The Tools & Techniques of Employee Benefit and Retirement Planning, 9th edition, Stephan R. Leimberg and John J. McFadden, The National Underwriter Company, 2005.

U.S. Master Tax Guide, Current Edition, CCH Editorial Staff Publication, CCH Incorporated.

CHAPTER TEN

Stock Bonus Plans/Employee Stock Ownership Plans (ESOPs)

• • •

Some employers are interested in providing their employees with a qualified retirement plan but are concerned about managing their cash flow. Committing to substantial qualified retirement plan *cash* contributions may also severely affect their financial flexibility. A stock bonus plan or employee stock ownership plan (ESOP) may be appropriate for this type of employer, provided the employer is willing to give up an ownership interest in the business. In this chapter, we will discuss stock bonus plans in general and in particular one variety of stock bonus plan known as an employee stock ownership plan (ESOP).

Upon completing this chapter, you should be able to:

- Distinguish between a profit-sharing plan and a stock bonus plan
- Discuss some of the advantages and disadvantages of a stock bonus plan
- Describe the income tax deduction and annual additions limits for a stock bonus plan
- Compare the voting rights of employer closely held stock held in a stock bonus plan to those of employer stock publicly traded on an established securities market held in a stock bonus plan
- Explain the income taxation of distributions from a stock bonus plan
- Compare a regular stock bonus plan to an employee stock ownership plan (ESOP)
- Explain what is meant by "qualifying employer securities" in an ESOP
- Discuss the treatment of gain on the sale of company stock by a retiring owner to the company's ESOP
- Describe the income tax treatment of cash dividends paid to ESOP participants

- Distinguish between a nonleveraged ESOP and a leveraged ESOP
- Explain what is meant by an "exempt loan" made to an ESOP by a disqualified person
- Describe the rules applicable to the diversification of ESOP investments by participants nearing retirement
- Identify the "put option" available to an ESOP participant receiving employer securities not readily tradable on an established securities market
- Distinguish between the general rules regarding commencement of benefit payments applicable to all qualified plans to those applicable to ESOPs

STOCK BONUS PLANS (IN GENERAL)

In this section, we will discuss the general attributes of a stock bonus plan. In the next section, we will discuss a specific type of stock bonus plan known as an employee stock ownership plan (or ESOP).

Definition, Purpose, and Pros and Cons

Stock bonus plans are defined contribution qualified plans that are similar to profit-sharing plans (discussed in chapter 9). The primary difference between stock bonus plans and profit-sharing plans is that the benefits from a stock bonus plan are payable in the form of the employer's *stock*, rather than in cash. Reg. Section 1.401-1(a)(3)(iii) defines a stock bonus plan as "a plan established and maintained by an employer to provide benefits similar to those of a profit-sharing plan, except that the contributions by the employer are not necessarily dependent upon profits and the benefits are distributable in stock of the employer company. For the purpose of allocating and distributing the stock of the employer which is to be shared among his employees or their beneficiaries, such a plan is subject to the same requirements as a profit-sharing plan".

A stock bonus plan: (1) provides a tax incentive for an employer to make its stock available to employees; (2) creates an additional market for the employer's stock; (3) permits an employer to expand the ownership of its stock (perhaps, for example, to help defend against a hostile takeover); (4) offers an incentive for employees to act in a manner that will increase the value of the employer's stock; (5) allows an employee to defer taxation on the unrealized appreciation of stock held in the plan until the stock is eventually sold (known as the "net unrealized appreciation" tax rule); and (6) permits an employer tax deduction for either cash or stock contributions to the plan. Cash contributed by the employer is used by the plan to purchase stock.

However, to achieve these benefits a stock bonus plan must meet *all* of the qualified plan requirements such as coverage, vesting, funding, reporting, and disclosure, among other requirements. Moreover, an employer must be willing to endure some dilution of its stock value. From the standpoint of the employees, investing a large portion of one's retirement funds in employer stock involves, at best, a large amount of unsystematic investment risk.

Plan Contributions

Annual contributions to a stock bonus plan are normally made in shares of the employer's stock, rather than cash. The ability to make cashless contributions helps a business manage cash flow while operating a qualified plan for its employees.

Most plans allocate plan contributions to participants based on employee compensation in a nondiscriminatory fashion. Only the first $210,000 of compensation (in 2005) may be taken into account in the plan's allocation formula. Employer contributions are deductible when made, up to 25 percent of covered employees' payroll. Stock bonus plans are subject to the normal defined contribution plan annual additions limit—the lesser of 100 percent of a participant's compensation or $42,000 (in 2005).

Moreover, as with any qualified plan, participants are not taxed on employer contributions at the time they are made and certain employers adopting a stock bonus plan may qualify for a business tax credit of up to $500 for "qualified startup costs."

Voting Rights

Shares held in plan participants' accounts are subject to specific voting rights. Closely held employer company shares (those not publicly traded on an established securities market) comprising more than 10 percent of the plan's assets carry with them specific voting rights for the plan participants, including the right to approve or disapprove any proposed corporate merger or consolidation, acquisition, recapitalization, reclassification, liquidation, or dissolution or the sale of substantially all employer assets and other similar transactions as specified in IRS regulations. Where the stock is publicly traded, voting rights extend to all issues.

Distributions

A distribution of employer stock or securities is not treated like other qualified plan distributions. If employer stock is distributed as a lump sum, the employee is *not* taxed at the time of the distribution on the appreciation in value of the stock that has occurred since it was contributed to the qualified plan by the employer. Further, this "unrealized appreciation" on the stock is taxed only as a capital gain when the employee actually sells or exchanges the stock. For example, if an employer contributes employer stock worth $1,000 to a participant's account that grows to $5,000 at the time of the employee's retirement, and if the participant receives the stock in a lump sum distribution, he or she will pay tax only on the $1,000 at that time. Taxation of the $4,000 of unrealized appreciation at capital gains rates is *deferred* until the participant sells the stock, unless the participant elects to pay the tax currently. However, if the stock is distributed to the employee in a nonlump-sum (periodic) distribution, only the portion of the unrealized appreciation that is attributable to the portion of the stock that was paid for by the employee may be excluded. All of this is what is referred to as the "net unrealized appreciation" tax rule.

In addition, a participant has the right to insist that distributions from a stock bonus plan be made in employer stock. If such stock is not publicly traded on an established securities market, a participant may exercise what is known as a "put option" to require the employer to repurchase the stock at a price determined by an independent appraiser.

EMPLOYEE STOCK OWNERSHIP PLANS (ESOPS)

An ESOP is a special type of stock bonus plan or combined stock bonus and money purchase pension plan (discussed in chapter 12) qualified under Code Section 401(a), which is designed to invest primarily in "qualifying employer securities." Congress has encouraged the growth of ESOPs through favorable legislation designed to broaden ownership of corporate stock, provide a source of funds for capital formation through tax-favored leveraging techniques, and to improve the economic performance of sponsoring corporations. Even an S corporation may now sponsor an ESOP although under somewhat different rules than those applicable to a regular C corporation.

Definition, Purpose, and Pros and Cons

In addition to complying with the general requirements imposed on defined contribution plans, ESOPs must also comply with requirements concerning voting rights, diversification, and account allocation restrictions, discussed later in this chapter. An ESOP must meet all the requirements relating to qualified stock bonus plans and, if applicable, money purchase pension plans. These include the participation, vesting, and nondiscrimination rules. The plan document must also formally designate the plan as an ESOP and specifically state that it is designed to invest primarily (or exclusively, if so stated) in "qualifying employer securities." While a stock bonus plan generally may be integrated with Social Security benefits, an ESOP created after November 1, 1977 is *not* allowed to integrate with Social Security benefits.

Qualifying employer securities are defined under Code Section 409(1) as common stock issued by the employer (or by a corporation which is a member of the same controlled group of corporations) that is readily tradable on an established securities market. If there is no common stock which meets this definition, then "employer securities" means employer common stock that has a combination of voting power and dividend rights at least equal to those classes of common stock having the greatest voting power and the greatest dividend rights. Employer securities also include noncallable preferred stock convertible at any time into qualifying common stock.

Because an ESOP is a qualified plan under IRC Section 401(a), employees defer recognition of income at least until the stock is actually distributed to them. The employer is able to fund the plan with contributions of stock, thereby avoiding any drain on cash flows. In addition to deducting up to 25 percent of compensation for contributions to the plan, the company may be able to deduct amounts above the normal qualified plan limits if special leveraging techniques are used (see Leveraged ESOPs).

Use of ESOPs for Closely Held Buyouts

ESOPs are often used to purchase the stock of a retiring owner in a closely held corporation. IRC Section 1042 permits certain owners to defer recognition of any gain realized upon the sale of company stock to the ESOP. To obtain this special treatment, the retiring owner must use the sale proceeds to purchase "replacement securities," meaning stock or securities of another corporation. The tax basis of the company's stock in the hands of the retiring owner carries over to the replacement securities (as does the holding period of the company's stock) with any taxation deferred until the replacement securities are eventually sold, provided the ESOP owns at least 30 percent of the company's stock after the buyout.

In order for the nonrecognition of gain to apply, however, several rules apply to the employer, the shareholder, the replacement property, and the ESOP. For example, the employer must be a domestic C corporation that has no outstanding stock readily tradable on an established securities market. In addition, the employer must give written consent to be assessed a 10 percent excise tax if the ESOP disposes of the shares acquired within 3 years of acquisition.

In the case of the shareholder, he or she must not have acquired the qualifying employer securities from a qualified plan through the exercise of statutory or nonqualified stock options, or from any other plan to which IRC Section 83 (property transferred in connection with the performance of services) applies. The shareholder must also have held the qualifying employer securities for at least 3 years before selling it to the ESOP. Finally, the shareholder must purchase the qualified replacement property within a 15-month replacement period, which begins three months prior to the sale. To the extent that any sale proceeds are not used to buy qualified replacement property within the requisite period, gain is recognized. The taxpayer or executor must make an election to have IRC Section 1042 apply to the sale of the securities to the ESOP.

The replacement property is any security (including stock, bonds, etc.) issued by a domestic operating corporation (more than 50 percent of its assets are used in the active conduct of a trade or business) where the corporation does not have passive investment income in excess of 25 percent of its gross receipts. Also, the corporation may be privately or publicly held but it may not be a member of the same controlled group as the one which issued the securities that were sold to the ESOP.

In meeting the 30 percent ownership requirement immediately after the sale, the ESOP may own 30 percent of either each class of outstanding stock of the corporation or the total value of all outstanding stock.

Valuation Issues

An extremely important issue is the value that is assigned to qualifying securities of a nonpublicly traded employer. There are several reasons for determining such a value, including:

(1) Determining the amount of a deduction for contributions of securities to the employer's ESOP

(2) Establishing the sales price for a sale of employer securities to an ESOP (otherwise, if the trustee paid an amount in excess of the fair market value, it is considered to be a prohibited transaction)

(3) Determining the amount of securities which may be allocated to participants' accounts for purposes of the IRC Section 415 contribution limits

(4) Establishing values for put options and rights of first refusal

A good-faith estimation of the fair market value (FMV) must be made based on all relevant factors. Such a determination of FMV must be made at least annually and be performed by an independent person who customarily makes such appraisals.

Dividend Deductions

Employers are permitted to *deduct* any cash dividends paid to ESOP participants. However, one of the following conditions must be met: (1) the dividends must be paid in cash directly to the participants or to their beneficiaries; (2) the dividend must be distributed through the ESOP to the participants or their beneficiaries within 90 days after the end of the plan year in which the corporation paid the dividend; (3) the dividend must, at the election of the participants or their beneficiaries, be payable as provided in either of the two methods above, or paid to the plan and reinvested in qualified employer securities; or (4) the dividend must be used to make payments on an exempt ESOP loan (for principal or interest), the proceeds of which are used to acquire the employer securities with respect to which the dividends were paid. The deduction is allowed for the corporation's year in which the dividend is distributed to the participants or used to repay the loan, rather than for the year in which the corporation paid the dividend. The employer is permitted a deduction even if participants elect not to receive any dividends. This deduction is in addition to the regular deduction limits allowed for contributions to an ESOP under IRC Section 404 and is not considered to be an annual addition to participants' accounts for purposes of the IRC Section 415 limits.

Dividends distributed to participants are not considered a return of any nondeductible employee contributions but rather are considered to be ordinary income to the recipient. They are not eligible for the reduced tax rates on dividends introduced by JGTRRA of 2003.

Types of ESOPs

Even though the purpose of an ESOP may not really be to provide for a participant's retirement, the plan nevertheless must meet all of the qualification requirements of IRC Section 401(a). An ESOP is a defined contribution plan that must contain a stock bonus plan element. There are basically two types of ESOPs-the nonleveraged ESOP and the leveraged ESOP.

Nonleveraged ESOPs

A nonleveraged ESOP is not designed to borrow money and carries the normal attributes of a stock bonus plan. Inasmuch as an ESOP may invest primarily, or even exclusively, in employer securities, it is exempted from the "prudent man" or fair return investment requirements. As mentioned previously, the normal deduction limitations (25 percent of the compensation of participating employees) of stock bonus plans apply to nonleveraged ESOPs.

Leveraged ESOPs (LESOPs)

A leveraged ESOP, or "LESOP," is a qualified plan that is specially designed to borrow money under the tax-favored provisions of Regulation 54.4975-7. A LESOP permits the employer to not only provide employee benefits, but to also obtain favorable debt financing through the deduction of *both* principal and interest for its contributions to the ESOP to repay the loan.

Generally, the lending and borrowing of money and the guaranteeing of such loans by qualified plans is a prohibited transaction. ESOPs are exempted from this general prohibition by IRC Section 4975. The trust of an ESOP is permitted to secure a loan from a lending institution with the employer guaranteeing to contribute to the ESOP enough money to repay the loan. The ESOP then may use the loan proceeds to purchase newly issued employer stock to provide the employer with working capital or funds for expansion, acquisitions, divestitures of subsidiaries, leveraged buyouts, and for buying out existing owners. The LESOP technique is shown in Figure 10.1.

Figure 10.1

LESOP

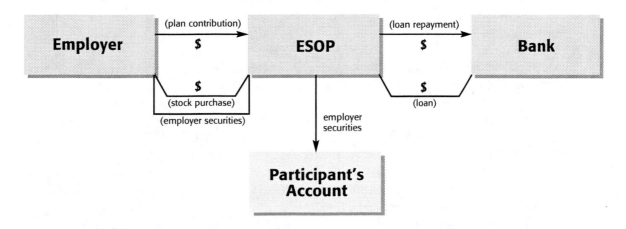

The LESOP must use an "exempt loan" which meets the requirements set forth in Regulation 54.4975-7 and 54.4975-11. An exempt loan is one that is made to an ESOP by a disqualified person or a loan made to an ESOP guaranteed by a disqualified person. The disqualified person, in this case, is the employer. The loan must be primarily for the benefit of the ESOP participants and their beneficiaries. In addition, the loan must be for a specific term, without recourse against the ESOP, and with only qualifying employer securities, either acquired with the loan proceeds or used as collateral on a prior exempt loan repaid with the proceeds of the current exempt loan, pledged as collateral. Finally, the ESOP's liability for repayment of the loan must be limited to: (1) the securities pledged as collateral on the loan; (2) any contributions made to the ESOP for loan repayment purposes; and (3) any earnings that are attributable to such contributions and collateral. An ESOP must also use exempt loan proceeds only to: (1) acquire qualifying employer securities; (2) repay such loan; and/or (3) repay a prior exempt loan.

As the employer makes contributions to the ESOP to repay the loan, the amounts representing interest are fully deductible, with only the amounts representing principal repayment subject to the regular 25 percent of compensation limitation. Accordingly, *the company is able to deduct both principal and interest on the repayment of the loan.* These additional deductions for ESOP loan principal and interest are not available for S corporations.

Additional Requirements for ESOPs

As discussed previously, in addition to complying with the general requirements imposed on defined contribution plans, ESOPs must also comply with requirements concerning voting rights, diversification, and account allocation restrictions. IRC Section 401(a)(22) specifies the voting rights applicable to all qualified stock bonus plans, including ESOPs. See the section on "Voting Rights."

Usually, the fiduciary of a qualified plan is charged with the responsibility of selecting proper investments and properly diversifying the assets of the trust to ensure a reasonable return. Because ESOPs invest primarily in employer securities, they are exempt from these requirements to the extent of their investments in qualifying employer securities. This means that qualifying employer securities held by an ESOP are not required to produce the return that would normally be expected from similar types of qualified plans. Courts have held that fiduciaries may only be liable for failure to diversify the trust investments in a plan that invests *exclusively* in employer stock, if the terms of the plan require a *primary*, but not *exclusive*, investment in employer stock.

An ESOP is required to permit employees who are near retirement age to diversify the investments in their separate accounts. Specifically, an ESOP must give each "qualified participant" an opportunity to have a portion of his or her account balance invested in investments other than employer securities each year during his or her "qualified election period." A "qualified participant" is any employee who is at least age 55 and who has participated in the plan for at least 10 years. The "qualified election period" is the six-plan-year period beginning with the plan year in which the individual first becomes a qualified participant. During the first 90 days of each of these plan years, a qualified participant must be allowed to elect to diversify up to 25 percent of his or her post-1986 stock, reduced by any amounts previously subject to diversification. In the final plan year, 50 percent of such employer securities are subject to the diversification election.

The diversification requirements may be met in one of three ways under IRC Section 401(a)(28)(B)(ii). First, the ESOP may offer at least three different investment options. Any investment option selected must then be implemented within 90 days after the end of the election period. Second, the ESOP may distribute the amount so elected to the participant within 90 days after the close of the diversification election period, either in cash or in stock (in which case the usual put option rules will apply). This amount is subsequently eligible for a rollover into an IRA or for a transfer to another qualified defined contribution plan that offers at least three investment options. Finally, the plan may permit the participant to direct a transfer of the diversification amount into another qualified plan providing for employee-directed investment and in which the required diversification options are available.

With regard to individual account allocations, the general rules of IRC Section 415(c) for allocating contributions among plan participants apply to ESOPs. Thus, the amount of "annual additions" to a participant's account is limited to the lesser of $42,000 (in 2005) or 100 percent of the participant's compensation. As in other qualified plans, "annual additions" include employer contributions (to all defined contribution plans in which the employee is a participant), forfeitures allocated to the participant's account, and employee contributions. Dividends paid on employer stock to an ESOP that are used to repay an exempt loan are *not* considered annual additions.

Two special provisions apply to ESOPs, both of which can substantially increase the amount of annual additions available to participants. Recall that "annual additions" include employer contributions, forfeitures allocated to an account, and employee contributions. Under IRC Section 415(c)(6), if no more than one-third of the employer contributions for a year are allocated to highly compensated employees (HCEs), then the following items will not be included in "annual additions" for purposes of applying the general limitations for defined contribution plans under IRC Section 415(c)(1):

(1) Forfeitures of stock acquired by the ESOP with an exempt loan

(2) Employer contributions to the ESOP used to pay interest on an exempt loan

Distributions

An ESOP may make distributions either in cash or in stock, but must provide participants with the *right* to demand payment in the form of qualifying employer securities. If the employer securities are not readily tradable on an established securities market, the participant must be given the "put option," discussed earlier, requiring the employer (not the ESOP) to repurchase the securities under a fair valuation formula.

All qualified plans are required to begin benefit payments under IRC Section 401(a)(14) no later than 60 days after the end of the plan year in which the latest of the following occurs: the participant (1) attains age 65 or an earlier normal retirement age under the plan; (2) reaches the 10th anniversary of his or her participation in the plan; or (3) terminates employment. Nonetheless, IRC Section 409(o) requires additional rules for ESOPs which allow for early distributions for separation from service before normal retirement age. Unless the participant otherwise elects in writing, the ESOP must begin benefit payments of the participant's account balance no later than one year after the close of the plan year: (1) in which the participant terminates employment due to retirement, disability, or death, or (2) which is the fifth plan year following the plan year in which the employee separated from service for any other reason, provided that he or she was not reemployed within this same five-year period. For these purposes, the participant's account balance does not include employer securities acquired with a loan in a leveraged ESOP until the close of the plan year in which the loan is repaid in full.

If the general rules were to require a benefit payment starting date sooner than the ESOP rules, those general rules, of course, must be followed if the plan is to remain qualified. Thus, the required starting date for distributions is the earlier of the general rules or the ESOP rules (i.e., IRC Section 401(a)(14) versus IRC Section 409(o)). In addition, there are rules governing the length of time over which a distribution may be made.

IRC Section 409(o)(1)(C) also provides rules that limit the length of time over which a distribution may be made. Unless the participant otherwise elects, the ESOP must distribute his or her account balance in substantially equal periodic payments over a period of no longer than five years. If the account balance exceeds $850,000 (in 2005), however, the payment term may be lengthened by one year for each $170,000 (in 2005), or fraction thereof, over $850,000, with a maximum payout period not to exceed ten years. The 2005 payout rules are as follows:

Account Balance	Maximum Payout Period
$1–$850,000	5 years
$850,001–$1,020,000	6 years
$1,020,001–$1,190,000	7 years
$1,190,001–$1,360,000	8 years
$1,360,001–$1,530,000	9 years
$1,530,001 and over	10 years

IMPORTANT CONCEPTS

Stock bonus plan

Participant voting rights

Unrealized appreciation on employer stock or securities

"Put option" for closely held employer stock

Qualifying employer securities

Diversification requirements for participants nearing retirement

Account allocation restrictions

IRC Section 1042 deferral of gain on sale of employer stock to ESOP

"Replacement securities"

Valuation of qualifying securities of a nonpublicly traded employer.

Dividend deduction rules

Nonleveraged versus leveraged ESOPs

"Exempt loan"

Deduction for principal and interest on repayment of exempt loan

Voting rights

Annual additions limit for ESOPs

QUESTIONS FOR REVIEW

1. What is the primary difference between a profit-sharing plan and a stock bonus plan?

2. What are some of the advantages and disadvantages of a stock bonus plan?

3. What is the deduction limit for employer contributions to a stock bonus plan?

4. What is the annual additions limit for a stock bonus plan?

5. How do participant voting rights differ between stock that is *not* publicly traded on an established securities market and stock that *is* so traded?

6. How does the income tax treatment of lump-sum distributions of employer stock or securities from a stock bonus plan differ from that applicable to a nonlump-sum distribution?

7. What is meant by a "put option" available to a participant in a stock bonus plan who receives stock not publicly traded on an established securities market?

8. How does an ESOP differ from a regular stock bonus plan?

9. What is meant by "qualifying employer securities"?

10. What entities other than a C corporation may adopt an ESOP?

11. What must be stated in the plan document for an ESOP?

12. Under what circumstances may an ESOP integrate its benefits formula with Social Security benefits?

13. What is the deduction limit for contributions to a LESOP?

14. What is the income tax treatment of gain realized on the sale of employer stock to the employer's ESOP by a retiring owner?

15. What constitutes "replacement securities" for purposes of IRC Section 1042 deferral of gain recognition on sale of employer securities to the employer's ESOP?

16. For what purposes is it important to establish a fair market value for qualifying securities of a nonpublicly traded employer?

17. What is the income tax treatment of cash dividends paid by an employer to its ESOP participants?

18. What are the two general types of ESOPs?

19. What is the basic process for an employer to obtain favorable debt financing through its LESOP?

20. What is meant by an "exempt loan" for purposes of Regulation 54.4975-7&-11?

21. How is an employer able to deduct both principal and interest on repayment of an exempt loan made to its LESOP?

22. What are the diversification requirements applicable to ESOP participants nearing retirement age?

23. What two special provisions applicable to ESOPs can substantially increase the amount of annual additions available to ESOP participants?

24. In addition to the normal rules applicable to the commencement of benefit payments under all qualified plans, what additional benefit payment rules are applicable to ESOPs?

25. How is the required starting date determined for the payment of benefits from an ESOP?

26. If a participant in an ESOP has a balance of $1,200,000, over what period of time must his or her balance be distributed in substantially equal periodic payments?

SUGGESTIONS FOR ADDITIONAL READING

The Tools & Techniques of Employee Benefit and Retirement Planning, 9th edition, Stephan R. Leimberg and John J. McFadden, The National Underwriter Company, 2005.

CHAPTER ELEVEN

401(k) Plans

• • •

Probably the best known qualified retirement plan is an IRC Section 401(k) plan, also known as a cash or deferred arrangement (CODA). A 401(k) plan is an arrangement that is part of a qualified profit-sharing or stock bonus plan under which an eligible employee may decide whether or not he or she will contribute to his or her own retirement fund. An employee may elect to have the employer contribute up to $14,000 (in 2005) plus "catch-up contributions" (if the plan permits this type of contribution) of up to $4,000 (in 2005) (for employees age 50 or over at the end of the plan year) to a trust under the plan, or to have the amount paid to the employee in cash. Other than the CODA option, a traditional 401(k) plan is much like any other profit-sharing plan (discussed in chapter 9). Indeed, a profit-sharing plan document must exist if the 401(k) plan feature is to be effective. Consequently, it must meet not only the general requirements for a profit-sharing plan but also additional special requirements for a 401(k) plan.

Upon completing this chapter, you should be able to:

- Describe the general characteristics of a 401(k), or CODA, plan
- Identify some of the advantages and disadvantages of a 401(k) plan
- Explain the various qualification requirements that a 401(k) plan must meet
- Describe a special provision of the general coverage tests that is applicable only to 401(k) plans
- Describe the actual deferred percentage (ADP) tests for nondiscrimination that must be satisfied by a 401(k) plan
- Discuss the "fail-safe" provisions in the Treasury Regulations applicable to 401(k) plans

- Identify some of the basic types of 401(k) plans
- Distinguish between a traditional 401(k) plan and a SIMPLE 401(k) plan
- Describe the features of a "safe harbor" 401(k) plan
- Explain how a 401(k) plan can incorporate a qualified Roth contribution program, beginning in 2006
- Identify the permissible types of contributions to 401(k) plans and the limitations to which they are subject
- Describe the treatment of excess contributions to a 401(k) plan
- Describe the general rules applicable to the distribution of employee elective deferrals under a 401(k) plan and the "same desk" rule
- Identify the types of distributions from a 401(k) plan that qualify as "hardship withdrawals" and satisfy the "immediate and heavy financial need" requirements
- Describe the vesting provisions applicable to various types of contributions to a 401(k) plan

DEFINITION AND PROS AND CONS

A qualified cash or deferred arrangement (CODA) (IRC Section 401(k) plan) is an arrangement within a qualified profit-sharing, stock bonus, pre-ERISA money purchase, rural electric cooperative, Indian tribal government, or tax-exempt organization plan under which a participant may elect either to receive current cash compensation or have the employer contribute an equal amount on a pre-tax basis to the qualified plan. The arrangement typically contains a salary reduction agreement under which employer contributions are made only if the participant elects to reduce his or her compensation or not take a pay increase in cash. The agreement may also give the participant the option to receive a portion of the elective amount in cash with the remainder contributed to the qualified plan.

Some of the advantages of such a plan include: (1) employees are empowered to determine how much to save for their retirement; (2) the employer receives an income tax deduction for up to 25 percent of covered payroll (including elective deferrals, or before-tax salary reduction contributions) plus the elective deferrals deposited in the plan; (3) the employer has the option of either relying solely on employee elective deferrals to fund the retirement plan or supplementing this funding by making matching or nonelective contributions; and (4) employees may be able to take in-service so-called "hardship" withdrawals, discussed later in this chapter.

A 401(k) plan does carry with it certain disadvantages, such as (1) the fact that because it is a defined contribution plan, a participant's account balance at retirement will *not* necessarily provide adequate retirement income; (2) an employee (who may be highly compensated) is limited to a salary reduction of $14,000 (in 2005) (plus another $4,000 (in 2005) if he or she is age 50 or over at the end of the plan year); (3) the plan (unless a SIMPLE 401(k) or Safe Harbor 401(k) plan) is subject to the actual deferred percentage (ADP) tests for nondiscrimination (discussed later in this chapter), which can be expensive, limiting, and difficult to administer; and (4) the employees bear the investment risk of their account balance.

GENERAL QUALIFICATION REQUIREMENTS

As discussed previously, in order to receive special tax treatment, a 401(k) plan must first satisfy the general qualification requirements for profit-sharing and stock bonus plans under IRC Section 401(a) (see chapters 9 and 10). In addition, a 401(k) plan must meet special provisions, which relate mainly to nondiscrimination, nonforfeitability, and distribution requirements.

As discussed previously, a 401(k) plan must be a part of a qualified profit-sharing or stock bonus plan. [Technically, it may also be a part of a rural electric cooperative plan, a plan maintained by Indian tribal governments, a plan maintained by tax-exempt employers, or a pre-ERISA money purchase plan.] A 401(k) plan cannot be a stand-alone program. Both the 401(k) plan and the underlying plan must meet their respective qualification requirements. For example, if the 401(k) plan meets the special rules applicable to it, but the underlying plan does not qualify under IRC Section 401(a), the entire arrangement is nonqualified for income tax purposes. The underlying plan that contains the 401(k) plan may still separately qualify as long as it meets the IRC Section 401(a) requirements, even though the 401(k) plan fails to meet the separate requirements. In this latter case, contributions made to the plan on account of elective deferrals are includible in the employee's gross income. However, this may, in turn, cause a qualification problem for the underlying plan due to the restrictions on nondeductible employee contributions (IRC Section 401(m)).

Nondiscrimination Requirements

As with other qualified plans, a 401(k) plan must *not* discriminate in favor of highly compensated employees (HCEs) with respect to coverage and benefits or contributions. Specifically, all 401(k) plans must satisfy the IRC Section 410(b) general nondiscrimination tests (discussed in chapter 7) and 401(k) plans, other than SIMPLE 401(k) plans or safe harbor plans (discussed later in this chapter), also must satisfy the special "actual deferred percentage" (ADP) tests.

With regard to the coverage or nondiscrimination tests, IRC Section 410(b) requires that a plan must satisfy *one* of two general tests: either a percentage test, a ratio test, or an average benefits test, as discussed in chapter 7. Since it is likely that a 401(k) plan would not satisfy the actual participation requirements due to the lack of contributions by many of the lower-paid employees, a 401(k) plan may, under IRC Section 401(a)(26)(C), treat all *eligible* employees, rather than just the *covered* employees, as benefiting under the plan. As a result, the 70-percent test of IRC Section 410(b)(1)(A) (discussed in chapter 7) is met if at least 70 percent of "all employees" are *eligible* to participate in the 401(k) plan, rather than if they actually do participate.

With regard to the special "actual deferral percentage" (ADP) tests relating to nondiscrimination as to benefits or contributions, ADPs must be calculated for the group of HCEs (as defined in IRC Section 414(q)) and the group of NHCEs. The ADP for each group is computed as the simple average of the employees' deferred percentages. Thus, the first step is to compute, for each employee who is eligible to make elective deferrals under the plan, the actual deferred ratio (ADR) of: (1) the amount of elective contributions actually paid over to the trust on his or her behalf for the plan year, to (2) the employee's compensation for the plan year. (Note: any special "catch-up" contributions, and earnings attributable thereto are disregarded when determining ADP ratios for a plan year). Next, the simple average of these ratios is computed for the group of HCEs and for the group of NHCEs. Any elective deferrals are counted as compensation, except that an employer may elect *not* to include as compensation any amount which is contributed by the employer pursuant to an elective deferral and which is not includible in the gross income of an employee under a cafeteria plan, 401(k) plan, tax-sheltered annuity, or SEP. As discussed in previous chapters, the amount of covered compensation that may be taken into account under any plan is limited to $210,000 (in 2005).

Having performed the calculations called for in the previous paragraph, a 401(k) plan must then satisfy, in actual operation, one of two of the following alternative ADP tests:

- Test 1: The ADP for eligible HCEs for the plan year is not more than the ADP of all other eligible employees *for the preceding plan year* multiplied by 1.25.
- Test 2: The ADP for eligible HCEs for the plan year does not exceed the ADP for other eligible employees *for the preceding plan year* by more than 2 percent *and* the ADP for eligible HCEs for the plan year is not more than the ADP of all other eligible employees *for the preceding plan year* multiplied by two.

Thus, the maximum spreads between the ADPs for the HCEs and the NHCEs are as follows:

Prior Year ADP for the NHCEs	Current Year Maximum ADP for the HCEs
0-2%	2 times that rate
2-8%	2 percentage points more
above 8%	1.25 times that rate

As just discussed, these tests require a specific comparison of the elective deferrals, expressed as a percentage of compensation, by HCEs and NHCEs. As described in both tests, this comparison is based on *prior* year data in determining the ADP for NHCEs, while *current* year data is used for HCEs. This enables the HCEs to know in advance the overall limit on their combined deferrals. Employers have the option to use current year data for determining the ADP for both HCEs and NHCEs for any plan year, but if an employer decides to change back to the prior-year testing method, such a change is subject to certain restrictions. Also, instead of applying two separate ADP tests, a plan may adopt a single ADP test that compares the ADP of the HCEs with the ADP of the NHCEs who are eligible to participate and who have met the minimum age and service requirements.

Here is an example of the calculation of the ADP for a group of employees.

> **Example:** Assume an employer maintains a profit-sharing plan with 401(k) provisions that permits employees to defer up to 10 percent of their total compensation, up to a maximum contribution of $14,000 for the 2005 plan year. Information for employees X and Y, who comprise the entire NHCE group, is as follows:

Employee	Compensation	Deferred Amount	ADR
X	$20,000	$2,000	10%
Y	10,000	-0-	0%

Thus, the ADP for the group is 5 percent, the average of 10 percent and 0 percent, and not 6.67 percent, which is the total deferred amount divided by the total compensation.

Once the ADP for each of the two groups of employees has been calculated, a comparison for discrimination is made. The standard method for this comparison is based on the prior-year ADP for NHCEs, while the current year ADP is used for HCEs. In the case of the first plan year, the ADP for the NHCEs is 3 percent, or at the employer's election, the ADP of the NHCEs for the first plan year.

Here is an example of how to apply the above rules:

> **Example:** Employees A, B, and C are the eligible employees and earn $30,000, $15,000, and $10,000 a year, respectively. These salary figures are used by the employer in determining contributions up to 10 percent of compensation to a 401(k) plan. Under the arrangement, each eligible employee may elect either to receive, in whole or in part, a direct cash payment of his or her allocated contribution in the current year or to have the amount contributed by the employer to the plan. For the plan year, A, B, and C make the following elections:

Employee	Salary	Elected Contribution to Plan	Cash Election	Total Compensation
A	$30,000	$2,000	$1,000	$33,000
B	15,000	750	750	16,500
C	10,000	400	600	11,000

Therefore, the ratios of employer contributions to the trust on behalf of each eligible employee to the employee's compensation for the plan year (calculated separately for each employee) are:

Employee	Ratio of Contribution to Total Compensation	ADR
A	2,000/33,000	6.06%
B	750/16,500	4.55%
C	400/11,000	3.64%

Finally, assume that A owns more than 5 percent of the employer's stock and is therefore an HCE, and that B and C are NHCEs. Accordingly, the ADP for the NHCEs group is 4.10% (the average of 4.55% and 3.64%, rounded to the nearest 0.01%). Thus, in the following plan year, A's maximum deferral is 6.10% of his compensation (i.e., 2 percentage points more than the ADP of the NHCEs).

"Fail-Safe" Provisions in Regulations

Now that the reader has been exposed to the ADP tests, it is easy to understand why a 401(k) plan must be concerned about satisfying these tests year after year in order to maintain its tax qualification. Thus, 401(k) plans are subject to the unpredictability of the NHCEs electing to defer a smaller percentage of their compensation in the next year. Although most of this uncertainty has been removed with the change to using the prior year ADP of the NHCEs in the discrimination test, it still exists for employers who elect to use current-year ADP ratios for the NHCE group. In light of this uncertainty, the regulations provide a "fail-safe" mechanism for employers to be able to exercise more control by making nonelective contributions and/or matching contributions, in addition to the employees' elective contributions.

For example, an employer could provide a nonelective contribution on behalf of all employees equal to 5 percent of salary and an elective contribution of 2 percent of salary. Thus, even if all of the NHCEs elected to receive the 2 percent in cash and all of the HCEs elected to have it contributed to the plan, the plan would still meet the ADP tests, since it is designed in such a way as to never fail the test. However, the price of being able to combine the employer's nonelective or matching contribution with the employees' elective contribution, for purposes of the ADP test, is that the nonelective or matching portion must comply with the distribution restrictions and full and immediate vesting provisions applicable to elective deferrals.

> **Example**: Assume that Plan XYZ is a qualified profit-sharing plan that contains a 401(k) plan. Plan XYZ elects to compute the ADP for NHCEs based on current year data. Assume that employer contributions on behalf of its 9 employees are as follows:
>
> 1. A qualified nonelective contribution (QNEC) of 2 percent of each employee's compensation, with such amounts subject to the distribution restrictions of IRC Section 401(k)(2)(B) and the full and immediate vesting requirements of IRC Section 401(k)(2)(C), and
>
> 2. Up to 2 percent of each employee's compensation that an employee may receive in cash or as an elective deferral into the plan.

For the plan year, employees 1 through 9 received compensation and deferred contributions as indicated below:

Employee	Wages	2% Non-Elective Contribution	2% Elective Contribution Deferred	Total Compensation (including non-elective deferrals)	ADR
1	$98,000	$2,000	$2,000	$100,000	2.00%
2	78,400	1,600	1,600	80,000	2.00%
3	58,800	1,200	1,200	60,000	2.00%
4	39,600	800	400	40,400	0.99%
5	27,700	600	300	30,300	0.99%
6	20,000	400	-0-	20,400	-0-
7	20,000	400	-0-	20,400	-0-
8	10,000	200	-0-	10,200	-0-
9	5,000	100	-0-	5,100	-0-

Finally, also assume that employees 1 and 2 are the only HCEs. In this case, the 2 percent elective portion (considered alone) does *not* satisfy the ADP tests. The ADP for the HCE group is 2.00 percent (the average ADR for employees 1 and 2), and the ADP for the NHCE group is 0.57 percent. However, since the 2 percent QNEC meets the distribution and vesting requirements, it may be considered in computing the ADP for the groups. The ADP for the HCE group, when the nonelective contributions are considered, is 4.00 percent, and for the NHCE group, the ADP is 2.54 percent. Although the plan does not meet the 1.25 ADP test, it does meet the second test (that is, 4.00 percent is less than 5.08 percent (2.54% x 2) and less than 4.54 percent (2.54% + 2.0%).

Other rules in this area are extremely complex and beyond the scope of this text.

TYPES OF 401(K) PLANS

There are five general types of 401(k) plans. These include the salary reduction, bonus, SIMPLE, safe harbor, and Roth types. We will discuss each of these types in the following sections.

Salary Reduction-Type Plans

Under the most common type of 401(k) plan, the salary reduction type, the employee elects to reduce his or her normal compensation for the coming year, or elects to forgo an increase in his or her current compensation, and have the amount instead contributed to the plan. Salary reductions must be elected by employees *before* the compensation is earned. For example, an employee may elect to have his or her salary reduced by four percent effective January 1 of the next year. Typically, an employee completes a salary reduction election form before the end of each calendar year effective for the next calendar year. Any amount that an employee elects to have contributed to the plan is not subject to federal income tax for the period in which it was earned (assuming the plan meets the special qualification requirements, described earlier). Consequently, if an employee elects to reduce his or her compensation by $100 per month, his or her net pay does not decline by the full $100 because the income tax applicable to this amount is no longer withheld from the employee's pay. These elective deferrals are, however, subject to FICA and FUTA taxes for the period in which they were earned.

Bonus-Type Plans

Under the bonus form of a 401(k) plan, an employee may elect to have the employer contribute to the plan all or any portion of an amount in excess of his or her normal compensation (e.g., a year-end bonus). If the employee does not so elect, the applicable amount may be paid to the employee in cash. For example, a 401(k) plan may permit participants to elect to allocate, in any proportion they see fit, five percent of their compensation (in the form of a bonus) between current cash or a contribution to the plan.

A bonus-type plan may not be particularly beneficial to lower-paid employees who may be hard-pressed to defer any portion of their compensation, even in light of the income tax benefits and the possibility of an employer matching contribution. Other employees may perceive a holiday bonus as an amount intended by the employer to help them pay their holiday bills and therefore should, instead, be taken as cash compensation.

SIMPLE 401(k) Plans

As we discussed in chapter 6, a Savings Incentive Match Plan for Employees (SIMPLE plan) may be either in the form of an IRA arrangement or adopted as part of a 401(k) plan. Also as discussed in chapter 6, SIMPLE 401(k) plans are available *only* to employers that: (1) employed 100 or fewer employees who earned $5,000 or more during the preceding year; and (2) do not maintain another qualified plan covering the employees who are eligible to participate in the SIMPLE 401(k) plan.

Special rules apply to SIMPLE 401(k) plans. First, SIMPLE 401(k) plans are *not* subject to the top-heavy rules (discussed in chapter 7). Second, eligibility for participation applies to all employees who have received at least $5,000 in compensation from the employer during any two preceding calendar years and who are reasonably expected to receive at least that amount during the current calendar year. Third, the plan does not have to satisfy the special ADP and actual contribution percentage (ACP) tests (for contributory plans) otherwise applicable to plans containing CODAs and matching contributions. Instead, those special tests are deemed met if:

1. Each eligible employee may elect to make salary reduction contributions for a year of up to $10,000 (in 2005)

2. The employer makes a matching contribution equal to the employee's salary reduction

contribution, limited to 3 percent of the employee's compensation for the year, or alternatively, makes a nonelective contribution for all eligible employees equal to 2 percent of the employee's compensation for the year

3. No other contributions are made under the SIMPLE 401(k) arrangement, nor are any contributions or benefit accruals under any other qualified plan of the employer covering the employees eligible to participate in the SIMPLE 401(k)

4. All amounts contributed under the SIMPLE 401(k) provisions are nonforfeitable (i.e., fully vested) at all times.

A SIMPLE 401(k) plan must use a calendar year as its plan year. Existing 401(k) plans not currently on a calendar plan year that want to adopt the SIMPLE provisions must convert their plan year to a calendar year.

Finally, a SIMPLE 401(k) must also permit each eligible employee to make or modify an elective deferral during the 60-day period immediately preceding each January 1. The employer must notify each eligible employee of the employee's right to make this election within a reasonable time period before the applicable election period. The plan must also allow a SIMPLE 401(k) plan participant to terminate an elective deferral at any time during the year.

Traditional 401(k) Plans versus SIMPLE 401(k) Plans

One of the drawbacks of the SIMPLE 401(k) plan is that annual employer contributions are *required*, whether the employer matches employee deferrals (up to 3 percent of compensation) or makes the 2 percent nonelective contribution (QNEC). As discussed previously, annual employer contributions are discretionary under a traditional 401(k) plan, except for years in which the plan is top heavy or years in which one of the safe harbor provisions is used to ensure that the ADP test is met.

In addition, SIMPLE plans could potentially have broader coverage, because each employee who earns over $5,000 is permitted to make an elective deferral that must be matched by the employer. If the alternative two percent nonelective contribution is made, an employer contribution is required for all eligible employees. Conversely, the traditional 401(k) plan requires only 70 percent coverage for eligibility, not participation.

The annual limit on elective deferrals under a traditional 401(k) plan is higher than the SIMPLE 401(k) plan ($14,000 versus $10,000 in 2005). However, the level of deferral for HCEs under a traditional plan is directly limited by the ADP of the NHCEs. No such limit applies to SIMPLE plans.

All employer-matching or nonelective contributions under a SIMPLE plan are immediately (100 percent) vested. Employer contributions under a traditional plan are subject to the normal vesting rules, unless the employer contributions are made in accordance with the fail-safe provisions, discussed earlier in this chapter. In either case, employee elective deferrals are nonforfeitable at all times.

Finally, employers adopting a SIMPLE 401(k) plan cannot make contributions other than those allowed under the SIMPLE provisions. Moreover, the employer cannot maintain any other qualified plan under which additional contributions or benefit accruals may be made. In addition, an employer who adopts a SIMPLE 401(k) plan must determine in advance of each calendar year whether it will match employee contributions or make the nonelective contribution (due to the 60-day notice requirement).

Safe Harbor 401(k) Plans

The Internal Revenue Code provides a "safe harbor provision" under which a traditional 401(k) plan may *automatically* satisfy the nondiscrimination rules. The safe harbor option requires an employer contribution that is either a matching contribution or a nonelective contribution. Similar to the fail-safe provision, employer matching and nonelective contributions used to satisfy the safe harbor rules must be nonforfeitable and subject to the distribution restrictions that apply to employee elective deferrals.

Under the matching contribution safe harbor, the employer matches each NHCE's elective contribution in an amount equal to:

1. 100 percent of the employee's elective contribution, up to 3 percent of the employee's compensation; and
2. 50 percent of the employee's elective contribution on the next 2 percent of the employee's compensation.

The match rate for HCEs may not be greater than the match rate for NHCEs at any level of compensation. As an alternative, the matching safe harbor is considered to be met if the employer's match rate does not increase as an employee's elective contribution increases, and the match amount equals at least the amount that would be made under the matching levels above.

Using the nonelective contribution safe harbor, the plan must require the employer to make a contribution, on behalf of each eligible NHCE, of an amount equal to at least 3 percent of the employee's compensation, without regard to any employee contribution.

Finally, a plan that intends to satisfy the safe harbor requirements for a plan year must, prior to the beginning of the plan year, contain language to that effect and must specify which safe harbor will be used. However, a plan is permitted to be amended, not later than 30 days before plan year-end, to use the safe harbor rules for that plan year. So, if it appears that a plan will not meet the ADP and ACP tests, an employer may adopt the safe harbor three percent employer nonelective contribution for the year as late as December 1 of that year. Moreover, a plan may also be amended during the plan year to forego the matching contribution safe harbor if it otherwise expects to meet the ADP and ACP tests.

Under either safe harbor contribution provision, each eligible employee must be given written or electronic notice of their rights and obligations under the plan within a reasonable period of time before the plan year or, for the year in which an employee becomes eligible, within a reasonable period of time before the employee becomes eligible.

Roth 401(k) Plans

Beginning in 2006, 401(k) plans may incorporate a "qualified Roth contribution" program. Under such a plan, participants may elect to have all or a portion of their elective deferrals treated as Roth contributions. Unlike regular 401(k) elective deferrals, Roth contributions are included in the participant's current income; however, as discussed in chapter 4, qualified distributions from a designated Roth account are *not* included in income.

Under a qualified Roth contribution program, participants are permitted to make designated Roth contributions in lieu of all or part of elective deferrals that they are otherwise allowed to make under the 401(k) plan. These Roth elective deferrals are subject to the same immediate vesting requirements and distribution restrictions normally imposed on regular 401(k) elective deferrals.

Because qualified distributions are not included in an employee's income, the plan must establish and maintain a separate "designated Roth account" for designated Roth contributions and attributed earnings for each employee. Failure to maintain this separate account and recordkeeping disqualifies the program.

Since they are part of a participant's eligible 401(k) elective deferrals, Roth contributions are subject to the same 401(k) contribution limits. Accordingly, Roth contributions are subject to the annual limit on elective deferrals, reduced by the amount of other elective deferrals under the 401(k) plan, as well as the ADP limits.

Qualified distributions from a designated Roth account are not included in a participant's income. A qualified distribution from a designated Roth account is equivalent to one made from a Roth IRA account. Thus, as discussed in chapter 4, the distribution must be made after a five-year "nonexclusion" period and:

1. Made on or after the date on which the participant attains age 59 1/2;
2. Made to a beneficiary (or to the participant's estate) on or after the death of the participant; or
3. Attributable to the participant's being disabled.

The five-year nonexclusion period is the five-year period beginning with the earlier of (1) the first tax year in which the participant makes a designated Roth contribution to any designated Roth account under the employer plan, or (2) if the participant has made a rollover contribution to the designated Roth account from another plan, the first year in which the participant made a designated Roth contribution to that previous plan.

Qualified distributions from a designated Roth account may be rolled over to either (1) another designated Roth account for the participant (if the new plan allows for rollovers), or (2) the participant's Roth IRA. Such rollovers are not taken into account for purposes of the annual limits on elective deferrals.

CONTRIBUTIONS

Two types of contributions may be made to CODAs. Employers may make nonelective contributions that are basically treated the same way for tax purposes as employer contributions to other qualified plans (that is, they are excludable income to the participant). The other type of contribution is elective deferrals that are made under a salary reduction plan. They are also excludable for income tax purposes when contributed, but are otherwise subject to FICA and FUTA taxes. The employer may also make matching contributions equal to the amount of or a certain percentage of the employees' elective contributions.

Under IRC Section 402(g), participants in traditional CODAs may make elective deferrals that may be excluded up to $14,000 (in 2005). In addition, as discussed previously, plan participants who are at least or will become age 50 before the end of the applicable calendar year, may make additional "catch-up" contributions of $4,000 (in 2005). Hence a catch-up-eligible participant may contribute a total of $18,000 (in 2005).

Excess Contributions

If the elective deferrals (including the qualified nonelective contributions and the qualified matching contributions) of the HCEs exceed the level permitted by the ADP tests, the plan must distribute the excess contributions (and income) to the HCEs by the end of the following plan year to maintain the qualified status of the plan. This distribution is *not* subject to the 10 percent tax on early distributions under IRC Section 72(t), but a 10 percent excise tax may be imposed on the employer for allowing these excess contributions. This excise tax may be avoided by the employer if the excess contributions (plus income) are distributed within 2 1/2 months after the end of the plan year in which the excess was contributed (March 15 for calendar year plans). As a result, if the distribution is made within the 2 1/2-month period, the plan will still be qualified, and no excise tax will be imposed. However, the excess contributions, and the income earned thereon, will still be taxed in the employee's taxable year in which they were made.

If the employer distributes the excess contributions after the 2 1/2-month period, but before the end of the next plan year, the penalty tax will be imposed but the plan will still be qualified. However, the employee will be taxed on the distribution (the excess contributions plus the income) in the year of the distribution, rather than in the year of the deferral.

Instead of distributing the excess contributions, the plan may permit the employee to recharacterize the excess contributions, and the earnings thereon, as distributions to the employee and then after-tax contributions by the employee to the plan. To be effective, such a recharacterization must take place no later than 2 1/2 months after the close of the plan year. The resulting presumed distribution is not subject to the early distribution penalty. However, since after-tax employee contributions must also meet an ADP test under IRC Section 401(m), such a recharacterization could place the underlying plan in danger of disqualification.

DISTRIBUTIONS

Employer and nonelective employee contributions to the underlying plan of a 401(k) plan are subject to the normal distribution restrictions discussed in chapter 7. However, the distribution of amounts that are attributable to an employee's elective deferral is further restricted. Such amounts may not be distributable earlier than:

1. Severance from employment, death, or disability
2. Termination of the plan without establishment or maintenance of another defined contribution plan, other than an ESOP (however, this rule applies only if the employee receives a lump-sum distribution because of the termination)
3. In the case of a profit-sharing or stock bonus underlying plan, the attainment of age 59 1/2, or
4. In the case of a profit-sharing or stock bonus underlying plan, if a hardship is experienced by the employee.

The Internal Revenue Code specifically prohibits employee deferred amounts from being distributable by reason of the completion of a stated period of participation or the lapse of a fixed number of years.

"Same Desk" Rule

Employees who continue to work the same job for a different employer (i.e., the "same desk") following a merger or acquisition of their former employer may receive distributions attributable to their elective deferrals, because they have severed employment from the former employer. However, a plan may provide that a severance from employment does *not* constitute a distributable event unless there is a sale of substantially all (at least 85 percent) of the assets of the former employer. Note that if there is a transfer of the plan assets and liabilities attributable to an employee's benefits from the former employer plan to a plan of the new employer (other than a rollover or elective transfer), then that employee is not considered to have severed employment with the former employer. Accordingly, a distribution of the employee's elective deferrals is not allowed under these circumstances.

Hardship Withdrawals

Plans are not required to permit hardship distributions, but instead are allowed to provide them if the plan complies with the hardship distribution requirements. Hardship withdrawals are not eligible for rollover and are subject to the normal withholding rules that apply to such distributions and to the 10 percent penalty tax imposed on early distributions.

In defining what constitutes a hardship, the regulations offer general guidelines. In order to be on account of hardship, a distribution must be because of "immediate and heavy financial needs" of the employee. Generally, for example, the need to pay the funeral expenses of a family member constitutes an immediate and heavy financial need. On the other hand, the purchase of a television or a boat generally would not meet this standard. A distribution is deemed to be made on account of immediate and heavy financial need of the employee if the distribution is on account of:

- Medical expenses
- Purchase of a principal residence for the employee
- Payment of tuition and room and board for the next 12 months for post-secondary education for the employee, his or her spouse, children, or dependents
- Payments to prevent the eviction of the employee from, or the foreclosure on the mortgage loan of, his principal residence

However, the foregoing list is not intended to be all-inclusive. There are other distributions that meet the requirement of immediate and heavy financial need.

The amount of a distribution which may be made on account of hardship is limited to that required to meet the immediate financial need created by the hardship and not reasonably available from other resources of the employee, such as assets of the employee's spouse or minor children. This amount may be "grossed up" to pay any federal, state, or local income taxes or penalties reasonably anticipated to result from the distribution. A distribution generally may be treated as necessary to satisfy a "financial need" if the employer reasonably relies upon the employee's representation that the need may not be met through reimbursement or compensation by insurance; by reasonable liquidation of the employee's assets, to the extent such liquidation would not itself cause an immediate and heavy financial need; by cessation of elective contributions or employee contributions to the plan; by other distributions or nontaxable loans from plans maintained by the employer (or by any other employer), or by borrowing from commercial sources on reasonable commercial terms.

The dollar amount of these distributions is generally limited to the amount of the employee's elective deferrals, reduced by any previous distributions on account of hardship. Earnings on the elective deferrals are *not* available for hardship distribution. In addition, employer matching contributions and nonelective employee contributions that are taken into account for the special nondiscrimination tests may not be distributed because of hardship.

Finally, a distribution will be deemed to be necessary to satisfy an "immediate and heavy financial need" of an employee if *all* of the following requirements are satisfied:

1. The distribution is not in excess of the amount of the immediate and heavy financial need of the employee
2. The employee has obtained all distributions, other than hardship distributions, and all nontaxable loans currently available under all plans maintained by the employer
3. The plan, and all other plans maintained by the employer, provide that the employee's elective contributions and employee contributions will be suspended for at least six months after receipt of the hardship distribution
4. The plan, and all other plans maintained by the employer, provide that the employee may not make elective contributions for the employee's taxable year immediately following the taxable year of the hardship distribution in excess of the applicable limit under IRC Section

402(g) for the next taxable year, less the amount of the employee's elective contributions for the taxable year of the hardship distribution. (Under proposed regulations, this last requirement would be eliminated).

As expected for a qualified plan, the hardship provisions must meet certain nondiscrimination standards. The determination of the existence of financial hardship and the amount required to be distributed to meet the need created by the hardship must be made in accordance with "nondiscriminatory and objective" standards set forth in the plan. However, no specific guidelines are provided in the regulations regarding the establishment of these standards.

VESTING

As discussed previously, the accrued benefit derived from employee elective deferrals contributed to the plan must be fully vested at all times. Accordingly, the provisions for forfeitures of vested benefits under IRC Section 411(b)(3) are not applicable to elective deferrals. Accrued benefits from employer contributions and nonelective employee contributions are subject to the regular vesting rules of IRC Section 411, with three exceptions. First, for the employer contributions or nonelective employee contributions to be "qualified," (i.e., taken into account for the special nondiscrimination requirements), they must be immediately and fully vested. Second, if the employer contributions or nonelective employee contributions are not separately accounted for (as discussed in the next section), they must also be immediately and fully vested. Third, any employer matching contributions made after 2001 are subject to accelerated vesting schedules (i.e., the 3-year cliff schedule or the 2-to-6 year graded schedule).

With regard to service requirements, no plan which contains a qualified 401(k) plan may require more than one year of service for participation.

Separate Accounting Required

Unless the plan provides a separate accounting of employee elective deferrals, the entire balance of the employee's account is subject to the distribution rules and full and immediate vesting provisions which were discussed in the previous section. As a result, all amounts held under the plan, including the accrued benefits derived from employer contributions, and even contributions made for years when the 401(k) plan was not qualified, are treated as employee elective deferrals.

As a rule, this separate accounting must allocate investment gains and losses on a reasonable pro rata basis, with adjustments for withdrawals and contributions. Any separate accounting will not be acceptable unless gains, losses, withdrawals, forfeitures and other credits or charges are separately allocated to the accrued benefits subject to the distribution and vesting requirements and other benefits on a reasonable and consistent basis.

FINAL REGULATIONS

On December 28, 2004, the Treasury Department and the IRS issued final regulations governing 401(k) plans. The regulations apply to plans that permit employees to make pre-tax contributions and to plans that have employer matching contributions or employee after-tax contributions. The existing regulations covering these plans were last updated in 1994. Since then, there have been significant statutory changes. Proposed regulations to comply with these changes were published on July 17, 2003.

These final regulations are the result of a long effort of gathering input from retirement plan participants, sponsors, and service providers. Specifically, they address many of the concerns raised by comments submitted in response to the proposed regulations. These final regulations will be fully effective for plan years that begin on or after January 1, 2006, although employers are permitted to use these new rules for any plan year that ends after December 28, 2004.

IMPORTANT CONCEPTS

Cash or deferred arrangement (CODA)

Actual deferred percentage (ADP) tests

SIMPLE 401(k) plan

Eligible versus covered employees

Actual deferred ratio (ADR)

"Fail-safe" provisions

Salary reduction-type plan

Bonus-type plan

Traditional 401(k) plan

Safe harbor 401(k) plan

Roth 401(k) plan

Designated Roth account

Excess contributions

Recharacterization of excess contributions

"Same desk" rule

Hardship withdrawal

Immediate and heavy financial needs of the employee

Separate accounting of elective employee contributions

QUESTIONS FOR REVIEW

1. Of what type of underlying qualified retirement plan is a 401(k) plan typically a part?

2. What is the meaning of the term CODA?

3. What are some of the advantages of a 401(k) plan?

4. What are some of the disadvantages of a 401(k) plan?

5. In addition to the general qualification requirements for profit-sharing and stock bonus plans, what categories of special qualification provisions must be met by a 401(k) plan?

6. What is the effect on contributions to a 401(k) plan if the underlying plan meets the general IRC Section 401(a) requirements but the 401(k) plan fails to meet the special requirements applicable to 401(k) plans?

7. What kinds of nondiscrimination tests must be satisfied by a 401(k) plan?

8. What are the three options for satisfying the IRC Section 410(b) coverage tests?

9. What special actual participation rule applies to 401(k) plans?

10. How does the actual deferred percentage (ADP) nondiscrimination test work for a 401(k) plan?

11. What is the treatment of elective deferrals in calculating a participant's compensation for purposes of the ADP test?

12. What are the two alternative ADP nondiscrimination tests either of which must be satisfied by a 401(k) plan?

13. What are the maximum spreads permitted between the ADPs for the HCE group and the NHCE group in a 401(k) plan?

14. What is the so-called "fail-safe" mechanism for employers to be able to exercise more control over satisfying the ADP tests?

15. What "price" does an employer pay for using the "fail-safe" mechanism to satisfy the ADP tests?

16. What are the five general types of 401(k) plans?

17. When must salary reductions be elected by participants in a 401(k) plan?

18. Why is it that an employee's net pay declines by less than the amount of his or her salary reduction amount?

19. While salary reduction amounts are not subject to income taxation, to what taxes, if any, are they subject?

20. How does a bonus-type 401(k) plan operate?

21. What requirements must be met by an employer wishing to adopt a SIMPLE 401(k) plan?

22. What are some of the special rules applicable to SIMPLE 401(k) plans?

23. What plan year must be used by a SIMPLE 401(k) plan?

24. What are some of the ways in which traditional and SIMPLE 401(k) plans are similar and ways in which they differ?

25. Under a SIMPLE 401(k) plan, what is the treatment of employer-matching or nonelective contributions from a vesting standpoint?

26. How does a traditional 401(k) plan become a safe harbor 401(k) plan?

27. What amount of contribution must an employer make to satisfy the nonelective contribution safe harbor for a 401(k) plan?

28. How does an employer satisfy the matching contribution safe harbor?

29. Beginning in 2006, how will a qualified Roth contribution program function as part of a 401(k) plan?

30. What is the limit on Roth contributions to a 401(k) plan?

31. What is the income tax treatment of qualified distributions from a designated Roth account of a 401(k) plan?

32. What are the two types of contributions that may be made to a CODA?

33. What is the total amount that can be contributed by a plan participant who is or will attain age 50 before the end of the plan year to his or her 401(k) account?

34. What must an employer do to maintain the qualified status of a 401(k) plan that has made excess contributions?

35. Amounts attributable to an employee's elective deferrals may not be distributable earlier than which events?

36. What is meant by the "same desk" rule regarding distributions attributable to a 401(k) plan participant's elective deferrals?

37. What constitutes a "hardship withdrawal" from a 401(k) plan?

38. What portion of a participant's 401(k) plan account is available for purposes of a hardship withdrawal?

39. How, if at all, do the vesting requirements differ for elective deferrals and nonelective employee contributions?

40. What is the purpose of separate accounting for employee elective deferrals?

SUGGESTIONS FOR ADDITIONAL READING

IRS Publication 560, *Retirement Plans for Small Business,* current edition.

Tools & Techniques of Employee Benefit and Retirement Planning, 9th edition, Stephan R. Leimberg and John J. McFadden, The National Underwriter Company, 2005.

Retirement Planning, by Carla Gordon, American Institute of CPAs, 2002.

U.S. Master Tax Guide, CCH Editorial Staff Publication, CCH Incorporated, current edition.

CHAPTER TWELVE

Other Defined Contribution Retirement Plans

• • •

In previous chapters, we have discussed the more significant types of defined contribution plans, including profit-sharing plans (chapter 9), stock bonus plans and ESOPs (chapter 10), 401(k) plans (chapter 11), and Keogh plans (chapter 8). In this chapter we will discuss the money purchase pension plan, the target benefit plan, and the savings/match or thrift plan.

Upon completing this chapter, you should be able to:

- Describe the basic provisions of a money purchase pension plan
- Identify some of the advantages and disadvantages of a money purchase pension plan
- Describe the limitations on contributions to a money purchase pension plan
- Identify the methods by which plan forfeitures may be treated in a money purchase pension plan
- Discuss the factors that determine a participant's benefits payable under a money purchase pension plan
- Describe the design of a target benefit plan as compared to a money purchase pension plan
- Explain how the contribution formula of a target benefit plan is determined
- Describe the design of a savings/match or thrift plan
- Identify the test for nondiscrimination applicable to both employee contributions and employer matching contributions in a savings/match or thrift plan.
- Describe the vesting requirements applicable to employer matching contributions in a savings/match or thrift plan

MONEY PURCHASE PENSION PLAN

A qualified pension plan is ordinarily a defined benefit plan because of the fact that the amount of retirement benefits to be paid to the participants is a determined amount, and the contributions to fund such benefits are determined by an actuary. In fact, Regulation 1.401-1(b)(i) states the following:

> "A pension plan within the meaning of Code Sec. 401(a) is a plan established and maintained by an employer primarily to provide systematically for the payment of definitely determinable benefits to his employees over a period of years, usually for life, after retirement. Retirement benefits generally are measured by, and based on, such factors as years of service and compensation received by the employees. The determination of the amount of retirement benefits and the contributions to provide such benefits are not dependent upon profits... A plan designed to provide benefits for employees or their beneficiaries to be paid upon retirement or over a period of years after retirement will, for purposes of Code Sec. 401(a), be considered a pension plan if the employer contributions under the plan can be determined actuarially on the basis of definitely determinable benefits, or, as in the case of *money purchase pension plans*, such contributions are fixed without being geared to profits."

The quoted Regulation states that money purchase plans are pension plans. They are so classified because their benefits, by virtue of a fixed contribution formula, are actuarially predictable. Money purchase plans, which are defined contribution plans, are the *only* exception to the general rule that pension plans are defined benefit plans.

Definition, Purpose, and Pros and Cons

As already discussed, a money purchase pension plan is a defined contribution qualified plan under which the employer is obligated to make definitely determinable annual contributions to the account of each participant in the plan. Unlike a profit-sharing plan, an employer's annual contributions to a money purchase pension plan are fixed, nondiscriminatory, and not based on profits or some other criteria. For example, under a money purchase plan, the plan may require that the employer contribute 5 percent of each participating employee's wages, regardless of whether the employer shows a profit for the year. As a result, money purchase plans have the advantage of being easily understood by participants.

There are numerous reasons why an employer may choose to establish a money purchase plan. As mentioned, one factor is that such plans are easily grasped by employees (e.g., we will deposit 5 percent of your compensation in your account each year) and are not difficult to operate. Also, if the employer has a relatively young labor force and wishes to encourage employment longevity, required annual contributions may be made over a substantial period of time so that they accumulate to a meaningful retirement nest egg for each employee. Another reason why an employer may consider creation of a money purchase plan is that the investment risk is transferred to the employees rather than being borne by the employer.

A money purchase plan offers tax-deductible annual employer contributions of up to 25 percent of the total payroll of the employees covered under the plan and the tax deferral on earnings characteristic of qualified plans. Annual additions to each participant's account are limited to the lesser of (1) 100 percent of the participant's compensation or (2) $42,000 (in 2005), as indexed. Moreover, participants in a money purchase plan may also reap the advantage of favorable investment results in their individual accounts or, alternatively, suffer the ill effects of poor investment choices.

However, participants who enter the plan when they are older will *not* have adequate time for the employer's required annual contributions to accumulate a meaningful retirement fund. The same result will occur where an employer adopts a money purchase plan when the key employees are reasonably close to retirement age. The disparity in retirement account balances between employees with many years of service and employees with significantly less years of service may be mitigated somewhat by the size of annual salary increases. Nevertheless, where annual salary increases have been relatively large, this disparity in account balances is smaller whereas the reverse is true where salary increases have been more conservative.

Due to the limitation on annual additions, HCEs in a money purchase plan typically receive a much smaller contribution as a percentage of total compensation than NHCEs. This is the result of the $42,000 cap (in 2005) on individual contributions and the limitation on the amount of compensation that may be taken into account for this purpose ($210,000 in 2005).

Another potentially negative factor in implementing a money purchase plan is that a participant's ultimate account balance at retirement is very sensitive to the actual investment return earned on his or her account. A difference of a few percentage points in the actual investment return may mean a significant difference in the size of one's account balance at retirement.

Finally, an employer adopting a money purchase pension plan is subject to the minimum funding requirements and must make annual contributions to the plan regardless of whether the employer has adequate profits or cash flow. If the employer contributes less than the minimum required amount (the amount specified by the plan's contribution formula), a penalty may be imposed on the amount of the shortfall.

Contributions

Under the law, employer contributions under a money purchase plan are a specified percentage of a participant's compensation (up to a maximum of 25 percent). For example, a plan's formula may call for 10 percent of the first $100,000 of annual compensation and 15 percent of earnings in excess of $100,000. Amounts contributed each year may not discriminate in favor of HCEs with only the first $210,000 of compensation of each participant (in 2005) taken into account in determining employer contributions.

An employer may contribute and take advantage of an income tax deduction for up to 25 percent of the payroll of participants covered by the plan. However, the limitation on annual additions to a participant's account is the lesser of $42,000 (in 2005) or 100 percent of the participant's annual compensation. Some money purchase plans incorporate into their contribution formula a factor for employee service with the employer; this may result in discrimination in favor of HCEs and threaten the overall tax qualification of the plan.

Plans that use uniform allocation formulas for making contributions to participants' accounts may take advantage of various "safe harbors" to avoid discrimination in actual plan operation. For instance, plans may satisfy the general nondiscrimination test for defined contribution plans discussed in chapter 9, restructure the relevant HCE and NHCE groups, or use cross-testing in plan design (for example, test defined contribution plans on the basis of benefits, rather than contributions) and vice versa for defined benefit plans.

Money purchase pension plans may also be integrated with Social Security benefits. This permits higher rates of employer contributions (within a "permitted disparity") for compensation *above* the so-called "integration level" than for compensation rates *below* that level.

Finally, salary reductions (elective deferrals) are *not* permitted in a money purchase plan as they are in a profit-sharing, SARSEP, SIMPLE IRA, or 403(b) plan. After-tax employee contributions are permissible but may easily run afoul of the nondiscrimination rules and are, therefore, understandably less popular.

Vesting

A money purchase plan may use any of the vesting provisions permitted by the Internal Revenue Code. 5-year cliff vesting is perhaps the most prevalent schedule used. Plan forfeitures left by nonvested or only partially vested plan participants terminating employment may be used to reduce future employer contributions or added to the accounts of remaining participants. As with contributions, if forfeitures are added to the accounts of remaining participants, they must also be allocated in a nondiscriminatory fashion, and are usually tied to participants' compensation, rather than current account balances.

Distributions

As with any defined contribution plan, benefits payable under a money purchase plan are based on a participant's account balance at the time the benefit payments are to begin. A participant's account balance is composed of: (1) employer contributions; (2) any forfeitures allocated to the participant's account; and (3) employee contributions. Benefits are normally distributed when a participant's employment is terminated or at the participant's "normal retirement age" (as specified in the plan). Historically, the account balance at this time is converted to an annuity and consequently the participant receives payments over the remainder of his or her life. As the reader may recall from the discussion in chapter 7, IRC Section 401(a)(11) requires a qualified plan to provide the accrued benefit payable to a participant, who does not die before the annuity starting date, in the form of a "qualified joint and survivor annuity" (QJSA). If the participant dies before the annuity starting date and has a surviving spouse, a qualified survivor annuity must be provided to the participant's surviving spouse. However, if a participant otherwise has the written consent of his or her spouse, he or she may elect a lump sum or some form of installment option.

Unlike profit-sharing plans, money purchase plans are generally *not* permitted to make "in-service" distributions before termination of employment. The portion of a participant's account balance attributable to employer contributions or earnings on the invested funds may not be distributed until the participant dies, retires, becomes disabled, terminates his or her employment, or the plan is terminated. Certain early distributions are subject to penalties.

TARGET BENEFIT PLAN

A target benefit plan is similar to a money purchase pension plan since the amount of employer contributions allocated to each participant is determined under a plan formula that does not allow employer discretion. Further, the plan is designed to generate the amount necessary to provide, for each participant, a specific benefit of the type provided by a defined benefit plan (i.e., a monthly pension). In other words, the benefit that the participant actually receives (and that the plan is legally obligated to provide) is based on the participant's account balance, but the objective is for the account balance to provide a specified periodic benefit. Target benefit plans are treated as defined contribution plans.

Definition, Purpose, and Pros and Cons

Although the term is used only once in the Internal Revenue Code, and is not defined in the Code, there are frequent references in IRS regulations and rulings to target benefit plans. A target benefit plan is a retirement plan that is a hybrid of a defined benefit pension plan and a money purchase pension plan. Under a target benefit plan, a "target" age-weighted, defined benefit is established, and contributions are determined by actuarial assumptions to fund the target benefit. Subsequently, after the initial plan contribution formula is established, no adjustments are made to that formula. In that respect, the plan is a defined contribution plan. Many of the other features of a target benefit plan are similar to those of money purchase pension plans. Consequently, the pros and cons of a target benefit plan are very much the same as those of a money purchase pension plan.

Contributions

As discussed previously, a contribution formula adequate to fund the "target (but not guaranteed) benefit" is determined by actuarial assumptions and, once calculated, is held constant thereafter. As a defined contribution plan, a target benefit plan is subject to the same contribution, deduction, and annual additions limitations as a money purchase plan.

A target benefit plan is required, under the minimum funding requirements, to make annual contributions in the amount specified in the plan formula. Penalties are applicable for failure to make the minimum annual contributions outlined in the plan. Also, like other defined contribution plans, the investment risk in a target benefit plan rests with the participant, not with the employer.

Employer contributions are tax-deductible when made as long as the plan continues to be "qualified" (i.e., as long as it meets the eligibility, vesting, funding, and other requirements). The employee is not taxed on contributions and plan earnings until withdrawn.

Vesting

A target benefit plan is subject to the normal vesting requirements imposed on defined contribution plans as discussed in chapter 7.

Distributions

As discussed previously, the benefit from a target benefit plan is *not* guaranteed and, unlike the traditional defined benefit plan (subsequently discussed in chapter 13), a participant's ultimate benefit from a target benefit plan depends on the plan's investment return. Since the retirement benefit is not guaranteed, a target benefit plan is not required by law to use the services of an actuary.

SAVINGS/MATCH OR THRIFT PLAN

While popular in the past as a free-standing qualified plan, the savings or thrift plan is now generally employed only as a *supplement to* a 401(k) plan. The most common form of savings or thrift plan features after-tax employee contributions and employer matching contributions. Beginning in 2006, Roth contribution programs (discussed in chapter 11) are expected to gradually replace savings or thrift contribution programs in 401(k) plans, due to the tax-free withdrawals permitted by a Roth program after the participant has met certain specific requirements.

Definition, Purpose, and Pros and Cons

A savings/match or thrift plan is a qualified defined contribution plan that has many of the characteristics of a profit-sharing plan (discussed in chapter 9). Under a savings plan, each participant elects to contribute a certain percentage of his or her compensation to the plan on an after-tax (nondeductible) basis, with the employer then matching these contributions in accordance with a prescribed formula. Such employee nondeductible contributions are *in addition to* any employee elective deferrals (limited to $14,000 in 2005 plus an additional $4,000 in catch-up contributions for qualifying participants). While not subject to the limitation on elective deferrals, thrift plan contributions are nevertheless subject to the actual contribution percentage (ACP) test for nondiscrimination, as first discussed in chapter 11 of this textbook.

A savings or thrift plan may be appropriate where the employer already has a 401(k) plan, wants to permit employee contributions beyond the elective deferral limits, and does not wish to adopt a Roth contribution program. Such a plan might also make sense for a relatively young employee population that has many years to build retirement funds and is willing to run some investment risk. A savings plan may also work well in tandem with a defined benefit pension plan by providing employees the opportunity to build additional retirement savings beyond those benefits guaranteed by the defined benefit plan.

While a savings plan does not offer before-tax employee contributions it does provide tax deferral on plan earnings and employer contributions until withdrawn by the participants. In addition, it offers employees the option of not contributing anything to their own retirement or, alternatively, making nondeductible contributions and receiving an employer match. Finally, like other defined contribution plans, a savings plan features individual participant accounts in which participants may benefit from favorable investment performance.

One drawback of such a plan is that it will not necessarily provide an adequate retirement benefit for participants, particularly if they fail to participate in a meaningful way. Also, older employees are limited both by annual contribution limits and by a short accumulation period. Investment risk is transferred to the participants but the administrative costs of keeping separate track of employee nondeductible contributions and employer matching contributions makes a savings plan more expensive to operate than other types of defined contribution plans.

Contributions

Employees are not required to participate in a savings/thrift plan but, if they do, they may elect to contribute a specific percentage of compensation within the limits established by the plan. As discussed earlier, these contributions are not tax-deductible by the employee. Generally, the employer matches the employee's contribution either 100 percent or at a percentage specified in the plan formula. Employer contributions are deductible as made as long as the plan remains tax-qualified (including meeting eligibility, vesting, funding and other requirements discussed in earlier chapters).

A savings plan has to satisfy the "actual contribution percentage" (ACP) test for nondiscrimination specified in IRC Section 401(m). The test is applicable to both employee contributions and employer matching contributions. Employee contributions must also satisfy the following test:

The average ratio (expressed as a percentage) of HCE contributions (both matched and non-matched) plus employer matching contributions to compensation *for the plan year* must not exceed the greater of:

1) 125 percent of the contribution percentage (i.e., ratio) for all other eligible employees (NHCEs) *for the preceding plan year*, or

2) the lesser of (a) 200 percent of the contribution percentage for all other eligible employees (NHCEs), or (b) such percentage plus two percentage points *for the preceding plan year*.

For example, if the total of employee contributions and employer matching contributions was 5 percent of the NHCEs' compensation in 2005, the applicable percentage for HCEs may be as much as 7 percent (5 percent plus 2 percent) in 2006.

In order to retain tax-qualification, the ACP test must be performed annually to determine the NHCE contribution level so that HCE contribution levels may be set for the subsequent year.

Employer matching contributions in a savings plan must also satisfy the ACP test by meeting the foregoing test used for employee contributions or by meeting any of two additional tests. The first additional test is that imposed on SIMPLE 401(k) plans, as discussed in chapter 11. The second additional test is that applicable to so-called "safe harbor plans" (also see chapter 11). A safe harbor plan, by virtue of the manner in which it is designed, satisfies (1) a contribution requirement, (2) a notice requirement, and (3) a matching contribution limitation.

The contribution requirement is fundamentally a matching contribution requirement under which the employer must match employee elective contributions 100 percent (up to 3 percent of compensation) plus 50 percent of employee elective contributions in excess of 3 percent but not exceeding 5 percent of compensation. Also, the matching rate for HCEs must not exceed the rate for NHCEs. Alternatively, the employer may make nonelective contributions equal to 3 percent of compensation. Each eligible employee must be provided with written notice, before the beginning of the plan year, that this will in fact be done so that the plan may be amended during the plan year to implement a nonelective contribution of at least 3 percent. The matching contribution limitation is considered met if: (1) no employer match is made for employee deferrals in excess of 6 percent of compensation; (2) the rate of match does not increase as the employee deferral rate increases; and (3) the matching contribution rates for HCEs are not as large as those for NHCEs.

If employer matching contributions use either of the last two tests (i.e., the one imposed on SIMPLE 401(k) plans or the safe harbor tests), annual testing of matching contributions is not necessary.

Vesting

Employer matching contributions must vest in the same accelerated manner as that applicable to top heavy plans (i.e., 3-year 100 percent cliff vesting or 6-year graded vesting (beginning after two years)).

Distributions

Savings plans generally offer liberal employee withdrawal and plan loan provisions. However, distributions from such plans must also generally comply with the rules applicable to qualified plan distributions.

IMPORTANT CONCEPTS

Money purchase pension plan

Pension plan

Definitely determinable annual contributions

Minimum funding requirements

Safe harbors for meeting nondiscrimination tests

Forfeitures

Composition of a participant's account balance

Target benefit plan

Actuarial assumptions

Savings/match or thrift plan

After-tax (nondeductible) employee contributions

Employer matching contributions

Actual contribution percentage (ACP) nondiscrimination test

SIMPLE 401(k) plan nondiscrimination test

Safe harbor nondiscrimination tests

Contribution requirement

Notice requirement

Matching contribution limitation

Vesting requirements for employer matching contributions

QUESTIONS FOR REVIEW

1. Why is a money purchase plan, which is a defined contribution plan, classified as a pension plan?

2. How do the annual contributions of a money purchase pension plan differ from those of a profit-sharing plan?

3. What are some reasons why an employer would establish a money purchase pension plan?

4. What is the limit on annual employer contributions to a money purchase plan and how does it differ, if at all, from the annual additions limit to each participant's account?

5. What are some of the disadvantages of a money purchase pension plan?

6. If a money purchase plan uses a uniform allocation formula for making contributions to participants' accounts, how can it avoid discrimination in its operation?

7. To what extent, if any, may a money purchase plan use salary reductions (employee elective deferrals)?

8. What is the treatment of plan forfeitures in a money purchase pension plan?

9. How is the benefit determined under a money purchase pension plan and, historically, how has it been provided to a participant?

10. What items make up a participant's account balance in a money purchase plan?

11. To what extent, if any, may money purchase plans make "in-service" distributions before termination of employment?

12. In what way, if at all, is a target benefit plan similar to a money purchase pension plan?

13. In what general classification of qualified retirement plan does a target benefit plan fall?

14. How are contributions determined under a target benefit plan?

15. To what extent, if any, is the benefit of a target benefit plan guaranteed?

16. What is the income tax treatment to both the employer and the employee under a target benefit plan?

17. In recent times, in what form is the savings/match or thrift plan used?

18. What is likely to cause the decline of savings/match or thrift plans?

19. What is the income tax treatment to both the employer and the employee of contributions under a savings/match or thrift plan?

20. While savings/match or thrift plan contributions are not subject to the limitation on elective deferrals, to what nondiscrimination test are they subject?

21. What are some effective ways in which a savings/match or thrift plan may be used in conjunction with other existing qualified retirement plans?

22. What nondiscrimination test must a savings/match or thrift plan satisfy?

23. How do the nondiscrimination tests differ, if at all, between employee contributions and employer matching contributions in a savings/match or thrift plan?

24. A safe harbor savings/match or thrift plan is designed in such a way that it satisfies what three requirements?

25. How would you describe the three requirements satisfied by a safe harbor savings/match or thrift plan?

26. What are the vesting requirements for employer matching contributions under a savings/match or thrift plan?

SUGGESTIONS FOR ADDITIONAL READING

Tools & Techniques of Employee Benefit and Retirement Planning, 9th edition, Stephan R. Leimberg and John J. McFadden, The National Underwriter Company, 2005.

Tax Facts on Insurance and Employee Benefits, The National Underwriter Company, latest annual edition.

CHAPTER THIRTEEN

Traditional Defined Benefit Plans

• • •

Workers who were employed by major corporations and who retired in the 1950s, 1960s, and 1970s probably knew only one kind of pension plan—the defined benefit plan. Under this classic qualified retirement plan, a worker knew that if he or she worked for a certain number of years at a particular salary level for his or her employer, he or she was guaranteed a specific monthly pension for the rest of his or her life. In those earlier years, employees tended to work longer for a particular employer due partially to the promised pension benefit, to a strong sense of employee loyalty, and to an employer's greater feeling of obligation to its employees than has been the case in more recent years. Over the years, employers have become less paternalistic and more concerned with their bottom line. In addition, employers have tended to transfer more and more of the responsibility and financial obligation to provide employees with a livable retirement income to their employees. Fewer and fewer employers today offer defined benefit plans. Once the gold standard of qualified retirement plans, the defined benefit plan has given way to various forms of defined contribution plans, principally the 401(k) plan, discussed in chapter 11.

In this chapter, we will discuss the design, operation, and administration of a traditional defined benefit plan and how it differs from the various types of defined contribution plans discussed in previous chapters.

Upon completing this chapter, you should be able to:

- Describe the main features of a defined benefit plan and how it differs from a defined contribution plan
- Identify some of the advantages and disadvantages of defined benefit plans
- Explain how defined benefit plans operate

- Compare the career average method to the final average method of determining a defined benefit plan participant's compensation
- Identify the four basic types of benefit formulas employed by defined benefit plans
- Identify the actuarial factors that must be considered in funding a defined benefit pension plan
- Describe the two general actuarial methods employed by defined benefit plans
- Explain the use of the "funding standard account"
- Identify the two general methods of calculating the cost of funding promised benefits under a defined benefit plan
- Identify the limit on a participant's annual benefit payable from a defined benefit plan
- Describe the various reporting and disclosure requirements imposed on defined benefit plans
- Describe the role of the Pension Benefit Guaranty Corporation (PBGC)
- Compare and contrast a defined benefit plan with a defined contribution plan

DEFINITION, PURPOSE, AND PROS AND CONS

For tax purposes, a defined benefit plan is *always* classified as a qualified employer pension plan. A pension plan provides for the payment of definitely determinable benefits to employees over a period of years, usually for life, after retirement. The determination of the benefits to be paid and the contributions that must be made in order to provide those benefits cannot be dependent on the employer's profits. In addition to a retirement benefit, a pension plan may provide for the payment of a pension due to disability or for the payment of death benefits. However, a pension plan may not provide for the payment of layoff benefits or benefits for illness or accident, except for retired employees. Unlike defined contribution plans, employer contributions to a defined benefit pension plan are *not* allocated to separate accounts for employees. Rather, a defined benefit pension plan guarantees a specific level of benefit at a participant's retirement.

An employer that assumes an obligation to provide a meaningful level of retirement income to all of its eligible employees and to allocate a higher level of contributions to older key employees would tend to select a defined benefit plan. A defined benefit plan would also be indicated where the principal(s) in a small professional practice wishes (wish) to defer the maximum amount possible for retirement and at the same time obtain the largest income tax deduction permissible for his or her (their) practice.

Some of the positive attributes of defined benefit plans include: (1) maximization of contributions for older HCEs; (2) guarantee of benefits by both the employer and the Pension Benefit Guaranty Corporation (PBGC), discussed later in this chapter; (3) tax deferral of retirement savings; and (4) provision of a meaningful benefit to older employees who enter the plan with only a few years left until their retirement.

The downside of defined benefit plans includes: (1) the high cost of establishing and operating such plans; (2) the complexity of such plans and the challenge of communicating to employees how their benefits are determined; (3) the lack of a meaningful benefit for employees who leave the employer before retirement; (4) the lack of flexibility in making required annual contributions even when employer profit or cash flow is inadequate to do so; and (5) the assumption of the investment risk by the employer, sometimes resulting in larger annual employer contributions.

DESIGN AND OPERATION

Under a defined benefit plan, each participant's retirement benefit is defined and guaranteed in terms of dollars or as a replacement for some percentage of pre-retirement compensation from the employer sponsoring the plan. The term "compensation" may be defined in terms of average career wages or final employment years' wages.

Under the **career average method**, the employee's compensation over the years of plan participation is averaged, with some portion of that average replaced by the plan during retirement. Clearly, this method suffers from its failure to keep up with wage inflation and to replace a portion of the compensation being earned at or near retirement.

The **final average method** is more favorable to employees since it determines the retirement benefit as a percentage of their compensation immediately preceding their retirement. Typically, a participant's final three-to-five years of service are considered in computing the final average (commonly referred to as the "high five" or "high three"). This method provides plan participants with protection against inflation. In most cases, a worker's wages are highest in the final years of employment with the plan sponsor. Of course, under either the career average or final average method, only the first $210,000 (in 2005) of each employee's compensation may be taken into account in calculating the average.

Once a method of determining a participant's average compensation has been chosen, then one of the following four types of **benefit formulas** *must* be selected:

1. **Flat amount formula:** Under a flat amount formula, all employees normally receive the same monthly dollar amount of retirement benefit regardless of pre-retirement compensation and/or years of service. For example, all covered employees receive a monthly pension of $750 beginning at their normal retirement age (e.g., age 65), reduced by some plans for employees with less than a minimum number of years of service as specified in the plan document. This formula fails to take into account the level of each employee's pre-retirement compensation. However, in the rare case where the level of compensation of covered employees is within a narrow range, the formula may provide some degree of equity.

2. **Flat percentage of earnings formula:** Benefits for covered employees are expressed as a flat percentage of compensation (either using career average or final average). For example, a benefit of 45 percent of salary may be paid at the normal retirement age. This formula is more commonly associated with plans using the final average compensation method and in

plans in which most participants earn relatively low salaries. As with the flat amount formula, the plan may reduce benefits for those participants not completing a minimum number of years of service. In plans where the key employees are relatively old, this type of benefit formula may also be very advantageous to these employees.

3. **Flat amount per year of service formula:** Under this formula, benefits are expressed as a stated dollar amount for each year of service to the employer. For example, this type of formula may provide $25 per month for each year in which the employee worked 1,800 hours or more. Accordingly, a participant with 30 years of service would receive a benefit of $750 per month ($25 x 30). Many defined benefit plans impose minimum years of service and minimum hours of service per year for a participant to be considered "covered" as a full-time employee. Accordingly, participants not meeting these minimums, will have their benefits reduced. On the other hand, a participant who does satisfy the minimum years of service requirement with at least 1,000 hours of service per year is entitled to some level of benefit under the flat amount per year of service formula.

4. **Percentage of earnings per year of service or unit credit or unit benefit formula:** A participant's retirement benefit is based on a benefit credit for each year of covered service. Typically, benefit credits operate differently for past service years versus future service years. The amount credited for the past years' service is normally lower than that credited for future years' service. Past service refers to years of a participant's service to the employer prior to the implementation of the defined benefit plan. For example, a defined benefit plan may credit only three quarters of a percent for each year the employee worked before the plan's inception; then one and one half percent for each year of service following the plan's inception. The advantage of this formula is that it considers both compensation and years of service and therefore tends to favor the business owner who typically has more years of service than the average employee. However, those hired only a few years before retirement receive a smaller amount of benefit since they are able to accumulate only a minimal number of years of service (even those with high salaries). This type of benefit formula, therefore, is most appropriate for an employer with a large disparity in participant compensation.

These formulas may also be integrated with Social Security benefits (see chapter 7) to provide a reasonable level of retirement income for all employees by taking into account their anticipated Social Security benefits. The effect of Social Security integration is to adjust the employer's total plan contributions by reason of these benefits.

Having selected both the method for determining average compensation and the benefit formula to be employed, a defined benefit plan must then be funded by the employer with periodic (usually quarterly) deposits calculated by an actuary to provide assurance that the plan will have sufficient funds to pay the promised benefit as each participant retires. The goal is to accumulate an amount of money for each participant that is capable of providing the promised benefit over the remaining lifetime of the participant. Certain defined benefit plans may also purchase an annuity for each retiring participant in order to discharge their continuing obligation to each participant.

An actuary performs a time value of money calculation to determine the size of the fund needed for each participant and, in turn, the periodic deposit that the employer will have to make to accumulate this fund. There are many factors to be considered in the actuarial calculations. Some factors are relatively easy to determine, such as the age and sex of each participant and the benefit payable to each participant at normal retirement age.

However, other actuarial factors must be estimated, or "assumed." For example, the rate of return on plan investments is not knowable in advance and must, therefore, be projected over the relevant timeframe. Higher rates of return will result in lower employer contributions and lower rates of return will result in higher employer contributions. Another factor requiring reasonable estimation is the extent of both voluntary and involuntary employee turnover. Greater turnover rates will result in fewer employees receiving full retirement benefits and hence, lower contributions by the employer. Conversely, lower turnover rates will result in more employees receiving full retirement benefits and hence, higher contributions by the employer. The estimation of the employee turnover rate is greatly influenced by the average age of the employee population since younger employee populations generally have higher turnover rates. An additional factor is the rate of mortality among the employee population. Employees dying prior to their normal retirement age will, of course, *not* receive a full retirement benefit resulting in lower employer contributions. Similarly, morbidity (or disability) rates must be estimated to predict how many employees will become disabled prior to normal retirement age and accordingly receive early distributions from the plan. A final factor to be considered is the number of employees who will retire at or before their normal retirement age. Clearly, as the actual results over the years differ from the estimates for these various factors, adjustments need to be made to the periodic employer contributions to be sure that the plan is adequately funded or, alternatively, not overfunded.

Having obtained the necessary information concerning the age, sex, and benefit amount for each participant and developed the necessary estimates of the other actuarial factors just described, the actuary then needs to select one of two general actuarial methods-the **attained age level method** or the **entry age normal with frozen past service liability method**. Most insurance companies and pension administrators prefer to use the attained age level method because it develops a "benefit cost" for each participant and therefore facilitates the purchase of individual annuities at retirement. The rationale behind this method is that the employer deposits the precise amount required to fund each participant's benefit over the years remaining until retirement. Further, an assumption is made that compensation will remain level from the date the calculation is performed until retirement. Then, each time a participant receives a salary increase, a separate calculation is performed for each such increment in compensation and added to the level funding calculated previously. The attained age level actuarial method will generally favor older employees who are usually the business owners.

Under the entry age normal with frozen past service liability actuarial method, a minimum and maximum contribution range is developed that provides the employer with flexibility in required annual contributions. The overriding assumption under this method is that the defined benefit plan has been in effect since the time the business was started. Using this assumption, the actuary then determines the amount of funding that would have been accumulated to date (that is, had the plan always been in effect). This amount is known as "unfunded past service liability." The plan administrator then selects the period of time (usually 10 to 30 years) over which it will amortize this unfunded past service liability. This approach provides the employer with the flexibility to aggressively retire unfunded past service liability in profitable years and reduce funding in low-profit years to cover current and only minimal past service costs. The difference between the minimum and maximum contribution range may be substantial and the employer has the flexibility of paying the minimum, the maximum, or some intermediary amount. The use of a long period, such as 30 years, for amortizing unfunded past service liability may be problematical when key employees elect a lump-sum settlement over a much shorter payment period. In this case, inadequate funding may be available to meet such requirements. For this reason, some plans align the amortization period with the remaining service years of the older key employees.

An actuary uses a hypothetical model known as the **funding standard account** to determine the amount of money that would be in the defined benefit plan's account if all the actuarial factors had actually occurred as forecasted by the actuary. If the actual amount accumulated is *less* than the funding standard account, the employer must make *additional* contributions to eliminate the deficit. Conversely, if the funds accumulated *exceed* the funding standard account, the employer may *reduce* future contributions.

Finally, an employer must calculate the cost to fund promised benefits using one of two general methods—the **accrued benefits cost method** and the **projected benefits cost method**. The accrued benefits cost method, also known as the unit credit, single premium, or unit cost method, bases costs on benefits actually earned as of the date on which costs are calculated. No funding is provided for future costs. This method is usually employed by plans that use either the percentage of earnings per year of service (or unit credit) benefit formula and the career average method of determining compensation or the flat amount benefit formula. The accrued benefits cost method results in constant increases in the cost of funding each participant's unit of benefit as each participant ages and, accordingly, has fewer years in which to accumulate the necessary funding.

The projected benefits cost method, as its name suggests, looks ahead for a specific period of time to calculate the total benefits the employer will have to pay during that time period. Then, the cost of funding those benefits is amortized over that future period. For example, if the plan's actuary projects that a participant will have earned a monthly benefit of $2,500 at his or her normal retirement age 15 years from now, this method will spread the cost of funding this benefit evenly over the 15-year period. The projected benefits cost method is generally used with flat benefit or unit benefit formulas.

By now it should be clear that the projected benefits cost method will result in more level and predictable funding than the accrued benefits cost method under which costs are constantly increasing. Moreover, past service costs (discussed previously in this chapter) may be funded using either of these two actuarial cost methods.

CONTRIBUTIONS

Annual contributions to a defined benefit pension plan by the employer must meet **minimum funding standards** under IRC Section 412. The purpose of these standards is to ensure that the employer will have provided sufficient funding to pay benefits to participants. In general, a "funding standard account" must be maintained by the plan to determine the amount of annual contributions required from the employer. Such funding standards apply to all qualified pension plans, including defined benefit, money purchase, and target benefit plans.

ERISA does not allow an employer to fund a pension plan on a "pay as you go" method (where pension payments are funded only as they become due), nor does it allow a terminal funding method (where the entire value of a retirement annuity is funded immediately at retirement). Instead, only actuarial cost methods, (whereby the cost of the projected benefits is funded over the service period of the employee), are required. Minimum funding includes amortization of past service liability as well as current plan costs. In determining the minimum funding standard for any tax year, amortized amounts are credited for investment gains in excess of projected experience and for decreases in pension liabilities. For instance, the funding requirements as applied to a money purchase pension plan (see chapter 12) are satisfied if the promised contributions are made in each year.

The IRS may temporarily waive the requirement for a particular year in the event of business hardship. The funding requirements are not qualification requirements. However, failure to meet and correct the minimum funding requirements for a defined benefit plan will subject the employer to a special 10 percent excise tax. The tax for underfunding is generally limited to the year of actual underfunding. Accordingly, where a corporation's plan is underfunded for 8.5 months of a year following an assessment of underfunding, but then is brought up to fully funded status by the next plan year, no excise tax will apply to that next plan year. If the funding deficiency is not paid by the employer within the 90-day period after the IRS mails the notice of deficiency for the initial tax, a penalty tax of 100 percent of the accumulated funding deficiency is imposed on the employer. The employer is also required to notify participants and beneficiaries that the plan did not meet its required minimum funding standards. If an employer fails to make such notification, the employer is liable for a penalty of up to $100 per day from the date of the failure as well as any other relief the court may order.

The deadline for making funding contributions may be extended for up to one year in the event of a presidentially declared terrorist action. Also, the Treasury may waive interest and penalties for up to one year.

VESTING

In the case of a defined benefit plan, the vested benefit is not one determined at the termination of a participant's employment. Rather, the benefit is defined in terms of payments once reaching "normal retirement age" under the plan. Accordingly, an employee must usually wait until normal retirement age to receive the present value of his or her vested benefit. Under a defined contribution plan, a participant's accrued benefit is the participant's account balance. Under a defined benefit plan, however, a participant's accrued benefit is determined by the manner of accrual as specified by the plan.

There are three general classes of vesting: (1) those relating to situations calling for full and immediate vesting; (2) those relating to the minimum vesting schedules for IRC Section 411(a)(2); and (3) those relating to compliance with the IRC Section 401(a)(4) nondiscrimination requirements. The situations that require full and immediate vesting are the attainment of normal retirement age, employee contributions, and the complete or partial termination of, or discontinuance of contributions to, a plan. The minimum vesting schedules of Section 411(a)(2) include 5-year cliff vesting and 3-to-7-year graded vesting, as well as 3-year cliff vesting and 2-to-6-year graded vesting for top-heavy plans and those plans that feature employer matching contributions. Finally, even if a plan adopts one of the two statutory vesting schedules, it is possible that a pattern of abuse under the plan may exist (e.g., dismissal of lower-paid employees prior to vesting in their accrued benefits). Therefore, determination of whether a plan actually discriminates in favor of HCEs is based on all the facts and circumstances. If a plan is found to be discriminatory, it is not considered as having met the required vesting schedules.

BENEFIT LIMIT

Since 1975, there has been a limit on the annual benefit that may be payable from the interest of a participant in a qualified defined benefit plan or in a tax-sheltered annuity arrangement (TSA) of the defined benefit variety. This limit is a qualification requirement, meaning that a defined benefit plan may not qualify for the favorable tax treatment unless so provided for in the plan. Finally, not only must the plan language so provide, but if tax qualification is to be maintained, benefits paid must also not exceed the limit in actual practice.

The limit is expressed in terms of the maximum annual payment under a single-life annuity. If a benefit is not paid in the form of a single life annuity, the limitation is converted to the actuarial equivalent of such an annuity. The limit is the *lesser of*:

- 100 percent of the participant's average compensation for the three consecutive years for which compensation is the highest ("compensation limit") or
- A dollar amount indexed for increases in the cost of living ("dollar limit")($170,000 in 2005).

If an employee is covered by both a defined benefit plan and a defined contribution plan maintained by the same employer (or related employers), there is a special overall limitation.

NONDISCRIMINATION REQUIREMENTS

IRC Section 401(a)(4) requires only that a plan not discriminate in relation to benefits or contributions, but not both. Generally, this requires defined benefit plans to demonstrate that they do not discriminate as to benefits. A plan is not considered to be discriminatory merely because its benefits bear a uniform relationship to total employee compensation. That is, just because the highly compensated group members receive a larger absolute amount of benefits does not automatically mean that discrimination exists. Rather, discrimination with respect to benefits is based strictly on the amount provided as a percentage of compensation.

Three safe harbors are available for determining whether benefits from a defined benefit plan are nondiscriminatory. If a plan does not satisfy one of these three safe harbors, it must then pass the general test for nondiscrimination. A plan must satisfy all of the following requirements, however, if it is to take advantage of these safe harbors:

1. The same benefit formula applies to all employees in the plan.

2. Annual benefits provided to all employees are payable in the same form, commencing at the same uniform normal retirement age, and are the same percentage of average annual compensation (computed over at least a 3-year period) or the same dollar amount for all employees in the plan who will have the same number of years of service at normal retirement age. Further, the annual benefit must equal the employee's accrued benefit at normal retirement age and must be the normal retirement benefit under the plan.

3. With respect to an employee with a given number of years of service at any age after normal retirement age, the annual benefit commencing at the employee's age is the same percentage of average annual compensation or the same dollar amount that would be payable commencing at normal retirement age to an employee who had the same number of years of service at normal retirement age.

4. Each subsidized optional form of benefit is available to substantially all employees in the plan.

5. The plan must not be a contributory plan (i.e., no employee contributions).

6. Each employee benefit must be accrued over the same years of service that are taken into account in applying the benefit formula.

The three safe harbor tests are quite technical and are beyond the scope of this text. As discussed previously, if a defined benefit plan does not satisfy any of the three safe harbors, it must pass the general nondiscrimination test for benefits. This test is met if each rate group under the plan satisfies the minimum coverage requirements of IRC Section 410(b). Again, the details of this test are very technical and beyond the scope of this text.

REPORTING REQUIREMENTS

ERISA imposes several reporting and disclosure requirements on defined benefit plan administrators. Since ERISA divides the jurisdiction over employee benefit plans among the IRS, the Department of Labor (DOL), and the Pension Benefit Guaranty Corporation (PBGC), certain reporting requirements are required by all three entities. In addition, ERISA requires that certain disclosures concerning benefits be provided or made available to plan participants and beneficiaries. To reduce duplication of reporting, the IRS, DOL, and PBGC have designed consolidated annual return/report forms. These annual report forms, filed with the IRS, generally satisfy the annual reporting requirements of all three government agencies.

The 5500 series of forms, including information concerning the plan's qualification, operations, and financial condition, must be filed annually with the IRS. Each of the 5500 series is due by the end of the seventh month after the plan year-end (July 31 for calendar-year plans). An automatic extension of two-and-a-half months may be obtained by filing IRS Form 5558 by the normal due date. The DOL may also assess a civil penalty of up to $1,100 per day against the plan administrator for failure or refusal to file an annual report. Form 5500 is used by plans having more than 100 participants. Form 5500-C/R is used by plans with fewer than 100 participants. Form 5500-EZ is filed annually by a one-participant pension benefit plan. Plan administrators must attach to the appropriate form the applicable schedules. Schedule B is for actuarial information while Schedule H is for large plan financial information and Schedule I is for small plan financial information. Schedule R is required for defined benefit plans otherwise subject to IRC Section 412. Schedule SSA provides details of plan participants who have separated from service with a deferred vested benefit that was neither paid nor forfeited. Large plans must also submit separate audited financial statements.

With regard to reports to the DOL, the Taxpayer Relief Act of 1997 eliminated the requirement that plan administrators automatically file summary plan descriptions (SPDs), separate plan descriptions with certain prescribed information, and summaries of material modifications with the DOL. However, many of these documents must now be furnished to the DOL upon request.

With regard to reports to the PBGC, an annual return for the payment of termination insurance premiums is required for all defined benefit plans subject to PBGC insurance. The premium for PBGC coverage for single-employer pension plans currently consists of a flat-rate premium of $19 per participant, plus a variable-rate premium of $9 for each $1,000 of unfunded vested benefits as of the end of the preceding plan year.

Finally, in addition to the normal annual report filed with the IRS on the IRS/DOL/PBGC 5500 series of forms, defined benefit pension plan administrators are required to file with the PBGC a notice of certain reportable events within 30 days of their occurrence. Generally, these events signal potential problems with the plan or sponsoring employer. The events include the following:

- A 20 percent reduction in active participants
- The failure to make minimum funding payments
- The inability to pay benefits when due
- Excess distributions to a substantial owner within a 12-month period
- A transfer of 3 percent or more of benefit liabilities outside the controlled group
- An application for minimum funding waiver
- A transaction involving a change in the contributing sponsor or controlled group
- The liquidation or dissolution of a contributing sponsor or a controlled group member
- The declaration of an extraordinary dividend or stock redemption
- A loan default of $10 million or more
- Bankruptcy, insolvency, or similar settlements with creditors

TERMINATION

The PBGC uses the premiums collected from defined benefit plans to maintain a fund to guarantee certain benefits to participants of pension plans, in the event that the plan's assets are insufficient to pay its promised benefits. As discussed previously, one of the "reportable events" is the intent to terminate a plan. In the event of a voluntary termination by the plan sponsor, the PBGC determines whether the plan has sufficient assets to pay its guaranteed benefits when they become due. If so, the PBGC gives approval to the termination but remains otherwise uninvolved. On the other hand, if plan assets are insufficient to meet the promised benefits, and the employer request qualifies as a so-called "distress termination," the PBGC will step in as the plan trustee and administer the payment of benefits. In this case, however, the sponsor remains liable to the PBGC for any shortfall, up to a statutory limitation.

The PBGC may also force the *involuntary* termination of a plan, although it does not often exercise this power. It may do so in the following situations:

- The plan has not met the minimum funding requirements of IRC Section 412
- The plan is unable to pay benefits when due
- The plan has made a distribution of $10,000 or more to a substantial (ten percent) owner and immediately afterward has unfunded vested liabilities
- The possible long-run loss to the PBGC is expected to increase unreasonably if the plan is not terminated

The PBGC does not guarantee the payment of *all* benefits promised under a plan. Rather, it guarantees only those *basic* pension benefits vested at termination of the plan, up to a maximum amount. The guaranteed benefit is payable in the form of a monthly straight life annuity commencing at age 65. The maximum monthly benefit is limited to the *lesser of* (1) one-twelfth of the participant's average annual compensation from the employer during his highest five consecutive years; or (2) an otherwise specified limitation (for 2005, $3,801.14).

The employer is liable to the PBGC for the amount of unfunded guaranteed benefits as of the termination date. If the liability exceeds 30 percent of the net worth of the employer (and members of the same controlled group), the PBGC provides commercially reasonable terms for the liability in excess of 30 percent of the employer's net worth. If the employer refuses to pay the amount of its liability, the PBGC may attach a lien on the employer's property.

Normally, a 50 percent excise tax is imposed by IRC Section 4980 on excess plan assets that revert to an employer from a terminating overfunded defined benefit plan, after benefits have all been paid out to participants. Under certain circumstances, if the excess assets are placed in a qualified replacement plan established by the employer, the excise tax is lowered to 20 percent.

Finally, IRC Section 401(a)(2) requires that, before the satisfaction of all liabilities (fixed and contingent), a plan's assets may *not* be used for any purpose other than for the exclusive benefit of employees and beneficiaries. Regulation 1.401-2(b), however, allows an employer to reserve the right to recover at the termination of the trust, any balance remaining in the trust that is due to erroneous actuarial computations during the previous life of the trust. Thus, any surplus arising from unanticipated excess earnings or a high level of forfeitures may revert to the employer after paying the benefits of participants, provided plan language so provides.

DEFINED BENEFIT PLANS VERSUS DEFINED CONTRIBUTION PLANS

As the reader has learned in previous chapters, qualified plans are divided into two major categories—defined contribution and defined benefit plans. The fundamental difference between defined contribution and defined benefit plans is that, under defined benefit plans, the employer has the risk and obligation to make sufficient contributions to the plan to insure that the benefits due the participant/employee are actually paid. Benefits are typically in the form of a monthly retirement pension based on levels of compensation and years of service. Contributions to the plan are actuarially calculated to provide the promised benefits and are not allocated to individual accounts.

Alternatively, under a defined contribution plan, the employee/participants are not entitled to any particular level of benefits, and the amount of benefits received is dependent upon the amount of contributions that the employer and employee make to the individual account of each participant as well as the earnings thereon. Forfeitures that are allocated to each individual account are also included. The employee, not the employer, bears the risk as to the amount of benefits that will be received under a defined contribution plan. Other differences between the two types of plans are that (1) typically, the benefits under defined contribution plans such as a Section 401(k) CODA plan are more "portable" (i.e., may be moved to other plans if changing jobs) than with defined benefit plans and (2) employees, in many cases, control how contributed funds are invested under defined contribution plans (for example, a "self-directed" employee plan), whereas, in defined benefit plans, the investment decisions are made by the qualified plan trustee.

These plan differences, other tax factors, and certain demographic factors including a shift in employment away from industries where employers have traditionally favored defined benefit plans (e.g., the steel industry), have led to a tremendous *increase* in the percentage of employers offering defined contribution plans. A Government Accounting Office (GAO) study found that in 1993, 88 percent of private employers with single-employer-sponsored qualified plans sponsored only defined contribution plans, compared to 68 percent in 1984. Those sponsoring defined benefit plans decreased from 24 percent to 9 percent over this same period.[1] In recent years, many major employers have converted their defined benefit plans to cash balance plans, discussed in chapter 14. Most likely this is due to the fact that the conversions reduce (and, in some cases eliminate for one year or more) future amounts that employers must contribute to the plan. The general impact of the conversion is a reduction in the amount that must be contributed on behalf of *older* workers. This occurs because contributions into cash balance plans are made more evenly over time (therefore benefiting younger workers), as contrasted to the traditional defined benefit plan where employer contributions increase as a worker nears retirement.

---

[1]General Accounting Office, "Private Pensions: Most Employers That Offer Pensions Use Defined Contribution Plan," GAO/GGD-97-1, October 3, 1996.

Defined benefit plans result in the deferral of more tax-deductible contributions than a defined contribution plan as employees age. According to Stephan R. Leimberg and John J. McFadden in their book *Tools & Techniques of Employee Benefit and Retirement Planning,* a defined benefit plan is more advantageous than a defined contribution plan for tax-deferring the maximum amount of retirement savings needed, once an employee attains the ages of 45 to 50.

Finally, it is possible for an employee to participate in *both* a defined benefit plan and a defined contribution plan of the same employer. ERISA originally limited the benefits available under both plans to a so-called "combined plan formula." However, this limit was repealed effective for plans established after 1999 making it now possible to obtain the maximum benefit payable under both types of plans. Nonetheless, as a practical matter, IRC Section 404(a)(7) still imposes an overall 25 percent of payroll limit (or the required funding for the defined benefit plan, if greater) on total annual employer deductions for the two plans.

IMPORTANT CONCEPTS

Qualified employer pension plan

Definitely determinable benefits

Career average method

Final average method

Benefit formulas

Flat amount formula

Flat percentage of earnings formula

Flat amount per year of service formula

Percentage of earnings per year of service or unit credit or unit benefit formula

Integration with Social Security benefits

Actuarial factors

Attained age level method

Entry age normal with frozen past service liability

Funding standard account

Accrued benefits cost method

Projected benefits cost method

Minimum funding standards

10 percent excise tax for underfunding a defined benefit plan

Annual defined benefit plan benefit limit

ERISA reporting and disclosure requirements

Pension Benefit Guaranty Corporation (PBGC)

5500 series of forms

Termination insurance premiums

Reportable events

Defined benefit plans versus defined contribution plans

QUESTIONS FOR REVIEW

1. What are some features that are unique to a defined benefit pension plan?

2. Why would an employer with a high percentage of older key employees select a defined benefit plan over other types of retirement plans?

3. What is the difference between career average compensation and final average compensation for purposes of determining the benefit under a defined benefit plan?

4. What are the four benefit formulas discussed in this chapter and how do they differ from each other?

5. What is the purpose of integrating a benefit formula with Social Security benefits?

6. How is the amount of contributions to a defined benefit plan determined?

7. What are the primary actuarial factors that must be determined or estimated in making the necessary actuarial calculations of defined benefit plan contributions?

8. What is the difference between the attained age level actuarial method and the entry age normal with frozen past service liability actuarial method?

9. What is the purpose of the funding standard account?

10. What is the difference between the accrued benefits cost method and the projected benefits cost method in calculating the cost of funding promised benefits under a defined benefit plan?

11. What is the purpose of the minimum funding standards under IRC Section 412 and to what types of qualified retirement plans do they apply?

12. What is (are) the penalty (penalties) imposed by the IRS for failure to meet and correct minimum funding requirements?

13. The vested benefit in a defined benefit plan is determined for distribution at what point in time?

14. What situations require full and immediate vesting under a defined benefit plan?

15. How is a determination made of whether a qualified retirement plan actually discriminates in favor of highly compensated employees?

16. What is the current limit on the annual benefit that may be payable from the interest of a participant in a qualified defined benefit plan?

17. Discrimination with respect to benefits provided by a defined benefit plan is based on what single factor?

18. What three federal organizations are involved in the regulation of defined benefit plans?

19. What series of forms must be filed annually with the IRS by qualified retirement plans?

20. To which organization must a defined benefit plan submit termination insurance premiums?

21. What are some of the "reportable events" that must be reported to the PBGC within 30 days of their occurrence?

22. To what extent, if any, does the PBGC guarantee the payment of benefits promised under a defined benefit plan?

23. To what extent, if any, may a plan sponsor recover at the termination of a defined benefit plan's trust any balance remaining in the trust which is due to erroneous actuarial computations during the life of the trust?

24. What are some of the principal differences between a defined benefit plan and a defined contribution plan?

25. What has been the recent trend in employer sponsoring of defined benefit plans versus defined contribution plans?

26. If employees participate in both an employer's defined benefit plan and defined contribution plan, what limitations, if any, apply to the total annual employer deductions for the two plans?

SUGGESTIONS FOR ADDITIONAL READING

Tools & Techniques of Employee Benefit and Retirement Planning, 9th ed., Stephan R. Leimberg and John J. McFadden, The National Underwriter Company, 2005.

Retirement Planning by Carla Gordon, American Institute of CPAs, 2002.

Retirement Benefits Tax Guide by Thomas F. Rutherford, CCH Incorporated.

U.S. Master Tax Guide, current edition, CCH Incorporated.

CHAPTER FOURTEEN

Cash Balance Pension Plans

• • •

Another type of hybrid defined benefit pension plan is the cash balance pension (cash balance) plan. Traditional defined benefit plans define the employee's benefit as a series of monthly payments for life to begin at retirement. In contrast, a cash balance plan defines this benefit in terms of a stated account balance at retirement. While benefits are not based solely on actual contributions and forfeitures, the cash balance plan does provide a definitely determinable benefit. It uses hypothetical individual accounts established for each participant whereby participants in the plan may elect to receive their benefits in either annuity form or as a lump sum distribution. Amounts to be contributed are then actuarially determined to arrive at the contribution level needed to insure the promised benefits.

Most cash balance plans began as traditional defined benefit pension plans but were converted in an attempt to provide a better benefit for younger participants and to reduce the costs for older participants. In some cases, these plan conversions have resulted in age discrimination lawsuits by older employees.

In this chapter, we will discuss the details of the cash balance pension plan and how it may be used to provide benefits given a particular employee profile.

Upon completing this chapter, you should be able to:
- Describe the main features of a cash balance pension plan and how it differs from a traditional defined benefit pension plan
- Identify some of the advantages and disadvantages of a cash balance pension plan
- Explain the operation of a cash balance pension plan
- Describe the two types of credits to a cash balance plan participant's theoretical individual account

- Identify the limit on a participant's annual benefit payable from a cash balance plan
- Describe the various ERISA reporting and disclosure requirements imposed on cash balance plans
- Describe the role of the Pension Benefit Guaranty Corporation (PBGC) in the regulation of cash balance pension plans

CASH BALANCE PLAN DESIGN

While a cash balance pension plan is technically a qualified defined benefit plan, it actually combines the features of a defined benefit plan and a defined contribution plan. As mentioned in the introductory section, traditional defined benefit pension plans define the benefit as a monthly payment in the form of a life annuity. Cash balance plans define the benefit in terms of a guaranteed account balance at retirement; however, a participant may take the benefit either as an annuity or a lump sum distribution.

The plan sponsor creates a hypothetical account for each participant and makes two types of credits to each account at least annually. The first type of credit is referred to as a "pay credit" calculated as a certain percentage (as provided in the plan document) of a participant's annual compensation. This credit may or may not be integrated with Social Security benefits.

The other type of credit is an "interest credit" or employer-guaranteed return on investment adhering to a formula specified in the plan. Typically, this rate is set at a very conservative level so that the employer will be able to easily achieve it; however, a participant's account may be credited with a rate exceeding the guaranteed minimum if such a rate is actually achieved. Certain plans tie the guaranteed rate to U.S. government bonds or to a rate specified by the Pension Benefit Guaranty Corporation. If the guaranteed minimum rate is not achieved, the employer then must make up the shortfall.

The crediting of the pay credit and interest credit to a participant's hypothetical account is analogous to the actual allocation of contributions and earnings to a participant's account under a defined contribution plan. That is why the cash balance plan is said to combine the features of a defined benefit plan and a defined contribution plan.

PURPOSE, ADVANTAGES, AND DISADVANTAGES

A cash balance plan will prove most beneficial to an employer whose workforce is made up mostly of younger workers who have the advantage of many years to accumulate a meaningful amount of retirement savings. Employers with a sizeable work force consisting primarily of middle income workers are able to allocate plan administrative costs over a large number of participants. This type of plan is especially advantageous in those cases where employees are apprehensive about the security of their retirement accumulation. Finally, sponsors of traditional defined benefit plans who want to enhance the benefit of younger workers and spend less on older participants' benefits will find conversion to a cash balance plan to be attractive.

As a qualified retirement plan, a cash balance plan offers the advantage of tax-deferred savings and, for plan participants born before 1936, 10-year income tax averaging for lump-sum plan distributions. From the standpoint of the employee/participant, investment risk is borne by the employer/plan sponsor and plan benefits (like those of other defined benefit plans) are guaranteed by the Pension Benefit Guaranty Corporation. Plans with 25 or more participants are generally required to pay PBGC premiums. Moreover, cash balance plans are relatively easy to explain to employees with younger employees tending to favor them over the traditional form of defined benefit plan.

Some of the attributes of cash balance plans include the following:

- The fact that older plan participants generally receive lower benefits than they enjoyed under a traditional defined benefit plan, which, of course, is one of the main reasons to convert to a cash balance plan.
- Cash balance plans involve somewhat more administrative burden than defined contribution plans, but are not as complex in design and administration as traditional defined benefit plans.
- Because the employer assumes the investment risk in cash balance plans, administrative costs tend to be higher.
- Due to the fact that the employer guarantees a particular balance at retirement, the services of an actuary are required to determine the annual cost.
- Unlike defined contribution plans, there are no actual individual participant accounts and participants have no voice in the selection of investments.
- Cash balance plans, like money purchase pension plans and profit-sharing plans, may accumulate meaningful funds for participants' retirement but they offer the additional advantage of the employer's guaranteed minimum investment return.
- Cash balance plans do not provide guaranteed benefits for participants, but they are much easier to design and administer than traditional defined benefit plans.
- While participant loans are permitted in a cash balance plan, most employers normally do not offer them because of the additional administrative burden caused by the lack of actual individual participant accounts.

CONVERSION OF TRADITIONAL DEFINED BENEFIT PLANS TO CASH BALANCE PLANS

As discussed in the introductory section, most existing cash balance plans were created through the conversion of traditional defined benefit plans. The primary impetus for these conversions is the reduced cost to the employer resulting from a lower accrual rate for participants' benefits, particularly for older employees. In fact, there is an effect referred to as a "wearaway" of benefits for older employees in some of these conversions. In such conversions, the older employees' benefits that have accrued under the traditional defined benefit plan are greater than the benefit they would have accrued under the cash balance plan (had it been in effect since they entered the traditional defined benefit plan). As a result, the employer normally does not need to make benefit accruals for a considerable number of years after the conversion; in some cases, perhaps not until after the participant's normal retirement date.

> **Example:** Assume that the present value of a 50-year-old participant's traditional defined benefit plan accrued benefit is $250,000 at the time that his or her employer converts the existing plan to a cash balance plan. This plan features a "pay credit" of 10 percent of salary plus an "interest credit" of 6 percent on the account balance. If the cash balance plan had been in existence since the participant's hire date, he or she would have had a theoretical cash balance plan account balance of $200,000. As a result, the participant does not receive additional benefit accruals until the $50,000 of additional accrued benefit in the previous traditional defined benefit plan "wears away" (i.e., is credited to his theoretical cash balance account). Accordingly, in this fact situation, the participant would likely not receive any additional accruals until he or she turned approximately age 56.

Proposed Treasury regulations issued in 2001 permit such conversions with "wearaway" provisions, but Congress to date has prevented Treasury from implementing those regulations. Moreover, Congress charged the Treasury Department with developing a method for converting traditional defined benefit plans to cash balance plans without the use of such provisions. Legislation to correct this problem is anticipated in coming years. It appears that such legislation would accomplish several things regarding plan conversions. First, plans would be required to include a statement that a cash balance plan is not, in and of itself, discriminatory. Second, plans could provide for distributions of a lump sum determined by reference to the participant's theoretical account balance. Third, and finally, plans would be forced to create "hold harmless" requirements permitting a participant in a converted cash balance plan to continue to accrue benefits under the *greater* of the old plan's formula or the new plan's formula for a minimum of 5 years.

Under existing law, if an employer either converts a traditional defined benefit plan to a cash balance plan or amends a traditional defined benefit plan resulting in a reduction in the rate of future benefit accruals, the plan administrator must provide a prescribed written notice to affected plan participants and beneficiaries. The penalty for failure to do so is $100 per day. Plans with less than 100 participants are generally exempted from this notice requirement.

INCOME TAX IMPLICATIONS

As a qualified retirement plan, cash balance plans offer the normal income tax benefits. Contributions are deductible by the employer as made. Employee/participants receive a deferral of taxation until the funds are withdrawn and may receive a maximum annual benefit of the lesser of $170,000 (in 2005) or 100 percent of the participant's high 3-year average pre-retirement compensation. In addition, the normal distribution rules apply, with certain premature withdrawals subject to penalties.

Cash balance plans also must comply with the minimum funding rules of IRC Section 412. As a defined benefit plan, cash balance plans are subject to the mandatory insurance coverage provided by the Pension Benefit Guaranty Corporation (PBGC) and, accordingly, must pay the required premiums to the PBGC. Moreover, cash balance plans are subject to additional ERISA reporting and disclosure requirements to participants, including the Summary Plan Description, Summary of Material Modification, Summary Annual Report, and other required notices. Finally, an income tax credit (business tax credit) of up to $500 may be available for the qualified costs of starting up such a plan.

TRADITIONAL DEFINED BENEFIT PLAN VERSUS CASH BALANCE PLAN VERSUS DEFINED CONTRIBUTION PLAN

In a traditional defined benefit plan, the contribution is determined on an actuarial basis whereas with a cash balance plan it is determined as a percentage of compensation, including actuarial aspects (as a result of the employer guarantee feature). A defined contribution plan simply uses a specific percentage of compensation.

In the case of both a traditional defined benefit plan and a cash balance plan, the investment risk is borne by the employer, while with a defined contribution plan, the investment risk is borne by the employee. Similarly, in the case of a traditional defined benefit plan and a cash balance plan, a participant has no voice in the choice of plan investments. In a defined contribution plan, a participant usually has a broader choice of investments and greater participation in choosing those investments.

Social Security benefit integration is available in all three types of plans.

Both traditional defined benefit plans and cash balance plans are subject to PBGC coverage and premiums, while defined contribution plans are not.

401(k) features are only available in a profit-sharing type of defined contribution plan—not in a traditional defined benefit plan nor in a cash balance plan.

Only a traditional defined benefit plan is designed to provide an adequate retirement benefit to older participants. Neither the cash balance plan nor the defined contribution plan provide an adequate benefit for such participants.

Finally, administrative costs are typically much higher for traditional defined benefit plans and cash balance plans than for defined contribution plans. The exception to this is where the defined contribution plan offers 401(k) features or grants employees investment discretion, which in turn, drives up the administrative costs of offering such plans.

IMPORTANT CONCEPTS

Hypothetical individual accounts

Conversion of traditional defined benefit plans

Guaranteed account balance at retirement

Pay credit

Interest credit

Employer-guaranteed return on investment

Pension Benefit Guaranty Corporation (PBGC)

"Wearaway" of benefits

5-year "hold harmless" requirement

ERISA reporting and disclosure requirements

QUESTIONS FOR REVIEW

1. In what way does a cash balance plan provide a definitely determinable benefit?

2. What is meant by a hypothetical individual account?

3. What are the main reasons that employers have converted traditional defined benefit plans to cash balance plans?

4. What has been one of the negative results of these plan conversions?

5. In what way does a traditional defined benefit plan differ from a cash balance plan in terms of how each defines the plan benefits?

6. What is meant by a "pay credit" and an "interest credit" as those terms are used in conjunction with cash balance plans?

7. What happens if the employer does not achieve the guaranteed minimum rate of return in a cash balance plan?

8. In what ways does a cash balance plan combine the features of a defined benefit plan and a defined contribution plan?

9. While both plans are similar in certain respects, in what way does a cash balance plan differ from a money purchase pension plan?

10. What type of employer workforce will benefit most from a cash balance plan?

11. Who bears the investment risk with a cash balance plan and how, if at all, does that differ from a defined contribution plan?

12. What is the effect on older participants when a traditional defined benefit plan is converted to a cash balance plan?

13. Why is it necessary to use the services of an actuary in determining the annual contribution to a cash balance plan?

14. What is meant by "wearaway" of benefits where a traditional defined benefit plan has been converted to a cash balance plan?

15. How does Congress intend to remedy the perceived problem of "wearaway?"

16. What are some of the more significant income tax implications of cash balance plans?

17. Compare and contrast a traditional defined benefit plan, cash balance plan, and a defined contribution plan with regard to how contributions are determined, who bears investment risk, Social Security benefit integration, PBGC coverage and premiums, use of 401(k) features, adequacy of retirement benefits for older participants, and administrative costs.

SUGGESTIONS FOR ADDITIONAL READING

Tools & Techniques of Employee Benefit and Retirement Planning, Stephan R. Leimberg and John J. McFadden, 9th ed., The National Underwriter Company 2005.

Retirement Planning by Carla Gordon, American Institute of Certified Public Accountants, 2002.

CHAPTER FIFTEEN

Qualified Plan Distributions

• • •

In selecting the manner in which to receive retirement benefits, an owner of such benefits may prefer the security of an annuity to a lump-sum distribution or a rollover, even though it may not be the best choice from a tax point of view. However, in the case of substantial interests in retirement plans, taxes are probably the most important consideration in selecting the form in which to receive retirement benefits.

In this chapter we will discuss the various considerations in advising clients as to how and when to claim their retirement benefits.

Upon completing this chapter, you should be able to:

- Identify the three basic options for taking distributions from a qualified plan
- Describe the special tax treatments for lump-sum distributions available to plan participants born before 1936
- Explain what constitutes a lump-sum distribution
- Identify the items that may constitute a participant's cost basis in a qualified plan
- Describe the two forms of survivorship benefits that pension plans must provide to spouses of plan participants
- Explain what constitutes an annuity distribution from a retirement plan
- Discuss the income taxation of annuity distributions from a retirement plan
- Explain what constitutes a rollover of a participant's accrued benefits in a retirement plan
- Compare a direct transfer to an indirect transfer in connection with the rollover of a participant's accrued benefits in a retirement plan

- Describe the rules applicable to all rollovers
- Explain what is meant by an in-service distribution
- Discuss the rules applicable to loans to participants from retirement plans
- Describe how a QDRO is used to transfer a retirement plan participant's accrued benefits to a spouse or former spouse
- Describe the minimum distribution rules
- Describe the minimum incidental benefit (MDIB) rule
- Explain some of the important issues in planning for retirement plan distributions

DISTRIBUTION OPTIONS AVAILABLE

In the case of a qualified plan, there are three basic options available in selecting the form of distribution:

1. A lump-sum distribution
2. An annuity or other installment form of distribution
3. Rollover to an IRA (including a SEP/IRA, but not including a SIMPLE IRA account or Roth IRA) or other eligible qualified plan

Lump-Sum Distributions

A lump-sum distribution may be desirable for retirement planning purposes; however, if the lump sum will be taxed in a high tax bracket, it may not be so desirable. After 1999, a lump-sum distribution (if not rolled over) is taxed as ordinary income unless the employee was born before 1936, in which case the distribution is eligible for the special tax treatment of 10-year averaging. Employees born before 1936 are also entitled to a 20 percent capital gain rate for the capital gain portion of pre-1974 accumulations, if any, and if so elected. However, this grandfather rule no longer benefits such persons in light of the lower capital gain rates enacted in 1997 plus the further rate reductions enacted by JGTRRA of 2003 (i.e., a maximum rate of 15 percent).

Furthermore, regardless of when an employee was born, if he or she takes part of his or her benefits in the form of an annuity and the remainder as a single sum, the single sum is *not* eligible for special tax treatment. Similarly, if the recipient receives a lump-sum distribution and rolls over a portion of that distribution, the retained portion is not eligible for special tax treatment.

In addition, lump-sum distributions may be subject to the early distribution penalty if taken before the recipient has attained age 59 1/2. Moreover, lump-sum distributions generally will be subject to mandatory withholding at 20 percent.

Definition of a Lump-Sum Distribution

A distribution is a lump-sum distribution if it meets all of the following requirements:

1. It is made by a qualified retirement plan (as discussed in Chapter 7) and not an IRA
2. It represents a participant's entire interest ("the balance to the credit" of a participant) in the plan
3. It is distributed within a single tax year of the recipient

Under the Internal Revenue Code, a lump-sum distribution is not entitled to special tax treatment unless it is made (1) on account of the death of the employee, (2) on account of the employee's separation from service, (3) after the employee has become totally and permanently disabled, or (4) after the employee has attained age 59 1/2.

Employee Contributions

The part of a lump-sum distribution that consists of accumulated deductible employee contributions (DECs) is *not* eligible for special tax treatment. However, the balance of the distribution is eligible if it otherwise qualifies.

Less Than Five Years of Participation

A lump-sum distribution made before the employee has been a participant in the plan for at least five tax years before the tax year in which the distribution is made is *not* eligible for special tax treatment, unless it is made on account of the death of the employee. This rule applies *only* in the case of a distribution made to the employee. Therefore, it does *not* apply to distributions made to a beneficiary of a deceased employee.

Participant's Entire Interest

With regard to determining what constitutes a participant's entire interest in the plan and whether it has been distributed within one tax year, if his or her employer maintains two or more qualified retirement plans, they may have to be treated as a single plan. Technically, all pension plans must be treated as a single plan; all profit-sharing plans must be treated as a single plan; and all stock bonus plans must be treated as a single plan.

In addition, only amounts that are vested as of the last day of the tax year of the recipient in which the distribution is made are taken into account in determining whether the employee's entire interest has been distributed.

Lump-Sum Distribution to the Employee

If the lump-sum distribution is made to the employee/participant, and he or she was born before 1936, he or she may:

1. Apply 10-year averaging to the entire taxable amount;
2. Apply 10-year averaging to the post-1973 portion of the taxable amount and pay a flat 20-percent tax on the pre-1974 portion;

3. Pay a flat 20-percent tax on the pre-1974 portion of the taxable amount and report the post-1973 portion as ordinary income; or

4. Report the entire taxable amount as ordinary income.

As discussed previously, if the participant was born after 1935, a lump-sum distribution is *not* eligible for special tax treatment of any kind.

If the participant is eligible for 10-year averaging, a tax is computed (using a special table set forth in the instructions for IRS Form 4972) on one-tenth of the excess of: (1) the portion of the distribution subject to averaging over (2) a minimum distribution allowance. The minimum distribution allowance is:

1. The lesser of (a) $10,000 or (b) one-half of the portion subject to averaging

LESS

2. 20 percent of the amount by which the portion subject to averaging exceeds $20,000

If the amount subject to averaging is $70,000 or more, the minimum distribution allowance is zero.

Net Unrealized Appreciation (NUA) in Employer Securities

If securities of the employer corporation are included in a lump-sum distribution, the net unrealized appreciation (NUA) in those securities is not subject to tax. Accordingly, it is ordinarily excluded from any of the tax calculations that may apply to the lump-sum distribution. However, the distributee may elect to have the NUA appreciation included in gross income for the year of the distribution. The distributee makes this election simply by including the NUA on his or her tax return for the year of the distribution. However, the distributee who makes this election is always free to have the entire NUA taxed as ordinary income.

Lump-Sum Distribution to Beneficiaries

If a beneficiary of a plan participant is the recipient of a lump-sum distribution and if the participant was born before 1936, the options are the same as those of an employee-distributee as discussed earlier-namely:

1. Apply 10-year averaging to the entire taxable amount

2. Apply 10-year averaging to the post-1973 portion of the taxable amount and pay a flat 20-percent tax on the pre-1974 portion of the taxable amount

3. Pay a flat 20-percent tax on the pre-1974 portion of the taxable amount and report the post-1973 portion of the taxable amount as ordinary income

4. Report the entire taxable amount as ordinary income

Multiple Distributees

If the total balance credited to the account of an employee is distributable to two or more beneficiaries and the share of each beneficiary is received within a single tax year of that beneficiary, the combined distribution is eligible for special tax treatment if all other conditions are satisfied. However, the tax calculation varies depending upon whether any of the distributees are trusts. Such calculations are beyond the scope of this text.

Annuity or Other Installment Form of Distribution

The second basic option in selecting the form of distribution from a qualified retirement plan is the annuity or other installment option. An annuity distribution received from a retirement plan in any tax year of the employee is taxable as ordinary income, to the extent that it exceeds the portion of the employee's basis in the plan allocated to that distribution. For this purpose, basis is determined as of the *later* of the annuity starting date or the date on which an amount is first received as an annuity. If the employee has no basis in the qualified plan (a common occurrence), the full amount of each annuity distribution is taxable as ordinary income.

A participant's cost basis could be composed of any of the following:

- The total of the participant's after-tax contributions made to a contributory plan
- Any employer contributions previously taxed to the participant, such as would occur if a nonqualified plan became qualified
- The amount of any plan loans (discussed later in this chapter) included in income as a taxable distribution
- The total cost of life insurance protection included in a participant's gross income in his or her income tax return, but only if the plan distribution is received under the same life insurance contract that provides the life insurance protection

In the case of annuities paid by defined contribution plans, the portion of the plan that consists of the participant's nondeductible contributions and earnings and gains attributable thereto may be treated as an entirely separate plan, if the plan so permits. After 2005, participants in 401(k) plans and salary reduction TSAs may elect to treat all or part of their elective contributions as includible in gross income. If this election is made, a "qualified distribution" of these "designated Roth contributions" is excludable from gross income in its entirety. If a distribution of designated Roth contributions is not qualified and takes the form of an annuity distribution, it is not excludable from income in its entirety, but is taxable under the annuity rules (discussed later).

All pension plans must provide two forms of survivorship benefits for spouses: (1) the **qualified pre-retirement survivor annuity (QPSA)** and (2) the **qualified joint and survivor annuity (QJSA)**, as previously discussed (see chapter 5). Stock bonus plans, profit-sharing plans, and ESOPs generally are *not* required to provide these survivorship benefits for the spouse if the participant's vested interest is payable to that spouse as a death benefit.

At the point that a participant's interest in a retirement plan vests, his or her spouse becomes entitled to a pre-retirement survivor annuity, payable in the event of the participant's death prior to retirement. In the case of a defined benefit plan, the amount of this annuity is the amount that would have been paid under a qualified joint and survivor annuity if the participant had either (1) retired on the day before his or her death (where the participant died after attaining the earliest retirement age under the plan); or (2) separated from service at the earlier of the actual time of separation or death and survived to the plan's earliest retirement age, then retired with an immediate joint and survivor annuity. While this explanation is difficult to decipher, the effect is to attempt to put the spouse in the same position he or she would have been in if the participant had lived, but either retired or otherwise separated from service prior to the normal retirement age.

An unmarried participant typically will receive a straight life annuity under a defined benefit plan— usually monthly payments for the balance of the participant's life, with no continuing payments after his or her death. Most plans offer, as an option to the joint and survivor or single life annuities, a **period-certain annuity**, which provides payments for a specified period of time (typically 10 to 20 years) even if the participant or the participant and spouse both die before the end of that period. This option guarantees an income stream to the participant's heirs even if both the participant and his or her spouse die during the specified period of time. Because of the guarantee involved in the period-certain annuity, the monthly benefit is normally lower than that payable under a life annuity. A participant and spouse in poor health or needing to provide for a survivor should seriously consider a period-certain annuity in lieu of the straight life annuity option.

A defined benefit plan may also permit a participant to elect a joint annuity with a beneficiary other than a spouse (such as a son or daughter). However, the benefit available to a much younger beneficiary under such an annuity option is severely limited by Treasury regulations to prevent an inordinate deferral of benefits beyond the participant's death. This will be addressed later in this chapter during the discussion of the required minimum distribution (RMD) rules. Money purchase plans, target benefit plans, and TSAs subject to ERISA must also meet the pre-retirement and joint and survivor annuity rules. Other defined contribution plans do *not* have to meet these rules if (1) there is no annuity option; and (2) the plan participant's account balance is payable to the participant's spouse upon the death of the participant.

In the case of a defined contribution plan, the statutory qualified pre-retirement survivor annuity (QPSA) is an annuity for the life of the surviving spouse that is the actuarial equivalent of at least 50 percent of the participant's vested account balance, determined as of the date of death.

The surviving spouse does not need to elect a pre-retirement survivor annuity. If he or she fails to make any other election, this type of annuity is *automatically* provided by the plan. A participant may not waive the pre-retirement survivorship benefit without the written, witnessed consent (including an acknowledgment of the effect of the waiver) of the nonparticipant spouse. The nonparticipant spouse should obtain competent legal and/or financial advice prior to agreeing to such a waiver. As a participant approaches the plan's normal retirement age, it may be beneficial to elect out of the pre-retirement survivorship benefit in order to increase the participant's post-retirement benefit. On the other hand, a participant may want to provide a pre-retirement survivorship benefit for a nonspousal beneficiary.

The qualified joint and survivor annuity (QJSA) provides a post-retirement death benefit for the plan participant's spouse. This survivor annuity may not be less than 50 percent nor greater than 100 percent of the annuity payable during the joint lives of the participant and spouse. In addition, annuity payments to the spouse, under such a benefit, must continue even if he or she remarries. As is the case with the pre-retirement survivor annuity, a participant may elect to receive another form of benefit, such as a straight life annuity, (if the plan so provides), but such a waiver of the joint and survivor annuity benefit requires the written, witnessed consent (again including an acknowledgment of the effect of the waiver) of the nonparticipant spouse. Such an election must be made within 90 days of the "annuity starting date" (the date when benefit payments should have begun to the participant—not necessarily the date when they were paid). Finally, participants must be provided with notice of the election period including an explanation of the effect of the election within a reasonable period prior to the annuity starting date.

What Constitutes Annuity Payments?

To be classified as an annuity, a distribution must satisfy each of the following requirements:

1. It must be received on or after the annuity starting date (defined later).

2. It must be payable in periodic installments at regular intervals (e.g., annually, semiannually, quarterly, monthly, weekly or otherwise) over a period of more than one full year from the annuity starting date.

3. Except in the case of a variable annuity, the total of the amounts payable must be determinable at the annuity starting date either directly from the terms of the contract or indirectly by the use of mortality tables, compound interest calculations, or both, in conjunction with those terms and in accordance with sound actuarial theory. The total of the amounts payable is not determinable if the payments will only continue or terminate at the discretion of the payor.

The annuity starting date is the *later* of (1) the date when the obligations under the contract become fixed, or (2) the first day of the period ending on the date of the first annuity payment. This period may be a year, a half-year, a quarter, a month, or any other period, depending on the interval at which payments are made.

Where a participant receives payments under an agreement stating that the retirement plan holds the entire value of the participant's interest in the plan and pays interest thereon, the payments are not taxed as annuity payments, but rather as interest.

Simplified Method of Taxing Annuity Distributions

The "simplified method" of taxing annuity distributions is now required by law. Under this method, the distributee recovers his or her basis as of the annuity starting date in level amounts over the number of anticipated monthly payments. Except in the case of payments that are made for a fixed period (rather than over a life expectancy or expectancies), the anticipated payments are determined under IRS Tables I through IV. In cases where the annuity payments are not monthly, an adjustment needs to be made to take into account the period on the basis of which the payments are made.

The amount excluded from each monthly payment remains constant even though the amount of the annuity payment changes (as where the annuity increases with changes in the cost of living or where the annuity decreases for the survivor after the death of the primary annuitant). If the amount to be excluded is greater than the monthly payment (as may be the case with a survivor annuitant), each payment is completely excluded from gross income until the entire basis is recovered.

Employers and administrators with respect to qualified plans and TSAs must employ the simplified method in reporting the taxable amount of an annuity on IRS Form 1099-R.

Here is an example:

> **Example:** At his retirement, John Farnsworth, age 65, begins receiving retirement benefits in the form of a joint and 50 percent survivor annuity to be paid for the joint lives of John and his wife, Marcia, age 64. John's annuity starting date is January 1, 2006. John contributed $31,000 to the plan, and has received no distributions prior to the annuity starting date. Under plan provisions, John will receive a monthly retirement benefit of $1,000 per month, and Marcia will receive a monthly survivor benefit of $500 upon John's death.
>
> Therefore, John's investment in the contract is $31,000. The expected number of monthly payments is 310 for two distributees whose combined ages are 129 (65 and 64) per IRS Table IV. Accordingly, the tax-free portion of each $1,000 monthly annuity payment to John is $100, determined by dividing John's investment ($31,000) by the expected number of monthly payments (310).
>
> Upon John's death, if Marcia has not recovered the full $31,000 investment, Marcia may also exclude $100 per month from each $500 monthly annuity payment. Any annuity payments received after the 310 monthly payments have been made are then fully includible in her gross income. If John and Marcia die before 310 monthly payments have been made, a deduction is allowed on the last income tax return equal to the amount of the unrecovered investment.

If the annuitant is not eligible for, or does not choose to employ, the simplified method of taxing annuity distributions, the following is the basic procedure for determining the taxable and nontaxable portions of annuity payments received in any tax year:

1. Determine the employee's basis in the retirement plan.
2. Determine the expected return from the annuity by multiplying the anticipated number of annual payments by the amount of the annual payment. In the case of annuities whose duration is measured in whole or in part by one or more lives, it is necessary to turn to actuarial tables to determine the life expectancy (or expectancies) of the annuitant(s). For this purpose, IRS Tables I through VIII are used.
3. Divide the amount determined in (1) by the amount determined in (2). Round the dividend to three decimal places. This is the "exclusion percentage or exclusion ratio."
4. Multiply the first regular annuity payment by the exclusion percentage. The result is the excluded (tax-free) portion of that annuity payment. The tax-free portion of each succeeding payment is the same dollar amount even though the payments may increase.
5. Multiply the tax-free portion of each payment by the number of full payments received during the year and add the taxable portion of any payment for a fractional period (as may be the case in the first year of the annuity). These computations result in the tax-free portion of the total payments received in the tax year.

6. Subtract the tax-free portion from the total payments received in the tax year. The balance is the taxable portion of the annuity.

Rollover to an IRA or Other Qualified Plan

The third basic option in selecting the form of distribution from a qualified retirement plan is the rollover of the distribution to either an IRA or to another qualified plan.

What Constitutes a Rollover?

Technically, a rollover is a direct or indirect transfer from one retirement plan to another of all or part of a taxpayer's accrued benefits, resulting by statute in (1) exclusion of the transferred benefits from the gross income of the owner, employee, or other person entitled to them and (2) disregard of the transferred benefits in determining the limit on contributions to the transferee plan by the employee or owner.[1]

A "direct transfer" is said to occur when the participant, the trustee, or other custodian who holds the assets making up the participant's accrued benefit transfers some or all of those assets to the trustee or custodian of another retirement plan. A "direct transfer" and "direct rollover" are synonymous in the tax law. An "indirect transfer" takes place when the trustee or custodian distributes the assets to the participant who, within a statutory time limit, transfers those assets to another retirement plan.

Originally, the Internal Revenue Code contemplated only indirect transfers; however, in 1992, the IRC was amended to expressly provide for direct trustee-to-trustee transfers from a qualified plan to an IRA or another qualified plan or from a TSA to an IRA or another TSA. Qualified plans (including TSAs and Section 457 plans) must allow an employee to direct the plan to accomplish a planned rollover by means of a direct trustee-to-trustee transfer of assets. If a direct transfer or rollover is not utilized by the employee, there is automatically withheld, for income tax purposes, 20 percent of the taxable amount of any distribution that is eligible for rollover, whether or not that amount is subsequently rolled over to another plan.

The foregoing direct transfer or rollover rules do *not* apply to amounts distributable by a traditional IRA (including a SEP/IRA), a SIMPLE account, or a Roth IRA. Accordingly, no 20 percent mandatory withholding applies.

What Constitutes an Eligible Plan?

Rollovers are available for benefits accumulated in the following types of retirement plans:

1. Pension, profit-sharing, and stock bonus plans that are qualified under IRC Section 401(a) (e.g., "qualified plans")
2. Traditional IRAs (including SEP/IRAs) (not discussed here)
3. SIMPLE accounts

---

[1] Retirement Benefits Tax Guide, 3rd edition, by Thomas F. Rutherford, CCH Incorporated, 2005.

4. Tax-sheltered annuity arrangements (TSAs)

5. Section 457 plans

Types of Statutory Rollovers

Rollovers that are permissible beginning in 2002 are listed in Table 15.1 below:

Table 15.1 Permissible Rollovers Beginning in 2002

Type of Plan	Distributions May be Rolled Over To	Rollover Contributions May Be Received From
Traditional IRA	IRA, Roth, QP, TSA, 457	IRA, QP, TSA, 457
Simple IRA Account	Simple IRA	Simple IRA
Roth IRA	IRA*, Roth	Roth
Qualified Plan	IRA, QP, TSA, 457	IRA, QP, TSA, 457
TSA	IRA, QP, TSA, 457	IRA, QP, TSA, 457
Governmental Section 457 plan	IRA, QP, TSA, 457	IRA, QP, TSA, 457

*A rollover from a traditional IRA to a Roth IRA is not free from income tax.

Table abbreviations used include:
IRA = Traditional IRA
Roth = Roth IRA
QP = Qualified Plan
TSA = Tax Sheltered annuity arrangement
457 = Governmental Section 457 Plan

Rules Applicable to All Rollovers

Important rules applicable to all rollovers include the following:

1. Both the transferor and transferee plans must satisfy all statutory requirements for treatment as an eligible retirement plan or IRA, as the case may be.

2. Required minimum distributions (discussed later in this chapter) may *not* be rolled over.

3. A distribution to an owner or participant from a traditional IRA (including a SEP/IRA), a SIMPLE account, Roth IRA, qualified plan, TSA, or a Section 457 plan must generally be transferred to an eligible recipient not later than the 60th day following the date of receipt of the distribution. The 60-day requirement may be waived by the IRS if the failure to waive would be against equity or good conscience, such as casualty, disaster, or other events beyond the reasonable control of the taxpayer.

Rules Applicable to Rollovers from Qualified Plans

A distribution of cash or other property from a qualified retirement plan may be rolled over to any of the following plans or arrangements:

1. A traditional IRA (including a SEP/IRA)
2. Another qualified plan
3. A tax-sheltered annuity arrangement (TSA)
4. A governmental Section 457 plan, provided it agrees to separately account for amounts rolled into it from a traditional IRA

If the distribution is rolled over not later than the 60th day after the day of receipt by the employee, it is excluded from the employee's gross income to the extent of the rollover. There is no requirement that a distribution represent any minimum percentage of the employee's interest in order to be eligible for rollover. However, a qualified plan does not have a statutory obligation to accept rollovers. It may limit the circumstances under which it will accept them or limit the type of assets it will accept.

As discussed previously, a proposed distribution from a qualified plan that is eligible for rollover treatment is subject to 20 percent withholding (i.e., 20 percent of the taxable amount of the distribution), unless it is rolled over by means of a direct trustee-to-trustee transfer of assets. The amount withheld as income tax from an eligible rollover distribution that is not directly transferred is considered to be part of that distribution. Therefore, it is eligible for rollover in the sense that an amount equal to all or any portion of it may be contributed as a rollover to an eligible retirement plan within the 60-day period. This amount is in addition to the net amount of the eligible rollover distribution actually received by the employee. In fact, any amount withheld that is not rolled over is subject to tax under the applicable rules relating to distributions from qualified plans.

> **Example:** John receives a lump-sum distribution from his former employer's 401(k) plan in the gross amount of $100,000, net of 20 percent withholding tax. Within 60 days of the receipt of the distribution, John decides to rollover the net amount of the distribution ($80,000) into his existing IRA. Accordingly, John endorses the $80,000 check to the trustee of his IRA and mails it to the trustee with the appropriate paperwork for an indirect transfer (or rollover). John may also transfer an amount equal to the 20 percent withheld as income tax (or $20,000) from the gross distribution, since it is considered to be part of the gross distribution of $100,000. In this manner, John will achieve a rollover of the entire gross amount of the distribution of $100,000.

The IRS has ruled that a rollover from a qualified plan to a SIMPLE IRA account is not possible, unless it is from another SIMPLE IRA account. However, a SIMPLE 401(k) plan may receive rollovers from qualified plans (including other SIMPLE 401(k)s). Similarly, a rollover from a qualified plan to a Roth IRA is not permitted.

An employee is not required to roll over the *entire* amount received from a qualified plan; he or she may roll only a *portion*. To the extent of the amount rolled over, the withdrawal is nontaxable. However, the amount rolled over is not treated as a contribution by the participant to a recipient plan or IRA. As discussed previously, the taxable portion of any amount not rolled over is treated as an ordinary distribution—and, therefore, not eligible for special 10-year averaging tax treatment.

Beginning in 2002, if a recipient of a distribution from a qualified plan is the participant's surviving spouse, he or she may roll the distribution to another qualified plan, TSA, traditional IRA, or governmental Section 457 plan on the same terms as if he or she were the participant.

Distributions Not Eligible for Rollover

As discussed previously, a distribution from a qualified plan may not be rolled over to the extent that it is required by the minimum distribution rules (discussed later in this chapter). In addition, beginning in 2002, a hardship distribution under the terms of the plan may not be rolled over. Moreover, a distribution by a qualified plan may not be rolled over if it is one of a series of substantially equal, at least annual, periodic payments to be made (1) over the life expectancy of the employee; (2) over the joint lives or joint life expectancies of the employee and his or her designated beneficiary; or (3) for a specified period of 10 years or more (a so-called "72(t) distribution" after the Internal Revenue Code section permitting such distributions).

The IRS has ruled that deductible dividends paid to participants by an ESOP are not eligible rollover distributions; nor are payments of life insurance premiums by a qualified plan for its participants.

Election of Rollover Treatment

For a contribution of an eligible rollover distribution to an IRA to qualify as a rollover, the distributee must elect, at the time the contribution is made, to treat it as such. This is accomplished by "designating to" (notifying) the trustee, issuer, or custodian of the IRA that the contribution is indeed a rollover. This election is irrevocable. This assures that, once the election is made, any subsequent withdrawal of the contribution from the IRA is taxable under the rules governing distributions from IRAs—not by the rules governing distributions from qualified plans. Accordingly, the withdrawal is also not eligible for the special tax treatment extended to lump-sum distributions from qualified plans or the exclusion from gross income for net unrealized appreciation (NUA) on employer stock distributed by a qualified plan.

Direct Rollovers

A direct rollover may be accomplished by any reasonable method ensuring that the transferred assets pass to the transferee plan without coming under the physical control of the participant. Reasonable methods include a wire transfer or the mailing of a check to the recipient plan. If payment is made by check, the check must be negotiable only by the trustee, custodian, or issuer; if by wire transfer, it must be directed only to the trustee, custodian, or issuer. In addition, the transferor plan may provide the distributee with a check and instruct him or her to deliver it to the transferee trustee, custodian, or issuer, provided that the check is made payable to that person. If the name of the distributee does not appear in the name of the plan, the check must indicate that it is for the distributee's benefit (e.g., "for the benefit of" or "FBO Jane Doe").

Rollovers from TSAs

Subject to the same exceptions that apply in the case of distributions from qualified plans, distributions from tax-sheltered annuity arrangements (TSAs) may be rolled over to any of the following plans or arrangements:

1. A traditional IRA (including a SEP/IRA, but not a Roth IRA or SIMPLE account)
2. Another TSA
3. A qualified plan
4. A governmental Section 457 plan

To qualify for rollover treatment, a distribution from a TSA must satisfy the same rules applicable to a distribution from a qualified plan, as discussed earlier.

Rollovers from Section 457 Plans

Beginning in 2002, a distribution by an eligible governmental Section 457 plan may be rolled over to any of the following plans or arrangements:

1. A traditional IRA (including a SEP/IRA, but not a Roth IRA or SIMPLE account)
2. Another governmental Section 457 plan
3. A qualified plan
4. A TSA

To qualify for rollover treatment, a distribution from a governmental Section 457 plan must satisfy the same rules applicable to a distribution from a qualified plan, as discussed earlier.

In-Service Distributions

In the previous sections of this chapter, we discussed annuity, lump-sum, and rollover distributions from retirement plans. In this section, we will discuss distributions that do not fall within any of those three categories. Primarily, these are nonrollover distributions made to a plan participant during the course of his or her employment—so-called "in-service distributions." Loans to participants by qualified and nonqualified plans are generally treated as in-service distributions.

Generally, in the case of an in-service distribution from a qualified plan or TSA, to calculate the tax-free portion of the distribution, one must divide the participant's basis in the plan by the value of the *vested portion* of the participant's interest. The resulting percentage is multiplied by the amount of the distribution to determine the amount that is excludable from the participant's gross income. The same basic rules apply in the case of distributions by IRAs as apply in the case of in-service distributions by plans qualified under IRC Section 401 and TSAs.

An exception to the general rule described in the previous paragraph is the "grandfather" rule for pre-1987 after-tax contributions to the plan. Contributions made before 1987 may be distributed to participants income tax-free until the total amount contributed has been recovered by the participant. Then, excess contributions are taxed in the manner described in the previous paragraph.

Taxable in-service distributions may be subject to the early distribution penalty and are generally subject to mandatory 20 percent withholding (unless transferred to an eligible retirement plan through a direct rollover, as discussed earlier in this chapter).

Loans to Participants

Subject to certain exceptions, a loan to a participant by a plan or arrangement that is, was, or was determined to be a qualified plan, a TSA, or a governmental Section 457 plan is treated as an in-service distribution to that participant in the amount of the loan. As such, it is taxed under the rules discussed in the previous section. It is also reported in the same way as other in-service distributions and may be subject to the penalty tax on early distributions.

A loan to a participant by a qualified plan may, under some circumstances, disqualify the plan, with disastrous consequences to both the employer and plan participants. If a plan is to remain qualified, loans to participants must satisfy the following conditions:

1. They must be available to all participants or beneficiaries on a reasonably equivalent basis
2. They must *not* be available to highly compensated employees in an amount greater than the amount made available to other employees
3. They must be made in accordance with specific plan provisions regarding such loans
4. They must bear a reasonable rate of interest
5. They must be adequately secured

These same conditions must be met if a plan loan to a participant who is a "disqualified person" or "party-in-interest" is to escape treatment as a prohibited transaction under the IRC or ERISA. If a loan is a prohibited transaction, it is subject, under the IRC and ERISA, to an excise tax of 15 percent of the amount involved in the transaction.

Under EGTRRA 2001, the previous (prior to 2002) prohibition against retirement plan loans to participants who are owner-employees (sole proprietors of, more-than-10-percent partners in an unincorporated business, or an S corporation employee who is a more-than-5-percent owner of the enterprise sponsoring the plan, or participants who are members of their families) was repealed.

If a participant or beneficiary assigns or pledges any part of his or her interest in a qualified plan, that part will be treated as a loan. Thus, unless an exception applies, it will be regarded as an in-service distribution from a qualified plan and taxed as such.

A loan is *not* treated as an in-service distribution if the loan must be repaid within five years or is used to acquire any dwelling unit which, within a reasonable time, is to be used as the principal residence of the participant. Such a loan is treated as a distribution only to the extent that, when added to the balance of all other loans to the participant (whenever made), it exceeds the *lesser of*:

1. $50,000 (which may have to be reduced under a complicated formula), or
2. One half of the present value (but not less than $10,000) of the participant's vested benefits under the plan.

In addition, loan repayments must satisfy certain level amortization requirements (i.e., at least quarterly payments) and the loan must be an enforceable agreement. Interest paid on a plan loan is generally treated as personal interest and, accordingly, *not* deductible unless the loan is secured by a home mortgage.

Death Benefits

Retirement and other deferred compensation plans often pay benefits to the survivors of deceased employees or deceased retirees. If these benefits are payable under a life insurance contract held by the qualified plan, the pure insurance amount of the death benefit is excluded from income taxation. The pure insurance amount is the difference between the policy's face amount and its cash value at the date of death. The taxable amount of the distribution is the face amount of the policy minus the pure insurance amount minus the participant's cost basis in the insurance policy (obtained either by paying a portion of the policy premiums or having paid tax on the insurance benefit provided by the plan). Treasury Regulations Table 2001 rates are generally used after 2000 in calculating the value of life insurance protection

If not paid from a life insurance contract held by the qualified plan, the benefits are compensation taxable under the general rules applicable to distributions from retirement and other deferred compensation plans. IRAs, including SIMPLE accounts, may *not* invest in life insurance policies. Therefore, post-death distributions from IRAs and SIMPLE accounts may *not* be excluded from income taxation as constituting the proceeds of life insurance.

A spouse may roll over the death benefit received from a participant to the spouse's IRA, or to another eligible retirement plan. This rollover option is *not* available to a nonspousal beneficiary (or any other entity-type beneficiary).

Distributions to Spouse or Former Spouse Pursuant To a QDRO

Normally, a participant's qualified plan benefit may not be assigned or "alienated" by the participant as his or her voluntary act or against his or her will. This rule is designed to protect the participant's benefit from his or her creditors.

However, when a participant in an employer's retirement plan or the owner of an IRA divorces or separates, the benefits under the plan are a divisible asset—at least to the extent that they have been accumulated during marriage. In virtually every state, this asset is taken into account in one way or another in finalizing a property settlement between the divorcing parties. In some cases, all or a portion of the benefits are awarded to the spouse or former spouse. When this happens, a number of special rules govern the tax consequences for participant and spouse when the benefits are distributed. In other cases, the participant or owner is permitted to retain all of the benefits, but the other spouse is compensated by a disproportionately large share of remaining marital or community property. In the latter cases, neither party recognizes gain or other income from the transaction; and subsequent distributions from the plan are taxed entirely to the participant. A plan participant's benefits also may be applied to satisfy his or her obligations for the support of a spouse, former spouse, or child of the marriage.

A distribution by a qualified retirement plan to an "alternate payee" who is a spouse or former spouse of the participant is taxable to the *spouse*, rather than the participant, *if* it is made pursuant to a "qualified domestic relations order" (QDRO). An alternate payee is a person who is recognized by a domestic relations order as having a right to receive all or a portion of the participant's benefits under the plan. A domestic relations order is a judgment, decree, or other order of a court issued under the domestic relations or community property law of a state that relates to alimony payments, child support, or marital property rights. It also includes judicial approval of a property settlement agreement between the spouses.

A domestic relations order is "qualified" (that is, constitutes a QDRO) if it satisfies all of the following requirements:

1. It creates or recognizes the existence of an alternate payee's right to, or assign to an alternate payee, the right to receive all or a portion of the benefits payable to a participant

2. It includes the name and last known mailing address of the participant and the name and mailing address of each alternate payee

3. The amount or percentage of the participant's benefits to be paid to each alternate payee or the manner in which the amount or percentage is to be determined is specified

4. The number of payments or the period to which the order applies is specified

5. Each plan to which the order applies is referenced

A QDRO may *not* assign a benefit that is already assigned under a previous order *nor* may it assign a benefit that the plan does not provide. Moreover, an alternate payee who is the spouse or former spouse of the participant and who receives a distribution pursuant to a QDRO may roll over the distribution in the same manner as if he or she were the participant.

MINIMUM DISTRIBUTIONS

A qualified retirement plan must provide that the payment of benefits must begin (unless the participant elects otherwise) not later than the 60th day after the latest of:

1. The end of the plan year in which the participant attains the earlier of age 65 or the normal retirement age under the plan;

2. The end of the plan year in which there occurs the tenth anniversary of the commencement of participation in the plan; or

3. The end of the plan year in which the participant terminates service with the employer.

While a participant may elect to have benefits begin later, Congress never contemplated that taxpayers would be able to make permanent or indefinite the tax deferral that is available for participants in qualified retirement plans, IRAs, and certain other deferred compensation plans. As a result, Congress enacted provisions requiring plans to make distributions to participants and their beneficiaries and to increase the likelihood that a participant's interest in a plan primarily benefits the participant rather than the participant's beneficiaries.

Final regulations specifying how required minimum distributions (RMDs) are to be made were issued in 2002 and became effective beginning in 2003. The minimum distribution rules (including the minimum distribution incidental benefit (MDIB) requirement, discussed later) apply to qualified pension, profit-sharing, and stock bonus plans, IRAs (including SEP/IRAs, SIMPLE accounts, and, to a limited extent, Roth IRAs), TSAs, and governmental Section 457 plans. Failure to comply with the minimum distribution and MDIB requirements may result in disqualification for a qualified plan and loss of status as a TSA, IRA, etc. In addition to disqualification, the plan may be subject to an excise tax of 50 percent of the amount by which the required minimum distribution exceeds the actual distribution made for a plan year.

Plans and arrangements may satisfy the minimum distribution requirements by making either annuity or nonannuity distributions. However, a qualified defined contribution plan, IRA (including a SEP/IRA, Roth IRA, or SIMPLE IRA account), TSA, or Section 457 plan may satisfy those requirements through annuity payments *only* if the payments are made under an annuity contract purchased from an insurance company. This is in contrast to a defined benefit plan that may either purchase a commercial annuity contract or make annuity payments directly to the distributee.

The Economic Growth and Tax Relief Reconciliation Act of 2001 (EGTRRA) directed the Treasury to issue revised tables to reflect the increased life expectancy of today's population and to replace the life expectancy tables under IRC Section 72. The final regulations, therefore, include three new tables: (1) a uniform table for determining the applicable distribution period during a participant's lifetime; (2) a single life expectancy table (also known as the single life table); and (3) a joint and last survivor life expectancy table for two individuals.

Under the final regulations, there is now a uniform and simplified method for determining a participant's required lifetime minimum distributions. Generally, the required minimum distribution for each calendar year is determined by dividing (1) the participant's account balance as of the last valuation date in the calendar year before the distribution calendar year by (2) an age-based factor from a uniform lifetime table. For lifetime required minimum distributions, the rules provide a uniform distribution period for all employees of the same age. The Uniform Lifetime Table (Uniform Table) (see Table 15.1) is used for determining the distribution period for lifetime distributions to an employee/plan participant (or IRA owner) *except* where the plan participant's spouse is the sole designated beneficiary and is more than 10 years younger than the employee (in that case, the joint and last survivor life expectancy table applies). The Uniform Table is also generally used by unmarried individuals.

Table 15.1

(Uniform Lifetime Table)*
(For Use by Owners)

Age	Distribution Period	Age	Distribution Period
70	27.4	93	9.6
71	26.5	94	9.1
72	25.6	95	8.6
73	24.7	96	8.1
74	23.8	97	7.6
75	22.9	98	7.1
76	22.0	99	6.7
77	21.2	100	6.3
78	20.3	101	5.9
79	19.5	102	5.5
80	18.7	103	5.2
81	17.9	104	4.9
82	17.1	105	4.5
83	16.3	106	4.2
84	15.5	107	3.9
85	14.8	108	3.7
86	14.1	109	3.4
87	13.4	110	3.1
88	12.7	111	2.9
89	12.0	112	2.6
90	11.4	113	2.4
91	10.8	114	2.1
92	10.2	115 and over	1.9

*From Final Regulations 1.401(a)(9)-0 through 1.401(a)(9)-8

Example: Earl Green is a 71 year old retiree with an account balance of $200,000. Under the current final regulations and the new Uniform Lifetime Table, Earl may base his distribution on an applicable distribution period of 26.5 years (the factor applicable to account owners who are 71 years of age). Therefore, his first year required distribution is $7,547 ($200,000 ÷ 26.5 = $7,547).

The single life expectancy table, referred to as the Single Life Table, is used for determining the life expectancy of a nonspousal beneficiary at the participant's death.

Distributions Commencing During the Participant's Lifetime

Except in the case of a five-percent owner and unless the retirement plan provides otherwise, distribution of the interest of a living participant in a qualified plan (not an IRA) must begin not later than April 1 of the calendar year following the *later of*:

1. The calendar year in which the participant attains age 70 1/2 or
2. The calendar year in which the participant retires.

The law does not require a plan to defer the commencement of required minimum distributions until the employee retires. A plan may provide for minimum distributions commencing no later than April 1 of the calendar year following the calendar year in which the employee attains age 70 1/2, even though the employee has not retired at that time.

The date when the distribution of benefits must begin is referred to as the "required beginning date" (or RBD). The first year for which a distribution is required is either the year in which the participant reaches age 70 1/2 or the year of retirement. The distribution for that year, however, need not be made until April 1 of the *following* calendar year. The annual distribution for each subsequent calendar year (including the year of death) must then be made no later than the end of that year. If a participant does not receive a distribution during the first calendar year for which a distribution is required, he or she must receive distributions for *two* calendar years in the following year as follows:

> **Example:** Fred Winter, a retired participant in a qualified plan, reaches age 70 1/2 on August 1, 2006. Therefore, he must receive the required minimum distribution for 2006 no later than April 1, 2007, and the required minimum distribution for 2007 no later than December 31, 2007. To avoid having to take two distributions in 2007 (and be subject to income tax thereon), Fred should consider taking the 2006 distribution no later than December 31, 2006 (or previous to the year when he must take such distribution).

In the case of a five-percent business owner, the distribution must be completed not later than April 1 of the calendar year following the calendar year in which the five-percent owner attained age 70 1/2. The date of retirement exception does not apply to such an individual. A five-percent business owner is any corporate employee who owns (or is considered to own, under the constructive ownership rules of IRC Section 318) more than five percent of the value of the outstanding stock of the corporation or stock possessing more than five percent of the total combined voting power of all stock of the corporation. In the case of an unincorporated business, a five-percent owner is any employee who owns more than five-percent of the capital or profits interest in the business.

In the case of the owner of an IRA (including a SEP/IRA and SIMPLE account, but not a Roth IRA), distributions must be completed or begun not later than April 1 of the calendar year following the calendar year in which the owner attained age 70 1/2 (see chapter 3). A Roth IRA is not required to make any distributions during the lifetime of the owner.

Death of Participant After Benefits Have Begun

Where a participant dies *after* plan benefits have begun to be paid, the minimum distribution rules for the post-death distributions (discussed below) apply to qualified plans, TSAs, Section 457 plans, traditional IRAs, SEP/IRAs, and SIMPLE accounts. The IRS has ruled that these post-death distribution rules do not apply, however, to Roth IRAs.

If a participant dies after distribution of his or her interest has begun, the remaining portion of that interest must be distributed at least as rapidly as under the method of distribution being used at date of death. What this means is that if, as of the participant's death, nonannuity distributions have begun that satisfy the minimum distribution requirements, the participant's remaining interest must, unless the plan or arrangement purchases an annuity contract, continue to be distributed so as to satisfy those requirements. In application of this rule, the distribution of a participant's interest is considered to begin on the required beginning date, even though payments have actually begun before that date.

Under the regulations, the "at least as rapidly" requirement is satisfied if each annual distribution is at least equal to an amount determined by dividing the account balance by the number of years in the applicable distribution period. Accordingly, if a participant dies on or after the date when distribution has begun and has a *designated* beneficiary, the applicable distribution period for calendar years after the date-of-death calendar year is the life expectancy of that beneficiary. If there is *no* designated beneficiary (for example, the participant's estate), the distribution period is the remaining life expectancy of the participant using the age of the participant as of his or her birthday in the year of his or her death.

When the Designated Beneficiary Is Not the Surviving Spouse

If the designated beneficiary is not the participant's spouse, the distribution period is determined by consulting Table I, using the beneficiary's age as of his or her birthday in the year following the year of the participant's death. The distribution period so determined is used in calculating the minimum distribution for the first year *after* the year of death (that is, no distribution is required in the year of the participant's death). In following years, the distribution period is reduced by one for each year that has elapsed since the year following the year of death. (Note: This is also commonly referred to by financial planning practitioners as the "minus one method.")

> **Example:** Ralph, age 70, dies in 2006 with a vested interest in a qualified retirement plan of $200,000. His son Frank, age 49, is the beneficiary of his father's interest in the qualified plan. The distribution period, beginning in 2007, is determined by consulting Table I (the Single Life Table) for a beneficiary age 50 (Frank's age in the year after Ralph's death). The applicable factor is 34.2. Therefore, the first distribution in the year 2007 (the year after Ralph's death) is $5,848 ($200,000 ÷ 34.2 = $5,848). No distribution is required to be made in 2006. The distribution is now fixed. The distribution for the year 2008 is determined by subtracting one from the first year's distribution period, resulting in a factor of 33.2 (34.2 - 1 = 33.2).

When the Designated Beneficiary Is the Surviving Spouse

If the sole beneficiary is the participant's surviving spouse, the distribution period for each year during that spouse's lifetime after the year of death is determined by consulting Table I, using the surviving spouse's age as of his or her birthday in that year. For the first year after the year of the *spouse's* death, the distribution period is determined under Table I, using the spouse's age as of his or her birthday in the year of his or her death. In later years, the applicable distribution period is reduced by one for each year that has elapsed since the year after the year of death.

When There Is No Designated Beneficiary

If there is no designated beneficiary (for example, the participant's estate or a qualified charity), the distribution period for each year is determined by consulting Table I, using the age of the employee as of the employee's birthday in the year of death. The distribution period so determined is used in calculating the minimum distribution for the first year after the year of death. In subsequent years, the distribution period is reduced by one for each year that has elapsed since the year of death.

Surviving Spouse as Successor to an IRA

If the owner of an IRA (including a SEP/IRA, SIMPLE IRA account, or Roth IRA) leaves his or her entire remaining interest in an IRA to his or her surviving spouse, the surviving spouse may elect to treat the IRA as his or her own (see chapter 3). The spouse may make this election at any time after the required distribution has been made for the calendar year in which death occurred. To make the election, he or she must be the sole beneficiary of the IRA and have an unlimited right to withdraw from it. This requirement is not satisfied if a trust is named as beneficiary of the IRA, even if the spouse is the sole beneficiary. However, the spouse may make the election by retitling the account in his or her name as IRA owner (rather than leaving it as the owner's IRA with the spouse as beneficiary).

Distributions Commencing After the Participant's Death

If a participant dies *before* the required beginning date, distribution of his or her interest in the plan or arrangement must be made under one of two rules:

1. **The five-year rule**—the deceased participant's interest must be distributed not later than December 31st of the calendar year in which falls the fifth anniversary of the participant's death.

2. **The life expectancy rule**—any portion of a participant's interest that is payable to (or for the benefit of) a designated beneficiary must be distributed (commencing not later than December 31st of the calendar year immediately following the calendar year of the participant's death) over the life of the beneficiary or over a period not extending beyond the life expectancy of the beneficiary. This is commonly referred to by financial planning practitioners as "stretching" the distribution. If there is no designated beneficiary, the five-year rule applies.

If a plan or arrangement has no plan provision regarding which distribution method is preferred and the employee dies before his or her required beginning date and has a designated beneficiary, the default rule applies. In this situation, the default rule is the life expectancy rule. The Single Life Table is used to calculate the remaining life expectancy of the designated beneficiary under the life expectancy rule, if there is a designated beneficiary. If the employee does *not* have a designated beneficiary, the 5-year rule applies.

A plan may provide that the five-year rule applies to distributions after the death of the employee even if the employee has a designated beneficiary. Or it may provide that distribution is to be made in accordance with the five-year rule in every case. Further, a plan need not have the same method of distribution for the benefits of all employees. Finally, a plan or arrangement may include a provision under which either the participant or a beneficiary may elect the method that will apply.

The foregoing rules are modified if the designated beneficiary is the participant's surviving spouse who does not, in the case of an IRA, elect to treat the decedent's IRA as his or her own.

The following table summarizes the current required post-death minimum distribution rules for IRAs and qualified plans.

Table 15.2

Beneficiary	Death Before RBD	Death After RBD
Surviving Spouse	Life expectancy	Life expectancy
Surviving Spouse Rollover	Available	Available
Child (or other non-spousal designated beneficiary)	Five-year rule or life expectancy of beneficiary less one each year (with election to switch to Single Life Table under Final Regulations)	Life expectancy of beneficiary less one each year (with election to switch to Single Life Table under Final Regulations)
Nonqualified trust*	Five-year rule	Remaining life expectancy of participant less one each year
Charity	Five-year rule	Remaining life expectancy of participant less one each year
Estate	Five-year rule	Remaining life expectancy of participant less one each year

* If the designated beneficiary is older than the participant, the designated beneficiary may use the participant's remaining life expectancy. Therefore, a limited "stretch" is possible.

Importance of Designating Beneficiaries

We have discussed the fact that the period over which distributions must be made and the amount of those distributions depend on whether or not the plan or participant has designated a beneficiary. A participant may have more than one designated beneficiary, but only one beneficiary (the one with the shortest life expectancy) is taken into account in determining required minimum distributions.

An individual qualifies as a designated beneficiary if he or she is designated under the plan or arrangement as a person who is entitled to a portion of the participant's benefit, contingent on the participant's death or other specified event. For example, if a distribution is in the form of a joint and survivor annuity over the life of the employee and another individual, it does not satisfy the minimum distribution requirement unless such other individual is a designated beneficiary.

Only *individuals* may be designated beneficiaries. Thus, for example, an estate may *not* be a designated beneficiary. Although a trust is not, as such, a designated beneficiary, IRS final regulations do permit certain "qualified trusts" (for example, a revocable living trust that becomes irrevocable at the grantor's death) to be treated under the rules applying to a designated beneficiary.

It should be apparent that it is very important to name a beneficiary for purposes of additional tax deferral of plan benefits.

MINIMUM DISTRIBUTION INCIDENTAL BENEFIT RULE

The IRS has long held the position that the principal purpose of a pension plan is to provide retirement benefits for employees and that the principal purpose of a profit-sharing or stock bonus plan is to provide deferred compensation for employees. Accordingly, the IRS has developed the principle that post-retirement benefits paid for any other purpose must be "incidental" to the primary purpose. As a practical matter, the post-retirement benefits that must be incidental are death benefits paid to beneficiaries of the participant. To assure that they are incidental, a special rule is designed to insure that, from an actuarial point of view, the value of distributions to be made to the participant are indeed greater than the value of the distributions to the beneficiary. This rule applies to qualified plans, TSAs, traditional IRAs, SEP/IRAs, SIMPLE accounts, and Section 457 plans.

For purposes of the MDIB rule, distributions from a defined contribution plan that do not take the form of an annuity automatically satisfy the MDIB requirement if they satisfy the basic minimum required distribution rules. If the participant's benefit is payable in the form of a life annuity for the life of the employee and it satisfies the basic annuity distribution rules, the MDIB requirement is considered to be satisfied. Where the participant's benefit is paid in the form of a joint and survivor annuity with his or her spouse as the beneficiary and the basic annuity distribution rules are satisfied, the distributions are considered to satisfy the MDIB requirement. Where the participant's benefit is paid in the form of a joint and survivor annuity with a nonspousal beneficiary, the MDIB requirement is satisfied, as of the date distributions commence, if: (1) the amount satisfies the basic annuity distribution rules and (2) the distribution option provides that annuity payments to the participant, on and after his or her required beginning date, satisfy the following condition: The periodic annuity payment payable to the survivor must not, at any time on and after the participant's required beginning date, exceed the applicable percentage of the annuity payment payable to the employee specified in a table provided for that purpose. This condition must be satisfied with respect to any benefit increase after the required beginning date, including increases to reflect increases in the cost of living.

The percentage referred to in the referenced table is based on the excess of the age of the employee over the age of the beneficiary as of their attained ages in a calendar year.

PLANNING FOR DISTRIBUTIONS

While income taxes are not the only factor to be considered in planning a participant's retirement distribution, they are certainly one of the most important considerations, particularly where there is a substantial vested interest involved. Even a long-time middle level employee/participant may accumulate hundreds of thousands of dollars in his or her account balance at either retirement or at termination of employment. As discussed earlier in this chapter, distributions from a qualified plan must take one of three forms:

1. A lump-sum distribution
2. An annuity or other installment form of distribution, or
3. Rollover to an IRA (including a SEP/IRA, but not including a SIMPLE IRA account or Roth IRA) or other eligible qualified plan.

To summarize the income tax rules surrounding retirement plan distributions, a lump-sum distribution is taxed as ordinary income unless the employee was born before 1936, in which case the distribution is eligible for special tax treatment (i.e., 10-year averaging). This is *not* the case if the recipient receives a portion of his or her benefits in the form of an annuity and the remainder as a single sum (i.e., the single sum is not eligible for special tax treatment). Similarly, if the recipient receives a lump-sum distribution and rolls over a portion of that distribution, the retained portion is *not* eligible for special tax treatment. Further, an annuity or other installment distribution is always taxed as ordinary income. A rollover is generally *nontaxable*. In the case of a distribution upon the death of a participant, a rollover is *not* available unless the distributee is the participant's surviving spouse.

In the case of a tax-advantaged plan (including a traditional IRA, SIMPLE IRA account, or employer plan that does not satisfy the requirements of IRC Section 401, but not including a TSA), there are fewer choices than in the case of a qualified plan. A distribution from a tax-advantaged plan may not be rolled over and a lump-sum distribution is *never* eligible for averaging or other special tax treatment. The best that a participant in a tax-advantaged plan (other than a TSA) may do is to arrange at the inception of participation to have the benefits paid over a period of years or otherwise deferred.

Distributions from a TSA may be rolled over to a traditional IRA, another TSA, a 401(k) plan, or a Section 457 plan, but lump-sum distributions are never eligible for special tax treatment.

Important Factors in Choosing the Form of Distribution from a Qualified Plan

In choosing the form of distribution from a qualified plan, several factors must be taken into consideration:

1. **The manner in which the benefit will be used by the participant**—if, for instance, the participant wants to purchase a retirement home, only a lump-sum distribution will suffice.

2. **Whether the participant has a need for the principal of the retirement benefits or just the income generated by it to support his or her retirement lifestyle**—under the rollover or lump-sum options, the participant assumes the risk of superannuation (outliving his or her assets).

3. **The amount of the retirement benefits**—a large amount of benefits receivable tends to favor a rollover to a traditional IRA after the first few years of the IRA's existence, while providing the option of invading principal to maintain a chosen standard of living.

4. **The beneficiary designations selected by the participant**—under a rollover, if the participant selects his or her estate as beneficiary of the IRA receiving the rollover, minimum required distributions are based on the participant's life expectancy.

5. **The expected date of death of both the participant and his or her designated beneficiary**—the amount to which a rollover distribution accumulates (and therefore the benefits) is greatly dependent upon the life expectancy of both the participant and his or her designated beneficiary as well as the order in which they die. Accordingly, the health of both the participant and the beneficiary must be considered.

6. **Whether the participant and his or her spouse (if any) will recalculate life expectancies on an annual basis, under the rollover option**—beginning in 2003, life expectancies, for the purpose of determining required minimum distributions must be calculated by using tables provided in final regulations issued in 2002. These tables appear in IRS Regulations Section 1.401(a)(9)-9. If the plan or arrangement does not provide otherwise, the life expectancy of the benefit owner as well as that of the owner's spouse must be recalculated each year. If life expectancies are not recalculated, the relevant life expectancy in the first required distribution year is reduced by one for each succeeding distribution year. Over many years, the life expectancies as redetermined are significantly higher than those that have *not* been redetermined. When the life expectancies are redetermined annually, the effect is to substantially reduce the required annual minimum distributions.

In evaluating distribution choices at retirement, one thing should be clear—there is no such thing as a single best answer for all possible situations.

Retirement Distribution Checklist

In helping clients plan for retirement distributions, the following checklist may prove useful:

1. Determine if the client has properly designated a beneficiary for each IRA and/or retirement account. A properly prepared beneficiary form should include a primary beneficiary or beneficiaries and a contingent beneficiary or beneficiaries. If a minor is designated as a

beneficiary, the beneficiary form should be prepared in a manner that avoids the jurisdiction of the probate court—either by making the interest of the deceased payable to a custodian under the Uniform Transfer (or Gift) to Minors Act or to a trust for the benefit of the minor.

2. If an account owner dies on or after his or her required beginning date, the required distribution that has not been paid to the account owner prior to the date of his or her death must be paid to the beneficiary of the account owner. This often overlooked rule is included in the IRS final regulations that were issued on April 17, 2002.

3. If an account owner has multiple beneficiaries, then the "separate share rule" should be timely implemented so that each nonspouse beneficiary may be able to use his or her life expectancy in determining his or her required minimum distribution from the account of the deceased owner. (Note: This rule means establishing separate IRAs for each designated beneficiary before making required distributions.) Required minimum distributions to nonspouse beneficiaries must start in the year after the year of death of the account owner, regardless of whether the account owner dies before or after his or her required beginning date. The "separate share rule" is also useful where multiple beneficiaries cannot agree on how to invest the assets in the decedent's account, where they cannot agree on the speed with which distributions should be taken, where they do not get along with each other, and where they want to designate different successor beneficiaries.

4. Determine whether the account owner has a power of attorney that covers the handling of retirement plan distributions.

5. Make certain that a nonspouse beneficiary timely commences required minimum distributions from a retirement account. These payments must start one year after the year of death of the account owner. Also, make sure that the nonspouse beneficiary is aware of the payout period that is applicable to him or her.

6. Make certain that the spouse beneficiary is aware of the spousal rollover rules and timely implements the spousal rollover. Also, make certain that the spouse does not roll over a required minimum distribution. Finally, determine that the spousal IRA rollover account has appropriate designated beneficiaries consistent with the spouse's estate plan.

IMPORTANT CONCEPTS

Lump-sum distribution

Annuity or installment form of distribution

Rollover

10-year averaging

Early distribution penalty

20-percent mandatory withholding

Deductible employee contributions (DECs)

Participant's entire interest in the plan

Net unrealized appreciation in employer securities

Participant's cost basis

Qualified pre-retirement survivor annuity

Qualified joint and survivor annuity

Straight life annuity

Period-certain annuity

Simplified method of taxing annuity distributions

Direct rollover

Indirect rollover

Rules applicable to all rollovers

Rules applicable to rollovers from qualified plans

Distributions not eligible for rollover

Rollovers from TSAs

Rollovers from Section 457 plans

In-service distributions

Loans to participants

Death benefits

Distributions to a Spouse or Former Spouse Pursuant to a QDRO

Minimum distributions

Required beginning date

Distributions commencing during the participant's lifetime

Death of participant after benefits have begun

Distributions commencing after the participant's death

Five-year rule

Life expectancy rule

Minimum distribution incidental benefit rule

Planning for distributions

QUESTIONS FOR REVIEW

1. What are the three basic options available in selecting a form of distribution from a retirement plan?

2. What is the special tax treatment afforded to lump-sum distributions from qualified retirement plans for participants born before 1936?

3. What is the early distribution penalty for distributions taken before the recipient has reached age 59 1/2?

4. What is meant by a participant's "entire interest" or "balance to the credit" in a qualified retirement plan?

5. What is the income tax treatment of a participant's accumulated deductible employee contributions (DECs) upon distribution from a qualified retirement plan?

6. What are the income tax options available to a participant born before 1936 who receives a distribution from a qualified retirement plan?

7. What is the income tax treatment of net unrealized appreciation in employer securities included in a lump-sum distribution received from a qualified retirement plan?

8. What is the income tax treatment of an annuity distribution received from a retirement plan?

9. What are the items that constitute cost basis for a participant in a qualified retirement plan?

10. What two forms of survivorship benefits must be provided to the spouse of a participant in a qualified retirement plan?

11. What are the features of a period-certain annuity?

12. With a qualified joint and survivor annuity, what percentage of the annuity payable during the joint lives of the participant and spouse is payable in the survivor annuity?

13. What is the "annuity starting date"?

14. How does a distributee recover his or her basis under the simplified method of taxing annuity distributions?

15. What constitutes a rollover of a participant's accrued benefits in a qualified retirement plan?

16. How does a direct rollover differ from an indirect rollover?

17. What types of plans or arrangements may receive rollovers of a distribution of cash or other property from a qualified retirement plan?

18. Which type (or types) of rollover distribution(s) is subject to mandatory 20 percent withholding?

19. What types of distributions from a qualified plan may not be rolled over?

20. What is meant by an "in-service distribution"?

21. How is the tax-free portion of an in-service distribution determined?

22. What types of loans to participants are *not* treated as in-service distributions?

23. What is the income tax treatment of death benefits paid to the survivors of deceased employees or deceased retirees?

24. What is the income tax treatment of a distribution by a qualified retirement plan to an "alternate payee" who is a spouse or former spouse of a participant, if made pursuant to a QDRO?

25. What is the purpose of the required minimum distribution rules?

26. What are the three life expectancy tables now used to calculate required minimum distributions from qualified retirement plans and how is each table used?

27. When must a distribution to a living participant (other than to a five-percent owner or if the plan provides otherwise) in a plan or arrangement (other than an IRA) begin?

28. What is the "required beginning date?"

29. When a participant dies after distribution of his or her interest in a retirement plan has begun, how must the remaining portion of that interest be distributed to his or her beneficiary?

30. If the owner of an IRA leaves his or her entire remaining interest in the IRA to his or her surviving spouse, what election is available to the surviving spouse?

31. What distribution rules are applicable in the situation where a participant dies before the required beginning date?

32. What is the purpose of the minimum distribution incidental benefit rule?

33. What are some of the important factors in choosing the form of distribution from a qualified plan?

SUGGESTIONS FOR ADDITIONAL READING

The Tools & Techniques of Employee Benefit and Retirement Planning, 9th edition, Stephen R. Leimberg and John J. McFadden, The National Underwriter Company, 2005.

Retirement Planning, Carla Gordon, American Institute of Certified Public Accountants, 2002.

U.S. Master Compensation Tax Guide, 4th edition, Dennis R. Lassila and Bob G. Kilpatrick, CCH Incorporated, 2003.

CHAPTER SIXTEEN

Regulatory Considerations

• • •

Retirement plans are regulated by both the U.S. Department of Labor and the Internal Revenue Service under the authority of the Employee Retirement Income Security Act of 1974 (generally known as ERISA). In order to protect the accrued benefits of retirement plan participants and beneficiaries, ERISA created an extensive framework of regulatory requirements that must be satisfied by plan sponsors. These requirements have been amended by Congress from time to time. A financial planner needs to be familiar with the principal provisions of ERISA, the reporting and disclosure requirements imposed upon plan sponsors, and the protections it affords to plan participants.

Upon completing this chapter, you should be able to:

- Identify the principal regulatory authorities deriving their jurisdiction or authority under ERISA and the role of each entity
- Identify the pension and welfare plans exempted from ERISA
- Explain how a pension plan is defined under ERISA and how it differs from the definition used for purposes of qualification under IRC Section 401
- Describe the ERISA reporting and disclosure requirements that must be met by pension plans
- Distinguish among a retirement plan summary plan description, annual report, summary annual report, and individual accrued benefit statement
- Identify the six prohibited transactions between a retirement plan trust and a so-called "disqualified person"
- Define a fiduciary under the provisions of ERISA
- Describe the principal obligations or responsibilities of a plan fiduciary
- Explain the "managed account option" available to participants in defined contribution plans

REGULATORY JURISDICTION OR AUTHORITY

The U.S. Department of Labor (DOL) is given its jurisdiction or authority to act in Title I of ERISA, which also spells out the reporting and disclosure requirements that both pension and welfare types of employee benefit plans must meet. Generally, an employee benefit plan is covered by ERISA *unless* it is specifically exempted by ERISA or the related regulations. The Internal Revenue Service tax qualification rules are found in Title II of ERISA, as subsequently codified in the Internal Revenue Code beginning in IRC Section 401. Moreover, ERISA created the Pension Benefit Guaranty Corporation (PBGC) as a federal insurance agency to assure that promised retirement benefits payable via a defined-benefit type of plan are in fact paid (within statutory limits).

Some of the pension and welfare plans exempted from ERISA include:

- Governmental (federal, state, or local) or governmental organization plans
- Religious organization plans except those that elect ERISA coverage
- Plans for nonresident aliens maintained outside the U.S.
- Unfunded excess benefit plans (a type of nonqualified deferred compensation plan)
- Workers' compensation, unemployment compensation, or disability insurance law plans (maintained solely to comply with such laws)

PENSION PLAN UNDER ERISA

A pension plan is defined more broadly under ERISA than under the Internal Revenue Code. In general, a pension plan under ERISA is any employee benefit plan that involves deferral of an employee's compensation until his or her retirement date or later (without regard to the method used to calculate contributions to the plan, the method used to calculate benefits under the plan, or the method used to distribute benefits from the plan) or, alternatively, provides retirement income to employees. The foregoing definition encompasses all qualified pension, profit-sharing, stock bonus, and similar qualified plans. Even certain types of nonqualified deferred compensation plans are included but may be exempted from ERISA's reporting and disclosure requirements. For example, an unfunded excess benefit plan (designed to supplement the qualified retirement benefits limited by IRC Section 415) is *not* subject to any ERISA requirements. It is very unusual for a plan to be exempted from *all* of ERISA's requirements.

A "top-hat" plan, as an unfunded nonqualified plan maintained by an employer primarily for the purpose of providing deferred compensation for a "select group of management or highly compensated employees," is exempt from all of ERISA's provisions except its reporting and disclosure requirements and its administrative and enforcement provisions. A top-hat plan satisfies the former requirement by providing plan documents, upon request, to the DOL, and by filing a simple, one-time statement about the arrangement with the DOL. The DOL has not yet clarified the definition of "highly compensated" for this purpose.

Nonqualified deferred compensation plans not meeting one of these ERISA exemptions must generally comply with most of the ERISA provisions applicable to qualified pension plans, including the vesting, fiduciary, minimum funding, and reporting and disclosure requirements.

Other than the foregoing exemptions specified in ERISA itself, the DOL issues regulations granting partial exemptions or special treatment for certain pension-like plans. For example, a severance pay plan does *not* have to comply with the reporting and disclosure requirements for pension plans but must comply with the more limited reporting and disclosure requirements for welfare plans. Specifically, reporting and disclosure to the DOL must occur if: (1) payments are not directly or indirectly dependent on the employee's retiring; (2) total payments under the plan are not more than twice the employee's annual compensation during the year immediately preceding the separation from service; and (3) all payments to any employee are generally completed within 24 months of separation from service.

A supplemental payment plan providing additional benefits to retirees to cover the cost of inflation also need not comply with numerous ERISA requirements under DOL regulations. SEP and SIMPLE IRAs as well as IRC Section 403(b) plans (TSAs), may be either exempt from ERISA's reporting and disclosure requirements or subject to lesser requirements. Refer to the applicable chapters discussing plan types for a brief discussion of ERISA requirements that must be met by various types of retirement plans.

See Table 16.1 for the reporting and disclosure requirements that must be met by pension plans. The principal requirements that all such plans must satisfy include:

1. The **Summary Plan Description (SPD)**, which describes the major provisions of the plan to participants in understandable language. An SPD must be furnished to participants within 120 days of the creation of a plan or 90 days after a new participant enters an existing plan. Supplements to the SPD are also required in the event that plan provisions are revised. While DOL regulations specify what must be contained in an SPD, there is no prescribed form for filing such document. Filing of an SPD with the DOL is only required if requested by the DOL.

2. The **Annual Report** (Form 5500 series), which includes financial information and is due by the end of the seventh month after the plan year ends. The report includes financial statements as well as an actuary's report (if a defined benefit plan) and information relative to any insurance contracts held by the plan.

3. The **Summary Annual Report (SAR)**, which summarizes the financial information from the annual report for the purpose of providing plan participants with such information within nine months of the end of the plan year.

4. An **Individual Accrued Benefit Statement** within 30 days, if requested by a plan participant, only once per year.

Table 16.1*

Major Reporting and Disclosure Requirements for Pension Plans				
I. Government Filings				
Form	**Description**	**Who Must File**	**When to File**	**Where to File**
5500	Annual Return/Report of Employee Benefit Plan.	Plan administrator.	On or before last day of seventh month after available—file Form 5558.)	Address indicated in instructions to Form 5500.
5500EZ	Annual Return of One-Participant (Owners and Their Spouses) Plans.	Plan administrator. May be filed for plans that cover only an individual or an individual and spouse who are the owners of a business. May also be filed for partnership plans that cover only partners or partners and their spouses.	Same as Form 5500.	Address indicated in instructions to Form 5500EZ.
Schedule A (Form 5500)	Insurance Information.	Plan administrator, where any plan benefits are provided by an insurance company or similar organization.	Attachment to Form 5500.	Same as Form 5500.
Schedule B (Form 5500)	Actuarial Information.	Plan administrator of defined benefit plan subject to minimum funding standards.	Attachment to Form 5500.	Same as Form 5500.
Schedule C (Form 5500)	Service Provider and Trustee Information.	Plan administrator.	Attachment to Form 5500.	Same as Form 5500.
Schedule E (Form 5500)	ESOP Annual Information.	Plan administrator.	Attachment to Form 5500.	Same as Form 5500.
Schedule G (Form 5500)	Financial Schedules.	Plan administrator.	Attachment to Form 5500.	Same as Form 5500.
Schedule P (Form 5500)	Annual Return of Fiduciary of Employee Benefit Trust.	Trustee or custodian of qualified trust or custodial account. (Begins running of statute of limitations.)	Attachment to Form 5500.	Same as Form 5500.
Schedule SSA (Form 5500)	Annual Registration Statement Identifying Separated Participants with Deferred Vested Benefits.	Plan administrator, if plan had participants who separated with deferred vested benefits during the plan year.	Attachment to Form 5500.	Same as Form 5500.

**Tools & Techniques of Employee Benefit and Retirement Planning*, 9th edition, Stephan R. Leimberg and John J. McFadden, The National Underwriter Company, 2005. Used with permission.

(continued on next oage)

Table 16.1* *(continued)*

Form	Description	Who Must File	When to File	Where to File
Schedule T (Form 5500)	Qualified Pension Plan Coverage Information.	Plan administrator.	Attachment to Form 5500.	Same as Form 5500.
PBGC Form 1-ES	Estimated Premium Payment (Base premiums for plans with 500 or more participants).	Plan administrator or sponsor of defined benefit plan (with 500 or more participants) subject to PBGC provisions.	Within two months after the end of the prior plan year.	Pension Benefit Guaranty Corporation P.O. Box 7247-7426 Philadelphia, PA 19170-7426
PBGC Form 1	Annual Premium Payment.	Plan administrator or sponsor of defined benefit plan subject to PBGC provisions.	Within 8 months after the end of the prior plan year.	Pension Benefit Guaranty Corporation P.O. Box 7247-7426 Philadelphia, PA 19170-7426

II. Disclosure to Pension Plan Participants

Item	Description	Who Must Provide	When Provided
Summary Plan Description	Summary of the provisions of the plan in plain language; includes statement of ERISA rights.	Plan administrator.	New plans: within 120 days after effective date. Updated SPD must be furnished within 210 days of every fifth plan year for plans that have been amended; otherwise SPD must be redistributed every 10 years. New participants: within 90 days after becoming a participant or benefits commence (in the case of beneficiaries).
Summary of Material Modification	Summary of any material modification to the plan and any change in information required to be in summary plan description.	Plan administrator.	Within 210 days after the close of the plan year in which the modification was adopted unless changes or modifications are described in a timely distributed summary plan description.
Summary Annual Report	Summary of annual report Form 5500.	Plan administrator.	Nine months after end of plan year, or within two months after close of extension period for plans filing that form.

* *Tools & Techniques of Employee Benefit and Retirement Planning*, 9th edition, Stephan R. Leimberg and John J. McFadden, The National Underwriter Company, 2005. Used with permission. *(continued on next oage)*

Table 16.1* *(continued)*

II. Disclosure to Pension Plan Participants *(continued)*			
Item	**Description**	**Who Must Provide**	**When Provided**
Notice of Preretirement Survivor Benefit	Written explanation of preretirement survivor annuity, participant's right to make an election (or revoke election) to waive the annuity, spouse's rights, and effect of election or revocation.	Plan administrator of plan required to provide	Within period beginning on first day of plan year in which participant attains age 32 and ending with close of plan year in which participant attains age 34. Election must be made within the period beginning on the first day of the plan year in which the participant attains age 35 and ending with the participant's death. For individuals who become participants after age 32, plan must provide explanation within three years of first day of plan year they become participants.
Notice of Joint and Survivor Benefit	Written explanation of joint and survivor annuity, right to make election to waive the annuity, right to revoke waiver, effect of election or revocation, and rights of the spouse.	Plan administrator of plan required to provide	Within reasonable period before annuity starting date. Election must be made no sooner than 90 days before the annuity starting date.
Notice to Terminated Vested Participants	Same information as provided to IRS on Schedule SSA (Form 5500) concerning participant's accrued benefit. Statement must include notice if certain benefits may be forfeited if the participant dies before a particular date.	Plan administrator.	No later than due date for filing Schedule SSA (Form 5500).
Individual Accrued Benefit Statement	Statement of participant's benefit accrued to date based on the latest available data. Statement must include notice of certain benefits may be forfeited if the participant dies before a particular date.	Plan administrator.	Within 30 days of participant's request. Need not be provided more than once in a 12-month period.

* Tools & Techniques of Employee Benefit and Retirement Planning, 9th edition, Stephan R. Leimberg and John J. McFadden, The National Underwriter Company, 2005. Used with permission.

Finally, Title IV of ERISA covers the plan termination insurance provisions and imposes various reporting and disclosure obligations on certain defined benefit pension plans. This information is provided to the Pension Benefit Guaranty Corporation (PBGC) pursuant to their role of insuring and protecting pension benefits for participants and beneficiaries.

PROHIBITED TRANSACTIONS BY A PLAN FIDUCIARY

ERISA requires that a plan fiduciary act solely in the best interest of the retirement plan participants or, under Title I of that Act, be prepared to incur *personal liability* if certain prohibited transactions are permitted to take place. There are six prohibited transactions between a retirement plan trust and a so-called "disqualified person," such as a plan fiduciary. They are as follows:

1. The sale, exchange, or leasing of any property
2. The lending of money or extending of any credit
3. The furnishing of goods, services, or facilities
4. The transfer to or use of plan assets by a fiduciary
5. A fiduciary dealing with plan income or plan assets for his or her own interest
6. A plan fiduciary receiving consideration for his or her own account from a party in a plan transaction involving plan income or plan assets

For each transaction that is prohibited under ERISA, there is currently imposed personally on the plan fiduciary a penalty tax of 15 percent on the amount involved for each year until the transaction is corrected. An *additional 100 percent tax* is imposed if the transaction is *not corrected* within a period of 90 days after the mailing of a deficiency notice by the IRS.

In part because of the punitive nature of the tax on prohibited transactions between a retirement plan and a plan fiduciary, it is therefore necessary to identify who is considered a fiduciary under the provisions of ERISA. Quite simply, a fiduciary is defined as any person who:

1. Exercises any discretionary authority or control over the management of the plan
2. Exercises any authority or control over the management or disposition of the plan's assets
3. Offers investment advice for a fee or other compensation with respect to plan funds or property
4. Has any discretionary authority or responsibility in the plan's administration

Accordingly, this definition includes the plan sponsor (usually the employer), plan administrator, plan trustee, any investment adviser providing services to the plan for a fee, and certain officers and directors of the employer. On the other hand, individuals whose duties are purely ministerial (e.g., the accountant who files certain reporting or tax forms on behalf of the plan) are *not* considered to be plan fiduciaries. It is also interesting to note that the DOL has ruled that broker/dealers who regularly provide only general research concerning securities to its customers, including ERISA plans, are *not* rendering investment advice. Rather, individualized advice that serves as the primary reason for a plan investment decision appears to be the triggering event for determining fiduciary liability.

Once fiduciary status is determined, certain obligations or responsibilities attach. One of these, the obligation to "act solely in the interest of plan participants and beneficiaries," has already been mentioned. However, there are others. Among these is the requirement to act with the "care, skill, prudence and diligence that a prudent person who is familiar with such matters would use under the circumstances then prevailing"—the so-called "prudent person rule." A fiduciary is also responsible for diversifying plan investments so as to minimize the risk of large losses unless it is clearly prudent not to diversify. Nevertheless, the practical, present-day standard for evaluating a fiduciary's prudence in investing plan assets "is one of conduct and not a test of the result of the performance of the investment." As a final prudence requirement, the fiduciary must comply with the documentation requirements of the plan and must invest only in assets subject to the jurisdiction of U.S. courts. This latter requirement does not preclude investing in international securities; it simply requires that the assets be held in a manner such that the U.S. courts may take jurisdiction (e.g., not held in an offshore trust).

A particularly interesting aspect of fiduciary responsibility is the obligation to attempt to achieve superior plan investment performance. This obligation has come into potential conflict with the multiplicity of present-day defined contribution plans (e.g., a Section 401(k) plan) permitting employees to direct the investment of their own individual accounts. Under these plans, employers and other plan fiduciaries are exempt from liability for investment returns that result from participant choices, provided that participants are given the opportunity to exercise control over the assets in their accounts and can choose from a broad range of categories. This exemption from potential liability is specified in ERISA Section 404(c) and Regulations specifying how and in what situations the employer will be protected from any liability for the bad investment decisions of its employees. For example, "safe harbor" provisions have been enacted protecting plan sponsors who offer at least three diversified categories of investments with materially different risk and return characteristics. The Department of Labor has also issued interpretative guidance to help the employer/sponsor distinguish between investment education for its employees (which will *not* subject the employer to potential liability) and investment advice (which probably *will* result in liability).

Since December 2001, a "managed account option" is now available for participants in defined contribution plans. Specifically, prior to that time, participants in self-directed 401(k) retirement plans were beseeching employers/plan sponsors to assist with investment decisions. However, as noted, employers were restricted by ERISA from offering investment advice. In addition, employers often hesitated in providing this service for fear of assuming fiduciary liability for poorly performing investment choices by their employees. To lessen this conflict, the DOL relaxed its regulations to provide for the "managed account option." The practical implementation of this option permits employee/participants in 401(k) plans to choose among money managers at several well-known investment companies (mutual funds) to advance the employees' retirement fund accumulation and wealth-building goals.

Finally, as a part of the regulatory considerations involved in the implementation and administration of a qualified retirement plan, several additional pieces of legislation need to be mentioned. The first is the Age Discrimination in Employment Act (or ADEA) that protects plan participants from discrimination on the basis of age. Specifically, under ADEA, an employee cannot be required to contribute more to a qualified plan simply because he or she has attained the age of 40 or more. The second is Title VII of the Civil Rights Act of 1964 that prohibits discrimination against participants on the basis of sex or sex-related conditions, such as pregnancy. A difference in the amount of employer plan contributions or benefits provided a participant is also prohibited based solely on gender.

IMPORTANT CONCEPTS

Employee Retirement Income Security Act of 1974 (ERISA)

U.S. Department of Labor (DOL)

Internal Revenue Service (IRS)

Pension Benefit Guaranty Corporation (PBGC)

ERISA definition of a pension plan

Unfunded excess benefit plan

Top-hat plan

Severance pay plan

Supplemental payment plan

Summary plan description

Annual report

Summary annual report

Individual accrued benefit statement

Prohibited transactions

Fiduciary

Prudent person test

Managed account option

Age Discrimination in Employment Act (ADEA)

Title VII of the Civil Rights Act of 1964

QUESTIONS FOR REVIEW

1. What are the three primary entities involved in the regulation of retirement plans and what is the principal function of each entity?

2. What are some of the pension and welfare plans exempted from ERISA?

3. In what way does the ERISA definition of a pension plan differ from the definition in IRC Section 401 for purposes of plan qualification?

4. What two types of unfunded nonqualified plans are partially or wholly exempt from ERISA's requirements?

5. Under Department of Labor regulations, what types of pension-like plans are either partially exempt from or receive special treatment under ERISA?

6. What are the principal ERISA reporting and disclosure requirements that all pension plans must satisfy?

7. What are the six prohibited transactions between a retirement plan trust and a so-called "disqualified person?"

8. What penalty is imposed on a plan fiduciary that permits a prohibited transaction to take place?

9. How does ERISA define a plan fiduciary?

10. What parties to a retirement plan are considered fiduciaries?

11. What are some of the obligations or responsibilities of a plan fiduciary?

12. What is the prudent person test?

13. From the standpoint of employer/plan sponsor liability, what is the effect of providing plan participants with investment education versus providing investment advice?

14. What is meant by a "managed account option" for participants in defined contribution plans?

15. What are the roles of the Age Discrimination in Employment Act (ADEA) and Title VII of the Civil Rights Act of 1964 in regulating qualified retirement plans?

SUGGESTIONS FOR ADDITIONAL READING

Tools & Techniques of Employee Benefit and Retirement Planning, 9th edition, Stephan R. Leimberg and John J. McFadden, The National Underwriter Company, 2005.

CHAPTER SEVENTEEN

Investment Considerations for Retirement Plans

• • •

Perhaps the foremost consideration in determining the composition of assets in which a qualified or tax-advantaged plan is invested is that of who bears the investment risk—the employer or the employee. As discussed in previous chapters, in an individual account/defined contribution type of plan, the investment risk is borne directly by the employee. As a result, sponsors of such plans typically provide participants with a choice of investment vehicles, among them fixed income investments, common stock, mutual funds, real estate opportunities and, sometimes, employer stock. In contrast, the investment risk under a pooled account/defined benefit type of plan is assumed almost entirely by the plan sponsor/employer. Accordingly, because this type of plan typically promises some fixed amount of benefit to the participant at his or her retirement (and for which this benefit requires pre-retirement funding), an employer is usually somewhat conservative in its choice of investment assets to fund the plan. Also, an employer/sponsor's choice of investments in a defined benefit type of plan, and therefore the resulting investment performance of the plan, may have a significant effect on the employer's financial results. In addition, the necessity of developing a written investment policy statement to assist in the meeting of investment objectives is much more critical for those employer/sponsors who have decided to implement a defined benefit type of plan.

In order to give proper advice to business clients, a financial planner needs to have a working knowledge of the investment considerations involved in the various types of retirement plans.

Upon completing this chapter, you should be able to:

- Explain the fiduciary obligations created by ERISA on plan sponsors, trustees, administrators, and others
- Describe the "exclusive benefit rule" as it applies to plan fiduciaries
- Describe the "prudent person rule" as it applies to plan fiduciaries

- Describe the factors considered in determining whether a plan portfolio violates the diversification rule
- Identify the prohibited transactions in which a "disqualified person" or "party-in-interest" may not engage and the most common exemptions from these rules
- Describe what is meant by a "directed investment" provision in a defined contribution plan
- Explain what constitutes unrelated business taxable income (UBTI)
- Identify the situations in which a plan fiduciary will not be relieved of all fiduciary responsibilities, after delegating such responsibilities
- Identify the three broad considerations that must be evaluated in establishing the investment objectives of an employer-sponsored retirement plan
- Describe the four primary characteristics of any investment vehicle that need to be considered in assessing its potential suitability as a retirement plan asset
- Explain the several benefits of including life insurance contracts on the lives of plan participants and/or annuity contracts in a qualified plan
- Identify the two incidental benefit tests one of which must be met by qualified plans including life insurance or annuity contracts
- Compare the funding of life insurance premiums between defined benefit and defined contribution plans
- Identify the three types of funding for life insurance policies purchased for plan participants in a defined benefit plan
- Identify the three general ways in which part of a participant's account can be used to purchase insurance on the participant's life in a defined contribution plan
- Describe the principal income tax implications of life insurance or annuity contracts in qualified plans

ERISA AND IRC FIDUCIARY REQUIREMENTS

In the type of situation that exists in a funded employee benefit plan where plan assets are held by a trustee or insurance company, at the direction of the employer, on behalf of plan participants and beneficiaries, a fiduciary relationship is present. Usually, fiduciary relationships are determined under state law. However, ERISA imposes specific federal fiduciary requirements that supersede state law in many cases and have a significant effect on qualified pension and profit-sharing plans.

As discussed in chapter 16, a fiduciary is any person who:

Exercises any discretionary authority or discretionary control with respect to the management of the plan or exercises any authority or control with respect to the management or disposition of plan assets; renders investment advice for a fee or other compensation, direct or indirect, with respect to any plan asset, or has any authority or responsibility to do so; or has discretionary authority or discretionary responsibility in the administration of the plan.[1]

---

[1] ERISA Section 3(21).

Also as discussed in chapter 16, the foregoing definition generally includes the employer, the plan administrator, and the trustee. Attorneys, accountants, actuaries, or consultants who render their specialized services to the plan are normally not considered fiduciaries simply because they provide those services. The same is true for broker/dealers or banks who simply execute buy-sell orders from the plan. Of course, a provider of investment advice is considered a fiduciary, but only in connection with the assets on which advice was rendered.

Each plan must indicate a "named fiduciary" simply to provide an initial defendant in a legal action against the plan. The named fiduciary is not necessarily the only fiduciary involved in the plan and others may be defendants in any legal action against the plan.

The duties of a fiduciary are spelled out in ERISA and are discussed in the following sections.

Exclusive Benefit Rule

Under ERISA Section 404, a fiduciary is required to "discharge duties with respect to a plan solely in the interest of the participants and the beneficiaries." In addition, he or she must "act for the exclusive purpose of providing benefits to participants and their beneficiaries and defraying the reasonable expenses of administering the plan." These obligations are generally known as the "exclusive-benefit rule."

Prudent Man [Person] Rule

Also under ERISA Section 404, a fiduciary must "act with the care, skill, prudence, and diligence under the prevailing circumstances that a 'prudent man [person]' acting in a like capacity and familiar with such matters would use in the conduct of an enterprise of a like character and with like aims." This is generally referred to as the "prudent man (person) rule." DOL regulations require a fiduciary to determine that a particular investment when included in a plan's portfolio is reasonably designed to achieve the investment objectives of the plan. Accordingly, the fiduciary must consider the effect on a plan portfolio's diversification, liquidity, current return relative to the plan's cash flow requirements, and the projected return relative to the plan's funding goals.

Fiduciaries should also keep detailed records of the actions taken and the factors that went into the decisions. In addition, they should make sure these records describe in detail the relevant circumstances prevailing at the time (the conditions under which the action was taken). Finally, fiduciaries should ascertain that all reasonable steps have been taken to acquire the information needed to make informed decisions.

Diversification Requirement

Section 404 of ERISA also requires a fiduciary to "diversify the investments of the plan to minimize the risk of large losses, unless under the circumstances it is clearly prudent not to do so." However, an individual account plan (e.g., profit-sharing, stock bonus, or ESOP plan that permits the holding of "employer real property" or "qualifying employer securities") may hold these items in any amount and as the sole plan assets. A significant advantage of such a strategy is the ability to benefit from the net unrealized appreciation (NUA) on employer stock and thereby defer a taxable event until subsequent sale of the stock, rather than upon its distribution from the plan. On the other hand, such a strategy sacrifices any semblance of diversification and may lead to significant employee relations problems if the employer stock does not perform well in the investment marketplace.

Other types of plans are limited to 10 percent of the fair market value of plan assets in holding employer stock.

The degree of investment concentration that would violate the diversification rule cannot be stated as a fixed percentage but depends on the facts and circumstances of each case, including the following factors:

- The purposes of the plan
- The amount of plan assets
- Financial and industrial conditions
- The type of investment made
- Diversification along geographic lines
- Diversification along industry lines
- The date the investment matures

For instance, an investment in real estate mortgages should not be concentrated in a particular region of the country or in a particular type of property. It is possible to meet the diversification requirement by investing plan assets in a bank's pooled investment fund, a mutual fund, or insurance or annuity contracts if the bank, mutual fund, or insurance company diversifies its investments within such a fund.

Liquidity Requirement

ERISA also requires a fiduciary to take into account the plan's cash flow requirements over time and not invest in assets that may have to be liquidated at a loss when funds are needed to distribute plan benefits.

Compliance with the Plan Document

A plan fiduciary also must follow the provisions of the documents and instruments governing the plan, unless those provisions are inconsistent with ERISA provisions.

Prohibited Transactions

As discussed in chapter 16, a "disqualified person" or "party-in-interest" is prohibited from engaging in specific types of transactions. A disqualified person includes any fiduciary, counsel, or employee of the plan; a person providing services to the plan; an employer, if any of its employees are covered by the plan; an employee organization, any of whose members are covered by the plan (e.g., a labor union); an owner, direct or indirect, of a 50 percent or more interest in an employer or employee organization described above; or various individuals and organizations related to those described above, under specific rules given in the IRC and ERISA.

Prohibited transactions, as listed in chapter 16, include the following:

- The sale or exchange, or leasing, of any property between the plan and a disqualified person
- The lending of money or other extension of credit between the plan and a disqualified person
- The furnishing of goods, services, or facilities between the plan and a disqualified person
- The transfer to, or use by or for the benefit of, a disqualified person, of any assets of the plan
- The acquisition, on behalf of the plan, of any employer security or employer real property in excess of the limits described previously in this chapter.

A statutory exemption permits loans to participants or beneficiaries under specific circumstances as described in chapter 16. Other statutory exemptions permit a loan to an ESOP by a disqualified person under certain circumstances and permit the ESOP to purchase employer securities or real property. Moreover, a disqualified person may provide legal, accounting, or other services to the plan at a reasonable fee without fear of violating the prohibited transaction provisions.

Finally, the DOL has exempted the sale of life insurance policies by participants to the plan or vice versa. DOL has also exempted sales by disqualified persons to the plan where such sales represent a very favorable investment for the plan.

Defined contribution plans are permitted to adopt a "directed investment" provision allowing a participant to select the investments in his or her individual account. Such provisions meeting ERISA requirements relieve the plan trustees from fiduciary responsibility for the participant's investment choices. Usually, the participant's selection of investments, under this provision, is limited; however, by law there must be at least three choices of diversified funds.

Violation of the prohibited transaction rules may result in an excise tax of 15 percent of the amount involved plus an additional 100 percent penalty if the transaction is not corrected within a certain timeframe. Such violation may also result in penalties for breach of fiduciary responsibility.

Unrelated Business Taxable Income (UBTI)

Generally, a trust fund under a qualified plan is exempt from federal income tax. However, qualified plan investment earnings may be subject to income tax to the extent that they represent "unrelated business taxable income (UBTI)" in excess of $1,000 annually. UBTI is gross income generated by a qualified plan trust that is not related to the function that is the basis for the trust's income tax exemption. This is generally so-called "nonpassive income" (such as a working interest in an oil and gas limited partnership) and leveraged retirement plan assets (such as dividends received from stock purchased on margin by the trust), subject to certain exceptions. Dividends, interest, annuities, royalties, and rents from real property or personal property leased with real property, as passive income, are specifically exempted from UBTI treatment.

Delegation of Fiduciary Responsibilities

A fiduciary may elect to delegate to others his or her responsibilities as a fiduciary. For example, a fiduciary may appoint a trustee or investment manager for the plan. However, under ERISA Section 405, this delegation of duties will not relieve the fiduciary of all responsibility in the following situations:

- If he or she participates knowingly in, or knowingly undertakes to conceal, an act or omission of another fiduciary knowing such act or omission is a breach
- If he or she fails to comply with fiduciary duties in the administration of his or her specific responsibilities that give rise to his or her status as a fiduciary and, therefore, enables another fiduciary to commit a breach
- If he or she has knowledge of a breach by another fiduciary, unless he or she makes reasonable efforts under the circumstances to remedy the breach

Need for Liability Insurance Coverage

In light of the aforementioned fiduciary responsibilities, an employer/plan sponsor should exercise great care in selecting a trustee and advisors and should ascertain that adequate liability insurance is in effect covering its plan fiduciary responsibilities.

INVESTMENT POLICY

In recent years, there has been a growing movement away from defined benefit (DB) plans and toward defined contribution (DC) plans. This has been fueled primarily by the growing complexity of administering a defined benefit plan (including the development and administration of the required formal investment policy statement). Also, it is clear that employer/sponsors generally do not want to assume the investment risks associated with DB plans. Therefore, employers have had to become more creative with encouraging and motivating employees to participate in DC plans and plan for their own retirement. A multiplicity of investment choices has been the result and it is here that a client/employee's financial planner may provide valuable advice. Among factors contributing to additional investment choices for employee/clients participating in a DC plan has been the growing public awareness of retirement planning and the need to provide for one's own future economic security, as well as the aggressive marketing efforts of leading mutual fund companies in attempting to provide more complete financial planning services to their investors.

In addition to the type of retirement plan that is adopted (i.e., defined benefit versus individual account), there are three broad considerations that must be evaluated in establishing the investment objectives of an employer-sponsored plan. These include: (1) the financial characteristics of the sponsor and the industry or profession in which it participates; (2) the demographics of the employee workforce; and (3) the possibility of plan termination and associated costs. If an employer is currently experiencing thin profit margins and high labor costs in a highly cyclical industry, it is, in turn, likely to have *less* tolerance for risk than that of an employer in a rapidly growing and dynamic industry. Similarly, demographics are important because a growth company with a young workforce has less concern for cash flow and investment liquidity than does a company with a more mature workforce and the need to provide an immediate or near-term pension to participants. Finally, the possibility of plan termination is an important consideration for companies with some risk of financial decline, merger, or other corporate acquisition since that employer must take into account the possibility of government assumption of plan liabilities to existing participants and the costs associated with the government (specifically, the Pension Benefit Guaranty Corporation) doing so.

There are four primary characteristics of any investment vehicle that need to be considered in assessing its potential suitability as a retirement plan asset. These include: (1) the investment's tax advantages; (2) its liquidity; (3) its stability in value; and (4) its ability to preserve purchasing power. Broadly, as with any investment, these factors may be categorized generally as characteristics of risk and expected return considerations and are relevant for each of the following classes of retirement plan assets:

- Common stocks
- Short-term and long-term debt (e.g., certificates of deposit, commercial paper, U.S. Treasury bills, U.S. Treasury bonds, corporate bonds, and other fixed income assets, including guaranteed investment contracts or GICs)
- Real estate (e.g., real property itself, mortgages secured by real estate, and real estate syndications)
- Equipment leasing (but must avoid UBTI treatment)
- Mutual funds
- Collectibles (not for IRAs)
- Options, commodity futures, and puts and calls

The tax aspects of an asset being considered for a retirement plan is important because of the tax-exempt status of the qualified plan trust that owns the asset. For example, it is not generally good investment practice to place an already tax-exempt asset (such as a municipal bond) in another tax-exempt vehicle (such as a qualified plan trust). In doing so, several percentage points of potential before-tax rate of return may be sacrificed. Also, the plan advisor needs to know the limitations on the tax-exempt status of qualified plans when selecting appropriate investment assets so that a particular investment does not trigger the UBTI, discussed earlier in this chapter.

Finally, investors who are accumulating money, shortly before retirement, need as high a compounded annual investment return as possible and, therefore, must assume the increased risk of volatility. It has been shown that volatility is a major threat to those already retired. In this regard, studies have shown that, in a retirement portfolio, moderate but consistent returns are much more valuable than high but sporadic returns (see, for example, the website www.fundadvice.com for several excellent articles on this phenomenon).

In light of the foregoing considerations, qualified plan investment advisers or investment managers seek to establish certain investment objectives consistent with the interests of plan participants and beneficiaries as well as that of the employer/plan sponsor. These investment objectives usually include: (1) high rate of return; (2) safety of principal; and (3) adequate liquidity. Often these objectives are at odds with each other; correspondingly, a balance must be achieved among them in arriving at an overall investment strategy. One must also consider the ERISA and IRC fiduciary requirements discussed earlier in this chapter. Additionally, ERISA Section 402 requires a "funding policy and method consistent with the objectives of the plan."

LIFE INSURANCE IN A QUALIFIED PLAN

One of the many permissible investments in a qualified plan is life insurance policies on the lives of plan participants. Such policies may be purchased by and owned by a qualified plan using deductible employer contributions to the plan to pay the premiums. The "pure insurance" portion of a qualified plan death benefit (death proceeds less policy cash values at death) is received by a beneficiary income tax free and may be used to pay estate taxes in the estate of the deceased plan participant. The purchase of life insurance policies is most often used in profit sharing or 401(k) plans or in other defined contribution plans.

Life insurance inside a qualified plan tends to have cost advantages over individual life policies provided by the employer outside the qualified plan or those personally owned by plan participants. Moreover, life insurance policies represent a very safe investment (including the guarantee of an insurance company) and provide highly predictable plan costs. Some experts believe that it is possible to structure insured plan death benefits to exclude them from the estate of the plan participant.

The benefit of life insurance policies must be provided to all plan participants under a nondiscriminatory formula related to the retirement benefit or to the plan contribution formula. In addition, such a plan must meet one of the two following incidental benefit tests:

1. A participant's insured death benefit must be no more than 100 times the expected monthly retirement benefit under the plan

2. The aggregate premiums paid (over the entire life of the plan) for a participant's insured death benefit are at all times less than the following percentages of the plan cost for that participant:

"ordinary life" insurance	50%
term life insurance	25%
universal life insurance	25%

While defined contribution plans typically use the above percentages, defined benefit plans have historically used the "100 x" limit. However, either type of plan may use either limit. In fact, defined benefit plans are increasingly using the percentage limits.

Life Insurance in Defined Benefit Plans

The cost of life insurance included in a qualified plan may be added to the maximum deductible retirement plan contribution with the total constituting tax-deductible dollars contributed by the employer. This differs from the treatment in a defined contribution plan where the costs of life insurance must be part of the contributions to each participant's account (that is, those contributions do not increase the Section 415 annual additions limit—lesser of 100 percent of compensation or $42,000 (in 2005)).

Defined benefit plans typically offer three general types of funding for life insurance policies purchased for plan participants. First is combination plan funding under which the retirement benefit is equal to the combination of policy cash values at death, plus an amount distributed from a "side fund" or "conversion fund." This type of funding offers the advantages of an insured death benefit, the investment security of cash surrender values, and an opportunity to invest more aggressively in the side fund. It tends to be used primarily by small plans due to the administrative costs of carrying life insurance policies on each plan participant. Such plans will also typically use the "100 x" limit.

The second type of funding is envelope funding under which the insurance policies are treated as plan assets just like any other asset. Such funding provides both a retirement and a death benefit and normally offers a lower initial contribution to the plan than combination plan funding.

The third type of funding is fully insured funding under which the plan funding consists of 100 percent life insurance policies or annuity contracts and in which there is no side fund. Such plans, known as "IRC Section 412(i) plans" after the Internal Revenue Code Section of the same number, are exempt from the minimum funding rules. A fully insured plan is one that:

1. Contains exclusively individual or group insurance contracts or annuity contracts
2. Has level premiums extending to retirement age for each plan participant
3. Offers insurance and/or annuity contract benefits guaranteed by a licensed insurance company
4. Pays premiums without lapse
5. Has had no rights subject to a security interest during the plan year, and
6. Has had no policy loans outstanding at any time during the plan year

Fully insured plans must be nondiscriminatory as to rights, benefits, and features. However, they enjoy more simplified ERISA reporting requirements, are not required to submit an actuarial certification, and are exempt from quarterly pension deposits. Nonetheless, they are still subject to PBGC annual premium requirements. Fully insured plans are characterized by larger initial annual deposits than uninsured plans and are actually the mirror image of traditional trusteed plans in which the initial annual deposits are relatively small and then increase as participants approach retirement.

Life Insurance in Defined Contribution Plans

In a defined contribution plan, part of each participant's account may be used to purchase insurance on the participant's life in one of three general ways:

1. Voluntary insurance is purchased by participants, using "directed account" or "earmarking" provisions
2. Insurance is provided automatically as a plan benefit
3. Insurance is provided on a nondiscriminatory basis at the option of the plan administrator

Of course, the amount of insurance must stay within the incidental benefit limits. As an investment hedge, many such plans maintain whole life insurance premiums at about one third of plan contributions so as not to run afoul of the incidental benefit limits. Plans that have been in existence for a considerable period of time (e.g., 10 years or more) may make large purchases of life insurance and still avoid the incidental benefit limitation, because of the fact that the tests are computed based on aggregate (or cumulative) plan contributions.

Income Tax Implications of Life Insurance in Qualified Plans

Employer contributions to the plan, including those used to purchase life insurance, are deductible if the amount of life insurance is within the incidental benefit limits. Secondly, the economic value of pure life insurance coverage on a participant's life is taxed annually to the participant based on the lesser of IRS Table 2001 values or actual life insurance company term rates for standard risks. Third, the pure insurance element of an insured plan death benefit, as well as the portion of the death benefit representing Table 2001 costs paid by the participant are income tax free (assuming that they are paid from the same insurance contracts that gave rise to the premium costs). The remainder of the death benefit is taxed as a qualified plan distribution. Finally, life insurance inside a qualified plan receives favorable tax treatment compared to personally owned or employer-provided life insurance (outside a qualified plan), due to the greater deferral of tax with insurance inside a qualified plan. While the death benefits received from qualified plans are generally included in a decedent's estate for federal estate tax purposes, a competent estate planning attorney may assist in structuring a method to eliminate them from the decedent's taxable estate.

IMPORTANT CONCEPTS

Plan fiduciary

Definition of a plan fiduciary

Named fiduciary

Exclusive benefit rule

Prudent person rule

Diversification requirements

Employer real property

Qualifying employer securities

10 percent limit on qualifying employer securities

Liquidity requirement

Compliance with the plan document

Prohibited transactions

Disqualified person or party-in-interest

Directed investment provision

Unrelated business taxable income (UBTI)

Investment policy

Incidental benefit tests

Combination plan funding in a defined benefit plan

Envelope funding in a defined benefit plan

Fully insured funding in a defined benefit plan

Fully insured plan

IRS Table 2001

QUESTIONS FOR REVIEW

1. How may an employer/sponsor's choice of investments in a defined benefit type of retirement plan have a significant effect on the employer's financial results?

2. What effect, if any, does ERISA have on plan fiduciary relationships as determined by state law?

3. What types of professionals who render specialized services to a retirement plan are normally not considered fiduciaries?

4. What is meant by the "exclusive benefit rule?"

5. How must a fiduciary act under the "prudent person rule?"

6. What is meant by the "diversification requirement" under a retirement plan?

7. In the case of profit-sharing, stock bonus, or ESOP plans that permit the holding of "employer real property" or "qualifying employer securities," what is the limit on such holdings?

8. How may a plan participant or beneficiary benefit from the net unrealized appreciation on qualifying employer securities?

9. To what extent may a defined benefit plan hold employer real property or qualifying employer securities?

10. What factors are normally considered in determining the degree of investment concentration that would violate the diversification rule for retirement plans?

11. What is the purpose of the liquidity requirement for retirement plans?

12. Under what circumstances may a plan fiduciary *not* follow the provisions of the documents and instruments governing the plan?

13. Who is considered a "disqualified person" or "party-in-interest" as relates to a retirement plan?

14. What are some of the statutory exemptions to the prohibited transactions rules?

15. What is meant by a "directed investment provision" in defined contribution plans?

16. What is the penalty, if any, for violating the prohibited transaction rules?

17. What is meant by unrelated business taxable income (UBTI) and what is its effect on the income taxation of the trust fund of a qualified plan?

18. Under what situations will a plan fiduciary *not* be relieved of fiduciary responsibilities after delegating such responsibilities to others?

19. What primary factors have contributed to the growing movement away from defined benefit plans and toward defined contribution plans?

20. What three broad considerations must be evaluated in setting the investment objectives of an employer-sponsored retirement plan?

21. What four primary characteristics of investment vehicles need to be considered in assessing their potential suitability as a retirement plan asset?

22. What are some of the investment objectives that qualified plan investment advisers or investment managers may seek to establish for retirement plan funds?

23. What are the two incidental benefit tests one of which must be satisfied by a qualified plan investing in insurance policies on the lives of plan participants?

24. How does the treatment of the funding of the cost of life insurance differ between defined benefit and defined contribution plans?

25. What are the differences among combination plan funding, envelope funding, and fully insured funding in qualified plans that invest in insurance policies on the lives of plan participants?

26. What are the three ways in which a part of each participant's account can be used to purchase insurance on the participant's life in a defined contribution plan?

27. What are the principal income tax implications of qualified plans that invest in insurance policies on the lives of plan participants?

SUGGESTIONS FOR ADDITIONAL READING

Tools & Techniques of Employee Benefit and Retirement Planning, 9th edition, Stephen R. Leimberg and John J. McFadden, The National Underwriter Company, 2005.

The Pension Answer Book, 2005 edition, Stephen J. Krass, Aspen Publishers, Inc., 2005.

CHAPTER EIGHTEEN

Plan Selection for Businesses

• • •

In the previous chapters of this textbook, the author has discussed retirement planning and the broad spectrum of retirement plans extending from tax-advantaged savings vehicles for individuals and government-sponsored programs to employer-sponsored plans for employees. The discussion has included plans that are qualified for income tax purposes under IRC Section 401(a) as well as plans that share some characteristics of qualified plans, yet are not strictly defined as such. Among the latter plans (which are best thought of as tax-favored or tax-advantaged) are plans for self-employed individuals (Keogh plans) and other individuals planning for their own retirement with use of such vehicles as an IRA, a SEP, or an employer-sponsored SIMPLE plan.

However, the assumption that the implementation of *any* retirement plan by a business owner will be in the best interests of those involved may *not* be appropriate. A financial planner is often in the position of advising his or her business client about the adoption of a retirement plan. This chapter explains factors or considerations that should be taken into account before implementing any retirement plan. It is designed to help a financial planner and/or a business owner make an informed decision about the selection, design, and adoption of a retirement plan that will be the most suitable plan to accomplish the employer/sponsor's business, personal, and employee motivational objectives. In many respects, selecting an appropriate retirement plan is a matching exercise in which the employer/sponsor's objectives are matched with the features offered by a specific retirement plan. This chapter requires the reader to apply all of the knowledge he or she should have acquired from the previous chapters to the difficult task of retirement plan selection.

Upon completing this chapter, you should be able to:
- Identify the preliminary considerations that should be taken into account prior to considering the adoption of a qualified retirement plan
- Identify the factual employer information that should be obtained prior to ascertaining the employer's retirement objectives in considering the adoption of a qualified retirement plan

- Describe the typical business owner's personal objectives and other personal factors that must be taken into account when considering the adoption of a qualified retirement plan
- Describe the typical objectives of the business itself in considering the adoption of a qualified retirement plan
- Describe the typical employee motivational objectives of a business in considering the adoption of a qualified retirement plan
- Compare the characteristics and features of various types of qualified retirement plans
- Identify techniques that may be used to maximize the owner's share of contributions to a qualified retirement plan
- Identify those retirement plans that constitute qualified retirement plans.
- Explain the process of adoption of a qualified retirement plan
- Explain the purpose of an "advance determination letter" in considering the adoption of a qualified retirement plan
- Distinguish between a master and a prototype qualified retirement plan
- Describe the common control rules as they apply to qualified retirement plans
- Describe the plan termination protection afforded by the Pension Benefit Guaranty Corporation (PBGC)
- Select an appropriate qualified retirement plan in a given client/business situation

PRELIMINARY CONSIDERATIONS

In many instances, the decision of whether to implement a retirement plan comes down to the threshold question of "Can we afford not to?" A primary reason why the implementation of a retirement plan may be so important is because it makes business sense. Retirement plans of any sort have become so popular and are so potentially advantageous for a number of reasons that a business must proceed or risk being left behind.

Nevertheless, the process of arriving at such a conclusion may not be as simple as it appears. First, a business owner (or an individual planning for his or her own retirement) should not consider the implementation of a retirement plan until following proper risk management techniques and both personal and business liability insurance policies are in place. In addition, adequate cash reserves, in the event of a business or personal emergency, need to be firmly established. Finally, as with most other financial planning decisions, it should be clear that a business or individual's current cash flow can adequately support such a major investment in one's financial future. Stated very simply, unless adequate discretionary income exists in the first place, the business owner should *not* proceed with the implementation of an employer-sponsored retirement plan.

In addition to the competitive business reasons, a business owner may want to implement a retirement plan because of one other primary motivation—to secure personal tax benefits while ensuring his or her *own* future financial security. This may appear self-serving; however, the fact remains that most business owners agree to cover the majority of employees *only* because of the tremendous attendant tax and investment advantages that they themselves enjoy. Nevertheless, these advantages come at a price—the considerable regulatory and fiduciary responsibility that is attendant to the implementation and administration of a qualified retirement plan.

As discussed in chapters 16 and 17, a qualified plan is subject to numerous reporting, disclosure, and investment requirements. The financial planner should discuss these requirements with his or her business owner/client. Specific annual reports, such as the Form 5500, must be filed with the IRS and/or Department of Labor (DOL) in addition to the sometimes considerable amount of paperwork that must be filed to implement the plan initially. There are also numerous other items that need to be provided to employees, either initially or annually, including the summary plan description (SPD) and summary annual report (SAR). In recent years, the desire to avoid at least some of the regulatory and disclosure requirements has led to the introduction of simplified employer plans (e.g., the SEP and SIMPLE).

Finally, the business owner, as sponsor of the plan, is in the role of a *fiduciary* and is required to discharge all duties in the interest of plan participants and beneficiaries. As such, this means that there is considerable potential liability in carrying out the responsibilities of this role. If the owner is either unwilling or unable to accept this liability, he or she should reconsider a qualified plan and perhaps install a nonqualified plan only for highly-valued employees or encourage employees to save for their retirement on an after-tax basis.

TYPICAL EMPLOYER/SPONSOR RETIREMENT PLAN OBJECTIVES/CONSIDERATIONS

Prior to ascertaining the client's objectives (discussed later), the financial planner first needs to obtain some very essential factual information, including (1) an employee census (i.e., a list of all employees with their compensation levels, ages, and years of service with the employer); and (2) current or previous retirement plans maintained by the employer.

Having obtained the employee census information and data concerning other employer retirement plans (current and past), the financial planner may then turn to the business owner's objectives. Specific business owner objectives in establishing a retirement plan usually fall into three general categories—(1) personal; (2) business; and (3) employee motivational. In most cases, the *personal* objectives will be of primary importance. Normally, the business and employee motivational objectives will be secondary, but will nevertheless be important in the plan's selection and design considerations.

In addition to the owner's objectives, other personal factors must be considered in selecting and designing an appropriate retirement plan. These factors include the owner's current age, the size of his or her retirement savings need, and his or her attitude toward investment risk. The closer the owner is to his or her own retirement date, the more he or she will want to ensure his or her own financial security. In addition, as the owner gets older, he or she will generally become more conservative in his or her approach to investment risk. Accordingly, this factor will tend to push the planner in the direction of a *defined benefit plan.*

Again, the closer the retirement date of the owner, the more immediate is the owner's savings need. He or she will probably wish to get as much money in his or her retirement account as quickly as possible. Accordingly, since the annual contributions to defined contribution plans are limited, the planner will again be influenced in the direction of a defined benefit plan.

As we discussed earlier in this text, in defined-contribution type plans, the employee assumes the investment risk. In defined-benefit type plans, the employer is the risk taker. Even though the owner may be older than his employees (and therefore would seem to be best suited to the lesser risk of a defined benefit plan) he or she may not wish to assume the risk of investment. Accordingly, the planner may be guided back in the direction of a defined contribution plan.

Finally, the ability of the business to sustain annual plan contributions will be *critical* in choosing between a defined contribution and a defined benefit plan. While all defined contribution plans do not provide flexible employer contributions, all defined benefit plans require *mandatory* annual employer funding. If the current or immediately foreseeable business cash flow will *not* support this mandatory contribution, the planner should orient his or her client's thinking toward a profit sharing or 401(k) type of *defined contribution plan* and away from a defined benefit plan.

As is the case with most financial planning issues, the planner is advised not to make a plan selection based upon any one of these factors, but to use his or her judgment in synthesizing all factors into the most appropriate recommendation for the client. This will usually mean that the planner must go further and investigate the client's specific objectives.

Business Owner's Personal Objectives

Some of the most common personal objectives of the business owner include the following:

1. To maximize retirement benefits for the owner
2. To provide a tax shelter for the owner
3. To provide estate liquidity for the owner
4. To allow the owner to withdraw funds prior to retirement

Business Objectives

Typical objectives of the business itself include:

1. To minimize plan costs by restricting contributions for lower-paid employees
2. To place the risk of investing plan assets on the employees

3. To provide for predictable annual plan costs

4. To maximize annual employer contribution flexibility

5. To provide for plan administrative convenience

6. To create a market for employer stock

7. To attract and reward key employees

8. To reduce employee turnover

9. To maximize the income tax benefits of the plan

Employee Motivational Objectives

Typical employee motivational objectives include:

1. To maximize retirement benefits for key employees

2. To maximize retirement benefits for older employees (typically management)

3. To provide a tax shelter for key employees

4. To allow employees to withdraw funds prior to retirement

5. To share business ownership with employees

6. To share business profits with employees

7. To increase employee satisfaction

8. To minimize employee turnover

9. To encourage retirement by providing retirement income for employees

10. To encourage employee savings by providing a savings medium that employees perceive as valuable

11. To create an incentive for employees to maximize performance

RETIREMENT PLAN CHARACTERISTICS AND FEATURES

Having discussed some of the more typical objectives of business owners in considering the establishment of a retirement plan, we now turn to the key characteristics and features of the various retirement plans discussed in the previous chapters. Table 18.1 contains a summary of those key characteristics and features.

Table 18.1 Retirement Plan Characteristics and Features

	Payroll Deduction Traditional IRA (tax-advantaged plan)	Payroll Deduction Roth IRA (tax-advantaged plan)	Simplified Employee Pension (SEP) (tax-advantaged plan)	SIMPLE IRA Plan (tax-advantaged plan)	Defined Contribution Plans							Defined Benefit Plans	
					401(k) Plan (regular)	Profit Sharing Plan	Money Purchase Pension Plan	Target Benefit Plan	Savings/Match Or Thrift Plan	Stock Bonus Plan	Employee Stock Ownership Plan (ESOP)	Traditional Defined Benefit Plan	Cash Balance Pension Plan
Key Advantage	Easy to set up and maintain	Easy to set up and maintain	Easy to set up and maintain	Salary reduction plan with little administrative paperwork	Permits higher level of salary deferrals by employees than other retirement vehicles	Permits employer to make large contributions for employees	Permits employer to make large contributions for employees	Plan formula does not allow employer discretion in contributions. Hybrid of DB and money purchase plan	Generally only a supplement to a 401(k) plan.	Benefit paid in employer stock rather than cash	Stock bonus plan which employer can use for borrowing from bank or other financial institution	Provides a fixed, pre-established benefit for employees	Provides a stated account balance at retirement in hypothetical individual accounts.
Employer Eligibility	Any employer with one or more employees	Any employer with one or more employees	Any employer with one or more employees	Any employer with 100 or fewer employees that does not currently maintain another plan	Any employer with one or more employees	Any employer with one or more employees	Any employer with one or more employees	Any employer with one or more employees	Any employer with one or more employees	Any corporation but only C corporations are eligible for all related tax benefits	Any corporation but only C corporations are eligible for all related tax benefits	Any employer with one or more employees	Any employer with one or more employees
Employer's Role	Arrange for employees to make payroll deduction contributions. Transmit contributions to IRA. No annual filing requirement for employer.	Arrange for employees to make payroll deduction contributions. Transmit contributions to IRA. No annual filing requirement for employer.	Set up plan by completing IRS Form 5305-SEP. No annual filing requirement for employer.	Set up plan by completing IRS Form 5304-SIMPLE or 5305-SIMPLE. No annual filing requirement for employer. Bank or financial institution processes most of the paperwork.	No model form to establish. May need professional advice. Annual filing of Form 5500 required. Also may require annual non-discrimination testing to ensure plan does not discriminate in favor of HCEs.	No model form to establish. May need professional advice. Annual filing of Form 5500 required.	No model form to establish. May need professional advice. Annual filing of Form 5500 required.	No model form to establish. May need professional advice. Annual filing of Form 5500 required.	No model form to establish. May need professional advice. Annual filing of Form 5500 required.	No model form to establish. May need professional advice. Annual filing of Form 5500 required.	No model form to establish. May need professional advice. Annual filing of Form 5500 required.	No model form to establish. Professional advice necessary. Annual filing of Form 5500 required. Actuary must determine annual contributions.	No model form to establish. Professional advice necessary. Annual filing of Form 5500 required. Actuary must determine annual contributions.
Contributors to the plan	Employee contributions remitted through payroll deduction.	Employee contributions remitted through payroll deduction.	Employer contributions only	Employee salary reduction contributions and employer contributions.	Employee salary reduction contributions and/or employer contributions.	Annual employer contribution is discretionary	Employer contributions are fixed.	Employer contributions that are not discretionary	After-tax employee contributions and/or employer matching	Primarily employer but employees may contribute also	Primarily employer but employees may contribute also	Primarily funded by employer.	Usually only the employer.

(continued on next page)

[1] Maximum compensation on which 2005 contribution can be based is $210,000.

Table 18.1 Retirement Plan Characteristics and Features
(continued from previous page)

	Payroll Deduction Traditional IRA (tax-advantaged plan)	Payroll Deduction Roth IRA (tax-advantaged plan)	Simplified Employee Pension (SEP) (tax-advantaged plan)	SIMPLE IRA Plan (tax-advantaged plan)	Defined Contribution Plans							Defined Benefit Plans	
					401(k) Plan (regular)	Profit Sharing Plan	Money Purchase Pension Plan	Target Benefit Plan	Savings/Match Or Thrift Plan	Stock Bonus Plan	Employee Stock Ownership Plan (ESOP)	Traditional Defined Benefit Plan	Cash Balance Pension Plan
Maximum Annual Contribution (Per participant)	$4,000 for 2005–2007; $5,000 in 2008; plus $500 catch-up (in 2005) for participants age 50 or over—$1,000 thereafter	$4,000 for 2005–2007; $5,000 in 2008; plus $500 catch-up (in 2005) for participants age 50 or over—$1,000 thereafter	Up to 25% of compensation[1] or a maximum of $42,000 in 2005	Employee: Up to $10,000 plus catch-up contributions. Employer: Either match employee contributions 100% of first 3% of compensation (can reduce to as low as 1% in any 2 of 5 yrs); or contribute 2% of each eligible employee's compensation.	Employee: $14,000 in 2005; $15,000 thereafter plus catch-up contributions Employer/Employee Combined: Up to lesser of 100% of compensation[1] or $42,000 in 2005. Employer can deduct amounts that do not exceed 25% of aggregate compensation for all participants.	Contributions per participant up to lesser of 100% of compensation[1] or $42,000 in 2005. Employer can deduct amounts that do not exceed 25% of aggregate compensation for all participants	Contributions per participant up to lesser of 100% of compensation[1] or $42,000 in 2005. Employer can deduct amounts that do not exceed 25% of aggregate compensation for all participants	Contributions per participant up to lesser of 100% of compensation[1] or $42,000 in 2005. Employer can deduct amounts that do not exceed 25% of aggregate compensation for all participants	Employee contributions not deductible. Employer contributions deductible as long as plan remains qualified.	Contributions per participant up to lesser of 100% of compensation[1] or $42,000 in 2005. Employer can deduct amounts that do not exceed 25% of aggregate compensation for all participants	Same as stock bonus plan except C corporation ESOP can deduct amounts that do not exceed 25% of aggregate compensation for amounts used to repay loan principal, with no limit on amounts used to pay interest	Actuarially determined contribution; annual benefit capped at $170,000 (2005).	Actuarially determined contribution; pay credit (% of compensation) plus an interest credit based on employer-guaranteed return on investment. Annual benefit capped at $170,000 (2005).
Contributor's Options	Employee can decide how much to contribute at any time.	Employee can decide how much to contribute at any time.	Employer can decide whether to make contributions year-to-year	Employee can decide how much to contribute. Employer must make matching contributions or contribute 2% of each employee's compensation	Employee can elect how much to contribute pursuant to salary reduction agreement. Employer can make additional contributions including possible matching contributions as set by plan terms.	Employer makes contributions as set by plan terms. Employee contributions (if allowed) as set by plan terms.	Employer makes contributions as set by plan terms. Employee contributions (if allowed) as set by plan terms.	Employer makes contributions based on actuarially-determined formula in 1st year and then held constant. Must make annual contributions in amount per plan formula.	After-tax employee contributions must meet ACP test. Employer contributions can meet ACP or one of 2 additional tests.	Employer makes contributions as set by plan terms. Employee contributions (if allowed) as set by plan terms.	Employer makes contributions as set by plan terms. Employee contributions (if allowed) as set by plan terms.	Employer required to make contribution as set by plan terms.	Employer required to make contributions as actuarially-determined.

(continued on next page)

Table 18.1 Retirement Plan Characteristics and Features

(continued from previous page)

	Payroll Deduction Traditional IRA (tax-advantaged plan)	Payroll Deduction Roth IRA (tax-advantaged plan)	Simplified Employee Pension (SEP) (tax-advantaged plan)	SIMPLE IRA Plan (tax-advantaged plan)	**Defined Contribution Plans**							**Defined Benefit Plans**	
					401(k) Plan (regular)	Profit Sharing Plan	Money Purchase Pension Plan	Target Benefit Plan	Savings/ Match Or Thrift Plan	Stock Bonus Plan	Employee Stock Ownership Plan (ESOP)	Traditional Defined Benefit Plan	Cash Balance Pension Plan
Minimum Employee Coverage Requirements	Should be available to all employees	Should be available to all employees	Must be offered to all employees at least 21 yrs. old, employed by employer for 3 of last 5 yrs. and had earned income of $450 (2005)	Must be offered to all employees who have earned income of at least $5,000 in any prior 2 yrs. and are reasonably expected to earn at least $5,000 in current year	Generally must be offered to all employees at least 21 yrs. old who worked at least 1,000 hrs. in a previous year	Generally must be offered to all employees at least 21 yrs. old who worked at least 1,000 hrs. in a previous year	Generally must be offered to all employees at least 21 yrs. old who worked at least 1,000 hrs. in a previous year	Generally must be offered to all employees at least 21 yrs. old who worked at least 1,000 hrs. in a previous year	Generally must be offered to all employees at least 21 yrs. old who worked at least 1,000 hrs. in a previous year	Generally must be offered to all employees at least 21 yrs. old who worked at least 1,000 hrs. in a previous year	Generally must be offered to all employees at least 21 yrs. old who worked at least 1,000 hrs. in a previous year	Generally must be offered to all employees at least 21 yrs. old who worked at least 1,000 hrs. in a previous year	Generally must be offered to all employees at least 21 yrs. old who worked at least 1,000 hrs. in a previous year
Withdrawals, loans and payments	Withdrawals permitted anytime subject to Federal income taxes; early withdrawals subject to tax penalty	Withdrawals tax-free if distribution made after 5 yr. period beginning with 1st taxable year that made a contribution; if made after age 59 1/2; if made to beneficiary or individual's estate; if due to total and permanent disability; if made for 1st-time home purchase	Withdrawals permitted anytime subject to Federal income taxes; early withdrawals subject to tax penalty	Withdrawals permitted anytime subject to Federal income taxes; early withdrawals subject to tax penalty	Withdrawals permitted after a specified event occurs (e.g., retirement, plan termination, etc.). Plan may permit loans and hardship withdrawals; early withdrawals subject to penalty tax.	Withdrawals permitted after a specified event occurs (e.g., retirement, plan termination, etc.). Plan may permit loans and hardship withdrawals; early withdrawals subject to penalty tax.	Payment of benefits after a specified event occurs (e.g., retirement, plan termination, etc.). Plan may permit loans; early withdrawals subject to tax penalty.	Target benefit not guaranteed. Depends on investment return. Distributions subject to normal rules for qualified plan distributions.	Generally offer liberal employee withdrawal & plan loan provisions. Distributions must comply with qualified plan distribution rules.	Distributions subject to same rules applicable to all qualified plans; employee has "put option" if receives stock not traded on established market (employer must repurchase stock under fair valuation formula & by independent appraiser). Net unrealized appreciation is deferred until sale of stock.	Same as stock bonus plan plus employees age 55 or over and participants for at least 10 yrs. have annual election to diversify investments in their accounts (25% of balance for 1st 6 years & 50% in last year). Net unrealized appreciation is deferred until sale of stock.	Payment of benefits after a specified event occurs (e.g., retirement, plan termination, etc.). Plan may permit loans but usually does not due to additional administrative burden; early withdrawals subject to tax penalty.	Payment of benefits after a specified event occurs (e.g., retirement, plan termination, etc.). Plan may permit loans but usually does not due to additional administrative burden; early withdrawals subject to tax penalty.

(continued on next page)

Table 18.1 Retirement Plan Characteristics and Features

(continued from previous page)

	Payroll Deduction Traditional IRA (tax-advantaged plan)	Payroll Deduction Roth IRA (tax-advantaged plan)	Simplified Employee Pension (SEP) (tax-advantaged plan)	SIMPLE IRA Plan (tax-advantaged plan)	Defined Contribution Plans							Defined Benefit Plans	
					401(k) Plan (regular)	Profit Sharing Plan	Money Purchase Pension Plan	Target Benefit Plan	Savings/ Match Or Thrift Plan	Stock Bonus Plan	Employee Stock Ownership Plan (ESOP)	Traditional Defined Benefit Plan	Cash Balance Pension Plan
Vesting	Contributions are immediately 100% vested	Contributions are immediately 100% vested	Contributions are immediately 100% vested	Employer and employee contributions are immediately vested 100%	Employee salary deferrals are immediately 100% vested. Employer contributions may vest over time according to plan terms.	Employer contributions may vest over time according to plan terms. Employee contributions if any are immediately 100% vested.	Employer contributions may vest over time according to plan terms. Employee contributions if any are immediately 100% vested.	Employer contributions may vest over time according to plan terms. Employee contributions if any are immediately 100% vested.	Employer matching contributions must vest in same accelerated manner as applicable to top-heavy plans	Employer contributions may vest over time according to plan terms. Employee contributions if any are immediately 100% vested.	Employer contributions may vest over time according to plan terms. Employee contributions if any are immediately 100% vested.	Right to benefits may vest over time according to plan terms.	Right to benefits may vest over time according to plan terms.
Maximum 2005 salary deferral				$10,000	$14,000								
Maximum 2005 catch-up				$2,000	$4,000								
Subject to compensation limit of $210,000 in 2005				No	Yes	Yes	Yes	Yes	No	Yes	Yes	Yes	

RETIREMENT PLAN SELECTION AND DESIGN

As with any financial planning opportunity, the planner must know the universe of alternatives that is available to satisfy his or her client's goals. In retirement planning for the business owner, these are the various types of qualified and tax-advantaged plans, as shown in Table 18.1. It is fortunate that, in recent years, eligibility for these types of plans has been standardized such that all are generally available to a business entity, no matter what the form. The only notable exceptions to this rule are: stock bonus plans and ESOPs, which may not be adopted by *unincorporated* entities such as a sole proprietor or partnership, and the Section 403(b) tax-sheltered annuity (TSA) which is only permissible for certain IRC 501(c)(3) nonprofit organizations and public schools. In addition, as discussed in chapter 6, Section 457 plans may be adopted only by nonprofits and state and local governmental entities. With these exceptions, however, all forms of defined contribution and defined benefit plans are permitted for all forms of business entity.

Many of the business owner's objectives may be met by any well-designed employer-sponsored retirement plan. If the financial planner is in doubt as to which plan to recommend, it is always advisable for the planner to select the *simplest* or least complicated plan that satisfies the client's retirement planning objectives.

In designing an appropriate retirement plan, it cannot be reiterated enough that to help the business, *the financial planner first needs to help the business owner satisfy his or her own personal retirement objectives*. In that spirit, here are some suggestions or techniques that may be used to maximize the owner's share of contributions to a qualified retirement plan. All have been discussed previously in the preceding chapters of this text.

1. Impose a minimum age and waiting period for initial plan eligibility. A qualified plan may require a minimum age of 21 and a waiting period of up to one year. However, if all employer contributions are fully vested at that time, this waiting period (except for a 401(k) plan) may be up to two years. If the business is one that experiences rapid turnover (such as many retail firms), it may be advisable to delay the eligibility date to two years from the date of an employee's hiring.

2. Impose a vesting schedule. A departing employee is only entitled to the vested portion of his or her plan benefit. The non-vested portion is forfeited and may be used either to reduce future employer plan contributions or reallocated among the remaining plan participants, with the major participant usually being the business owner.

3. Impose a requirement that a participant work at least 1,000 hours during the plan year or be employed on the last day of the plan year to receive an allocation or accrue a benefit.

4. Integrate the plan with Social Security benefits using the "permitted disparity rules." This results in plan participants whose compensation does not exceed a specified integration level not receiving an additional qualified plan allocation.

5. Adopt an age-weighted profit sharing plan or target benefit pension plan, which favors an older business owner/employee. Both of these types of plans permit a greater allocation of the employer's contribution to an older employee and, in the case of the age-weighted plan, does not require a mandatory annual employer contribution.

RETIREMENT PLAN INSTALLATION

While a client's financial planner normally will be the client's most trusted advisor with regard to the selection of an appropriate retirement plan, installation of the plan (whether customized or prototyped) is best left to a pension advisory firm, also known as a third-party administrator (TPA). A TPA provides consulting services in the installation of, most particularly, a qualified corporate retirement plan. A TPA will also serve as the administrator of the plan that is implemented, thereby carrying out the duties of communicating regularly with plan participants/employees.

Before we discuss the process of installing a qualified retirement plan, let us first review which of the plans discussed in this text constitute qualified (or IRC Section 401(a)) retirement plans. Qualified plans include:

- Section 401(k) plans
- Profit sharing plans
- Money purchase pension plans
- Savings match or thrift plans
- Stock bonus plans, including ESOP plans
- Cross-tested/Age-weighted/Target benefit plans
- HR 10 (Keogh) plans
- Traditional defined benefit pension plans
- Cash balance pension plans

Plan Adoption

The first step in installing a qualified retirement plan is plan adoption. While a SEP may be adopted any time through the due date for filing the employer's tax return for the year the employer wants to make the plan effective, a qualified plan must be adopted during the calendar year in which the employer wants the plan to be effective. An employer may elect to make the plan effective on the first day of the year of adoption.

Adoption is effected by a corporation through a resolution of its board of directors. Unincorporated businesses may simply adopt a written resolution in a similar form. It is critical that a valid plan trust be adopted before the end of the year of adoption.

Small employers (no more than 100 employees with compensation in excess of $5,000 for the previous year) may qualify for a business tax credit of up to $500 calculated on 50 percent of plan startup costs or expenses incurred in educating employees about the plan. However, at least one NHCE must be covered by the plan.

Determination Letter

Some employer/sponsors apply to the IRS for an "advance determination letter" that the proposed plan satisfies the plan qualification requirements in the Internal Revenue Code. The purpose of doing so is to gain advance assurance that the plan as proposed constitutes a qualified plan in its initial year and all subsequent years. Failure to obtain a determination letter places the employer at risk of a subsequent disqualification upon audit by the IRS. In the event of an IRS audit, not only might the employer's income tax deduction be disallowed but the plan trust might lose its tax-exempt status and employee/participants may be taxed on their vested benefits. As retirement plan law is in a constant state of flux, plans must be constantly amended to retain their qualification. Each time a significant amendment is made, the plan administrator/employer should request a new determination letter. However, if a plan is found by the IRS to be discriminatory *in operation*, rather than in its plan provisions, a determination letter will be of no value. Also, the Internal Revenue Code permits "retroactive amendment" to correct disqualifying plan provisions up to the filing date (including extensions) of the year audited.

Custom/Master or Prototype Plans

Due to the significant costs involved, very few employer/sponsors custom design their qualified plan. Most employer/sponsors use what is referred to as a "master" or "prototype" plan offered by various financial institutions, such as insurance companies, banks, mutual fund companies, and various service providers, to encourage the plan sponsor to purchase its investment products in funding the plan. These master or prototype plans use standardized language previously approved by the IRS while they still permit the sponsor to make certain plan choices, such as the plan vesting schedule and contribution or benefit formula. A "master plan" is one offered by a single financial institution for a number of employers. Adoption of the master plan locks the plan sponsor into using that particular financial institution. On the other hand, a "prototype plan" provides sponsor flexibility in selecting a funding institution or medium.

When an employer/sponsor uses either a master or prototype plan, not only is plan installation made easier but so too is the determination letter process since the IRS needs to determine only whether the vesting schedule and contribution or benefit formula are nondiscriminatory.

COMMON CONTROL RULES

Throughout this text, we have made the simplifying assumption that a plan sponsor is a single business entity (incorporated or unincorporated business) and not part of a larger group of businesses owned or controlled in common by the same interests. Under IRC Section 414(b), all employees of all corporations in a "controlled group of corporations" (defined later in this section) are treated as employed by a single employer for coverage, nondiscrimination, and other plan purposes. In effect, this rule keeps an employer from creating various related business entities and moving employees around to avoid the coverage, nondiscrimination and other qualified plan rules. For example, in the absence of such rules, an employer could place all employees it wishes to benefit from a plan in one company while placing other employees in subsidiary or other related companies that offer either lesser plan benefits or no benefits.

There are actually three sets of **common control rules** that are quite complex. The first of these rules requires, among other things, that the participation and coverage tests of IRC Section 410 be applied to the entire controlled group of corporations, rather than to any single corporation in the group. IRC Section 414(c) adds partnerships and proprietorships to these rules. The second of the common control rules, under IRC Section 414(m), deals with an **affiliated service group** (defined later in this section) and requires that employees of such a group be treated as employed by a single employer. Primarily, this rule applies to medical doctors who form several clinics and then attempt to cover only selected employees. The third common control rule, under IRC Section 414(n), requires that a **leased employee** (defined later in this section) be treated as an employee of the lessor corporation under circumstances specified in Section 414(n).

Under IRC Sections 414(b) and 414(c), all employees of members of a controlled group of corporations or controlled group of trades or businesses (whether or not incorporated) that are under common control are treated as employed by a single employer for purposes of most provisions of the qualified plan law. Of main importance are the coverage requirements of IRC Section 410. This means that all employees or employers in a controlled group must be taken into account when determining whether a qualified plan maintained by any employer in the controlled group satisfies the percentage participation tests or the discriminatory tests. Under IRC Section 1563(a), there are three types of controlled groups: (1) **parent-subsidiary controlled groups**; (2) **brother-sister controlled groups**; and (3) **combined groups**.

A *parent-subsidiary controlled group* is one or more chains of corporations connected through stock ownership with a common parent corporation if at least 80 percent of the total combined voting power of all classes of stock entitled to vote or at least 80 percent of the total value of shares of all classes of stock is owned by one or more corporations in the group and the common parent corporation satisfies the same 80 percent test with at least one other corporation in the group. With regard to unincorporated trades or businesses, the 80 percent test is applied to an interest in profits or to a capital interest. For example, if Atlantic Corporation owns 80 percent of the total combined voting power of all classes of stock entitled to vote of Pacific Corporation, and Pacific Corporation, in turn, owns stock that possesses at least 80 percent of the total value of shares of all classes of stock of Gulf Corporation, then Atlantic is the common parent with the parent-subsidiary controlled group made up of Atlantic, Pacific, and Gulf.

A *brother-sister controlled group* is made up of two or more corporations in which five or fewer individuals, estates, or trusts own stock possessing at least 80 percent of the total combined voting power or value of all classes of stock (other than nonvoting preferred stock) of each corporation and more than 50 percent of the total combined voting power or value of all classes of stock (other than nonvoting preferred stock) of each corporation, taking into account the stock ownership of each owner only to the extent that the owner's interest is identical in each corporation. For example, let us assume that Atlantic Corporation, Pacific Corporation, and Gulf Corporation have only one class of stock owned by five unrelated individuals as follows:

Investor	Percentage of Ownership in			Identical Ownership in
	Atlantic Corp.	Pacific Corp.	Gulf Corp.	APG
A	20%	10%	20%	10%
B	20	30	10	10
C	20	20	30	20
D	20	20	20	20
E	20	20	20	20
Total	100%	100%	100%	80%

Corporations Atlantic, Pacific, and Gulf constitute a brother-sister controlled group because five or fewer individuals, estates, or trusts own stock possessing at least 80 percent (100 percent in this case) of the total combined voting power or value of all classes of stock of each corporation, and more than 50 percent (80 percent in this case) of the total combined voting power or value of all classes of stock of each corporation, taking into account the stock ownership of each owner only to the extent that the owner's interest is identical in each corporation.

A *combined group* is three or more corporations each of which is a member of a parent-subsidiary group or a brother-sister group and one of which is a common parent of a parent-subsidiary group and also is included in a brother-sister group. For example, assume that Keith, an individual, owns 80 percent of the total combined voting power of all classes of stock of Atlantic Corporation and Pacific Corporation. Also assume that Pacific Corporation owns 80 percent of the total combined voting power of all classes of the stock of Gulf Corporation. Atlantic and Pacific are members of a brother-sister controlled group. Pacific and Gulf are members of a parent-subsidiary group. Pacific is the common parent of the parent-subsidiary group and also a member of the brother-sister group. Therefore, Atlantic, Pacific, and Gulf constitute a combined group.

For the purposes of calculating the foregoing percentages, some types of stock are excluded in the controlled group tests. For instance, both nonvoting preferred stock and treasury stock are not taken into account. In addition, there are several other types of stock which are excluded. The primary purpose of these stock exclusions is to keep employers from defeating the controlled group tests by transferring stock to various trusts or other entities.

The Attribution Rules

Even stock owned indirectly (by certain related parties) may be deemed to be owned by an individual in determining the existence of a controlled group. For example, in the case of both parent-subsidiary and brother-sister controlled groups, having an option to acquire stock is treated the same as owning the stock for these purposes. Similarly, stock owned by a partnership is considered owned by any partner having a 5 percent or more capital or profits interest in the partnership. A beneficiary of an estate or trust (other than a qualified trust) having a present value interest of 5 percent or more in stock owned directly or indirectly by the estate or trust is treated as being owned by the beneficiary to the extent of his or her actuarial interest. Finally, stock owned directly or indirectly by or for any portion of a grantor trust is considered owned by the grantor. Additional attribution rules (not discussed here) apply only in the case of a brother-sister controlled group.

Affiliated Service Group

Prior to the enactment of IRC Section 414(m), professional corporations or partnerships that did not want to include rank-and-file employees in qualified plans established for the professional owners used creative methods to exclude such employees. For example, if two doctors entered into an equal partnership (or formed two one-person professional corporations which in turn entered into a partnership) and then formed a separate business to provide all support services for the medical practice, having the support business employ all of the support employees, each doctor would own only 50 percent of the support business. Under the other aggregation rules (other than the affiliated service group rules), each doctor could adopt a qualified plan covering only him- or herself and none of the support employees. However, the affiliated service group rules now prevent this type of activity. Basically, the rule provides that the employees of an affiliated service group must be included in any qualified plans that benefit the owners. The affiliated service group is deemed to include both the professional organization and the service organization. The rule treats all employees of an affiliated service group as employees of a single employer.

The applicable proposed regulations apply primarily to service organizations of the type that provide professional services in the field of health, law, engineering, architecture, accounting, actuarial science, performing arts, consulting, or insurance. As an example of the operation of the affiliated service group rules, assume that Doctors A and B each incorporate and that the two corporations form a partnership. Each corporation and the partnership of these two corporations constitutes an affiliated service group, because the corporations are service organizations in partnership with each other and each one is regularly associated with the partnership in performing services for third parties.

Because of the complexity and subjectivity of the affiliated service group rules, it is strongly recommended that an IRS ruling be obtained as to whether a particular organization is a member of an affiliated service group.

Employee Leasing

IRC Section 414(n) was designed to reduce the discrimination resulting from employers leasing employees from an independent employee leasing organization, rather than retaining such employees directly on their on payroll. By so doing, employers hoped to be able to exclude such persons from their qualified plans.

IRC Section 414(n) provides that a leased employee is considered the employee of the lessee organization for which the services are performed if the employee has performed services on a substantially full-time basis for at least one year, and the services are "performed under the primary direction or control by the recipient."

An exception is if the leasing organization itself maintains a "safe-harbor" plan for the leased employees meeting certain minimum requirements. Because of the one-year requirement discussed in the previous paragraph, the leasing provision does not affect most short-term temporary help.

RETIREMENT PLAN TERMINATION

The purpose of this final section of this text (prior to a sample case illustration) is to explain the plan termination protection afforded by the Pension Benefit Guaranty Corporation (PBGC), the different types of plan terminations, and the possibility of assets reverting to the employer in the event of plan termination.

Unfortunately, there are some times when an existing retirement plan must be terminated. This may happen frequently in the merger of two companies or the acquisition of one company by another. However, even though the plan's termination may be viewed as a detriment to a participant's retirement planning goals, the participant is protected where vesting provisions are a part of the plan. In that instance, the participant (no matter in what percentage vested) becomes 100 percent or fully vested in his or her (otherwise forfeitable) accrued benefit. In addition, further guarantees are provided for those employees participating in a traditional defined benefit or cash balance pension plan. (For example, monthly benefit amounts in defined benefit types of plans are insured up to the amount of $3,801.14 in the year 2005).

As discussed previously in this text, defined benefit plans promise specific benefits to participants and are required to pay regular premiums to the PBGC to insure these guaranteed benefits. Such benefits include nonforfeitable benefits and any death, survivor, or disability benefits due or in payment status. Plan-specified benefits that are *not* guaranteed by the PBGC include any death and disability benefits not in payment status and any retirement benefits that exceed the PBGC guaranteed monthly amount. For a plan benefit to be guaranteed by the PBGC, it must meet the three following prerequisites:

1. The benefit must be nonforfeitable (vested) and payable other than by reason of acceleration because of plan termination.
2. The benefit must be payable as an annuity or as one or more payments as an annuity.

3. The participant or his or her beneficiary must be entitled to the benefit according to any one of several legally-specified reasons (e.g., the benefit was in pay status on the date of plan termination).

The payment provided for in the PBGC-provided benefit is limited to a specified monthly amount that is indexed for inflation periodically and is a figure payable in level amounts over the participant's lifetime as a single-life annuity commencing at age 65. A lump sum payment is not available as a PBGC benefit, *regardless* of plan provisions indicating otherwise. A defined benefit qualified plan, either in the traditional pension form or in the more recent cash balance pension variation, pays for the guarantee of this benefit through the assessment of additional set premiums payable to the PBGC over the active lifetime of the plan.

A qualified plan that is subject to PBGC coverage may only be terminated voluntarily by the sponsor in the event that the plan meets the requirements for either a so-called standard or distress termination. For a standard termination to occur, an employer must generally have sufficient assets to pay *all* plan benefits. However, a plan without sufficient assets to pay these benefits may still qualify for a standard termination if the employer agrees to make up the deficiency in a single payment. If a plan does not have sufficient assets to pay benefits, it may qualify for a voluntary distress termination in any one of the following three circumstances:

1. The employer is being liquidated or reorganized in bankruptcy proceedings.
2. The employer is unable to pay debts as they become due and will not otherwise be able to remain in business.
3. The employer can show that the cost of providing coverage is unreasonably burdensome as a result of a decline in the workforce.

The PBGC may also undertake *involuntary* termination proceedings in a U.S. District Court in a jurisdiction where the employer/sponsor of a subject plan does business if the PBGC finds that either the plan does not comply with the required minimum funding standards applicable to a pension plan or that the plan is unable to pay benefits when they will become due.

Finally, what happens if any qualified plan is terminated and there is a reversion of at least some of the residual assets to the employer rather than the plan participants? Residual assets are equal to the plan funds remaining after the satisfaction of all plan liabilities. While Department of Labor regulations provide that an employer/sponsor may *not* recover any surplus plan assets until it has fully vested all participants' benefits and has made any requisite payments, a reversion of assets is quite common in the event of an overfunded pension plan. If a reversion occurs, there is now generally a 50 percent excise tax penalty on the amount recovered under the reversion. This penalty is reduced to 20 percent if the employer shares the reversion amount in some stipulated manner with the active participants of the terminated plan.

SAMPLE CASE ILLUSTRATION

Note: The following sample case is intended to help the reader apply the information presented in this text and select a qualified retirement plan in a given situation.

Consider the situation of Sharon Fortis, the 90 percent owner of a small software development firm doing business as an S corporation. Robert is also involved in the business as a 10-percent owner. Sharon is 45 years old and has an annual retirement savings need of $20,000 per year. She plans to retire at age 62, some 17 years from now. She is willing to take some moderate risk to achieve her desired retirement lifestyle, but wishes to spread this risk among the employees of her business, if possible. The business exhibits a fluctuating cash flow, but generally could afford to fund retirement plan contributions of approximately $60,000 per year. In addition to these general facts, Sharon also has the following specific objectives when considering the implementation of any retirement plan for herself and her business:

- To maximize tax benefits for herself
- To maximize retirement benefits and allocable plan contributions for herself and Robert
- To exclude as many employees as possible from plan coverage, but at a minimum the two hourly (non-salaried) employees of the business
- To retain current employees and minimize employee turnover to the extent possible
- To offer a competitive retirement plan as a recruitment tool for new hard-to-find employees, including sharing future business profits, if necessary
- To encourage employees to save for their own retirement

You are planning as of calendar year 2005.

The current employee profile for the business to use in designing and implementing a retirement plan for Sharon and her business is as follows:

Employee	Age	Yrs. of Service	Annual Compensation	HCE*	Key Employee**
Sharon	45	20	$150,000	X	X
Robert	48	18	100,000	X	X
Joan	42	15	85,000	X	
Harold	35	10	60,000		
Ralph	35	10	50,000		
Rhonda	32	3	35,000		
Julie	30	2	30,000		
Felipe	24	2	25,000		
Jessica	22	1	hourly		
Amy	21	1	hourly		

*Highly compensated employee for 2005.
**Key employee for purposes of top-heavy plan rules.

The first step in recommending a retirement savings alternative for Sharon is to consider whether to implement some form of qualified retirement plan using the business entity or have her save individually (outside the business). Since Sharon's annual retirement savings need is greater than what may easily be achieved through some form of personal retirement vehicle (such as an IRA) and there are good business reasons for a qualified corporate plan, the decision to implement such a plan is relatively straightforward.

Next is the general decision of whether to design a defined contribution, defined benefit, or simplified form of retirement plan. Sharon is under the age of 50 and still has 17 years until her retirement. She indicated that she would prefer to have the employees of her business bear the investment risk in saving for their own retirement, but will also share future business profits with them, if necessary. Finally, the cash flow of Sharon's business is fluctuating; therefore, she should avoid a mandatory employer contribution to any retirement plan that is implemented. All of these considerations guide you, the planner, in recommending some form of defined contribution plan, probably a profit sharing plan. While Sharon could install a SEP and/or SIMPLE plan to achieve administrative simplicity, she will lose some flexibility in excluding employees and/or delaying their potential vesting (which is important to Sharon as a method of discouraging employee turnover).

Now proceed on to three special plan design features—plan eligibility provisions, an appropriate vesting schedule, and the possibility of integrating the plan with Social Security benefits. The first of these—plan eligibility—addresses Sharon's goal of excluding as many employees from the plan as possible. The second—vesting—addresses her goal of retaining and motivating employees; however, this must be tested against the top-heavy rules to determine which type of vesting schedule is permissible. Finally, the third plan design feature—integration of the plan with Social Security benefits—will permit more money to be contributed on behalf of Sharon and Robert, the owners of the business.

Plan eligibility requirements (that is, the number of employees who actually are covered by the plan) must comply with the general nondiscrimination rules applicable to all qualified plans. Accordingly, for the plan to be considered nondiscriminatory, it must meet either the ratio percentage test or the average benefits test. In analyzing to see if the first test (ratio percentage) is satisfied, we find that 8 of 10 otherwise eligible employees will actually participate. The two eligible, but hourly, employees are excluded from coverage. Therefore, 100 percent of the highly compensated employees (3 of 3) participate and five of seven of the nonhighly compensated employees (or 71 percent) participate. Since the participation percentage of nonhighly compensated employees exceeds 70 percent of the HCE percentage, we pass this test and may proceed.

Now we must decide which vesting schedule is appropriate. This depends on whether the plan is classified as top-heavy, in which case an accelerated vesting schedule (either 3-year "cliff" vesting or 2 to 6-year graded vesting) must be used. The rule here is that the "key employees'" (in this case, Sharon and Robert) retirement account balances may not exceed 60 percent of the total account balances for all covered employees. As this is a new plan, and we do not yet have account balances, we must compare Sharon's and Robert's total percentage of compensation to the total to determine if the plan will be top-heavy. In performing this calculation, we find that their total percentage of compensation is only 47 percent (or $250,000 divided by $535,000), so the plan is not top-heavy and we are free to use the normal vesting schedules of either 5-year "cliff" vesting or 3 to 7-year graded vesting. Since Sharon is most concerned about employee retention and turnover minimization, it is probably prudent to install a 5-year "cliff" vesting schedule.

Finally, possible integration of the proposed profit sharing plan is investigated. We know that the maximum annual deductible contribution for a profit sharing plan is 25 percent of the annual compensation paid to all covered employees. However, we also know that Sharon has estimated that her business may contribute only approximately $60,000 per year. In taking these two factors into consideration (as well as simplicity), we determine that a 10 percent annual contribution to the profit sharing plan is appropriate or a total of $53,500 based upon the covered employees' current compensation level. This means that a contribution of $15,000 or 28 percent of the total will be made on behalf of Sharon and $10,000 or 19 percent of the total will be allocated to Robert's account. If we integrate the plan and use the "permitted disparity" rules for defined contribution plans, we can increase Sharon's and Robert's allocated amounts and percentage of total contribution as follows:

Sharon: $15,000 + (5.7 percent of pay greater than Social Security wage base of $90,000 in 2005) = $15,000 + $3,420 = $18,420 or 34 percent of total contribution

Robert: $10,000 + (5.7 percent of pay greater than Social Security wage base of $90,000 in 2005) = $10,000 + $571 = $10,571 or 20 percent of total contribution

In recalculating the total annual plan contribution in light of these additions, we find the total to be $57,491. This is still well within Sharon's stipulated maximum contribution figure of $60,000. Further, for Sharon alone, she is now able to apply a total of $18,420 per year towards her specified retirement savings need of $20,000 annually.

In summary, based upon a consideration of all relevant factors, we determined that an integrated 10 percent defined contribution, profit sharing plan is most appropriate to meet Sharon's retirement savings need. In doing so, we also met the business and employee motivational objectives that Sharon specified as most important. Truly, to use an overworked phrase, the end result is a "win-win" situation for everyone.

IMPORTANT CONCEPTS

Employee census or profile

Business owner's personal objectives

Objectives of the business

Employee motivational objectives

Qualified retirement plan characteristics and features

Techniques to maximize the owner's share of plan contributions

Third party administrator

Plans that constitute qualified retirement plans

Plan adoption

Advance determination letter

Custom, master or prototype plans

Common control rules

Controlled group of corporations

Affiliated service group

Leased employee

Parent-subsidiary controlled groups

Brother-sister controlled groups

Combined groups

Attribution rules

Retirement plan termination

QUESTIONS FOR REVIEW

1. What are some of the preliminary considerations to be taken into account in determining whether to establish a qualified retirement plan?

2. What type of factual information about a business should be obtained prior to ascertaining the client's retirement objectives?

3. What are the three general categories of business owner objectives in considering the adoption of a qualified retirement plan and which of these categories will generally be primary?

4. What other personal factors, in addition to the owner's objectives, must be considered in selecting and designing an appropriate retirement plan?

5. What are the most common personal objectives of a business owner in considering the adoption of a qualified retirement plan?

6. What are some of the typical objectives of the business itself in considering the adoption of a qualified retirement plan?

7. What are some of the typical employee motivational objectives in considering the adoption of a qualified retirement plan?

8. What are some of the most important characteristics and features of qualified retirement plans to be taken into consideration in selecting an appropriate plan?

9. Which types of qualified retirement plans may not be adopted by unincorporated entities?

10. Which type of retirement plan may be adopted only by nonprofit organizations and public schools?

11. Which type of retirement plan may be adopted only by nonprofits and state and local governmental entities?

12. What techniques may be used to maximize the business owner's share of contributions to a qualified retirement plan?

13. Installation and administration of a qualified retirement plan is usually best left to what type of entity?

14. Which of the retirement plans discussed in this text constitute qualified retirement plans?

15. How is plan adoption effected?

16. What is the purpose of obtaining an "advance determination letter" prior to establishing a qualified retirement plan?

17. What is the difference between a master and a prototype plan?

18. What are the three sets of common control rules?

19. What is meant by an affiliated service group?

20. What is the treatment of a leased employee for purposes of the IRC Section 414(n) nondiscrimination requirements?

21. What are the three types of controlled groups and how do they differ from each other?

22. What is the significance of the attribution rules?

23. For a benefit of a defined benefit plan to be guaranteed by the PBGC, what three prerequisites must it meet?

24. In what form is a PBGC-provided benefit paid?

25. What is the difference between a voluntary standard and distress termination and an involuntary termination by the PBGC?

26. What are the rules surrounding reversion of residual plan assets to the employer upon termination of a qualified retirement plan?

SUGGESTIONS FOR ADDITIONAL READING

Tools & Techniques of Employee Benefit and Retirement Planning, 9th edition, Stephan R. Leimberg and John J. McFadden, The National Underwriter Company, 2005.

Retirement Planning, Carla Gordon, American Institute of Certified Public Accountants, 2002.

Index

• • •

trusts for and Medicaid, 62-63

Disclosure requirements, ERISA, 290-291

Discretionary provision, profit-sharing plans, 181

Distress termination, defined benefit plans, 243

Distributions, 257-282

  annuity payments, 261-265

  and beneficiaries, 271-272, 276-279

  checklist, 281-282

  early. *See Distributions, early; Hardship withdrawals*

  in-service, 269-270

  lump-sum, 258-261

  minimum. *See Minimum distributions; Required minimum distributions (RMDs)*

  planning/choosing form of, 280-281

  rollovers, 265-269

  See also specific retirement plans

Distributions, early

  annuities, 105

  IRAs, 76, 78, 82-83, 125

  SIMPLE IRAs, 131

  termination of plans, 243

  See also Hardship withdrawals

Diversification

  employee stock ownership plans (ESOPs), 198

  fiduciary requirements, 299-300

Divorce

  IRA transfers, 78, 271

  qualified domestic relations order (QDRO), 155, 272

  and qualified retirement plans, 155

E

Early distributions. *See Distributions, early*

Early retirement, Social Security benefits, 37

Earned income, defined, 119

Education expenses

  education IRAs, 69

  permissible distributions, 82, 216

Elective deferrals

  options, 119

  to SARSEP, 124, 126

  tax-sheltered annuity plan limitations, 136-137

Eligible rollover distribution, IRAs, 77

Employee Retirement Income Security Act (ERISA), 288-294

  Annual Report, 289

  disclosures to plan participants, 291-292

  fiduciary, prohibited transactions, 239, 293-294

  fiduciary duties, 298-299

  Individual Accrued Benefit Statement, 289

  IRAs authorization, 68

  plans exempt from regulation, 288

  plans under, 288-289

  reporting requirements, 241-242, 290-291

  requirements for planners, 5

  Summary Annual Report (SAR), 289

  Summary Plan Description (SPD), 289

  See also Fiduciary requirements

Employees, retirement planning calculations, 17-18

Employee stock ownership plans (ESOPs), 194-200

  annual additions, 199

  and closely held buyouts, 195

  defined, 194

  distributions, 199-200

  diversification requirements, 198

  dividend deductions, 196

  functions of, 194

  leveraged, 197-198

  nonleveraged, 196

  pros/cons of, 194

  tax advantages to employers, 196-198

S